Charles Horton Cooley

Charles Horton Cooley
Imagining Social Reality

GLENN JACOBS

University of Massachusetts Press
Amherst and Boston

LC 2005023232
ISBN 1-55849-519-3
Designed by Sally Nichols
Set in Adobe Caslon
Printed and bound by The Maple-Vail Book Manufacturing Group

Library of Congress Cataloging-in-Publication Data

Jacobs, Glenn, 1940–
Charles Horton Cooley : imagining social reality / Glenn Jacobs.
p. cm.
Includes bibliographical references and index.
ISBN 1-55849-519-3 (cloth : alk. paper)
1. Cooley, Charles Horton, 1864–1929.
2. Sociologists—Biography.   3. Sociology—Philosophy.   I. Title.
HM479.C66J33 2006
301'.092—dc22   2005023232

British Library Cataloguing in Publication data are available.

CONTENTS

ACKNOWLEDGMENTS

The advice, help, and assistance of a number of people contributed to the birth of this book. First I want to thank Paul Wright, editor of the University of Massachusetts Press, for shepherding the book from the presentation of the prospectus before the editorial board through review of the completed manuscript. Paul has provided calm and patient support throughout. Norman Denzin's kind comments encouraged me to complete, and Mary J. Gallant's helpful suggestions provided a useful reference point for, my revisions. Conversations with my colleagues Jorge Capetillo-Ponce, Behrooz Tamdgidi, and Siamak Movahedi provided me with stimulating perspectives on Cooley and my own interpretation of his work. I am grateful for the help, kindness, and cooperation given to me by Karen Jania of the Bentley Historical Library at the University of Michigan, especially when these were extended during the critical final stages of revision. I am beholden to the Bentley Library and its staff for their courtesy and efficiency in giving me access to the Cooley papers. Archibald Hobson's thorough and erudite copyediting, initially evoking panic in me, turned out to be an invaluable educational experience. Carol Betsch of the University of Massachusetts Press has been an able and considerate editor providing me with advice and cooperation during the latter stages of readying the manuscript for publication. Siri Colom read parts of the manuscript at different stages of its development and provided perceptive commentary on writing style and sociological content. Her love, support, and encouragement have been invaluable to me. I am indebted to Lynn Perlman for being a helpful *nudge*! On a joyous note I salute my patron *orisha, Shangó*: *Shangó e wa 'ye. O ma yo. E ayó. Kawo kabiosile* [Shangó you are sought for life. You are truly overbrimming. You are happiness. Let us see you. Let us beget life in the house.] Finally, I salute my mother in *ocha*, Ochún—*Yalode, La Caridád del Cobre, "Cachita." ¡Ye yeo! Con cariño*.

I am grateful to the Bentley Historical Library, University of Michigan, for permission to quote from material in the Charles Horton Cooley papers in their collection.

Box 1: letter to Albion W. Small to Cooley, Dec. 2, 1902
Box 2: journals, 1882, 1887–1888, 1889–1891; journal of trip to Colorado, 1882; undated journal; undated lecture notes; remembrance of Cooley to Jacob Billikopf; index to Cooley's journal compiled by Glenn Jacobs, 1979
Box 5: journals, V. 6, 10–17, 18a, 18b, 19
Box 6: journals, V. 20–24
Box 7: diary of trip through Great Smoky Mountains; notebook of political philosophy lectures of John Dewey

PREFACE

Charles Horton Cooley has been an intellectual companion of mine and source of inspiration—an unblinking looking-glass—for more than forty years. His writing represents the courage to live by one's intellectual lights, to defend the democracy of difference, to recognize the spiritual in the social, to defend the valor of intuition, and to love art and proclaim its kinship with sociology. I don't agree with everything he says, but one does not need to do that with one's friends. From the time I was introduced to him I could love the open-heartedness of what he said one moment, be transported by his insight, and be impatient with his naivete—his occasionally charming, yet sometimes exasperating, lack of street smarts—practically an instant later. Thus I feel at home with him. As Willard Waller says of him, "He captures the feeling-states and impressions that are too swift for us and shows us their anatomy. Such men are rare and valuable. They live forever because the human race cannot afford to let them die" (1942, p. 1).

I decided to write this book following the deaths of Al Lee in 1992 and Leo Chall in 1993. Both were teachers of mine who kindled my interest in, and encouraged my scholarship on, Cooley. Their deaths followed a period in which I had become disenchanted with much of the canon in sociology's subdisciplines, including theory, a feeling fostered by personal as well as the social and political circumstances of the post–Vietnam War period. When Al died I was jolted into reflecting on how much he had given me that had carried right through my period of conscious rejection of the profession.

I will always think of Al as the most significant person inspiring me to become a sociologist: he was my mentor, and his wise spirit continues to guide me. Al, whose conception of "attitudinal multivalence" was inspired by William James's social self, viewed pervasive inconsistency as a principle underlying the formation of social personalities and the operation of social processes creating the bewildering mix of appearances and realities we know as society. As a new graduate student in the early 1960s I was deeply impressed by his talent for observing society "clinically," as he preferred to say, much as an experienced physician might employ an intuitive diagnostic ability, or a seasoned and somewhat cynical news reporter a kind of knack in grasping the inner reaches of his or her beat, whatever it might be. (The use of the term *clinical* has, by the way, been greatly transformed and expanded since Al coined it, becoming a kind of rationale for organizational development or therapy called "clinical sociology.")

At Al's suggestion I read *Human Nature and the Social Order* and was exhilarated by Cooley's insights about human nature and his novel way of seeing agency and structure—the individual and society—as two aspects of the same thing. As a young man seeking insight into his own existence and into the world around him, I found that Cooley stimulated my curiosity and satisfied a taste for percipient writing awakened in my undergraduate years by essayists such as Henry David Thoreau and E. B. White. I soon read everything of Cooley's I could get hold of, and his adage about society itself being a work of art stuck with me alongside the aphorism "The surest way to get to know men is by having simple and necessary relations with them," his sagacious understanding of human nature, and his resolution of the agency-structure conundrum. Al, who proudly called himself an "indigenous American radical," liked Cooley's homegrown, albeit *not* so radical, humanistic theoretical acumen; it was clear that Cooley's genius owed little to European sociology.

Leo Chall, the founder of *Sociological Abstracts* and champion of the open international exchange of sociological ideas, who taught me undergraduate theory and social stratification at Brooklyn College, and for whom I worked as an abstracter in the early to mid-1960s, presented to me, along with an entire photocopy and microfilm of them sometime around 1973, the idea of analyzing Cooley's journals for my doctoral dissertation.[1] His aim was to eventually produce a book, perhaps an abridgment of the journals derived from my work, which would be published by the *Abstracts'* subsidiary, Essay Press. I was enrolled in the doctoral program at Temple University at the time, and was studying sociological theory with Dean Maccannell, who had acquainted me with structuralism and semiotics and was completing *The Tourist.* Maccannell thought the idea of dealing with the Cooley journals as a "back region" (a term he borrowed from Erving Goffman) of his theory building was a good one and he agreed to be my adviser. The dissertation was completed, but unfortunately the book project was stalled under the pressures Leo constantly faced as impresario and editor in chief of *Sociological Abstracts.*

Working on the dissertation taught me a great deal about Cooley, but also about qualitative research methods, including the coding of data and the close connection between theory and method; the thousands of pages of diary were my data, and they had to be made sense of. Working on a single case or many presented identical problems of coding. The key issues were first, that as with all such textual data, I had to decide which of the journal's themes to select as major, which were subsidiary, and which were of minor importance; second, there was the matter of the role of the journal as a personal document, and discerning its significance in Cooley's life and in his work as a sociologist and a writer. Third, I needed to explicate the role played by the journal in Cooley's method or style of theory construction. I found that the richest source of ideas for my analysis was the dialectic stemming from the intuitive associations prompted by my reading of the journal, and their transformation into cues prompting further investigation. Often these cues were suggested by feelings evoked by reading journal material. So, for example, an initial response of boredom and a judgment of effeteness to Cooley's ruminations on style and Walter Pater's writing led me to probe both my response and some of Cooley's own ambivalence toward Pater. This led to my own rumination on the nature of influence as it pertained to Cooley's aestheticism.

Soon, indeed at the outset, it became clear that the three aforementioned concerns formed a web, and that much of this interrelatedness constituted more than mere linkages. The fragmentariness and ubiquitous autobiographical referentiality, even the disparities, of the materials were the sum and substance of Cooley as a thinker. As I came to understand the diary as a literary genre intimately related to his participation in the essay tradition, it occurred to me that Cooley's journals were a clearinghouse, an intellectual field where things he read and ideas he found in them glanced against and mixed with the material of his inner life, his self-observation, observations of his family and children, everyday events, the university and department he taught in, colleagues and professional involvements, travels, craft projects, intellectual plans, and so on.

At the same time, Cooley was the impresario of his corner of the journal-writing field, at times defining its lineaments and boundaries, at other times entering into it as though a spectator; that is, he would allow the genre's form to guide him until his authorial self might step in, exerting a strong declamatory hand, leaving its imprint page after page, afterwards being combed to reappear in published form. While all personal diaries bear the impresses of their authors, this may be unintentional or intentional. Cooley might simply record observations and events, or copy passages from favorite authors, or he might display a keen consciousness of journalkeeping and of his place among other writers and essayists. Becoming intimately familiar with the journal, I could see *it* as well as Cooley's authorial self as a whole, and better understand the textual interrelations underlying the theoretical connections within Cooley's work. Beyond my dissertation there remained the task of coming to a fuller and deeper understanding of the intellectual matrix of Cooley's thinking.[2]

But between my dissertation and the completion of my doctorate and this book there fell teaching, the deaths of my wife and my parents, a health crisis, a rocky remarriage, a long-term psychoanalysis, divorce, and a continuing romance with Cuban society and culture and with the Afro-Cuban religion, Santería. Returning to graduate school (1971–1976) had earlier caused personal and marital strains that were not alleviated by my appointment to a department undergoing severe conflict and offering no mentorship to new members. In a society experiencing economic and corporate restructuring, recession and massive unemployment ("stagflation"), a growing permanent cadre of the homeless, and transforming itself into a burgeoning information-purveying, service-based leviathan plunging into yet another phase of global adventurism—leaving universities scrambling to accommodate to a new lean-and-mean vocation-alism—I became disenchanted with academic sociology. I turned to a Marxian interpretation of social issues as a plausible alternative to what I viewed as a jumble of establishmentarian rationales for the preservation of the status quo. In 1979, at the height of my disenchantment, I published a piece analyzing Cooley's economic sociology. While I treat my subject here from some of the same critical presuppositions, I have shorn my treatment of the bitterness that underlay it, and tempered it with an appreciation of Cooley that I had under-stated in 1979.

After the country's illusionary moonwalk through the 1980s, I realized that Marxian sociology, while offering adroit critique, had failed to appreciate or understand what I understood as elemental precepts of social organization and social process, and thus was prevented from formulating effective strategies for changing them. It came to me that fundamentally important as political economy is, it does not replace sociological analysis, but must incorporate it. I remained a socialist yet leavened my political and economic sentiments with sociological understanding.

My health crisis (a heart operation in 1987), and Al's death in 1992, were wake-up calls prompting me to reflect on my life and experience and the means I had used to understand them. After the operation I was inspired to write about a long-standing interest in Afro-Cuban culture, and published two pieces on the composer and singer Bola de Nieve, one of my subtitles identifying this talented performer as a "creative looking-glass" for race relations and his African cultural patrimony in Cuba. At that time I had become familiar with the Cuban anthropologist Fernando Ortiz's notion of "transculturation," of cul-ture change as a creative process, reminiscent of the way Cooley described the tentative, "sympodial" social process. Clearly, Cooley had remained with me and aided me in my intellectual renewal. In addition, between 1989 and 1994, I engaged in participatory action research on privatization of the city of Chelsea's public schools of Boston University. It was a passionate project in which I truly was a participant observer using my sociological understanding to assist the opponents of the hijacking of their schools in resisting the BU juggernaut. That struggle represented an attempt to make democracy work by groups, in this case, working-class Latinos, often discounted as troublesome, ignorant, and apathetic. Instead we capitalized on these stereotypes and often took the new managers of the schools by surprise in publishing accounts and analyses of their shenanigans in a bilingual newspaper, doing community organizing, and successfully assisting Latino candidates running for public office. The struggle epitomized Cooley's faith in the vital role played by dissident groups in a democracy, for it revitalized a public sphere that had formerly been dominated by the white power structure or dismissed by the BU public school management team as of trivial importance.

Al had bequeathed tools for the understanding of society that were staples in my teaching and writing even during my disillusionment. From him I learned to distrust scholasticism and formal reason, and that to penetrate society's facades I had to look outside the pronouncements of public officials, clergy, teachers, and other purveyors of conventional wisdom—"societal surrogates"—seeking answers through what he called "participating observation." The subtle difference between participat*ing* and particip*ant* comes close to Cooley's dictum that sociology is systematic autobiography; the former connotes a dynamic principle for the conduct of one's life, the latter the more static facticity of a method of social research. What Cooley and Al Lee shared was the conviction that sociology could be a path toward wisdom; one viewed it as a means of understanding the "larger life," the other as augmenting the virtue of "looking and seeing" society for what it is, with all its sordidness, oppression, inequalities, and hypocrisy—much cloaked by the veils of orthodoxy and legitimacy—as well as its possibilities for, and occasional achieving of, human potential.

Al Lee's and then Leo Chall's deaths spurred me to complete a process, to pay my debts to Cooley and my mentors. Cooley has been treated inaccurately and I think unfairly by the discipline, which, although providing him a place in the canon as a progenitor of symbolic interactionism and the formulator of the notion of the primary group, has done so rather narrowly and in some cases dismissively (owing in part to G. H. Mead having self-servingly written him off).

My mission here, therefore, is to draw attention to the fact that—and the reasons why—Cooley was the first American sociologist to develop a viable conception of the social as part of a comprehensive theory of the self and of social organization. In addition to elucidating the literary "genre matrix" underlying his approach I am awakening sociologists to his pathbreaking methodological contributions and to his virtually unknown economic sociology. In attempting these things, I hope that this imagining of his imagination will tempt the reader to explore Cooley further; I will then consider my mission accomplished. In rendering my portrait of Cooley I have drawn extensively on his own unpublished and published writing and have striven in many places to let him speak for himself. In the spirit of Cooley's vigilance against his own vanity and pride, though, I accept responsibility for any faulty thinking and logical errors that might appear to be Cooley's, when in fact they should be my own.

Charles Horton Cooley

INTRODUCTION

My aim in this book is to explain the sources of inspiration and influence shaping the theory of Charles Horton Cooley (1864–1929). The first American sociologist to construct a viable notion of the social whose point of view compares in sophistication with that of his European cousins, Cooley stands as a unique figure among sociologists in the United States. Alongside his thinking virtually all of the American founders' work appears a collection of bric-a-brac.[1] Moreover, only Cooley has continued to inspire contemporary thinking, even if at times his contribution amounts only to small rivulets of scholarship and re-presentation on a range of subjects, from his views on human nature, nurture, and intelligence (Jacoby and Glauberman, 1995) and the genesis and lineaments of the social self and identity (Franks and Gecas, 1992; Scheff, 2003; Scheff, 1994; Reitzes, 1980; Calhoun, 1994, pp. 284–85; Johnson, 1992, p. 196), to his conception of the societal foundation of economics (Jacobs, 1979), the analysis of democracy, tradition, social change, and social organization (Clark, 1994), and literary-critical approaches to the analysis of sociological theory (Green, 1988).

Beginning with his unique conception of the social, I discuss the aspects of his thinking that set him apart from the first and second generation of sociologists of the United States. In comparison with the lacunae, patchwork, and false starts of his predecessors and contemporaries, Cooley worked out a sound conception of the social that served as a foundation for his sociological theory. This conception is elegant, and as with the rest of his thinking, expressed in a clear and engaging style that both conceals and reveals the depth of literary understanding contributing to his wisdom—conceals it through its deceptive easy flowing quality, and reveals it through its penetration into profound questions of the meaning of social life and that of the lives of individuals as they mutually affect each other. I follow this opening theme with exploration of his ideas and of those nonsociological literary influences inspiring them that clarify the points of intellectual leverage of Cooley's thought.

It would appear that the tracing of the sources of Cooley's sociological theory already has been accomplished (Jandy, 1942; Cohen, 1967; Schubert, 1998; Schwartz, 1985). So, for example, it is by now a truism that pragmatism and Emerson's transcendentalism are formative influences and that these, especially the latter, enabled Cooley to divest himself of the Spencerian hegemony over much or most of the sociology of the founding generations in the United States. But for the most part, these sources, offering only partial explanations, are little more than glosses of Cooley's multidimensional sociological theory.

I contend that although Cooley shared what Dorothy Ross (1991) calls the creed of American exceptionalism, it is the distance he kept from the intellectual and professional currents of his time, and the singular manner in which his exceptionalism manifested itself, that render him unique. Cooley's conception of the social, founded upon the communicative and sympathetic basis of the self and social organization and grounded in the concept of the organic tie between the individual and society, is the outcome of a synthesis of several intellectual currents: his involvement in and absorption of the essay tradition, pragmatism, and the lesser-known ideas of Adam Smith. Initially, I stress the conception of the social more than the ideas for which Cooley is now principally remembered—such as the looking-glass self and the primary group—because, despite their incorporation into the sociological canon, they are bare textbook ideas, unelucidated by the broader context of his thinking. Beyond the perfunctory mention of Cooley's role in creating the symbolic interactionist tradition, beyond characterizing him as a vestibular link to George

Herbert Mead, or noting his association with the ideas of the Chicago School, these textbook and summary treatments give little or no sense of the intellectual matrix underlying these notions. Their connection with Cooley's broader organic view of society, social organization, social process, social psychology, and sociological methodology—and, most important, their derivation from his literary aestheticism—remains hidden. Thus his vision of society, whether from a microscopic social psychological or a macrosociological vantage point, can be exclusively categorized neither as pragmatic on the one hand, nor as organicist (despite his use of this word) on the other. Rather, I call Cooley's perspective aestheticist, referring to its foundations, and meaning that he envisions the social process as intrinsically creative, and society itself as a work of art.

A little more than a decade after Cooley's passing a philosopher characterized him as an apostle of creativeness (Levin, 1941). Cooley viewed creativity as synonymous with the life process; human nature, incarnated in the social process, is creative in its "sympodial" development, like a vine tentatively sending out shoots and growing by trial and error in unforeseen ways and new directions. Furthermore, the social process manifests itself as "social intelligence" in the interwoven imaginative-scenaric schemas of actors' operations in social fields. In this fashion Cooley conceives social actors and action as creative—and by extension, social science as well, in its utilization of the method of sympathetic introspection in order to plumb social action (1918, pp. 351–62). Thus "the life of men . . . seems to include a creative element which must be grasped by the participating activity of the mind rather than by computation" (p. 401). As a result, he had no trouble expressing the connection between the individual and society as homologous works of art. He tells us that "Our individual lives cannot, generally, be works of art unless the social order is also" (1927, p. 142).

Creativeness is the integument of all of Cooley's thought and of the influences upon it. It is a value connecting his inner life with his sociological theory, his private with his public self. Creativeness is a hallmark of his liberal vision of democracy viewed as the occasionally tarnished emblem of the onward human struggle for self-realization and self-expression, which evades finality, being, rather, a process of becoming, a movement.

Cooley's exaltation of creativeness sets him apart from his precedessors, his contemporaries, even his successors. As I discuss below, it was his penchant for living and thinking by his literary lights and his membership in the essay tradition that gave him the freedom, insight, and inspiration to formulate his pathbreaking conception of the social. However, as I note in connection with his novel view of the economy as a value-based social institution, Cooley's exaltation of the aesthetic could occasionally be a stumbling block, as with his apotheosis of the medieval guild to restore the ideals of craftsmanship—which he conceived as an antidote to venality—in the industrial age. Here aesthetic romanticism led him into the same cul-de-sac as Émile Durkheim, whose corporatism promised redemption from anomie. Such idealizations are double-edged swords. On the one hand they proffer democratic freedom or solidarity as a healthy and enlarged collective self-expression. On the other hand, as Levin wrote of Cooley during the early stages of World War II, when the shadow of fascism threatened to engulf the world, during periods of immense destructiveness when democracy and rationality are under assault, they offer "vain solace" by playing into the hands of reaction (Levin, 1941, p. 229).

This caveat notwithstanding, Cooley's aesthetic vision also incorporated the translation of his spiritual awareness into sociological insight. This awareness transcended mere religiosity: it was product of inner work or acute self-observation granting him the freedom to observe himself and the social world simultaneously and with impartiality. In this way too, he carved out a place for values in social science. Frequently overlapping to the point of congruence, art and spirituality are very close: art conveys a sense of the boundlessness of the imagination, pushing feeling beyond the capacity of reason to penetrate life's mysteries, thereby enabling self-transcendence. Hence Cooley was attuned to "the ecstasy associated with the best achievements of poets, artists and saints." His thought "gives ample recognition to the pervasive importance in human experience, of mystical, intuitive, and spontaneous elements" (Levin, 1941, p. 221). His distinctive achievement was to demonstrate how this aesthetic and spiritual quality is essentially social. John Dewey's amalgamation of the aesthetic and spiritual with everyday life and activity captures the essence of this, but Cooley makes it truly sociological. Incorporating the insights and sensibilities of the essay tradition, Cooley embeds creativity in society, and society in creativity. To borrow his phrasing, they are both aspects of the same thing.

Sociologists are only just now developing conceptions of society and culture as explicitly creative, agent-centered phenomena. As Paul Willis suggests, "the raw materials of everyday lived cultures . . . [are] living art forms" (2000, p. ix). By decentering the text and granting authorial status to the reader as well as the writer, this view would appear to be postmodern. But once we understand that many of postmodernism's precepts (such as its anti-foundationalism, inter-textuality, and decentering of the text), actually antedate it, it will come as no surprise that Cooley's view of society as art, owing to his subscription to the essay tradition, can be viewed as freestanding and does not require postmodern trendiness to justify it.

It should be noted that while Cooley was not a postmodernist, his position on what postmodernists call foundationalism remains part of a stream of antipositivist sentiment in the social sciences. "Foundationalism" here refers to the certainty that social reality rests on the same factual (read measurable) or objective foundation as the natural world and so may be studied with the methods used by the natural sciences (Rosenau, 1992, pp. 9–11, 109–37). In these terms Cooley is consistent in his view of society as art and the methodology he advances for its study.

Having said this, it is important to note that Cooley's idea of the social is premised upon a novel way of resolving the structure-agency problem. Put another way, at one pole the problem of scale has loomed for microsociologists or symbolic interactionist social psychologists (who have been accused of "a-structural bias") as an inability to account for structural forces such as power and inequality; at the opposite pole, structuralists of varying stripes and acknowledged and unacknowledged political persuasions have been accused of dehumanizing society by making the individual an epiphenomenon of it. While a variety of solutions have been entertained, Cooley offers a method of dealing with this conundrum that I call his "perspectival gear-shifting apparatus." In asserting that society and the individual are simply aspects of the same thing ("self and society are twin-born"), there being only a difference in vantage point, Cooley is suggesting that the issue is a nonproblem, perhaps calling for different ideas appropriate to each level of analysis (Cooley, 1902, rev. ed. 1922, pp. 35–50; 1909, pp. 5–12).

The insight derives from Cooley's organic view, and represents what Lewis Coser, opening his essay on Cooley, calls "the organic link and the indissoluble connection between self and society" (1971, p. 305); but more than the individual and societal spheres being distinctive linked *levels* of reality, they are differences "in our point of view" rather "than in the subject we are looking at: when we speak of society, or use any other collective term, we fix our minds upon some general view of the people concerned, while when we speak of individuals we disregard the general aspect and think of them as if they were separate" (Cooley,

1909, p. 37). Here Cooley's literary insight is the fulcrum of his understanding, and this understanding stems from his familiarity with the connection between style, authorial personality, and social types, or the Emersonian representative man, of which I have more to say in chapters 2 and 4. Cooley arrived at such understanding from two starting points: the development of his personality throughout his life and intellectual influences from his wide reading within and beyond sociological literature.

Cooley the Person: A Biographical Portrait

Cooley's known family history begins in New England.[2] His grandfather, Thomas Cooley (a direct descendant of Benjamin Cooley, who before 1640 settled in Springfield, Massachusetts, and became a town selectman), left Springfield in 1804, settling on a farm in Attica, New York. He had fifteen children to support, and the family suffered poverty, requiring them to obtain education for themselves. The eighth child, Thomas McIntyre Cooley (1824–98), was to become Charles Horton's father. He received a high school education and at age eighteen, not finding farming to his liking, was apprenticing in a law office in Palmyra, New York. Being an ambitious sort, he headed west toward Chicago, winding up in Adrian, Michigan, and began his law career with admission to the bar in 1846. In Adrian he met and married Mary Elizabeth Horton, with whom over a twenty-five-year period he had six children.

Thomas McIntyre Cooley is described as being of delicate physique, with a feminine voice, but, although modest in manner, ambitious and intrepid in striving for success. He is also described as having a literary inclination. In 1857 he was made compiler of laws for the state, and in recognition of the high caliber of his work, recorder of Supreme Court decisions. Appointed as one of a faculty of three to start the University of Michigan Law School at Ann Arbor in 1859, he became its first dean. In 1864 he was elected to the state Supreme Court, where he served for twenty years. In 1887 he was appointed by U.S. president Grover Cleveland as the first chair of the Interstate Commerce Commission, serving until 1891, and in 1893 he was elected the sixteenth president of the American Bar Association. The author of books on constitutional law, treatises on taxation and torts, and numerous articles on legal subjects, Cooley, a Jacksonian, "viewed the premises of democratic law to be derived from the commonplace morality of self-governing citizens." As such, he saw law as an educating force that "could help the citizenry elevate their behavior better to reflect their own republican values of social equality, political self-restraint, tolerance, and mutual respect" (Carrington, 1997, pp. 523, 527).

In 1864, the year of Thomas McIntyre Cooley's election to the state Supreme Court, Charles Horton, their fourth of six children, was born in a house on State Street across from the University campus. Jandy describes Judge Cooley as being deeply interested in his family, firm in his commands toward his children "but . . . judicious . . . rather than authoritative." He took a keen interest in the children's diction, "both oral and written, and would prune their sentences of all irrelevant matter."[3] The wishes of the children were always respected by both parents, and "[a]ll in all, theirs was a congenial family life, for each parent had a large measure of sympathy and tolerance" (1942, p. 12).

Charles was a small, shy child, slight of physique, frail and of poor health from the age of eight until young adulthood. Separated in age by seven years from both an older sister and a younger brother, he was paid a great deal of attention because of his frailty and his brightness. Consequently, he developed a passion for approval and applause, but because of his self-consciousness and timidity kept to himself and dwelled in fantasy. In addition, from early boyhood he suffered from chronic constipation ("costiveness" of the bowel) that affected his temperament and his psyche. In addition, having contracted malaria at age sixteen, he suffered bouts of it for several years. It was not until age nineteen, when he went to Europe and climbed the Tyrolean and Swiss Alps and completely changed his diet, that these conditions began to disappear. Jandy states that the intestinal condition "probably left scars on his personality in the form of intermittent irritability, obstinacy, and a high sensitiveness to encroachment on his domain of thought and power," which "manifested themselves again and again throughout his life" (p. 16). In his journal he frequently observes his coldness and emotionally withholding nature, coexisting with emotional turmoil and wrenching anxiety about facing new experiences, public appearances, and meeting new and strange people. In an entry concerning this discomfort, Cooley observes: "Sometimes I think I am fit for nothing but a cloister. To have a visitor on my hands for half a day destroys a night's sleep and leaves me unfit for society the next day. After very little stress I feel exiled from myself" (V. 16 [9/19/02–6/17/03] 12/4/02, p. 33). Cooley's shyness could manifest itself as coldness. Jandy tells us that it was his "outward coldness" serving as "a kind of ectoplasm exuded from their innermost selves" that made Emerson's personality resonate with Cooley's and inspired Cooley's discipleship before the age of eighteen (Jandy, 1942, p. 42).

His undergraduate education at Michigan gives no hint of the career he would finally choose. The majority of the record consists of study of four languages, some history, and a specialization in mechanical engineering and related scientific subjects. Cooley entered college at age sixteen, but because of ill health took seven years to finish. In the summer of 1882 he went on an adventure-filled surveying trip to Colorado, with the hope that outdoor life would toughen him. In 1883 he again headed for mountain country, this time in Asheville, North Carolina, where "he spent as many as ten hours a day in the saddle, going through heavy laurel thickets, over log barricades and rock-strewn ground" (Jandy, 1942, p. 21). Then, in January, 1884, he traveled to Europe—to London, Munich, Lucerne, Dresden, and Berlin. After nearly a year—by the end of it, having, it seemed, to vanquish the malaria and the sluggish bowel that had plagued him—he returned home in December, and resumed his studies at the university, where he finished his education in mechanical engineering.

Of this extended college career Coser observes, "Cooley's unusually long period of apprenticeship and preparation may be accounted for in part by ill health but also by the fact that he was the son of well-to-do parents, who could afford to let their son take his time in deciding upon a career. Moreover, Cooley suffered from the fact that he stood under the shadow of a famous father. He once wrote to his mother: 'I should like as an experiment to get off somewhere where Father was never heard of and see whether anybody would care about me for my own sake'" (1971, p. 315).

After graduation Cooley returned to Michigan for another year of engineering and in the summer of 1888 he practiced draftsmanship at Bay City. That year he began to read Spencer and, intending to do graduate work, returned to Ann Arbor. Upon his father's advice to get more experience in the real world, however, Charles joined him in 1889 in Washington and worked for the Interstate Commerce Commission, and later the Census Bureau. He stayed for two years and utilized his training in statistics to investigate transportation problems (with the aim of reducing railroad accidents). He wrote a paper, "The Social Significance of Street Railways," and read it in 1890 at a meeting of the American Economic Association. At that meeting he met Franklin Giddings and Lester Ward, both of whom encouraged him to go on in sociology. Cooley carried on a correspondence with Ward for several years, asking advice. Giddings was to compose the sociology questions for Cooley's doctoral examination in 1894; much later on he would offer him a position at Columbia.

In 1890 Charles Cooley married Elsie Jones. Both were twenty-six years old. Elsie, whose father had been appointed dean of the university's Homeopathic Medical College in 1875, had been a bright student and had literary interests and talents. Her romance with Charles flowered during the time they spent in the Samovar Club, a group formed to discuss literature. Jandy tells us: "Although she was a much more sociable person than Cooley, she cared as little as he did for the conventional social life of Ann Arbor. In summer, boating on the Huron River and picnicking along its banks were favorite diversions for them and their circle of friends" (1942, p. 33). Upon graduation, Elsie taught Greek and Latin at a girls' school at North Wales, Pennsylvania, and then at the Hyde Park High School in Chicago. Since at the time of their marriage Charles was working in Washington, they resided there, and when he finished his research work the couple traveled to Florence, Italy for six months in 1891–92. They both learned Italian and studied Italian literature: these were some of the happiest months of a long companionship. They returned to Ann Arbor, where Cooley began a lengthy teaching career at the university. Of Elsie Cooley, Jandy says:

> Like her husband, Mrs. Cooley was of slight build, but unlike him, she was very energetic and sociable by nature. They led a life of simplicity, quiet, and dignity. Their reading together in the fields of biography, travel, poetry, and art became a lifetime habit. Mrs. Cooley was, moreover, an able literary critic and had a rich command of language. It was natural, therefore, that she should be both an inspiration and a help when Cooley came to write his own books. To the end of his life, Cooley found her a sympathetic companion, a wise counselor, and an understanding friend. (1942, p. 33)

Jandy concludes: "Without her sympathetic insight into his nature and needs, Cooley could scarcely have enjoyed the kind of domestic milieu which his type of personality and scholarship urgently needed" (p. 34). It is interesting to speculate on what kind of career the talented and perspicacious Mrs. Cooley would have embarked upon, and what kind of accommodation the couple would have worked out in an age more conducive to women's rights and ambitions. She could have earned a doctorate and perhaps secured an appointment at the same university, thus enabling the couple to maintain a family and a lifestyle similar to the one they actually lived. The Cooleys had three children—Rutger Horton, in 1893; Margaret Horton, in 1897; and Mary Elizabeth, in 1904—who "became for Cooley a domestic laboratory for the observation and study of the genesis and development of the personality" (Jandy, 1942, p. 34). The couple kept extensive notes on their children, and Cooley mined the rich material of their observations for his work on the genesis of the self.

During his college years and after, Cooley had read widely, but not greatly, in sociology. He tells us, "I can hardly say that any writer commonly reckoned a sociologist was of the very first importance in my mental growth." He then mentions Emerson, Goethe, and Darwin as having initially inspired him. Nonetheless, feeling "the need of a system to serve as a frame-work for my accumulating ideas . . . in pursuit of this I came, for a while, under the spell of Herbert Spencer, from whom I got my first outline of a general scheme of evolutionary knowledge" (Cooley, 1928 in 1930, p. 4). In 1890 he decided to return to Michigan to do graduate work in political economy, and was given a half-time instructorship in that subject. He minored in sociology and statistics and in 1894 took his examination, with questions in sociology sent by Giddings. In 1894–95 he continued his half-time appointment, and was made an assistant professor in 1899, an associate professor in 1904, and a full professor in 1907.

As a faculty member Cooley took little interest in committee work, meetings, and department administration. He was a member of a number of campus social and academic groups, but participated in them sporadically. He abhorred contact with administrators, especially if this entailed bartering or explaining policy, or involved personal gain or advancement. Such encounters "would bring Cooley back to his office plainly nervous, agitated, and exhausted" (Jandy, 1942, p. 63). As a lecturer he appeared somewhat awkward and ill at ease. Jandy describes his classroom performance as follows:

> When a slender, slightly nervous hand would push the notes he had placed on the long table away from him, it was a first sign that he was about to start lecturing. He would take one step forward, give his notes another little flip away from him, cup his left hand behind his left ear—he was slightly deaf—clear his throat with vehemence several times, and begin. His voice was in harmony with his aesthenic form—thin, somewhat weak, slightly feminine; it was as hard to control as his emotions. There was a nervous, strained quality to it, as if it threatened each moment to break completely. His words were carefully chosen, his sentences short, and his transitions easy; the subject matter was connected and amply studded

with illustrations. It was not the lectures at which one could direct criticisms, but rather at these mannerisms, which an unsympathetic undergraduate might find irksome. (p. 64)

Despite these mannerisms and his lack of initiative in directing their work, many graduate students found it a privilege to attend his seminars and were inspired by his searching intellect, his posing of different questions, and his new ways of thinking about problems.

While he felt strain and discomfort in public and in situations outside the orbit of his family, he nonetheless was active professionally. He participated in the formation of the American Sociological Society in 1905 and attended most of its annual meetings, but found them stressful. In 1918 he became president of the society, and he thereafter found the meetings more enjoyable, perhaps because of the success he enjoyed having published two well-received books in 1902 and 1909 and another in 1918, thereby acquiring prestige among his sociological peers and his university. Jandy describes the last decade of his life as Cooley's happiest. Late in 1928 his health began to fail; his trouble was subsequently defined as cancer. He died on May 7, 1929.

Plan of the Book

There is no "school" explicitly founded on Cooley's thought, although with respect to his theories of the self, his methodology, and his reliance upon the pragmatic philosophical tradition he generally is grouped with the Chicago tradition, including symbolic interactionist social psychology. The absence of such a school perhaps betokens the creativity of his work, for it is not easily reduced to formulae or crystallized into orthodoxy. The closest European analogue, whose wide influence on modern sociology resembles Cooley's, is Georg Simmel, who evinces a similar type of literary and aesthetic turn of mind. Both sociologists, to borrow Simmel's metaphor, are perceived and responded to as strangers—types in, although not entirely of, the academic communities (here Simmel more than Cooley) and discursive traditions they dwelled and worked within—and the purported diffuseness of their work is regarded with mixed admiration and puzzlement. Certainly their discursive marginality reflects Levine's attribution to Simmel of "a studied ambivalence toward the canons and claims of 'objective' scholarship" (1971, p. xii). Here Cooley's own observation of Simmel reads as one of a kindred soul: "Simmel's *Soziologie* is ideally German—penetrating, amazingly patient and thorough, the work of a man who loves his thought and expects only a few readers" (*Journal* V. 186 [2/16/08–1/1/10] 7/22/09, p. 58). In 1919, musing over his life as a professional sociologist, he characterizes himself as an "innovator" who has been "in practice, a somewhat isolated adventurer, acting alone in great things and as I could or must in small ones a pioneer rather than an organizer." The sociological group produces textbooks, but "[m]y part is in forming the ideas for the group to live by" (*Journal* V. 22 [5/20/19–5/25/25] 9/4/19, p. 12).

With respect to the matter of Cooley's distance from the orbit of professional sociology, in chapter 1, "The Exceptional Exceptionalist: Cooley's Rescue of Sociology from the Graveyard of European Liberalism," I open my analysis with a discussion of his pioneering development of a viable conception of the social, as a whole comprising the interchangeability of individual and societal perspectives, the organic view and the social self and its relation to the Scottish moralists. I then take up Comte's and Spencer's liberal perspectives, their goodness of fit with the American exceptionalist ethos, their incorporation in Ward's synthesis, and Cooley's contrasting rejection of Spencer. The social science and sociological "movements," however, did not reject Spencer out of hand, but incorporated him, adapting his sociology piecemeal, according to the needs of sociologists who sought professional autonomy and legitimacy as purveyors of useful knowledge in a maturing capitalist society. Small, Giddings, and Ross each in his own fashion exemplified the patchwork syntheses that characterized the sociology of Cooley's contemporaries. In view of this I discuss Cooley's place in the development of sociological theorizing in the United States and his role within the "sociological movement," pointing to his first steps in crafting the concept of the social, based on the properties of communication.

In short, this chapter analyzes the intersection of sociological theorizing with the emergence of sociology as a profession. Sociology's travail in this case is due to the challenge made by economists and political scientists to sociologists, namely that sociology has no proper subject matter, the economy and the state already falling under their jurisdiction, and also to U.S. sociologists' tardiness in defining the social. In this respect, Cooley shares with his sociological peers an emended version of the American exceptionalist creed—an adherence to a belief in the immunity of the United States to rigid class differences and "the rich particularity of the European past" (Ross, 1991, p. 245). The manner in which he does so, though, is more sophisticated in its reliance on a viable conception of the social. In addition, he maintained faith—following his father's Jacksonian values—in the vitality of American democracy as sustained in part through the hybridity of a highly differentiated society.

Chapter 2, "The Social Self: Human Nature, Imagination, and Perception," discusses Cooley's notion of "the empirical self," deriving from pragmatism and William James's idea that the self is to be understood as a phenomenon of everyday life, as well as from James Mark Baldwin's perspective on the child's self-development, synthesized from Gabriel Tarde's notion of imitation and the ideas of the Hegelian philosopher Josiah Royce, and from pragmatism (Martindale, 1981, p. 288). While George Herbert Mead gets the lion's share of the credit for his concept (most likely owing to Mead's location at the University of Chicago, and, in effect, his writing of Cooley's intellectual obituary), Cooley's concept precedes Mead's as the first viable sociological predecessor.

Cooley's idea of the self clearly is based on a view of human nature, including dispositions toward sociality, and on emotional awareness. These ideas, and the recognition of Cooley's pioneering formulation of them, are only recently coming into vogue among sociologists. The insights that sympathetically derived intersubjectivity is its foundation and that the individual actively interprets others' perceptions and constructs his or her self, essentially are the basis for Cooley's idea. In addition, Cooley builds the self out of the components of the personal symbol and the personal idea, a kind of semiotic derivation incorporating appearance, as opposed to reliance on a stark discursive or cognitive foundation. In addition, Cooley takes up questions such as egotism versus egoism, vanity and pride, and the meaning of "I," much of this stemming from his inner work, and (as I discuss in chapter 4) his reading of the essay tradition and the French moralists.

Finally, I discuss at length the damage done to Cooley by Mead's labeling him a solipsist and his notion of the self "mentalistic." I suggest that Mead's fateful attributions are inaccurate, the products of stylistic differences between his and Cooley's writing and thinking. Moreover, these differences reflect even more fundamental disparities in their reckoning of the epistemological foundations of the study of human behavior and its scientific understanding. They are ultimately reducible to the values of the two men and their scholarly dispositions, and they have broad methodological implications in the social and behavioral sciences. These questions are taken up in more detail in my discussion of Cooley's contribution to methodology in chapter 6. The fact that issues of style remain occult in sociology accounts for the mechanical way in which Mead's impugning of Cooley has been reproduced and transmitted by subsequent generations of sociologists of the symbolic interactionist school founded in Mead's name.

In chapter 3, "Communication Writ Large: Cooley's Concept of Social Organization," I discuss the expansion of Cooley's insights around the derivation of the social. For Cooley social organization is inextricably tied to social process—it is built up through a process of tentative growth and is knit together by communication and public opinion. Here he tells us "visible society is, indeed, literally, a work of art" (1909, p. 21). This notion is more than metaphorical for Cooley, and marks him as truly ahead of his time. As I said earlier, only recently has it begun to surface as an idea that makes serious sociological sense. Cooley's notion is tied to his "organic view," a varied structure of differentiated thought and symbols. He tells us "Both consciously and unconsciously the larger mind is continually building itself up into wholes—fashions, traditions, institutions, tendencies, and the like—which spread and diversify like the branches of a tree, and so generate an even higher and more various structure of differentiated thought and symbols" (ibid.).

When it comes to matters of social class and competition, Cooley is liberal in his views. Following the example of his intellectual hero Emerson, he sees competition (Emerson's allusion is to "property") as a process that is transcendentally emblematic and as the only viable alternative to the status as the "ordering principle" of society. He subscribes—following his father, the jurist T. M. Cooley, and his mentor Henry Carter Adams—to the doctrine of regulated competition embodying high standards of service in society.

There is a naive ring to the optimism of some of Cooley's material on social organization; it stems from his faith in the onward movement of democracy and a vitalized public opinion that he sees as an antidote to the conservative, or even reactionary, tendencies represented by eugenics and anti-Semitism. This exceptionalist sentiment could on the other hand also include both an intolerance of slavery and subscription to milder, more polite doubts about the inherited endowment of African Americans. Much of Cooley's communicatively based democratic faith now resembles Jürgen Habermas's fealty to the rationality and fair play of the public sphere, and reflects Cooley's unwillingness to bow to cynicism. Instead of directly deriving the vitality of American democracy from the Enlightenment heritage, as Habermas does, Cooley rests his optimism on his influential idea of the primary group and the ideals it nurtures, which had their origin in European societies but which effloresced on the geographic and social frontiers of the United States. In either case, whether we are speaking about the communicative optimism of Cooley or the "communicative competence" of Habermas, both perhaps represent a faith in "democratic togetherness," or the idealized happy gemeinschaft.

In chapter 4, "Cooley and the Essay Tradition, Part I: The Influences of Montaigne and Emerson," I turn, having summarized Cooley's sociology, to its infrastructure, that is, its literary/aesthetic underpinnings. It is an oft repeated truism that Cooley is a "literary" sociologist, with commentators invariably alluding to his consummate writing style and his early admiration of Emerson; but that is as far as analysis customarily goes. Beyond the naming of the authors he read and the fact that Emerson was a transcendentalist, we are left with little material with which to unpack Cooley's intellect.

With brief reference to the matter of style I take up the influence of his genre matrix on Cooley's work, beginning with a discussion of the literary analysis of influence. Here, in addressing the contending notions of influence versus intertextuality, the sociologist encounters parallels between the methodological imputation of causality and the hermeneutics of understanding, but more centrally we may face the same issues as literary critics do in seeking to ascertain the origins of and influences on textual production when we analyze the influences on sociological writing. To what extent, for example, do we impute the influence of the ideas of a precursor on a sociological theorist? How do we ascertain the textual boundaries of genres of sociological theory, and how do we gauge the impact of texts and text fragments on a theorist's work?

Cooley confers upon himself membership in the essay tradition as one among "a larger society of men who live for the ages as well as the hours, and by virtue of their representative minds, speak to each other from century to century" (*Journal* V. 21 [1913–19] 8/8/18, p. 161). He typifies this "society's" members and, in particular, the essayists' conversation as being sub specie aeternitatis—"under the aspect of eternity," that is, for the ages. I examine Montaigne, the founder and labeler of the essay genre, and explore the signal textual features of the essay—its multivocality, its intertextuality and polysemy, and, importantly, in Cooley's case, its self-referentiality and emphasis on feeling. The very features of the essay genre suggest Cooley's manner of discussion of the self.

The essayistic underpinnings of Cooley's conception of the self ramify into his treatment of egoism, egotism, vanity, pride, and leadership. These are traceable to Montaigne and the French moralists. Moving from there I discuss Cooley's donning of the mantle of the "oratorical self," that is, the confessed influence of Emerson on him, particularly with respect to the development of character and representative men. Cooley adopts Emerson's representative man, a figure who is "hieratic" or transcendentally emblematic, who mediates between the human and cosmic realms. For Emerson and Cooley this heroic figure is a model articulating the focal concerns of society. The theme of character development is a leitmotif of this notion and is important to the young Cooley. Emerson's intellectual posture embodies that of the orator, a type of public folk figure encompassing politicians, scholars, and itinerant lecturers. The orator, as Emerson conceives of him in his famous essay "The American Scholar," embodies the representative "man thinking," and the "man of the world." He epitomizes social potency and serves as the young Cooley's ego ideal.

As Cooley matures and becomes established in his career, he undergoes a shift of intellectual emphasis wherein style—man writing—succeeds speech as the apogee of intellectual evolution. Character development and inner work remain as anchorage points throughout his life, but style increasingly dominates his intellectual persona. Chapter 5, the second part of my discussion of the essay tradition, "The Template Completed: Walter Pater and Cooley's Literary Aestheticism," commences with a discussion of style and its relevance to sociological concerns. I here analyze this shift in cathexis from Emerson to Walter Pater (1839–94), a pre-Raphaelite writer whose hieratic quality rivals Emerson's. It marks a transformation of Cooley's oratorical into an "authorial" self.

Pater's aestheticism, which eulogizes art for art's sake, is adopted by Cooley, who emulates him while at the same time infusing the former's aesthetic credo into a phenomenology of the self based upon the impression. Pater's emphasis on style, incorporated into Cooley's notion of the "writer's personality," melds with and no doubt influences Cooley's notion of the personal idea. As much of the writing on intertextuality implies, tracing influence is not an all-or-nothing game, since it is absurd, beyond ascertaining major or minor scalar impact, to quantify it. Cooley's acquaintanceship with Pater spans the years 1897 through 1929, the end of his life, and so overlaps the period of Cooley's most notable

work on self and social organization. Finally, Pater's aestheticism is transubstan-
tiated into Cooley's view of society as a work of art and the creative/aesthetic
quality of social process. Moreover, the aesthetic sensibility, stemming from
Pater's appreciation of the grotesque in art (which Cooley literally includes
in his statement about society being a work of art), is incarnated in Cooley's
conceptions of the differentiated quality of modern society (which I call "the
aesthetic of difference") and the operation of "social intelligence." These "mis-
prisions" (distortions and inaccuracies), as Harold Bloom describes them, are
creative distortions, and in some measure transform Pater's effete aestheticism
into a more liberal democratic ideal inspiring Cooley's vision of social organization and process. Their creative reinterpretation must be viewed in light of
both Pater's and Cooley's intellectual matrices.

There is no denying Cooley's aestheticism, and its particular sources are numerous. Yet it is clear that the essay tradition looms large as a source, and that
tradition intersects with the diary tradition that figures so eminently in his intellectual practice (Jacobs, 1976). Cooley's journal spans his whole adult life. It is
repeatedly sifted and selections from it appear in one form or another in the majority of his writing; his last book, *Life and the Student* (1927), derives almost exclusively from it. In calling sociology "systematic autobiography," Cooley "transposes the essayists' conversational yardstick onto sociological methodology."

In chapter 6, "Life and Death at the Aesthetic Center: Cooley's Methodology," I discuss Cooley as an important architect of qualitative method, beginning with his signal essay, "The Roots of Social Knowledge," which stands as
a classic supporting the epistemological foundation of qualitative methods. I
show here how Cooley's distinction between "spatial" and "social" science derives from Pascal's distinction between the mathematical and intuitive minds.
Again, the matter of influence here is sealed by inspection of Cooley's journal,
for he copied passages from Pascal's *Pensées* discussing this distinction.

Social knowledge is based upon "the inter-communicating behavior of men,"
and "human knowledge is both behavioristic and sympathetic" (1926 in 1930,
pp. 294, 295). Cooley's use of "mind" and "behaviorism" is reminiscent of Mead's
terminology but really anticipates it, as the latter's published record of these
notions ranges between six and ten years later than Cooley's (Mead, 1964).

It is in "The Roots of Social Knowledge" that Cooley states that "sympathetic introspection" is the basis of social science methods. Anticipating
Thomas Kuhn's limning of "normal science," he suggests that all science is

socially grounded, and notes that even its standard units of measurement derive from group consensus. With respect to its level of sophistication, and its importance as both a manifesto and epistemological rationale, this essay stands as both the qualitative analogue and rebuttal to Durkheim's declaration and establishment of social facts as measurable phenomena in *The Rules of Sociological Method* (1895).

Drawing on entries concerning a trip to New York's Lower East Side in 1904, observations on Jane Addams and Hull House in Chicago, the death of his daughter Margaret, and his own impending death, I explore how Cooley's journal serves him as a repository of ethnographic field notes. It is evident that there is no canonical format for writing fieldnotes (Jackson, 1990; Sanders, 1996; Lederman, 1990; Sanjeck, 1990a; Ottenberg, 1990; Sanjeck 1990b); in effect, Cooley's journals at least overlap with this genre of data collection. The record of his trip to New York's Lower East Side is a fascinating account because, while not meticulously detailed, it does evidence the manner in which Cooley seeks to grasp the varying perspectives of the people he meets—for example, the different points of view of family members considering the possibility of a mother moving in with her daughter, or a precocious young boy's sense of life on the street. In addition, a reminiscence of Cooley's visit by his 1904 guide to the Lower East Side Jewish community, Jacob Billikopf (1942), provides confirmation of Cooley's genuine interest in and empathy for those he encountered in his intense foray into that community. In reminiscing about Cooley's thinking during his visit, about the hospitality norms of immigrant Lower East Siders and Cooley's own cultural precepts, Billikopf underscores Cooley's capacity to think and analyze sociologically on his feet. Cooley's journal entries on Jane Addams and Hull House demonstrate his artful description of the institution and the person. Each reflects, but is not engulfed by, the other. When he shifts gears into the observations of a family tragedy, the death of his daughter, we learn that a description of the most intimate and personal events conveys great emotion without succumbing to maudlin prose; instead, we get a sensitively drawn description of his daughter and the family's response to her passing. Similarly, the last pages of his diary reveal a human being who can think and feel deeply with rare composure.

Finally, chapter 7, "The Economy and the Whole: The Theory of Pecuniary Valuation," discusses a relatively unknown portion of Cooley's thought, an original contribution to economic sociology.[4] In some ways it rivals, as does his vantage point on method, Durkheim's approach, by building a sociological foundation for economic institutions, not by simple assertion but through an analysis of value. In other words, it is Cooley's holistic approach—the understanding of society as a *totality*—that undergirds his economic thinking. Values, such as primary ideals (ideals developed by and passed down through primary group membership), or institutions, which give form to and appraise them, are part of "organic mental life."

Cooley criticizes political economy for rooting the market institution in human nature, and wishes to re-embed it in society: the market's apparent uniformity reflects that institution's molding of individual estimate, eventually straitjacketing value into price or pecuniary standardization. I discuss here some of the contradictions in Cooley's approach, as revealed in his ambivalence toward the market and his belief in the virtues of competition—albeit regulated competition. His analysis leads him to idealize production and to converge with Durkheim's idealization of occupational groupings—in Cooley's case expressed as an anachronistic romanticization of the medieval guild. Interestingly, both sociologists come to similar conclusions concerning the desirable endpoint of societal evolution: the development of a vibrant social/occupational realm. Thus the productive sphere is not discussed as a contestable arena. It is instead the centerpiece of the good society. Cooley seeks to rescue the economy from banality and rapacity through pursuit of the ideals of function and service, and through the intrinsic creativeness of productive activity.

Cooley was critical of the economics of his time, particularly the marginal utility approach, which, as a consumer- or price-based schema beginning with demand or final degree of utility as determined by the rationally calculating human being, is opposed to identifying the economic locus in the cost of production and is thus based on consumer sovereignty. The neoclassicists, as they are now called, position the economic root behind the mirage of the household economy, and disturbances of demand or insufficient production are seen as the fault of the consumer. In Cooley's view, this makes market values supervene all others. The marginal utility approach strikingly resembles contemporary rational choice theory in economics and sociology; it is a kind of sterile reification of what economic rationality is thought to be, and an extirpation of economics from its social context.

Institutional economics was a contemporary approach that included Cooley's formulation. Currently institutionalism appears to be lapsing into the same trivialities as its forerunners. The most noteworthy first-generation exponents of institutional economics were Cooley, Thorstein Veblen, and B. M. Anderson (followed later by Robert F. Hoxie and Wesley Claire Mitchell).

It is clear that Cooley has made a significant contribution to the sociological analysis of the economy, and along with Veblen views the economics of his time as diversionary. He seeks, as contemporary sociological approaches to economics do, the re-embedment or grounding of the economy in society. Contemporary approaches, however, sometimes appear hyperrationalized (as is the case with rational choice theorizing, which suffers from the same faults as the marginal utility approach), or, in identifying economic activity, for example, as coterminous with "networks," falling on the horns of the agency/structure dilemma (Granovetter, 1985, 1993, 2002).

There are contemporary approaches (Beckert, 1999) to economic sociology that are returning to the pragmatists and that seek to locate the construction of economic meaning intersubjectively (interpersonally) in the action (interaction) process so that actors' economic behavior, as all other social behavior, embodies reflexivity: it is not calculating, but becomes so or appears so when routines fail. Thus economic behavior is envisioned as scenaric—plans and ideas are formulated, rehearsed, and revised. This comes strikingly close to Cooley's understanding of social intelligence, which he calls "dramatic."[5] I suggest that contemporary exponents of economic sociology take a look at Cooley to see what insight can be derived from his notion of valuation, economic action, institutional definition, and social process.

I hope that my analysis of the underpinnings of Cooley's thought will add to its understanding and the appreciation of its depth, for as I have strongly emphasized, appreciation requires us to expand our awareness of the kinds of influences that impinged upon it. In the course of this work, for example, I was no longer able to think of terms such as "art," "literature," "creativity," and "imagination" in the way I had originally done so. I could no longer ponder the self in the same way, nor society, nor the social process. These terms and others became more nuanced for me. Moreover, I came to understand Cooley himself differently, because in the process of immersing myself in his genre matrix I developed, more than an appreciation of who he was intellectually, a sense of what he was, both intellectually and psychologically. I was able to empathize— or, in his terms, sympathize—with his feelings and thoughts about the matters he felt were important. Beyond comprehending him as the biographical Cooley,

I came to understand his sensibility—the way he thought and felt about much of what he considered important. In this respect, I could see how both his feeling and his thought were unified with respect to the key themes of his life and work. I hope that this presentation of Cooley's ideas and its analysis will inspire reconsideration of his place in the development of sociological theory— not only of its rightful position, but also with respect to the leads his ideas can provide in assisting sociologists to develop and reinvent their approaches to issues such as creativity, agency, social action and the self, social process, social and economic organization, and sociological methods and methodology. In other words, far from starkly suggesting that Cooley prefigures sociologists' thinking today, a reconnaissance of his work can stimulate the development of new ideas and approaches—which, after all, is part of the stock and trade of social theory.

CHAPTER ONE

THE EXCEPTIONAL EXCEPTIONALIST

Cooley's Rescue of Sociology from the Graveyard of European Liberalism

> We speak of an English *graveyard* with some sympathetic re-
> alization of what it has meant to a community of people like
> ourselves.
>
> GEORGE CRABB, *Crabb's English Synonyms*

> If social science were well begun and clear general conceptions
> were accepted, I would not unwillingly confine my work to some
> comparatively narrow department. But as things are, to do any-
> thing you must do everything; you must first make the science
> you wish to pursue.
>
> CHARLES HORTON COOLEY, *Journal,* November 23, 1895

Charles Horton Cooley's formulation of the social is truly momentous, for it
represents a turning point in the history of sociological theory in the United
States. So original is his formulation that its discontinuity with social science
tradition in the United States seems virtually unique. The nature of the en-
trenched thoughtways of U.S. sociology represents the largely unrepeated if
not untold story of the liberal American exceptionalist heritage, one that leads
up to but does not fully explain Cooley's creative synthesis of certain ingredients overlooked by his predecessors and contemporaries, as well as others
that impeded their thinking. In spite of its uniqueness, Cooley's formulation
of the social, as a result of his break with the intellectual traditions comprising
liberal and methodological individualism (the "graveyard" of European liberal
thought), has been inadequately explained.

After briefly discussing the reasons for Cooley's embarkation on a more sophisticated theoretical road toward the social, emanating from the liberalism
of the Scottish moralists, I will discuss the influence of European liberalism,

which, refracted through the sociologies of Herbert Spencer and August Comte, and clothed in the garb of the American exceptionalist ideology, became the basis of most sociological thinking in nineteenth and early twentieth century United States, carried forward by the impulse toward professionalization of the discipline: the "Sociological Movement." It was Cooley's departure from the Spencerian hegemony, his "role distance" from the "Sociological Movement," and his immunity from the ideas that bogged down his contemporaries (Small, Ross, and Giddings) that afforded him the opportunity to craft his pathbreaking conceptions of the social—the "organic view"—and his notion of the looking-glass self, his integral idea of the group stemming from his formulation of the primary group, and his ideas about social organization.

Cooley's Synthesis of the Social and the Scottish Moralists

Cooley's unique notion of the social rests upon the integration, not the separation or opposition, of the individual and society. So artfully and simply stated is it, however, that its elegance belies the sophistication of the underlying analysis. Cooley is a consummate writer, and it is no accident that this fact has been taken for granted, as has writing style in general by sociologists who have tacitly incorporated certain style canons into their judgments on scientific appropriateness. The uncovering of the belletristic/essayistic background contributing to both his style and substance I will leave for later. For now, let us look at the way Cooley opens his two best-known books, *Human Nature and the Social Order* (1902, rev. ed. 1922) and *Social Organization* (1909), with a discussion of the interchangeability of society and the individual.

Cooley simply states that society and the individual "do not denote separable phenomena." He tells us, "the individual is not separable from the human whole, but a living member of it." Accordingly, "a separate individual is an abstraction unknown to experience" (1902, rev. ed. 1922, pp. 37, 35, 36). It follows that self-consciousness is inseparable from social consciousness, and "we may view social consciousness either in a particular mind or as a cooperative activity of many minds." Consciousness of oneself "is largely a direct reflection of the ideas about himself *he attributes to the others* [my italics]" (1909, pp. 10, 11). Hence society and the individual are "simply collective and distributive aspects of the same thing," and insofar "as there is any difference between the two, it is rather in our point of view than in the object we are looking at" (1902, rev. ed. 1922, p. 37).

This statement is unusual when measured against either the "sociologism" of a Durkheim or the naive imputation of something like mass psychology to the social by most of Cooley's predecessors and contemporaries.[1] To say that society and the individual are aspects of the same thing suggests further exploration of what that thing is. The fact that we are compelled to probe more deeply into the properties of this thing testifies to the heuristic value of the notion. In this respect, Cooley's unique organic view is encapsulated in the notion that the social mind "is an organic whole made up of cooperating individualities," on which, when we study it, "we merely fix our attention on larger aspects and relations rather than on the narrower ones of ordinary psychology" (1909, p. 3). Its unity "consists not in agreement but in organization, in the fact of reciprocal influence or causation among its parts, by virtue of which everything that takes place in it is connected with everything else, and so is an outcome of the whole" (p. 4).

This view, while retaining the organic reference, marks Cooley's defection from Herbert Spencer's sociology. His abandonment of Spencerianism, which I discuss below, was the outcome of two processes: Cooley's construction of the ideas of the social and the self, and his allegiance to a body of literature—the essay tradition—outside the boundaries of the social sciences. Postponing the latter for awhile, let us look more deeply into Cooley's formulation of the social. As we have seen, it is deceptively simple and elegantly stated. Thus, "self and society are twin-born . . . and the notion of a separate and independent ego is an illusion" (p. 5). The "organic view" and its inclusion of the social self, appearing seven years after Cooley's formulation of the looking-glass self in *Human Nature and the Social Order* (1902, rev. ed. 1922, p. 184), derives from his root concept of sympathy, the integument both of the social process out of which the self arises and of social organization. Sympathy, as the faculty responsible for intersubjectivity, is crafted into "sympathetic introspection," the "principal method of the social psychologist" (1909, p. 7).

Cooley's utilization of sympathy as a root concept used in the derivation of his notion of the social, and the basis of the looking-glass self, is prefigured by the Scottish moralist Adam Smith's use of the term and the notion of the "impartial spectator" to explain the formation of our moral standards and their internalization as "self command." These ideas offer the beginnings of a true social psychology, one that requires a certain kind of inspiration for its flowering.

Adam Smith, whom we remember chiefly as the sire of classical economics —the author of *An Inquiry into the Nature and Causes of the Wealth of Nations*

(1776)—distinguished himself as a moral philosopher and contributor to the Scottish Enlightenment. Seventeen years earlier he published *The Theory of Moral Sentiments* (*TMS*) (1759), an analysis of the sources of virtuous, unselfish action transcending a special inborn human moral sense (Ross, 1995, pp. 161–63), which Smith based on the responses to the real and imagined approval and disapproval of one's neighbors designated as "sympathy" (Smith, 1976 [1759], pp. 9–10, 12). Thus, Smith tells us: "As we have no immediate experience of what other men feel, we can form no idea of the manner in which they are affected, but by conceiving what we ourselves should feel in the like situation" (p. 9). Furthermore, and this is crucial to Cooley's construction of the self, "it is by the imagination only that we can form any conception of what are his sensations" (ibid.).[2] Imagination is a critical link because it denotes the human capacity to conceive of others and their feelings and sentiments while no longer in their immediate presence. As such, imagination provides a foundation for awareness. As a recent biographer notes, "Smith is extending the meaning of sympathy beyond the concept of sharing someone's feelings to that of an individual's *awareness* that he is sharing another person's feelings" (Ross, 1995, p. 164). This point is critical for Cooley, who makes the same distinction in his definition of sympathy, a cornerstone for his theory of the social. Cooley tells us that sympathy "denotes the sharing of any mental state that can be communicated, and has not the special implication of pity or other 'tender emotion' [such as compassion] that it very commonly carries in ordinary speech" (1902, rev. ed. 1922, p. 136). As such, relying on the essential ingredient of communication, it is a vehicle carrying thought and sentiment, important components of personal ideas, which, in turn, are building blocks of character and of selves, springing from and contributing to "the general life of society" (1902, rev. ed. 1922, pp. 138–39).[3] These personal ideas are derived from our imagination of others' appearance and behavior, and our sense of self, in turn, is derived from our imagination of our appearance to others.

The idea of sympathy incorporates Smith's account of human conduct by "spectators" external to oneself as well as the internal spectator operating on two levels: one's imagination of a hypothetical spectator's reaction to one's conduct; and one's judgment or judgment by conscience, thus, "the man within your breast" as "impartial spectator" (Smith 1976 [1759], pp. 21–22, 128–29, 134, 137, 147, 148, 153, 154, 157, 189, 215, 226–27). Thus we see the first two elements of Cooley's looking-glass self adumbrated. Cooley's looking-glass self has three aspects: one's imagination of one's appearance to another, one's imagination of the other's judgment of that appearance, and some sort of resulting self-feeling such as pride or mortification (Cooley, 1902, rev. ed. 1922, p. 184).

Smith used the term "impartial spectator" in lieu of "'conscience' for his self scrutinizing agency because he wished to avoid orthodox religious overtones here." Consequently "Smith reckons that it is society that provides a mirror in which we can see these things." In other words, "we can become spectators of our own behaviour and appearance, and so make judgments" (Ross, 1995, p. 166). The formulation of the impartial spectator adds depth, complexity, and perspective to the idea of sympathy inasmuch as it imputes a mental faculty to the human being enabling the objectification of one's self and one's behavior, that is, reflexivity. Smith anticipates Cooley in the same use of the looking-glass, when he says, "We suppose ourselves the spectators of our own behaviour, and endeavour to imagine what effect it would, in this light, produce upon us. This is the only looking-glass by which we can, in some measure, with the eyes of other people, scrutinize the propriety of our own conduct" (Smith, 1976 [1759], p. 112). Hence, as one scholar tells us, "Smith's conception of the social self is hardly distinguishable from Cooley's 'looking-glass self,' the sense of self that is evident whenever one's 'self-feeling' is determined by imagination of how one appears to another" (Shott, 1976, p. 43).

Dorothy Ross suggests that the addition of a focus on (inner) social control to what she calls the revisionist tendency in the liberal ideology of exceptionalism infusing nineteenth-century U.S. sociology derives from a European liberal base.[4] European liberalism is not monolithic; it is "subject to differing interpretations and is put to different uses, depending upon what implications are drawn from the view that the individual is 'self possessed'" (1991, p. 11). So it is clear that Smith's notions of sympathy—aside from his more familiar economic ideas—as awareness, and the impartial spectator, anticipate the integration of society and the individual (the internalization of the social, or the socialization process) through the reflective awareness that Cooley, then Mead (via role-taking), and later, the symbolic interactionists, placed at the base of the social. Indeed, some time ago this prompted Shott and other recent authors to point out that several of the concepts of the Scottish moralists, especially those of Smith, anticipated those central to symbolic interactionism, whose foundation supports the work of Cooley and Mead (Shott, 1976; Costelloe, 1997; Wilson and Dixon, 2004; Dingwall, 2001; Stryker, 1980, pp. 3–30).

Shott contends that the Scottish moralists "propounded the symbolic interactionist assumptions that society is necessarily antecedent to the individual, self and mind develop through interaction with others, self-control derives from social control, and people are actors as well as reactors" (1976, p. 39). While this attribution of identity is perhaps framed too closely in contemporary language and verges on retrospective reification, Shott accurately describes some of the Scottish moralists' thought as the precursor to Cooley's, Mead's, and the symbolic interactionists' approaches to society, self, and mind—including that "Most of the Scottish moralists shared the view that people are not born human, but derive their humanness from society" and that "only an impulse toward gregariousness is given by nature; all other qualities that make people human are mere latent capacities until developed through participation in social life" (p. 40). Other writers largely agree about the Scottish moralists' concord on sociability as foundational for that intellectual movement (Roger Emerson, 2003; Berry, 2003; Denby, 2004, p. 94; Ross, 1995, pp. 52, 176). Here the moralists' views remarkably resemble Cooley's ideas about a teachable human nature endowed with sociability.

Given Cooley's formulation of the social, its possible derivation from Adam Smith's notions of sympathy and the impartial spectator, and noting the similarities in their views of human nature, what does all of this say about the *historical* context of these ideas? The metaphor from Crabb's *Synonyms* about the community of meaning of the English graveyard suggests a key theme: a well-worn and nearly moribund English liberalism was imported and embedded in the ideology of American exceptionalism. While their use of liberal thought enabled social scientists in the United States to underscore a connectedness or sense of community with European thought, it also left many American sociologists to resurrect or warm over stale thinking; this both retarded and enhanced their theoretical acumen concerning the social. In Cooley's (and Mead's) case some of these ideas perhaps were inspirational, but their influence, at least so far as sympathy is concerned, remains somewhat recondite, as there are no pointed references to the moralists in their works. Nonetheless, I maintain that Cooley was probably influenced by Smith as a result of his training in economics and because he knew the work of Giddings, whose notion of "consciousness of kind" was based on Smith's ideas.[5]

But why did Cooley, and *not* his predecessors and contemporaries (including Giddings), accomplish the synthesis necessary to produce something fresh—a viable conception of the social—without rehashing clichés? The answer is that their subscription to the exceptionalist credo was not leavened by the influences that liberated Cooley's thinking, namely a broad background in and love of literature and art, including his clear identification with the essay tradition, and his reading of pragmatism. What motivated the pragmatic philosopher Mead to do so was the inspiration of Cooley's and William James's notions of the self and his search for an explanation of action shorn of the impediments of psychological parallelism (the simultaneous locating of events—consciousness—in the central nervous system with the experience paralleling them), which could answer the empirical requirements of scientistic behaviorism. Thus the sociologists turned into the blind alleys left to them by their exemplars Herbert Spencer and August Comte, and were forced to make do with the detritus of British liberalism and the leftovers of the other social sciences in the United States that had professionalized before sociology.

In sum, sociology in the United States, from the immediate post–Civil War period through the turn of the twentieth century, was shaped by three forces: (1) American exceptionalism, a national self-conception or ideological framework, which contends "that America occupies an exceptional place in history . . . based on her republican government and economic opportunity" provided by a continent of virgin land which set the country on a millennial course (Ross, 1991, p. xiv); (2) European liberal social thought, chiefly represented by the positivism of August Comte and the synthetic sociology of Herbert Spencer; and (3) the Sociological Movement, or the drive toward professionalization and the differentiation of sociology from the general body of social science in the United States. It is Cooley's exception to, or distance from, the latter two that distinguishes him from his predecessors and contemporaries. Thus, early in his career he fell away from the Comtean and Spencerian liberal dominion, which shaped the work of Lester Ward, and later on of Albion Small, Franklin Giddings, and Edward Allsworth Ross, and he did not fall victim to the eclecticism and reformist preoccupation of the Sociological Movement.

Exceptionalism and U.S. Sociology: The Liberal Heritage of Comte and Spencer

Regarding their revolution as a success, in contrast to the way Europeans regarded the French Revolution, and haunted by the fall of the Roman Republic,

Americans conceived of the "millennial newness" of the United States as an escape from European republican decay. This American attitude, though, was initially at base a mythical projection of European utopian fantasies onto the New World. The American creed's direct transposition of Lockean philosophy quite easily framed virgin America as a return to Locke's (free) state of nature, envisioning it in libertarian terms, suffused with property rights (Ross, 1991, pp. 10–11, 25). Moreover, Americans did follow the lead of Adam Smith, who had abandoned the republic, and mostly adapted his *economic* ideas to a burgeoning industrial economy, which at the nineteenth century's end, because of the tremendous increase in scale of corporate and public bureaucracies, fairly begged for government regulation. Thus they retained the republican state and maintained that "modern Western society [the United States] could for a long time come to escape the stasis or decline that had befallen all other societies by freeing the transformative energies of commerce and industry" (Ross, 1991, p. 6). In sum, more than simply evincing a glancing affinity with British liberalism and, in Cooley's case, the Scottish Enlightenment, sociologists in the United States frequently adapted these ideas by annealing their perspectives in the exceptionalist flame. These adaptations largely included subscriptions to and revisions of Spencerian sociology and Comtean positivism.

Dorothy Ross suggests that "the term 'liberal' was first adopted in the early nineteenth century by English and continental radicals who sought to destroy the remains of feudal and mercantilist power in the state and to place justice, representation, and economic activity on individualistic bases." This view emphasized the rights, powers, and potential of the individual. Along these lines, Adam Smith conceived of individual liberty as protected by an accountable government with limited legislative functions that "could be consigned to little else beyond securing individual rights from the interference of others" (1991, pp. 10, 11). But "capitalist development was already producing consequences Adam Smith had not foreseen," and liberals found themselves charged by conservatives with creating not harmony "but political chaos, social disorganization, and the exploitation of labor." Moreover, "only an organically integrated society . . . could be stable and just" (p. 12).

August Comte (1798–1857) responded to this critique by developing an organic conception of society as an entity (constituted of a "harmony" of interrelated parts) bound together by spiritual ties (Bryant, 1985, pp. 18–20; Coser, 1971, p. 10; Martindale, 1981, p. 78; Ross, 1991, p. 12). Conceiving of society, the sciences, and human beings as ineluctably developing through three stages—the theological, the metaphysical, and the positive—Comte believed that modernity (that is, the French Revolution and its aftermath) was producing moral and social chaos, which obscured the ultimate revelation of society's inevitable progress toward the positive stage within which scientific knowledge and understanding would emerge to provide social guidance. Hence liberal progress would produce the force creating social order. Largely disdaining political economists, Comte had high regard for Adam Smith, whom he saw as a moral philosopher "with a sense of what constitutes a true scientific method" (Simpson, 1969, p. 35).

Herbert Spencer soon followed and "put the last piece of liberal social science in place by developing a liberal version of sociology from the sociological materials implicit in Smith's political economy" (Ross, 1991, p. 15). Borrowing Smith's conception of progress through differentiation via the division of labor, he conferred upon this idea the status of a cosmic law of evolution serving as a prolegomenon to a massive synthetic philosophy (Spencer, 1873; 1896, 3 vols.; Cooley, 1920 in 1930, pp. 263–79; Barnes, 1948, p. 81–108; House, 1936, pp. 120–31; Schwendinger and Schwendinger, 1974, pp. 39–57; Martindale, 1971, pp. 81–85; Coser, 1971, pp. 89–127; Fine, 1956, pp. 32–46; Raison (ed.), 1969, pp. 76–91; Hofstadter, 1955, p. 31–50; Westby, 1991, pp. 146–68; Turner, 1985).[6]

In brief, from the key postulate establishing differentiation as an outcome are derived the respective principles of inorganic, organic, and "superorganic" evolution and the "factors of social phenomena" (Spencer, 1896, I, pp. 3–15). Spencer's "inductions" of sociology, applying principles of organic evolution to the phenomena most remote from the psychological evidence on which the theory is based, are used to trace the development of society as an organic analogue: the laws governing the organism and society are the same (p. 450). Thus Spencer traces their parallel development in size, structure, and function (and "equilibration") from homogeneity to heterogeneity, likening military and state structures and functions to organic defense systems, industry to digestion (the "sustaining" system), transportation and communication to vascular circulation (the "distributing" system) and the state and government to the neuro-motor mechanism (the "regulating" system) (pp. 459–536). He acknowledges that language and intellect and the human association based on them rendered society a breed apart from an organism with a "sensorium" (centrally located brain or nervous system), yet refuses to view society as more than a sum total of individuals. It "exists for the benefit of its members not its members for the benefit of society" (pp. 449–50). While positing its ineluctable moral evolution, Spencer simultaneously stresses society's analogy to an organism and refuses to acknowledge its progressive evolution by the aid of the evolved sensorium (government and the state).[7] His utilitarian view of happiness and his adherence to laissez-faire individualism thus prevented him from following through on his evolutionary principle beyond the assertion that society would achieve social integration permitting the evolution of industrialism and social peace (pp. 537–75).[8] Indeed, as Ross tells us, he drew "out the vision of harmony implicit in Smith's liberal ideal" and "pictured the functionally integrated, contractual, industrial society as a cooperative as well as competitive world, one which would produce altruism in its members and a peaceable world order" (Ross, 1991, p. 15). Beyond mere conferral of the superorganic label on society, however, Spencer's adherence to the organismic analogy, combined with his fixation on the negative state, prevented him from conceiving of a viable notion of the social.

Speaking of the influence of Spencer on nineteenth century social science in general, Cohen, in his study of the historical context of Cooley's work, remarks that "Spencer's sociology provided a model for American social scientists in the late nineteenth century. His conceptions of society and the proper ways of thinking about it were shared by both his defenders and critics. Notwithstanding differences on matters of practical social policy, there was a marked consensus of assumptions. Only when this consensus broke, did Americans transcend the Spencerian model and definitely refute it" (1967, p. 11).

One of the things that made Spencer so attractive to social scientists in the United States was his anticlericalism, bolstered by the cloaking of his laissez-faire antistatism in evolutionary and scientific garb. So plausible was he that as late as the immediate post–World War II period Harry Elmer Barnes could still write, "Few would today uphold so extreme a policy of laissez faire as Spencer sanctioned or wait so patiently for the impersonal laws of evolution to work out a program of reform as he assumed to be willing to do. Yet we cannot well doubt the wisdom of his advice to beware of the doctrine of the possibility of manufacturing progress by legislation that is not based on the widest possible knowledge of the sociological principles involved" (1948, p. 134). Suffice it to say that the nearly uniform consensus had a nearly paralytic effect on sociologists' conceptualization of the social. It was left to Cooley to dispel the Spencerian miasma. Of Cooley's break with Spencerianism I shall have more to say, but before I do this I wish to briefly summarize Lester Ward's synthesis, since Ward systematically integrated Spencer and Comte.

Lester F. Ward (1841–1913) appears as the first systematic sociologist in the United States. With respect to his notions concerning evolution, the use of biological analogies, and the role of sociological knowledge in social improvement and the amelioration of social problems, Ward's approach synthesized Comte and Spencer. Ward would appear to have liberated himself from the Spencerian model, but he chiefly takes issue with Spencer's laissez-faire while taking the organic analogy one step further, toward the socially liberal aims of the welfare state. Ward regards social evolution as a phase of cosmic evolution and therefore conceives of sociology as an evolutionary science (Chugerman, 1939; Barnes, 1948, pp. 173–90; Cohen, 1967, pp. 43–49; Commager (ed.), 1967; Gerver (ed.), 1963; Hinkle, 1980, pp. 68–72; Hofstadter, 1955, pp. 67–84; Martindale, 1960, pp. 81–85; Schwendinger and Schwendinger, 1974, pp. 163–97; Westby, 1991, p. 239). Following Spencer, he used natural science analogies, especially biological and botanical ones. Society develops "sympodially," like plants branching, and produces new syntheses ("synergy"). Mind emerges from this "zoism" (life process), which produces awareness or the capacity to distinguish pain from pleasure: feeling and desire are its forces, and intellect, a higher product, is directive. Nature in its nondirective and nonintentional fashion is wasteful, improving only by natural selection ("genesis"). Following Comte's emphasis on the progressive emergence and use of social knowledge, "telesis" or conscious intervention by mind is epitomized in the development of the state. The state is the chief element through which conscious control of the social process is effected vis-à-vis knowledge of the nature and operations of social forces. Education plays a central role, since it provides information useful to the state in its implementation of social or collective telesis.

In contrast to Spencer's view, government checks license and has prevented man from losing liberty (Barnes, 1948, p. 128–41; Hofstadter, 1955, pp. 67–84; House, 1936, pp. 232–35; Page, 1969, pp. 32–69; Schwendinger and Schwendinger, 1974, pp. 168–97). Like Spencer, however, Ward considers the state analogous to the brain of the organism. Humans thus participate in evolution, and laissez-faire is now nugatory, an impossibility.[9]

Both Ward and Spencer conceive of society as a new level of organization. Ward chiefly differs from Spencer in his championing of the positive state, but like his exemplar he stops short of probing the critical question of the relation between the individual and society. Consequently, "Ward's excessive reliance on biological analogy fails on conceptual and methodological grounds" (Furner, 1975, p. 300). Ward's sociology, in attempting to subject history and society to positive change, thus succumbs to the anachronistic deficiencies and nonviable conceptions of the social of his progenitors, Spencer and Comte. His sociology is, as Dorothy Ross tells us, "the first major statement in American social science of the new liberalism," but he has "little insight into the distinctively social aspects of psychology and society, which would ultimately become the focus of the field" (1991, pp. 91, 94). Hence, it may be true that, as the first systematic U.S. sociologist Ward put sociology as a profession on its feet, but barely erect; lacking a viable conception of the social it could at best stumble forward theoretically. Cooley does take the insight of society's sympodial growth and development from Ward as a hallmark of social process, typifying it as the "tentative method."

Cooley's Liberation from Spencer

"We read Spencer at twenty-five but prefer Montaigne at fifty," is Cooley's pronouncement in his last book, *Life and the Student* (1927, p. 63), a volume culled from his journal. Chronologically and thematically these are Cooley's last words on Spencer, for they aptly attest to his liberation from the Spencerian pall through the literary sensibility he had acquired long before his middle age. The formative literature of his youth, to be sure, differed from that of Spencer, whose youthful experience Cooley describes as follows:

> His mind was active, but chiefly upon inquiries of his own—into mechanics, natural history, or ethics—and even then he showed signs of that incapacity for sustained reading which was pathological in his mature years. . . . Nor does it appear that he ever studied history, literature, or philosophy, except as he was incited to occasional reading in these subjects by the requirements of his own work. . . . We may think of him, then, as a bright, argumentative boy, rather disagreeably self-confident, well supplied with ideas, many of them original, regarding mathematics, natural science, and the conduct of life, but notably deficient in the foundations of traditional culture. (Cooley, 1920 in 1930, p. 264)

The result, in Spencer, was "one who does not need to pore over the records of the past, but is already competent, by virtue of natural gifts and a philosophy of his own device, to instruct the world on these questions," that is, one displaying "a cocksureness that does nothing to reconcile us to his insufficiency" (p. 268). So while, as Cooley states in an essay describing Spencer's childhood and temperament, their bearing on his sociology and a description of his work, "I imagine that nearly all of us who took up sociology between 1870, say, and 1890 did so at the instigation of Spencer," he also informs us that "nearly all of us fell away from him," noting that his own defection "was one of the earliest and most complete" (1930, p. 263).

Cooley's perspective differs from his colleagues in sociology, not so much in his disenchantment with Spencer, as in the reasons for it. He judges Spencer's blindness to style (which Cooley conceives as a kind of personal communication) and consequent lack of empathy, a product of a "schoolmasterish sort of egotism" and a "defect of sympathy" (pp. 266, 267). This insensitivity is, perhaps, one of the most serious defects from which all of Spencer's other faults derive: "he does not seem interested in the fact—if indeed he perceives it at all—that at least half of style is the communication of personal attitudes, and this by means so subtle as to defy the rather mechanical analysis which he employs" (p. 266). In other words, this mode of representation is beyond Spencer's ken. As we shall see, the personal element of style is pivotal both for Cooley's practice of writing and for his way of conceiving of society, social organization, social change, and the self.

Spencer's organicism Cooley sees as the dead mechanism of system-building. There is great consistency in his published and unpublished writing, such as his journal, concerning his distaste for the system-building of Spencer and of those, such as Giddings, who followed him. In "Reflections Upon the Sociology of Herbert Spencer" (1920 in 1930, pp. 263–79), he credits Spencer with inspiring American scholars to take up sociology: "Whatever we may have occasion to charge against him, let us set down at once a large credit for effective propagation" (p. 263). Having paid his respects, and praising Spencer for the "energy of his speculative impulse," Cooley sallies forth, stating that Spencer is "inclined to domineer over his facts, instead of listening with open mind to what they had to say" (p. 269). By the same token, "Spencer spun a theory from any material he happened to have and collected facts to illustrate it" (p. 270). Spencer is conceived as a person "deficient in those sympathetic qualities which are, after all the only direct source of our knowledge of other people" (p. 265). Thus "both his analysis and his synthesis were *a priori*" (p. 270). And while Spencer himself saw his work as obliterating prior theological foundations, "his work belonged . . . in a class with the systematizers of theology—Thomas Aquinas, perhaps, or John Calvin—rather than with the true men of science" (ibid.).

As to the particulars of Spencer's doctrine, he is faulted for omitting a viable social psychology and for relying on a utilitarian model coupled with the Lamarckian idea of the cumulative inheritance of acquired mental traits to explain the social sentiments. From these Spencer arbitrarily dichotomizes the higher sentiments as either egoistic or altruistic, rather than "just social" (pp. 271–72). Likewise, Spencer's conception of justice fails "to see that it also represents the accumulated wisdom of the past transmitted through language. His process is not social but biological and individual" (p. 272). While Spencer's social organism does encompass "a differentiated and co-ordinated society, . . . this is conceived almost as if it were continually reproduced from biological roots" (p. 273).

So Spencer had little conception of a social order, or of persons and their relations within it. Cooley also objected to Spencer's doctrine of the negative state (laissez-faire) and denied that this was a corollary of Darwinism.[10] While his notions of differentiation, coordination, and life of humans as progressive organization gave Cooley in the 1880s "an animating and assuring perspective," he is put off by Spencer's insensitivity to life "summed up in terms of life, not translated into another language" (p. 275). Spencer "lacked direct and authentic perception of the structure and movement of human life, and . . . he conceived these phenomena almost wholly by analogy" (p. 269).

Cooley's view, as we know, while retaining use of the term "organic," in no way descends into the literal application of the biological analogy to society. It more resembles John Dewey's liberal exceptionalist conception wherein democracy "'approaches most nearly the ideal of all social organization; that in which the individual and society are organic to each other'" (quoted in Ross, 1991, p. 163). Furthermore, "Such an organic society was not an authoritarian state nor a biological organism"; rather society is a type of organism wherein the individual "joins his will with the whole in cooperative, coordinated action" (ibid.). Such a view conceives of society as a gestalt, and in Cooley's case this is done utilizing a viable conception of the social derived from an interpretive or reflexive social base.

Communication: Cooley's Transition into Self and Social Organization

A key element liberating Cooley from Spencer, and serving as well as a spring-board for his approach to self and social organization, is his early focus on communication, which he conceives as embedded in and as the instrumentality deeply interpenetrating both the individual and society. His early mention of communication appears in his theory of transportation, first discussed in two papers, one becoming his doctoral thesis. Of this initial focus on communication Cooley reminisces, "Communication was thus my first real conquest, and the thesis a forecast of the organic view of society I have been working out ever since" (1928 in 1930, p. 8). The paper on transportation (1894), coauthored with his father, Thomas McIntyre Cooley, still bears traces of Spencerian influence in its stress on the analogy between the "body politic" or social organism and the physical body. "The Theory of Transportation" of the same year (1894 in 1930, pp. 17–118), while also retaining vestiges of Spencer—for example: "the economic idea is held to be, at bottom, the nourishment idea" (p. 62), emphasizes the reciprocity between transportation and social development. Here we see the homologous stress on communication and transportation within the organismic approach:

> Sociologically considered it [transportation] is a means to the physical organization of society. Development or evolution, the organization of social forces, implies unification of aim, specialization of activities in view of a common purpose, a growing interdependence among the parts of society. *Such organization, such extension of relations, involves a mechanism through which relations can exist and make themselves felt. This mechanism is Communication in the widest sense of that word; communication of ideas and physical commodities, between one time and another and one place and another* [my italics]. (p. 40)

Linking the physical aspects of communication with the communicative aspects of transportation (for example, communication as "thought transportation"), Cooley surmises that "material transportation and the communication of thought make use in part of the same instruments . . . and are analogous in their functions when highly organized. . . . Thus a century ago the 'post' carried light commodities and was also a vehicle of the transfer of thought" (p. 60). Nonetheless, "transportation is physical, communication psychical"

(p. 61). Viewed from this standpoint and the organismic context within which Cooley places it, communication could, indeed, serve as the ineffable "missing link" that Small speaks of (see below), for Cooley's early writings indicate that it is communication that establishes a clear distinction between the social and biological realms. Moreover, human nature is conditioned by communication (1897; see also Cohen, 1967, pp. 75–81). This focus of communication, however, does not pop up ex nihilo in Cooley's thinking; it is fostered, in great measure, although by no means exclusively, by Cooley's exposure and subscription to the premises of pragmatism.

Standing now upon the threshold of the parturition and maturation of Cooley's approach, the question that comes to mind is: Yes, Cooley sees through Spencerianism, but is the source of his insight into the fecundity of communication merely negative? In other words, what keeps him from throwing out the baby (society) with the bathwater (organicism à la Spencer), as Giddings had done with Smith's sympathy and the impartial spectator? To simply ascribe his thought to his genius is to mystify the matter. Clearly it comes from somewhere, but certainly only indirectly from Europe. While Cooley spent some of his youthful *Wanderjahr* in Germany in the 1880s, he apparently was not inspired by German thought at this time, although a later reading of Albert Schäffle provided him with intellectual weaning from Spencer.[11]

The acknowledged catalyst is pragmatism, especially in its social scientific implications in the work of William James and John Dewey (Cooley, 1902, rev. ed. 1922, p. 125 ff.). Pragmatism's conception of action unmoored from instinct, that is, from biological determinism and from the biologistic rooting of society in the Spencerian evolutionary meshes, supplies a philosophical grounding for Cooley. As we shall see, pragmatism's efficacy in this regard is both philosophical and rhetorical, for its conception of action and language and thought as action weds its perspective to common sense and the social world. Moreover, James's notion of the self directly inspires Cooley's own formulation.

The inability to adequately conceptualize the social, except by biological analogy, which Ward shared with his successors Small, Giddings, and Ross, is attributable to the historical context provided by the Social Science Movement of the post–Civil War period and the subsequent branching off of the individual social science associations, whereupon sociology, being the last to achieve professional autonomy, was left with the dregs of the others.

The Social Science and Sociological Movements

In the United States, sociology initially appears more as a sectarian movement than as a scientific discipline. As in the case of the halting development of the natural sciences and the professions earlier in U.S. history (Daniels, 1968; Calhoun, 1965; Gilb, 1966; Gerstl and Jacobs, 1976), sociology had to fend for itself amid a welter of competing movements in and out of the academy. While it could brag of its purist scientific and abstract character, as an offshoot of the American Social Science movement it had roots in philanthropic and liberal-reformist praxis as well.

The Social Science Movement began in the immediate post–Civil War period among an eclectic congeries of concerned citizen-amateurs devoted to humanitarian causes, that is, among social reformers and activists as well as academic social scientists (Furner, 1975, pp. 1–34). In this respect, social science replaces the energizing facility of religion as a means of addressing pressing social issues and problems, and so for the reform-minded, "Social Science was a substitute religion for those whom the ferocious and moss-grown old New England theology had alienated from more conservative churches" (p. 545). Soon there developed a search for a common denominator, but despite its tortured quest for one, it was clear that this "Social Science must not be confused with Socialism, with Radicalism, nor even Philanthropy" (Bernard and Bernard, 1965, p. 574).

Concomitant with the emergence of corporate capitalism in the latter half of the nineteenth century, tensions concerning the proper roles of social scientists as advocates of reform, social causes, and social groups, as opposed to disinterested gatherers and analysts of scientific data, began to appear (Furner, 1975, p. 8). By the 1890s these tensions culminated in the various social science professions establishing their autonomous associations. It is largely out of this movement toward professionalization that sociology grows. The American Social Science Association represented an unstable fusion of ideals that were finally split and segmented into different disciplines representing an overriding schism between reform and academic interests:

> The social reform ideal, harnessed now to prosaic and concrete problems of charity and philanthropy, delinquency and dependency . . . was finally separated from the other disciplines and became the disciplines of social work, social legislation, and various other social welfare disciplines. The scientific ideal, freed from practical applications, gradually emerged as economics, sociology, and political

science, and the American Economics Association [1885], the American Sociological Society [1905], and the American Political Science Association [1894] became the child and the grandchildren of the American Social Science Association. (Bernard and Bernard, 1965, p. 529)

Even the leading figures in the field, while abjuring their identification with philanthropists and social workers, "could not agree where they stood in relation to other academic disciplines" (Furner, 1975, p. 297). Professional sociology emerged still unclear as to its scientific jurisdiction, and was indistinguishable from social science to many. Indeed, so identified with social science was sociology through the 1890s that "writers used the term [social science] more or less interchangeably with sociology." And so complete was the confusion that late in the 1880s the frequent identification was "rather striking" (Bernard and Bernard, 1965, p. 657).[12] This correlative development is referred to as the "rationalization of philanthropy" (House, 1936, pp. 219–27),[13] or the legitimation of reform (Oberschall, 1972). The gathering consolidation of professional sociology "was not of a spontaneous growth. . . . It was an administrative movement, synthetic rather than expansive in character. . . . Thus it was decidedly a movement 'engineered' from the top and consciously directed" (Bernard and Bernard, 1965, p. 528). This was largely due to the efforts of sociologists like Albion Small, who at the time "seemed to regard this synthesis as the chief function of the sociologists and of Sociology" (p. 595). Thus "as the most immediate successor to Social Science, [it] was accused of the same grandiose temerity as Social Science was guilty of, in undertaking such a synthesis" (ibid.). To accomplish this it had to withstand the onslaughts of more established competitors such as history, economics, and political science, disciplines emphasizing differentiation rather than synthesis. Its synthetic posture plus its unclear and often vague conception of its subject matter left sociology "content to serve humbly by developing the neglected and minor aspects of the social sciences in the college curricula. Thus it gained the reputation academically of being sort of a catch-all, but it thrived reasonably under such a dispensation" (Bernard and Bernard, 1965, p. 595).

In securing a disciplinary foothold, sociology's position was legitimated by figures such as Franklin Henry Giddings and Albion Small, who built the first independent departments, at Columbia University and the University of Chicago (House, 1936, pp. 245–46). The fortunate correlation of the expanding

universities at the turn of the century with the hatching of sociology as a discipline in an expanding academic market offered an opportunity to "a group
of upwardly mobile men who otherwise would not have moved into university positions through the already established disciplines" (Oberschall, 1972,
p. 189).[14] In this context sociology's miscellaneous character, inherited from
its social science forebear, was camouflaged by the illusion of systematization,
largely provided by the production of college textbooks for the field. As one
early historian of the field observes:

> Instructors in charge of college classes find that they are compelled to reduce their
> subject to the orderly and logically unified form in order to be able to present it
> effectively to immature students as anything but a collection of unrelated items. *It
> is no mere coincidence that the outstanding general treatises in sociology that have been
> produced in the United States in recent years have been written by authors who were
> also university professors and who had in view, in the preparation of their treatises, the
> needs of college classes* [my italics]. (House, 1936, p. 251)

In short, sociology compensated for its marginal heterogeneous and hybrid
qualities by seeking academic legitimacy. This resulted in a largely *didactic* or
rhetorical systematization. As Louis Wirth contended, during the first decade
of the twentieth century sociologists could, on the one hand, claim an autonomous subject matter, or, on the other, all of social life as their domain "and
justify themselves as an academic department by their efforts to understand
social life from a special viewpoint" (Bramson, 1961, p. 83). The ramifications
of this are manifested in a quandary, which continues to plague us. This Wirth
called our "Cinderella complex":

> Sociologists could not, however, be content for long in their humble positions
> as devotees of a science of leftovers. Nor could the need for adjustment to and
> securing status in the American hierarchy . . . fail to generate grave dissatisfaction
> among the more logical thinkers in the field with the state of sociology as an
> *omnium gatherum*. As is often the case among those who are afflicted with the
> Cinderella complex, there developed a goodly number of sociologists with the
> aspiration to assume the role of generalissimo of the social sciences. Wherever
> these delusions of grandeur developed, however, they were soon met by rebuffs
> which in turn led to a reconsideration of the proper scope of sociology and its
> place among the sciences. This reflection has been proceeding uninterrupted ever
> since. (quoted in Bramson, 1961, pp. 83–84)

This complex, as Furner observes, enshrouded the discipline by the 1890s. Sociology developed two modalities in order to adapt to the emerging academic environment: in one, conceived as a coordinating or synthesizing master discipline as Comte and Spencer had originally envisioned, in the other as a science devoted to topics that its "critics did indeed consider leftovers: marriage, the family, poverty, crime, education, religion, and sex" (1975, pp. 297–98). A graduate student at Chicago, Ira Howerth, sending a questionnaire to academics connected with sociology, found among his respondents "'a chaotic condition of social thought,'" with respect to sociology's substantive purview and its relationship to neighboring fields. Nonetheless "the great majority thought it should occupy a separate university department. Professional ambitions obviously outran intellectual development" (Howerth quoted in Ross, 1991, p. 131).

Perhaps an even more trenchant related matter concerns the conceptions of the social, groups, and the scope of the discipline held by Cooley's most eminent contemporaries. Comparison of Cooley with his contemporaries reveals the leap he took in capturing the essence of the social as a foundation for sociology as a freestanding discipline. I use the expression "the social" to refer to the articulation of what constitutes a social phenomenon in the spirit of Durkheim's enunciation of "social facts" or Cooley's "social knowledge" (Durkheim, 1938; Cooley, 1926 in 1930). While Cooley and Durkheim derive significantly contrasting methodologies from these conceptions, it is important to note that both clearly and explicitly address the issues of the ontology and epistemology of social phenomena. This discussion was a severe and limiting omission among U.S. sociologists of the nineteenth and early twentieth century, and had critical theoretical consequences, as revealed in the work of Small, Giddings, and Ross. They are instructive as much for what they omit as for what they postulate in their conceptions of the social, and their ideas thus serve as useful comparisons with Cooley's.

Small, Giddings, and Ross

Sociology's miscellaneous quality epitomized the work of Albion Small, whom Barnes calls "Promoter of American Sociology and Expositor of Social Interests" (1948, pp. 409–35). Besides building the Chicago department he produced, in collaboration with Vincent, the first introductory textbook. Moreover, Barnes notes that Small's books all grew out of his classroom lectures and seminar discussions (p. 413). Finally, this chief spokesman of the "sociological movement" developed a social psychology whose basic ontological unit was the individual joined to a social process centering around interest groups (Kress, 1970, p. 89–106)[15] and deriving from "'the reappearance in the social realm of the physiological phenomenon of the somatic building of organisms,'" that is, from a Spencerian and organicist revisionist base (Schäffle, Schmoller and Wagner—the Bismarckian "socialists of the chair"). One scholar (Kress, 1970, p. 103) comments that it was Small's commitment to the sociological movement and the expediencies of professionalization that cost him more thorough analysis: he was "much less prepared . . . to dismiss his predecessors as incompetent or mistaken" and "the compromises, the patchwork, and the stopgaps that Small employed are more likely to reflect the course a discipline will pursue in the short run."[16]

In a rejoinder to an article by a Princeton political scientist criticizing sociology as a discipline without a de facto subject matter (Ford, 1909, p. 259), Small makes a puerile attempt to parry the accusation, and can do no more than offer sociology's undiscovered "missing link" as a retort:

> Professor Ford demands acceptance of the a priori that *the state existed before the individual* [Small's italics]. This is like denying scientific value to biology until it solves the riddle of the priority of chick or egg, and deduces the details of biological knowledge from that a priori. *In as much as we have not produced the missing link* [my italics], and do not know its habitat and its habits, we should be somewhat premature, whether we called ourselves sociologists or anything else. . . . What we do know is that wherever human experience has been observed one of its elements has been an incessant reciprocating process between individuals and their groupings. (p. 259)

The missing link Small alludes to is *the social*, which he baldly states remains undiscovered and is not understood beyond the "reciprocating processes" between individuals and groups. This is all the more striking considering the fact that Small cites Cooley's two major books, *Human Nature and the Social Order* (1902, rev. ed. 1922) and *Social Organization* (1909), in his "Vindication . . ." (1909, p. 9)—books in which Cooley clearly expounds on the relation between society and the individual, the self, social interaction, primary groups, communication, public opinion, social classes, and so on. One can only conclude that Small either had not read them, or if he had, failed to make the proper connections between their content and his argument.[17] Or perhaps we might understand this lapse as reflecting the hiatus encountered between the conceptions of the innovator—in this case Cooley—and the level of understanding prevalent among his peers, for whom these formulations have outstripped their understanding. Judging by Small's fixation on the level of Spencerian organic analogues, and his careerist and entrepreneurial bent, it is understandable that he was unable to rise to the occasion of clearly enunciating the unique ontological character of the social.

A similar argument can be made in the case of Giddings, Small's contemporary who presided over the rival Columbia department. Giddings (Ross, 1991, pp. 127–32; Northcott, 1948; Martindale, 1960, pp. 317–21; Odum, 1951, pp. 86–94; Cohen, 1967, pp. 50–61) derived an approach emphasizing first principles, and Spencer authenticated his short summary of his sociological theory (Barnes, 1948, p. 85). Giddings emphasized positivism in his missionary zeal for statistical or quantitative approaches, stressing the positive role of sociology (as does Ward) serving civic reform. Martindale (1960, pp. 317–21) calls him a "pluralistic behaviorist," because, in deriving the principles of association from Spencerian postulates, notions such as "like-mindedness" and "reflective sympathy" leading to the emergence of "consciousness of kind," are merely proxies for Tarde's "imitation." Giddings stresses parallel responses to parallel stimuli over interaction. Social behavior is simplistically conceived as plural individual behavior.

Giddings's theory of the social mind, or the objectification of society qua human self-consciousness, derives from language that puts the individual into contact with the "general fund," the residual store of experiences common to all (Giddings, 1896, p. 132). Instead of pursuing this insight vis-à-vis communication and/or a naturalistic approach to custom, however, he elaborates on the differences between the individual and social minds and lapses into the more sterile Tardean orientation of mass psychology:

> The social mind is a concrete thing. It is more than any individual mind and dominates every individual will. Yet it exists only in individual minds, and we have no knowledge of any consciousness but that of individuals. The social consciousness, then, is nothing more than the feeling or thought that appears at the same moment in all individuals. . . . The social mind is the phenomenon of many individual minds in interaction, so playing upon one another that they simultaneously

feel the same sensation or emotion, arrive at one judgment and perhaps act in concert. It is, in short, the mental unity of many individuals or of a crowd. It is therefore a product of what M. Tarde has called a social logic, which binds the products of individual logic into more complex wholes. (1896, p. 134)

Giddings's pluralist view, conceiving of society as a sum total of individuals, marks the retention of Spencer's individualism. The hearkening back to Tarde's imitation-based formulation is especially ironic since consciousness of kind is founded upon Giddings's reading of sympathy encountered in Adam Smith's *The Theory of Moral Sentiments* (1976 [1759]). Sympathy, however, is merely a synonym for contagion in Giddings's approach, which is nestled in the overarching parameters of the Spencerian organismic perspective: it is tantamount to "attraction (*sympathie*) in the broadest sense of the word" (Tarde, 1969, p. 224 ff.), and Giddings, who is unable to see the forest for the trees, naively equates it with fellow feeling, the name Smith uses for sympathetically *derived* social behavior, and which Giddings baldly applies to the imitation-derived group as "a conscious perception of likeness" (Ross, 1991, p. 130). Nowhere does Giddings incorporate or integrate sympathy with Smith's impartial spectator, as Cooley does—sympathy supplying the connective tissue for the intersubjective or reflexively based operation of the imagination in social interaction and both the constitutive and operative processes of the self.

As to why Giddings misses the boat despite using the term, Joas assists our understanding (1996, p. 186) in offering the observation that sympathy is a notion more associated with literature than philosophy—that is, academic writing: "only in literature does 'sympathy' play a constitutive role for the ego as actor." Representing the "right wing" of the liberal exceptionalist revisionists Ross refers to, Giddings was a staunch positivist whose theory literally conceived the arithmetic plurality of individuals as constituting society. He was so influenced by Tarde, who focused on "small-scale repetitions of personal acts in interaction," and was so positive that "these could be—and ultimately had to be—analyzed statistically" (Martindale, 1960, p. 318), that he never went on to develop the concept beyond consciousness of kind.[18] His Spencerian-derived evolutionary view prompted him to call "for precise or quantitiative study by the statistical method" (Northcott, 1948, p. 762). Ross views his conceptual transformations as symptomatic of Giddings's formulation of the exceptionalist ideology: "Giddings had found the classical conception of liberal society, and drawn from it a double-edged sword fit for the modern industrial world. His evolutionary theory [incorporating consciousness of kind] put these invidious conflicts [racial hatred and class prejudice] on the road to ultimate extinction, but in the interim, it fixed them in natural law" (1991, p. 130). Thus, as Giddings put it, "Of all the modes of socially distributed surplus energy, the most important are sympathy and allied elements in the consciousness of kind. Given this force, the transformations of the weak by the strong necessarily become to some extent an uplifting instead of an exploitation. Given the equilibration of energy through uplifting, there is a necessary growth of equality and an increasing possibility of successful democracy of the liberal type" (quoted in Northcott, 1948, p. 758).

As a result of his wholesale acceptance of the Spencerian paradigm, Giddings felt no need to focus on sympathy as more than a mechanical building block for the social mass mind rather than the medium for intersubjectivity. Thus, the sins of the Spencerian father were visited upon the son: Spencer's schizoid dissociation of his notion of society as the superorganic from his individualism prevented him from analyzing the social as such. Beyond the motivation of having his own notions of morality serve as a springboard for his theory, Spencer cannot, as Durkheim would, bring morality into the sphere of sociological analysis. Similarly, Giddings could not truly integrate Smith's notion of sympathy reflexively. For Giddings the social mind is merely a plurality, or a literal compounding—à la Tarde—of individual minds.

By and large, E. A. Ross, who was considered a social psychologist with a strong reform emphasis (Barnes, 1948, pp. 819–32; Martindale, 1960, pp. 321–24; Kolb, 1948, pp. 448–61; Faris, 1967, p. 5), went no further than Giddings. Ross defined social psychology as collective behavior ("planes" and "currents" of feeling) also analyzed from the standpoint of Tarde's notions of conventionality and custom based on imitation.[19] Thus, his social psychology missed the pragmatic influence that fostered Cooley's and Mead's conceptual flowering, and his discussions of "social forces" (based on desires motivating human beings) and social process, were thought by an earlier commentator, Harry Elmer Barnes, to lack a level of coherence that other systematic thinking already had achieved. This "minimizes the possibility that his system as such will ever have a great deal of importance for formal sociological theory" (Barnes, 1948, p. 831).

The Tarde-Giddings-Ross intellectual axis, representing extreme sociological naïveté with its emphasis on segmentalized, pluralistic—as opposed to truly

social—action, was easily accommodated with quantitative analysis. The joining of segmentalized social psychology with the quantitative emphasis, a tendency that has persisted and become hegemonic through the present and has
even permeated aspects of the symbolic interactionist tradition (such as the
Iowa School), comfortably accommodates theories of the middle range. Frac-
tionalization and quantification make companionable bedfellows. Historically,
statistics became the fellow traveler of sociology when, after its sectlike beginnings in the late 1830s, it evolved from its "almanac period" through its attempts
to rationalize reform (1860s), thence into its crisis, when it sought academic legitimacy and joined with the social science course at Columbia in the late 1880s
(Bernard and Bernard, 1965, pp. 641, 783–831).

While the affinity of a "segmental pluralism" for quantitative approaches
enhanced its professional standing in the short run, it could not solidify sociology's theoretical vantage point. Sociology could only enhance sovereignty over
a fragmented and ambiguous territory (Small's *omnium gatherum*") by developing a solid theoretical foundation, that is, by clearly articulating the nature of
the social and defining the group as something quite other than a sum total of
individuals. This task was handicapped by the legacy of Spencer, whose iron-
clad evolutionary system, resting on possessive individualism, failed to produce
a viable and heuristic conception of the social and the group.

Sociology's historical context as an offshoot of reform and the Social Science Movement, and the exigencies of securing for itself academic legitimacy,
left it comprising little more than an assortment of miscellany. Indeed, even
after social psychology had gotten under way, the problem persisted, and while
Spencer's organicism was now crumbling, social scientists "were after a theory
that filled the gap between the social state of mind in the individual and the objective fact of social interaction" (Cohen, 1967, pp. 101–2). Furner (1975, p. 304)
accurately states that by the 1890s "[i]t was no longer possible to establish a
discipline by proclamation" and that at the twentieth century's turn "the most
original and productive scholars . . . wanted to know what the social group was,
where it came from, how it functioned, how it lasted, how it controlled its
individual members, and how it might be destroyed" (pp. 305–6). She places
Cooley and his notion of the primary group at the head of her list, followed by
Giddings's consciousness of kind and socialization, William Graham Sumner's
folkways and mores, and Ross's social control. Sumner represents an interesting case because his discussions of in-groups and out-groups, ethnocentrism,

institutions, and the components of culture (folkways and mores) do come to grips with the social; that is, his analysis of social groups from the standpoint of the components of societal and group cultural codes does not reduce these to simplistic formulae. Unfortunately Sumner's insights are eclipsed in contemporary discussions by his reputed conservatism, his fixation on laissez-faire, and his antistatist politics. Yet, as Ross says, "Sumner spelled out the tenets of possessive individualism, as Cooley articulated the new liberal organicism," and "[b]oth drew immediate criticism from their contemporaries for their extreme moods" (1991, p. 247). She avers that "the analytic power and ideological resonance of both gave their work remarkable vitality through the twentieth century" (ibid.).

Cooley and the Sociological Movement

Because Cooley was able to sufficiently emancipate himself from organicist doctrine, he had no trouble in tunneling to the social from the opposite directions of self and society. Nor did he, despite his use of the term "imitation," joined with "sympathy," early in his career, fall into the Tardean trap of imitation and like-mindedness. Robert E. L. Faris's classic summary of trends and events in early U.S. sociology notes that the Tarde-Ross-Giddings treatment of imitation and attraction of the like-minded is merely a halfway step toward "true sociology." He argues that it is perhaps the intense rivalry between Durkheim and Tarde that influences the neglect of the former in the United States, and which sidetracked sociologists from the insight that "persons are drawn together into organizations, not by imitation or like-mindedness, but by the fact that [as Durkheim saw] their very differences fit into a complementary pattern in which properties not present in the individual appear" (1967, p. 8). Faris suggests that this ignorance set sociology back for more than thirty years (until the early 1920s). On the heels of this, Faris says that "about the turn of the century Charles Horton Cooley set out to give a clear formulation to the essence of sociological cohesion in his two books [*Human Nature and the Social Order* (1902, rev. ed. 1922) and *Social Organization* (1909)]. . . . In words which still read well today he characterizes the nature of primary groups, which are founded on likenesses among members, and of social organizations, which are not" (p. 9).[20] Faris's Chicago bias perhaps also forces his omission of Cooley as the first formulator of a sociological concept of self (it preceded Mead's), but he accurately discerns why Cooley's thought and the Michigan department, despite Cooley's having had "the clearest vision" of the proper direction to be taken by a viable sociological tradition, do not become dominant in the field:

> At this point it might seem that Michigan should have achieved a considerable lead over other American Universities in the building of a sound sociological tradition since in the first decade of the century Cooley appeared to have the clearest vision of its proper direction. But . . . a variety of factors play a part in this process, and the diffident and literary Cooley, who was no organizer or promoter, did not offer a model of research activity which graduate students could emulate. His contribution was to a wider world of sociology more than to the Michigan campus. (ibid.)

Cooley's account of sociology at Michigan (Cooley, 1928 in 1930) bears out Faris's comments. He informs us that the growth of sociology was slow. The Michigan department, still joined with economics and business administration at the end of World War I, had Cooley occupying its sole full-time position until 1913, when he was able to add another position. Cooley mentions that Michigan shared in the general expansion of universities following the war, mentioning several appointments of new members between 1925 and 1927 (pp. 13–14). As far as graduate work was concerned, Cooley tells us that he was "never without a group of able graduate students, though none, during the first ten years, took his Doctor's degree at Michigan in the subject" (p. 11). That he was not a professionalizer and maintained role distance from his professional involvement speaks both to Cooley's attitude toward his participation in, and his promotion of the organizational and entrepreneurial life of, the discipline, and the kind of energy he invested in these activities.

Being one whose orbit lay outside the professionalizing round of his sociologist peers, and being an intellectual loner as well, gave Cooley a reputation as a nonconformist, as attested to, for example, by his view of textbooks, written in prose reminiscent of Thoreau: "Is a good text-book possible? Or is a text-book in its nature a machine, uncongenial to the free growth of the soul? Some day, probably, I shall come to writing one. At present I am exploring and describing the country, not laying railroads so that every one may follow me at two cents a mile" (*Journal* V. 18b [2/16/08–1/1/10] 7/8/08, p. 14). His sentiment toward this kind of writing was recognized by the sociologists of his day, a clue to which is provided by a review of his first book, *Human Nature and the Social order* (1902, rev. ed. 1922) in which the reviewer, George E. Vincent, coauthor with Albion Small of the first textbook in the field, refers to Cooley's work as "something of an anomaly in sociological literature." It is "none the less welcome for its very non-conformity." Vincent's review of Cooley's second book, *Social Organization* (1909), says that it is not primarily a textbook since it "lacks on the one hand the technical arrangement and apparatus for the work of the classroom, and on the other the 'source' material now so much in demand to supplement library facilities" (Vincent, 1909, p. 418). This view persisted despite the fact that Cooley appended classroom study questions to both books.

Cooley's detachment from the Sociological Movement, that is, the professional/institutional position of sociology in the universities and colleges of the United States and the professional associations of the discipline, can be overstated. He participated in the affairs of his academic department and university, was active in the life of his profession, and attended professional meetings throughout the country: he assisted in the formation of the American Sociological Society in 1905, attended annual meetings of the organization, and served as its eighth president in 1918.

But while he participates in it, he did maintain a kind of role distance, a mental reserve, toward the discipline and its tendencies. Cooley's sentiments and predilections regarding professional sociology and science evince aloofness from the profession and from department-building academic activity. Thus, on December 30, 1905, returning from a trip where he has assisted in the formation of the American Sociological Society, Cooley comments ambivalently: "I have no great expectations of the movement: [I] even doubt whether such an organization is not, to me personally, more hindrance than help. Organizations foster mediocrity. Still it will probably make for sound cooperative thinking in the long run" (*Journal* V. 18a [9/9/04–2/11/08] 12/30/05, pp. 58–59). Thus, on the one hand, anticipating the upcoming combined meetings of the American Economic Association and the American Sociological Society, Cooley could muse on the possibility that "I might share in moulding the growth of sociology not only by writing but by direct intercourse with the men who are of that growth," and by getting "to know somewhat intimately the significant men and what they are trying to do, to exchange views with them and help capable men to find suitable positions." He adds he might "help in so conducting our Society [ASS] to make it a center of cooperation, encouragement and guidance for younger students." On the other hand, this participation was a trial to him, as is evident from his reflection on the meeting afterwards: "I got thro [sic] the meeting with rather less exhaustion and chagrin than formerly" (*Journal* V. 20 [10/31/11–11/1/13] 12/1/12, pp. 50–51). At the end of 1928, having just returned from the ASS annual meeting in Chicago, where he read a paper on the life-study method, he reports that the nominating committee's choices for the presidency were defeated, and William Fielding Ogburn was nominated and chosen from the floor. He concludes: "Our association has become so prosperous and influential that the offices are become an object of ambition and, a little perhaps, of intrigue." Two days later, he adds: "I find I am seriously disturbed by a cloud on the future of our enterprise to which I have in some degree devoted myself—the Sociological Society, for example, which seemed at the meeting to be developing questionable tendencies" (*Journal* V. 24 [10/4/28–4/7/29] 12/30/28, 1/2/29, pp. 8–9). He does not elaborate on what these tendencies were, but, despite his active participation, he retained a skeptical eye.

In 1907, with a well-received book, *Human Nature and the Social Order* (1902, rev. ed. 1922), behind him and with a foot into the prime of his career, Cooley weighed his choices: "I must choose between research and diffusion. There are things I might do to advance sociology in the university, but which I can do only at the expense of my scholarship. . . . There are plenty of others to welcome the crowd" (*Journal* V. 18a [9/9/04–2/11/08] 5/23/07, pp. 121–22). It is apparent that he conceives of scholarship as a solitary activity as opposed to funded team research in an organizational setting. Later in life (1925), reminiscing about his aloofness from research entrepreneurship, he notes,

> I have not been notably successful in "organizing research." That is, I have not developed a line of study wherein, under my direction, men of mediocre talents could achieve substantial results. This should be possible, and I have serious compunctions, now and then, for not having done it. My feeling, however, is that a man with any real gift for research will provide the interest and initiative himself, on some hint that he gets from study or observation, and will need only encouragement, and guidance as to where to find what he wants. . . . Is it worth while to *think* for students? (*Journal* V. 22 [4/20/19–5/25/25] 7/20/22, p. 80)

A few pages down, he adds, "Social science is likely to flourish and vulgarize. Most of what is written will be by men of no insight or distinctive force, and, like enough, in controversial spirit" (p. 82). How different from a precocious sociologist of today, who might gauge intellectual productivity and academic

success and security by the magnitude of his or her success in organizing research. Similarly, Cooley recognized the practical value of sociology as a policy
science, but "[I]t will not make wisdom easy. It will do for social policy what
the study of military history and tactics will do for a strategist or the study of
economics for a financier, or the study of psychology for a teacher" (*Journal* V.
18b [2/16/1908–1/1/1910] 5/11/1909, p. 51). Clearly, even as a sociologist he had
other priorities.

Thus, as one somewhat detached from the Sociological Movement, at least
in the sense of being a *promoter and professionalizer*, Cooley just quietly worked
on sociology. In contrast to many of his contemporaries, he has weathered well,
and his thought lives among us, perhaps not so much for its popularity (he has
been neither a fashionable figure nor the sole founder of a school), as for the
contemporaneousness of its wisdom. As I say in the introduction to this volume,
his thought has been incorporated into contemporary sociological literature,
and manifested in the slow but steady trickle of current scholarship tracing his
ideas. But this is an oversimplification: for as we shall see, his idea of what sociology should be—that is, what it meant to him—was something quite different
from that of his contemporaries, and, in some ways, even from ours today.

Cooley's aloofness and selectivity was *selectively* applied most trenchantly to
those figures incorporated into his thinking, his meticulousness regarding his
own personal evolution, and his observations of science and society. For example, while he states: "I resorted to writers of little system, but great wisdom" for
his inspiration, in the same place, "The Development of Sociology at Michigan," he observes that Giddings was the figure who turned his attention to the
"*academic* possibilities of sociology" [italics mine]. He notes, "I may add that I
had made the acquaintance of Giddings, probably at the 1890 meeting of the
American Economic Association at Washington, where, at least, I remember
hearing him speak, and that he had given kindly encouragement to my sociological aspirations. It was he more than any other who led me to believe that
sociology might have become a university subject, and myself a teacher of it"
(1928 in 1930, p. 5).

Giddings's influence was chiefly *vocational and professional*, since the 1890s
were formative years for the new science and for Cooley's career. Thus despite
the fact that Cooley cared little for Giddings's sociology, this did not prevent
him from establishing friendly relations with one who wielded formidable professional influence. Cooley's biographer, Edward C. Jandy, notes that the latter

offered Cooley a position at Columbia at the 1910 meeting of the American Sociological Society in St. Louis, which he turned down a month later. It is clear that he did not turn his intellectual distance into personal distance from those he associated with. It is to be expected that Cooley's criticisms of Giddings are similar to those of Spencer: "I note the following objections to Giddings (in his Inductive Sociology[:] Too much abstract, scholastic system; too much commonplace; owing to the preceding, a lack of that feeling of reality and significance that all writing ought to give; a tendency to view things in a physical way and a lack of thoroughly organic or vital ways of thinking" (*Journal* V. 17 [7/8/03–8/28/04] 10/16/03, p. 26). But Giddings did more than stimulate his interest: it was Giddings who composed the Ph.D. examination questions in sociology that Cooley took in 1894. The questions were sent from Columbia, and Cooley remarks that he doubts that anyone ever read his answers. As to Ward, "I had and have the greatest respect for Ward . . . but it would be untrue to say that his writings had any large part in forming my own conceptions of the subject" (1930, p. 5). If not Spencer, Ward, Giddings, and company, then who? From what does Cooley's framing of the social derive? The short answer is belles lettres and pragmatism.

Cooley's approach to sociology is both inter- and suprapersonal. His formulation of the social, the notion that society and self are twin-born, is fed by three rivers, each, in turn nourished by several streams: (1) the probable influence of Adam Smith; (2) the world of academic philosophy, sociology, and psychology, including pragmatism exemplified by John Dewey, William James, and the psychology of James Mark Baldwin, and (3) belles lettres, the essay tradition begun by Michel de Montaigne, that is, the great conversation traversing the ages whose representative contributors to Cooley's thought I discuss in chapters 4 and 5. In the next chapter I first discuss Cooley's approach to the self, then Mead's distorted view of it, and, finally, the influence of pragmatism in shaping his framework of the social.

CHAPTER TWO

THE SOCIAL SELF
Human Nature, Imagination, and Perception

A self-idea . . . seems to have three principal elements: the imagination of our appearance to the other person; the imagination of
his judgment of that appearance, and some sort of self-feeling,
such as pride or mortification. The comparison with a looking
glass hardly suggests the second element, the imagined judgment, which is quite essential. The thing that moves us to pride
or shame is not the mere mechanical reflection of ourselves, but
an imputed sentiment, the imagined effect of this reflection upon
another's mind.

CHARLES HORTON COOLEY,
Human Nature and the Social Order

Although Wm James had insight into the social nature of the
self, he did not develop this into a really organic conception of
the relation of the individual to the social whole. His conceptions are intensely individualistic, or, if you please, mystically
social, but not organically or intelligibly so. . . . He saw men as
separate individuals, not as, in any intelligible sense, members
of one another. A social, or perhaps I should say a sociological,
pragmatism remains to be worked out.

CHARLES HORTON COOLEY, *Journal,* April 7, 1921

Does Cooley's psychological account of the self lying in the mind
serve as an adequate account of the social individual in the collective life of society? The crucial point, I think, is found in Cooley's
assumption that the form which the self takes in the experience
of the individual is that of the imaginative ideas which he finds in
his mind that others have of him. And the others are the imaginative ideas which he entertains of them.

GEORGE HERBERT MEAD,
"Cooley's Contribution to American Social Thought"

Cooley's tripartite idea of the looking-glass self is a self-contained idea. Its definition immediately denotes the self as a reflexive entity or process deriving from sympathy or empathy, as imaginatively constructed, as perceptually based, and as embodying feeling. Moreover, it clearly emerges out of a social process in response to the other, leaving great latitude in determining that behavior of the other to which the self is responding. While the self exists in the minds of the members of society, Cooley is *not* saying that we blankly base our idea of ourselves on the actual opinions others hold of us. Rather, their opinions are perceptually filtered by our own minds. As he puts it, "I do not see how any one can hold that we know persons directly except as imaginative ideas in the mind" (1902 rev. ed. 1922, p. 120). No matter. It is clear that selves reflect, and, in turn, influence, the interactive mix, that is, they shape and are shaped by the intersubjective field(s) of action comprising the mundane world.

Considered in this way, Cooley's notion of the self has been characterized as the "empirical or social self," that is, a concept that has turned away from the individually based Cartesian *cogito,* representing the self as "disembodied, separated, and distinguished from the very corporeal body upon which it was otherwise philosophically mused and cast judgment," and, oppositely, a concept resting on the mundane construction of the self as found in everyday usage (Holstein and Gubrium, 2000, p. 18). Cooley immediately corrects the Cartesian frame for the self as "one-sided or 'individualistic' in asserting the personal or 'I' aspect to the exclusion of the social or 'we' aspect, which is equally original with it." Thus "Descartes might have said 'We think' *cogitamus,* on as good grounds as he said *cogito*" (Cooley, 1909, pp. 6, 9).[1]

Cooley's Conception of Human Nature: A Foundation of the Social Self

Cooley's notion of the self is directly predicated on his general view of human nature occupying the opening discussion of first book, *Human Nature and the Social Order* (1902, rev. ed. 1922). There he defines "the evolutionary point of view" as meaning "all our life has a history." In other words, "Every word we say, every movement we make, every idea we have, and every feeling, is, in one way or another, an outcome of what our predecessors have said or done or thought or felt in past ages. There is an actual historical continuity from their life to ours" (1902, rev. ed. 1922, pp. 3–4).

For Cooley history and social influence precede biology; evolution is defined in historical terms. Only after this proclamation does he insert the Darwinian principle that life "is all one great whole, a kinship, unified by a common descent" (p. 4). But having said this, Cooley is not ready to discard the body, biological disposition, and the social process, which influence each other. Thence Cooley characterizes heredity and the environment (defined as synonymous with communication or social transmission) as a stream (heredity) with a road (environment) running along its bank. "The road is more recent than the stream: it is an improvement that did not exist at all in the earliest flow of animal life, but appears later as a trail . . . and finally develops into an elaborate highway" (pp. 4–5). The germ plasm (heredity)—the antecedent body—is the main source of bodily traits, mental endowment, tendencies to "a sort of physical development" and "capacity, aptitude, disposition, lines of teachability, or whatever else we may call the vague physical tendencies that all of us are born with" (p. 7). From social transmission "come all the stimulation and teaching which cause these tendencies to develop in a definite form" (ibid.). Moreover, "even if our mode of life has no direct effect upon heredity," it is possible "for us to influence it by an indirect process known as Selection" (pp. 9–10).

Selection as used here is distinct from *natural* selection. It refers to the potential to influence development of the species through conscious or intelligent selection, which Cooley suggests contains many difficulties. He acknowledges that "social improvement and eugenics are a team that should be driven abreast" (1902, rev. ed. 1922, pp. 14–15). Cooley's purpose here is to dissociate natural selection as a process of biological evolution from social issues and from social change itself. Thus, early in his career as a sociologist he dissociates himself from biological reductionism and from the crude "social Darwinism" of the eugenics movement.

Cooley's essay "Genius, Fame and Comparison of the Races" (1897 in 1930) repudiates Francis Galton's claims in *Hereditary Genius:* that fame is a sufficient test of genius; that social conditions are not comparable in this regard with natural capacity; and that the number of geniuses a race is capable of producing from a given population is a gauge of the ability of a race. Cooley demonstrates the inconsistencies in Galton's argument and argues, citing historical examples and cases drawn from art and literary history, that "Every able race probably turns out a number of greatly endowed men many times larger than the number that attains to fame" (1897 in 1930, p. 122). Moreover, whether any of these achieve fame "is determined by historical and social conditions, and these vary so much that the production of great men cannot justifiably be used as a criterion of the ability of races" (ibid.). So cogent is Cooley's reasoning on this issue that the editors of a recent casebook on *The Bell Curve*, Russell Jacoby and Naomi Glauberman (1995, pp. xi–xii) find his "reflections . . . breathe of unsurpassed good sense" and have reprinted an abridgment of Cooley's essay (pp. 417–37). Thus, as Barry Schwartz's analysis of the influence of Emerson's notion of the hero on Cooley's thought avers, the essay demonstrates that "Cooley saw greatness only in the context of collective needs and interests; he therefore believed . . . that the use we make of the great man far outweighs the virtue of the man himself" (1985, p. 110).

Cooley's theme that social improvement must be considered in any discussion of eugenic selection is taken up in the same year as "Genius, Fame and the Comparison of Races" in an essay, "The Process of Social Change." Here he distinguishes social change from natural selection: "it is apparent that natural selection of . . . [the] simple, animal sort, is not the ordinary process of social change" (1897 in 1998, p. 68).[2] He states that the

> process which generates opinions, moral standards and institutions, and which results in progress or decadence . . . rests upon the imitative, sympathetic and intellectual faculties, and is related to natural selection through the probability that these faculties have an evolutionary history in which natural selection plays a part. . . . [I]t is sufficient to note that our ascendancy over other creatures is associated with a flexibility of nature that comes from imitation and sympathy, and makes us apt for social change. (p. 68)

Natural selection may be responsible for the evolution of the human species, but thereafter the evolution or change of human society works by different principles. Human history "is a process possible only to a species endowed with teachable instinctive dispositions, organized partly by reason, into a plastic and growing social whole" (1902, rev. ed. 1922, pp. 30–31). In this sense, Cooley's view is incontrovertibly social, but being so does not obviate the body's role in its formation. In this sense, Cooley's virtue also is his vice, for at one and the same time he could subscribe to Darwin's qualification that "heredity takes on a distinctively human character only by renouncing, as it were, the function of predetermined adaptation and becoming plastic to the environment," and the belief in rational control of the population by the "social science of eugenics [which] aims . . . to set a standard of propagation for the human race" (1918, pp. 206, 385). This would extend to "a practical eugenics, which shall diminish the propagation of degenerate types and perhaps apply more searching tests to immigrants" (p. 347).

As I discuss in chapter 3, this view has especially pernicious implications with respect to his views on race. As skeptical as he was concerning positivism, his faith in scientific intervention in social issues perhaps served as a mask for commitment to social values enshrouded and made plausible by intellectual elitism, history, and convention.

Clearly, what separates human nature from animal nature is its *teachability* or *plasticity*. Human nature consists "not of tendencies to do particular things that life calls for, but of vague aptitudes or lines of teachability that are of no practical use until they are educated," whereas the "mental outfit of the animal, on the other hand, is relatively definite and fixed, giving rise to activities which are useful with little or no teaching" (p. 19). Human dispositions lack the fixity of animal instincts. As for instinct, humans have little of it, if by this term is meant innate behavior patterns—actions performed by many individuals the same way without knowing for what purpose. Cooley concedes there is no sharp line drawn between humans and animals in this matter. Although humans' outward behavior has ceased to be determined by heredity, "it seemed that we still had inward emotions and dispositions that were so determined . . . [which] had an immense influence on our conduct." Cooley prefers to call this component of human nature "instinctive emotion" (pp. 23–24).

Instinctive emotions "predetermine, not specific actions, but, in a measure, the energy that flows into actions having a certain function with reference to our environment" (p. 26). They represent impulses "whose definite expression depends upon education and social expression" (p. 27). The environment in significant measure includes the social environment. What distinguishes the social environment from the biological one is communication: "A man's social environment embraces all persons with whom he has intelligence or sympathy, all influences that reach him. . . . In other words, the social influences act through a mechanism; and the character of their action depends upon the character of the mechanism. The existing system of communication determines the reach of the environment" (1897 in 1998, p. 71).

Here Cooley's conception follows that of William James, who defined the self in terms used in ordinary, everyday language, as socially grounded, and who also conceived of it as embodied. Its origin is neither naively ideational nor seen in idealized terms, as cognitively or spiritually privileged, as transcending society and standing above the round of everyday life. Thus the appropriative self, which Cooley derives from James, is concretely manifested in its mundane aspects in people's propensity to identify themselves with what they possess, create, and affiliate with, and is signified by the pronominal "I," "me," "mine," "my," and "myself." James's multivalent conception of the social self is also anchored in groups, that is, one "has as many social selves as there are distinct groups of persons about whose opinion he cares" (1963 [1892], p. 169).

Thus Cooley incorporates James's frame in two ways in his construction of the self: (a) imaginative refracting, or reflective consideration of the multiplicity, or the multivalence, of others' and other groups' images and opinions of and by the individual; and (b) the incorporating of the appropriative tendency, including the body and its conception by the individual, into the self. This is what James meant by the "empirical self."

As we are beginning to see, Cooley carefully treads a path between nature and nurture for the sake of a discourse that lies squarely within the social. In positing a "plastic" human nature along with its species receptivity toward sociality, he can simultaneously provide a ground for inchoate feeling and its socialization. In this sense, he brings the body back in to sociology, but in another, carefully dispenses with it as a foundation for the self and social process. While Cooley understands that the self cannot be reduced to the original nature of the human being, nevertheless the "plastic" or "teachable" quality of human nature springs from an inchoate sociability marking the human constitution, and this sociability supplies a ground for the self's emergence and development.

Finally, Cooley caps his contribution by actually placing feeling at a critical point in the rooting of the self in the social process insofar as it engages in imaginative reflection, evaluation, and registering feeling. Feeling, or the affective aspect of the self, is grounded, as are reflection and evaluation, in social interaction. If for no other reason, Cooley's close association of feeling with the reflexive process constituting the self renders his notion useful, and unique among the founders and leading lights of the symbolic interactionist tradition (Scheff, 2003). Nonetheless, as I discuss below, particularly in the last section on Mead, this has not always been the perception of Cooley's views on self and society.

Cooley's conception of the self stepped out onto risky ground, for, in being emotionally as well as cognitively freighted, it opened itself to the criticism of being "mentalistic," and, in resting on "personal ideas" as well, left Cooley open to the charge of solipsism. Moreover, the grounding of the self's "impulse" or origin in human nature's sociable predisposition, makes the conception vulnerable to the suspicion justifiably leveled at cruder instinct-based theories. I contend, however, that all of the criticisms are misplaced and that the originality of Cooley's notion, which has stood the test of time, despite its having been seen as succeeded or even surpassed by Mead's, is perhaps more heuristic than the latter's.

The Self, the Individual, and the Social World

Predicating the self upon a teachable human nature, one in which instinct plays at most an attenuated part with the social environment forming and contextualizing it, also presupposes the existence of the social selves constituting it. Cooley's premise, consistent with the precepts of the hermeneutical circle, bears repeating: "Self and society are twin-born, we know one as immediately as we know the other, and the notion of a separate and independent ego is an illusion" (1909, p. 5). And once again, both the individual and society represent the same entity: "the individual is not separable from the human whole, but a living member of it, deriving his life from the whole through social and hereditary transmission as truly as if men were literally one body" (p. 35). Therefore, to repeat Cooley's adage quoted in the previous chapter, "A separate individual is an abstraction unknown to human experience, and so likewise is society when regarded as something apart from individuals" (p. 36). Moreover, awareness of society or social consciousness "is inseparable from self consciousness, because we can hardly think of ourselves excepting with reference to a social group of some sort, or of the group except with reference to ourselves" (p. 5).

There is no place for dualism here. What would appear to represent a dualism of the individual versus society resolves itself as simply a matter of one's vantage point, as when "one takes his stand in a field of corn when the young plants have begun to sprout, [and] all the plants in the field . . . appear arranged in a system of rows radiating from his feet; and no matter where he stands the system will appear to centre at that point." Thus, any standpoint represents "a point of vantage from which the whole may, in a particular manner, be apprehended" (1902, rev. ed. 1922, p. 150).

Cooley therefore does not proceed from the same sociologistic assumption as Durkheim, who, positing an ineluctable tension—a dualism—between society and the individual, resolves it by the coercive impinging of the social, in the form of moral rules, on the individual. Thus society via the internalization of rules limits, regulates, channels, directs, and verily coerces the individual's desires and propensities. However, the two sociologists come to a similar conclusion: society exists within and beyond ourselves. In answer to the question, Is society anything more than the sum of the individuals? Cooley says: "In a sense. Yes. There is an organization, a life process, in any social whole that you cannot see in the individuals separately. To study them one by one and attempt to understand society by putting them together will lead you astray. . . . You must see your groups, your social processes, as the living wholes that they are" (1902, rev. ed., 1922, p. 48).[3]

Social Feeling: Bringing the Body Back In?

Following his discussion of society and the individual in *Human Nature and the Social Order* (1902, rev. ed. 1922, pp. 81–135), Cooley discusses social feeling, on which the personal idea, a building block of the self, is crafted.[4] Social feeling, or sociability, is plastic and vague. This is not caprice but "a necessary form of thought, flowing from a life in which personal communication is the chief interest and social feeling the stream in which, like boats on a river, most other feelings float" (p. 88). Social feeling is instinctive in origin—an instinctive emotion—according to Cooley: "I take it that the child has by heredity a generous capacity and need for social feeling, rather too vague and plastic to be given any specific name like love." He adds, "this material, like all other instincts, allies itself with social experience to form, as time goes on, a growing and diversifying body of personal thought, in which the phases of social feeling developed correspond . . . to the complexity of life itself" (pp. 86–87). Here Cooley specifies the significance or meaning of the body as opposed to its physical characteristics. Social feeling, asking "little from others except bodily presence and an occasional sign of attention," is expressed in infanthood by the joyous reception of the attentions of others (p. 87). In other words, Cooley recognizes the body's significance as object and as a source of sociability, and Holstein and Gubrium recognize the originality of his contribution, asserting that, while Cooley imputes instinctively based "crude feelings" to the self, these "are also shaped and transformed with our experience in the world." Thus, "with experience, self-feeling forms into the social self . . ." and, therefore, "what is

original for us as human beings, then, are the bodily underpinnings for stimulating our activities as social entities" (2000, p. 26).

Social feeling actually is a *species-receptivity* to sociation. As such, it thus is
an aspect of human nature, and in this sense, has a physical basis. Moreover,
throughout Cooley's writing, thinking and feeling are conjoined, not dissociated, Joas's recent work on the theory of action makes exactly this point, namely
that "more than merely the cognitive construction of reality in the development
of the small child . . . the constitution of reality [is] a process which is also affective in nature" (1996, p. 164). However, Joas does not tell where this feeling
comes from or what it is rooted in. Moreover, the individual forms a "body
schema" that is constituted through the infant's prelinguistic communication.
In his discussion of the process of the formation of the infant's body schema Joas
notes that Mead in an unpublished paper dealing with this question insists "that
the organism is already tied into the structure of social interaction, even if at that
point it does not yet have an awareness of the boundaries between itself and the
social or physical world" because "it has already started to react to the gestural
language of partners in interaction and to articulate itself by means of gestures
that can be understood as gestures, or expressions that can be understood as
gestures." This serves as the basis "for the human being's assumption of a role
vis-à-vis objects such as her/his body" and thus the "young, pre-linguistic infant
is embedded in communicative interaction" enabling it to recognize the body
as its own, or in other words, as a constituted object (p. 183). The prelinguistic
foundation of the self had been remarked upon earlier in symbolic interactionist
literature. But what gives the human being its receptivity to sociation and the
capacity to gauge the body's meaning? Indeed, there is no avoiding the matter
of constitutional endowment vis-à-vis the issue of capacity.

Cooley's formulation of the partial grounding of the self in the body, that
is, inchoately instinct-based self-feeling, is not a clichéd sociobiological one.
Neither is it, with its inclusion, yet gingerly handling, of instinct, one lending
itself to a trendy postmodern conceit about "embodiment." The reluctance of
sociologists and philosophers to recognize the body's role beyond its place in the
cognitive social matrix betrays an ambivalence often "reflected in the scholarly
attempts to reach an understanding of the phenomena in which the boundaries
of the self are transgressed" (Joas, 1996, p. 190). Such measured reluctance is
expressed in Cooley's case in declaring that "instinctive self-feeling" is initially
"associated chiefly with ideas of the exercise of power, of being a cause, ideas

that emphasize the antithesis between the mind and the rest of the world." So the child's earliest thoughts associated with self-feeling "are probably those of his earliest endeavors to control visible objects—his limbs, his playthings, his bottle, and the like" (1902, rev. ed. 1922, p. 177). Nonetheless, the commonsense impression that the "verifiable self, the object that we name with 'I,' is usually the material body . . . is an illusion" (p. 175). This caution reflects the fact that Cooley ventures between the shoals of heredity and environment.

The objectification of one's body, consistent with Cooley's notion of the species receptivity to sociation, is conceivably prelinguistic and still social. Cooley's positing of the human bodily disposition to sociation vis-à-vis the inchoate social and self feelings is not an all-or-nothing proclamation. As Cooley says, the "emotion or feeling of self may be regarded as instinctive. . . . It is thus very profoundly rooted in the history of the human race." Like other human predispositions, however, it is "to be defined and developed by experience, becoming associated, or rather incorporated, with muscular, visual, and other sensations; with perception, apperceptions, and conceptions of every degree of complexity and of infinite variety of content; and especially, with personal ideas" (1902, rev. ed. 1922, pp. 170–71). Having established the dispositional basis and character of social feeling Cooley analyzes the role and function of the imaginary interlocutor or playmate in the socialization of the child.

The Conversational Matrix of the Self:
Imaginary Playmates and Personal Ideas

The child seeks to "continue the joys of sociability by means of an imaginary playmate" which, as I quote Cooley above, he emphasizes "is not an occasional practice, but, rather, a necessary form of thought, flowing from a life in which personal communication is the chief interest and social interest the stream in which, like boats on a river, most other feelings float" (p. 88). The key word here is "life," denoting the social character of the context from which mind develops. Thus, "after a child learns to talk about the social world in all its wonder and provocation opens on his mind, it floods his imagination so that all his thoughts are conversations" (pp. 88–89).

Here it might be objected, in the vein of Mead's charge of solipsism, that Cooley is conceiving of mind as existing prior to the child's involvement in the social world. I do not think he believes this. The opening page of *Social Organization* commences with a discussion of "social and individual aspects of mind." Hence, "the view that all mind acts together in a vital whole from which the individual is never really separate . . . makes it increasingly clear that every thought we have is linked with the thought of our ancestors and associates, and through them with that of society at large" (1909, p. 1). So it is clear that mind develops out of a social process. Cooley's equation of all thought with conversation prompts him to aver that these "conversations are not occasional and temporary effusions of the imagination, but are the naive expression of a socialization of the mind that is to be permanent and underlie all later thinking (1902, rev. ed. 1922, pp. 88, 89).

Drawing on material on his own children from his personal journal and observational notes, Cooley develops the idea that the inner conversation constitutes mind: "It is true of adults as of children that the mind lives in perpetual conversation" (p. 90), for while the imaginary dialog may become more reticent in adulthood, it never ceases. Language, mind, and interaction can never be dissociated. Significantly, communication becomes the habit of mind, so much so that even solitary souls, the "uncomprehended of all times and peoples have kept diaries for the same reason" (p. 92). Cooley's tracing of the close developmental association of mind with, and its derivation from, the role-taking conversation with the imaginary playmate, underscores his understanding of the social nature of mind. By no accident, as I discuss in chapter 4, his notion of the socially based mind is richly leavened by Cooley's familiarity with the essayists, the masters of literary conversation—Montaigne, Emerson, Thoreau, Goethe, à Kempis, Lamb, Stevenson, and others.

Cooley mentions Thoreau to illustrate how even that reclusive but sententious writer manifested and expressed his sociality, and notes: "No man ever labored more passionately to communicate." Thus, "he took to the woods and fields not because he lacked sociability, but precisely because his sensibilities were so keen that he needed to rest and protect them by a peculiar mode of life, and to express them by the indirect and considerate method of literature" (p. 93). The urge to communicate necessarily presupposes this sociability, because one "strives to communicate to others that part of his life which he is trying to unfold in himself"; and this is "a matter of self-preservation, because without expression thought cannot live" (p. 94). The obverse is true as well:

"The imagination, in time, loses the power to create an interlocutor who is not corroborated by any fresh experience," and so if "the artist finds no appreciator for his book of pictures he will scarcely be able to produce another" (p. 95).

The boundary between the imaginary and real interlocutor, or between the inner and outer life is, therefore, seamless, for we trace the lineaments of the former from the latter, that is, from those we have been in contact with; in short, they are drawn "from the accessible environment." Cooley has now arrived at the point where he can announce: "It is worth noting here that there is no separation between real and imaginary persons; indeed, to be imagined is to become real, in a social sense" (ibid.).

In effect, a physical "sensible presence is not necessarily a matter of the first importance." What makes a person real to us is the "degree in which we imagine an inner life which exists in us . . . and which we refer to him." The distinction between imaginary (that is, thought) and real persons, resembling that between the individual and society, is one of perspective: "thought and personal intercourse may be regarded as merely aspects of the same thing: we call it personal intercourse when the suggestions that keep it going are received through faces or other symbols present to the senses; reflection when the personal suggestions come through memory and are more elaborately worked over in thought." In sum, "the life of the mind is essentially a life of intercourse" (pp. 96–97).

Dipping again into his notes on his children, which Holstein and Gubrium (2000, p. 25) credit as "exemplary," in order to "consider . . . the way in which ideas of people grow up in the mind," Cooley concludes: "Apparently, then, facial expression, gesture, and the like, which later become the vehicle of personal impressions and the sensible basis of sympathy, are attractive at first chiefly for their sensuous variety and vividness, very much as other bright, moving, sounding things are attractive" (p. 103). The personal impression is the "sensuous element" constituting the personal symbol, and collections of personal symbols representing persons constitute personal ideas—that is, personal ideas are for us congeries of symbols. I emphasize the sensuousness of personal impressions in view of Mead's criticism of Cooley's "mentalist" approach, for here we encounter the human organism engaged in an interpersonal interactive process requisite to the emergence of self. Our breadth of perspective widens with our experience of persons, until our store of images is rich. Personality is thus personal milieu (p. 106).

The personal symbol is a vehicle for feeling as much as for communication: "personal sentiments are correlative with personal symbols" (p. 115). Personal symbols evoke these feelings. As a result "sentiment and imagination are generated, for the most part, in the life of communication, and so belong with personal images by original and necessary association, having no separate existence, except in our forms of speech" (p. 118). As we shall see, Cooley follows through on the inclusion of feeling as a component of personal ideas to his formulation of the self. Feeling is necessarily recalled "along with symbols of the persons who have suggested it" (p. 118), and the sentiment "was in its inception associated with a personal symbol" (p. 118 ff.). Hence the contention that "society . . . *is a relation among personal ideas* [Cooley's italics]" (p. 119) automatically transcends a starkly cognitive derivation of the self. Conceiving of persons as symbols and aspects of persons as personal symbols broadens the social process within which the self emerges to one not narrowly circumscribed by spoken or written language. What is important is that this portable personal trading card or snapshot collection is incorporated in and serves as a matrix for reflective consciousness of the self.

If society is a relation among personal ideas, then "the imaginations which people have of one another are the *solid facts* of society, and . . . to observe and interpret these must be a chief aim of sociology." Speaking methodologically, Cooley is here asserting that, in effect, society has an objective existence, and the social scientist must use his or her imagination to study it. Indeed, "we have to imagine imaginations" (pp. 121–22). As we shall see in chapter 6, on Cooley's methodology, this entails sympathetic introspection, a refinement of the reflective practice encountered in the social process. The conclusion drawn from this is that the alleged split between self and other is as fatuous as Spencer's (and Comte's and Durkheim's) egoism-altruism dichotomy (pp. 126 ff.–127 ff.)—all are socialized ideas inasmuch as they are references to others; thus, even hostility is "hostile sympathy."[5] Society, self, and personal intercourse are all phases of life, and may be considered in their primary aspects "or in secondary aspects, such as groups, institutions or processes" (p. 135). This verifies Cooley's opening premise concerning social organization: "separateness is an illusion of the eye and community the inner truth" (1909, p. 9).

But how do these personal ideas and the self that is their intersecting point form? They form through sympathy or understanding by entering into and sharing the minds of other persons; the sympathetic (or empathic) process denotes the communication of mental states including sentiment. In effect, "social experience is a matter of imaginative, not of material, contacts" (1902, rev. ed. 1922, p. 139). Here, as I have pointed out in chapter 1, Cooley specifies that sympathy refers to "entering into and sharing the minds of other persons," or the "sharing of any mental state that can be communicated, and has not the special implication of pity or other 'tender emotion' that it very commonly carries in ordinary speech" (p. 136). Sympathy thus is compassion, not communion (pp. 136 ff.–137 ff.). It is, in effect, empathic and thus represents the mechanism of role-taking discussed by Mead, or Weber's interpretive understanding—*verstehen.*

The range of one's sympathy measures the breadth of his or her character. It is a requisite of social power—the ability to empathize with others; and the "strong men of our society . . . are very human men, not at all the abnormal creatures they are sometimes asserted to be." Insanity is a "confirmed lack of touch with other minds" (pp. 141, 144).

The modern temper requires both selectivity and diversification of sympathy. As though taking a page from Simmel's "The Metropolis and Mental Life," Cooley observes the type of public armor donned by the individual in a modern urban setting, in which if one

> is assailed all day and every day by calls upon feeling and thought in excess of his power to respond, he soon finds that he must put up some sort of a barrier. Sensitive people who live where life is insistent take on a sort of social shell whose function is to deal mechanically with ordinary relations and preserve the interior from destruction. They are likely to acquire a conventional smile and conventional phrases for polite intercourse, and a cold mask for curiosity, hostility, or solicitation. (p. 146)

Just a bit further down, commenting on the spirit of a differentiated age and society, once again reminiscent of Simmel expounding on the web of group affiliations, Cooley tells us: "A man may be regarded as the point of intersection of our indefinite number of circles representing social groups, having as many arcs passing through him as there are groups" (p. 148).[6] Certainly William James's notion of the plurality of the social self is inspirational for Cooley, but Cooley the sociologist moves beyond the social self, to exploring the societal context of both groups and the individual. Thus he informs us: "The complexity of society takes the form of organization, that is, of a growing unity and breadth sustained by the co-operation of differentiated parts, and the man of the age must reflect both the unity and the differentiation; he must be more distinctly a specialist and at the same time a man of the world" (p. 149). In this chapter on sympathy, Cooley's discussion of the consequences of a differentiated social order squares with his ability to connect societal issues with biography and fulfills C. Wright Mills's criteria for the sociological imagination.

Do You See What I See?: The Looking-Glass Self

Eschewing formal definitions, and by way of clearing away the mystique of "I," Cooley starkly defines the self as "the my-feeling or sense of appropriation" (1902, rev. ed. 1922, p. 169). As such, self-feeling may appear to be instinctive, but as with other instinctive emotions, it needs "to be defined and developed by experience" (p. 171). But having said this, Cooley is careful to stipulate that the "social self is simply any idea, or system of ideas, drawn from communicative life, that the mind cherishes as its own." Accordingly, "self-feeling has its chief scope *within* the general life, not outside of it" (p. 179). Thus, the impression that the "verifiable self" is naively coequal with the material body "is easily dispelled by any one who will undertake a simple examination of facts" and "in not more than ten cases in a hundred does 'I' have reference to the body of the person speaking" (pp. 176, 177). Drawing upon James's appropriative aspect of the social "me," Cooley claims that it "is strongly suggested by the word 'gloating.' To gloat . . . is as much to think 'mine, mine, mine,' with a pleasant warmth of feeling (pp. 174–75). James (1963 [1892], p. 188) calls it the cloaking of Me with "warmth and intimacy." But Cooley is careful to qualify this feeling as not necessarily synonymous with one's *identification* with the body (1902, rev. ed. 1922, pp. 176, 181); rather, it is located squarely in language and communi- cation: "That the 'I' of common speech has a meaning which includes some sort of reference to other persons is involved in the very fact that the word and the ideas it stands for are phenomena of language and the communicative life" (p. 180). Again, drawing upon his observations of his children (pp. 189–200) Cooley meticulously etches the development of "I" from the child's appropria- tive use of pronouns, such as "my," which, contra Baldwin, "*could not be copied* [imitated; Cooley's italics]" (p. 190) and which is learned by associating it with other phenomena despite its use by others! The meaning of "my" (and "me") Cooley notes to be a product, say, of fighting over toys among his children—

their appropriativeness. Speaking of the genesis of the appropriative self-feeling in his daughter "M" he says: "From the first week she had wanted things and cried and fought for them. She had also become familiar by observation and opposition with similar appropriative activities on the part of R [his son]. Thus she not only had the feeling herself, but by associating it with its visible expression has probably divined it, sympathized it, resented it, in others" (pp. 190–91). And noticing the use of "I" ("I want it") in older people, the child facilely makes the connection between "I" and "my": "as I recorded in my notes at the time, . . . 'my' and 'mine' are simply names for concrete images of appropriativeness, embracing both the appropriative feeling and its manifestation" (p. 191). Thus "I" and "my" are learned as many other meanings are "by having the feeling, imputing it to others in connection with some kind of expression, and hearing the word along with it" (p. 192). Likewise, and probably derived from Baldwin (his notion of agency), Cooley associates the appropriative use of these pronouns with ideas of the exercise of power: "The first definite thoughts that a child associates with self-feeling are probably those of his earliest endeavors to control visible objects. . . . Then he attempts to control the actions of the persons about him, and so his circle of power and of self-feeling widens" (p. 177).

As a phenomenon, the social self—self-feeling—"finds its principle field of exercise in a world of personal forces" (p. 179). It thus sets the stage for the emergence of the looking-glass self through the formation of connections between one's "own acts and changes in those movements; that is they perceive their own influence or power over persons" (p. 196). Following James, the "young performer soon learns to be different to different people, showing that he begins to apprehend personality and to foresee its operation" (p. 197). Hence once again we encounter Cooley's recognition of a social process serving as a matrix for the self. Cooley informs us that "there is no sense of 'I,' as in pride or shame, without its correlative sense of you, or he, or they" (p. 182). Accordingly, "this social reference takes the form of a somewhat definite imagination of how one's self—that is, any he appropriates—appears in a particular mind, and the kind of self-feeling one has is determined by the attitude toward this attributed to that other mind. A social self of this sort might be called the reflected or looking-glass self" (pp. 183–84). The looking-glass metaphor describes the imaginative anticipation that enables us to "perceive in another's mind some thought of our appearance, manners, aims, deeds, character, friends, and so on" (p. 184).

The self, founded on feeling, entails a reflective process that ramifies into self-feeling. Consequently, "a self idea of this sort seems to have three principal elements: the imagination of our appearance to the other person; the imagination of his judgment of that appearance, and some sort of self-feeling, such as pride or mortification" (p. 184). The looking-glass analogy is not literal, for the "thing that moves us to pride or shame is not the mere mechanical reflection of ourselves, but an imputed sentiment, the imagined effect of this reflection upon another's mind" (ibid.). This proves to be critical, for as I say in my discussion of Mead's fateful diatribe about Cooley's conception of the self, the imaginative elements Cooley attributes to the self are easily misconstrued as a clichéd conception, wherein the self-concept is literally equated with the images others hold of the individual. Rather, as Reitzes recognizes, "Cooley is able concurrently to stress the role of others in validating and confirming self concepts, while locating the process within the perceiving individual" (1980, p. 632). In addition, one cannot overemphasize the integral place that feeling holds in Cooley's conception of self. As Thomas Scheff suggests in his recent portrayal of Erving Goffman as a symbolic interactionist "in the Cooley line," Cooley's framework of the self, referring to both thought and feelings, was larger than Mead's. This emphasis on feeling, especially the focus on shame as the third element of the looking-glass self that Goffman's perspective elucidates as embarrassment, constitutes a "Cooley-Goffman version of symbolic interaction [which] could open up a whole new area of study of discourse, built around the dynamics of the looking-glass self, and Goffman's extension of it into a fourth step, the management of the resulting emotions" (2005, pp. 148, 163). As Scheff tells us, "the shame triad . . . violates the principle of the self-contained individual" and thus the canon of individualism. Hence "individuals, as well as being separate units, may also be joined together as components of larger units, such as pairs, threesomes, and still larger groups" (2005, p. 156). As I discuss below, Mead's entirely cognitive conception of the self remained individually based, as were his notions of society and the generalized other.

So now we have a clear vantage point on Cooley's notion of the self. It incorporates the body and reflexivity, encompassing both cognitive and affective components. If the writing is merely skimmed and not read carefully, it is easy to misconstrue Cooley's understanding of the concatenations of body, mind, the imagination, emotion, and the self as banal reductions of behavior to "human nature," or to individual psychology. In this case it is necessary to keep in mind Cooley's stipulation of the plasticity of human nature and the fact that he, as we shall see, develops a truly sociological conception of the group. On the other hand, the cognitive conception of the self offered by Mead "largely ignores questions of motivation and the emotions" (Joas, 1996, p. 183). Cooley is free to explore the self in a wholly different manner, one in which "I" and the "me" are not so distinctly divided into logic-tight compartments.

The Inner Eye Apprehends the "I"

While Cooley disdains mystiques of the self or "I," the fact that he focuses on "I" as opposed to "Me" hints that his thinking proceeds from a different point from that of the pragmatists, especially Mead, whose own notion of the self postdates Cooley's.[7] It is a perspective fed by different currents of thought, as demonstrated in my treatment of Cooley's aestheticism and the belletristic sources of his thinking. Mead's theory embroiders on James's "I"—the subjective, spontaneous, acting, me-apprehending self. In this respect the "I" by Mead's own estimation remains virtually untouchable. Thus, in his essay "The Mechanism of Social Consciousness," Mead states:

> The "I" therefore never can exist as an object to consciousness, but the very conversational character of our inner experience, the very process of replying to one's own talk, implies an "I" behind the scenes who answers to the gestures, the symbols, that arise in consciousness. The "I" is the transcendental self of Kant, the soul that James conceived behind the scene holding on to the skirts of an idea to give it an added increment of emphasis. (1909 in Reck [ed.], 1964, p. 141)

Mead might argue that the "I" discussed by Cooley is, in actuality, the "Me," for it might be taken to represent the reflected "I": "One presents himself as acting toward others . . . and the subject of this presentation can never appear immediately in conscious experience" (1913 in Reck [ed.] 1964, p. 144). But, Mead says little beyond this about the "I," as though, in fact, the intrinsic impossibility of the individual observing his or her own "I" is shared by the observer. Indeed, one might say that observers of social behavior are always observing "Is" in action; they just do not emphasize this. In Cooley's extensive discussion of the self—the "I" as the emergent self—and in his discussions of egotism, pride, and vanity, this ground is thoroughly covered.

Mead himself gives an interesting clue to Cooley's own innovativeness in his discussion of "I" and "Me," where he distinguishes the conventional individual who "is hardly more than a 'me'" from "the person who has a definite personality, who replies to the organized attitude in a way which makes a significant difference." In this case, "it is the 'I' that is the more important phase of the experience" (Mead, 1962 [1934], p. 100). Cooley's emphasis on the "I" reflects both his own nonconformity to academic sociology and his membership in the essay tradition. Cooley's treatment of this aspect of the self underscores the fact that his manner of portraying it actually constitutes material ordinarily treated by ethnographers, novelists, painters, playwrights, philosophers, and other observers. This approach is neither an "over-socialized" nor an overly romanticized one.

Chapter VI (pp. 211–63) of *Human Nature and the Social Order*, on "Various Phases of 'I'" is unique because of its intellectual candor and intimacy and because it marks an analysis of material that sociologists do not ordinarily treat: egoism versus altruism, the inner life, pride and vanity, and representative men. It is material that reveals Cooley's lifelong concerns about character and its development, and to the reader who fails to recognize the belletristic derivation of the discussion may convey an air of diffuseness. As a result, much of this material is passed over by sociologists. Indeed, because it smacks too much of the "I," it is territory sociologists fear to tread; but if nothing else it bears witness to the essayistic context of Cooley's sociology.

The theme of egoism-altruism is in many ways a continuation of Cooley's already familiar argument against Spencer, that the dichotomy is false. On the other hand, Cooley explores these mislabeled phenomena, which are more appropriately construed as self-assertion, selfishness, and creativity. What we take to be egotistical behavior is "at bottom a matter of moral judgment" born out of disagreement or resentment. Indeed, the charismatic founders of religion and social movements might be considered egotists (1902, rev. ed. 1922, p. 215), as might those who lack tact on the level of face-to-face interaction (ibid.). On this note, Cooley passes onto the second part of his disquisition on the social self—"Various Phases of 'I'"—and a discussion of egotism, pride, vanity, humility, and their relation to the inner life and spirituality. Hence,

> there is perhaps no sort of self more subject to dangerous egotism than that which deludes itself with the notion that it is not a self at all, but something else. It is well

to beware of persons who believe that the cause, the mission, the philanthropy, the
hero, or whatever it may be that they strive for, is outside of themselves, so that
they feel a certain irresponsibility. . . . [I]n our own time the name of religion,
science, patriotism, or charity sometimes enables people to indulge comfortably
in browbeating, intrusion, slander, dishonesty, and the like. *Every cherished idea
is a self.* It is healthy for everyone to understand that he is, and will remain, a
self-seeker, and that if he gets out of one self he is sure to form another which
may stand in need of control [Cooley's italics]. (pp. 216–17)

Egotism is not the opposite of altruism, since the mind does not have self
versus other motives to choose from. It has "the far more difficult task of seeking a higher life by gradually discriminating and organizing a great variety of
motives not easily divisible into moral groups," such as broadness versus nar-
rowness of feeling or greater sympathy (p. 220). Outward doing develops the
inner life. The intrusion of "I" is not obnoxious so long, as in Montaigne's case,
it is a pertinent "I" and "not merely a random self-intrusion" (p. 223). Self-love
may really connote the joy of dwelling in the inner life, in one's self as Goethe
conceived it (pp. 225–26). Artists are thus covetous of their work in its early
stages until it is deemed ready for public scrutiny: "The Self, like a child, is
not likely to hold its own in the world unless it has had a mature development." Artistic production requires intense self-feeling in the artist: "It is only
as we have self-consciousness that we can be aware of those special tendencies
which we assert in production, or can learn how to express them, or even have
the desire to do so" (p. 228). By the same token, superficiality and vagueness
of character stem from a lack of "collectedness" and self-definition (p. 229).
Moreover, true substance in character manifests an enduring "need to *be,* and
cannot be guilty of that separation between being and seeming that constitutes
affectation" represented, for example, by pride and vanity (p. 236).

Cooley's discussion of pride and vanity actually stems from his own inner
work, and it is intimately and amply recorded in his personal journal. This
material provides great insight into how and why Cooley's formulation of the
self is unparalleled by the academic symbolic interactionist treatments. It also
derives from Cooley's familiarity with the Western hermetic tradition. Here he
restates his adage concerning the permeable membrane between the inner and
outer: "Outside and inside in human life mutually complement and interpret
each other" (*Journal* V. 22 [4/20/19–5/25/25] 7/30/33, p. 81). In this case, he is
not confining himself to the discussion of the social self but to inner work and

the *evolution* of the self. In an early (undated) volume of the journal, perhaps before the age of eighteen, Cooley posts the task of arriving at self-knowledge, which he defines as the "comprehension of my thoughts and feelings in their relation to my whole character and its development." By this he refers to "the ability to measure the deep currents of my life and to regard each experience in its connection with these currents" (*Journal* Undated, p. 12). From the outset he states that "Gradually a determined man brings his outer life into accord with his inner," thus emphasizing his practice of monitoring and maintaining the linkage between inner and outer (*Journal* 1889–91, pp. 55–56). Much of his inner work involves pondering the "higher life" and transcendent reality; but most significantly it entails disentangling and unencumbering himself from the meshes of the looking-glass self, that is, observing his own feelings of pride and vanity and the blows to his composure dealt by dwelling on his imagination of others' perceptions of him. Consider this rumination of January 24, 1898: "It is true, as Thomas [à Kempis] says, that when we lose peace there is a reason for it in our attitude toward men and circumstance. We want something that depends upon other persons; and so have to busy our imaginations with their states of mind. In this way we are degraded and miserable. If one wishes to have an inner higher life he must cut off his lower aims [Cooley's strike-through]" (*Journal* V. 12 [5/2/1897–7/31/1898] 1/24/1897, p. 67). All of the elements comprising the looking-glass self are explicitly or implicitly evident here, including the part played by imagination. Thus one's preoccupation with, and even torment over, others' views and judgments, which we too often ascribe to teenage insecurity, always stays with us and is explicitly recognized by certain schools as an obstacle to liberation of the self. G. I. Gurdjieff, the bazaar-hustling mystic from the Caucasus, calls this particular demon "internal considering."[8] As Cooley says, it is through finding one's way through the "chagrins" of suffering over not having attained the ideals of others that one "learns to define himself" (*Journal* V. 15 (12/24/01–9/12/02) 6/18/01, p. 49). Such intentional suffering, because of the willingness to pick through it without self-pity, is not masochism; it is the work of evolving, of developing character and consciousness. Regarding this theme of development, Cooley informs us: "There is always a part of us which we do not understand; and that is apt to be the most important part of all" (*Journal* V. 18b [2/16/08–1/1/10] 8/2/08, p. 16). We only come to see that part through special effort, that is, by self-observation, meditation, contemplation, or the performance of spiritual exercises designed to aid us in cultivating self-awareness.

Closely connected with the matter of preoccupation with one's image in the minds of others is Cooley's interest in the issue of pride and vanity ("forms of self-approval that strike us as disagreeable or egotistical"), which follows his discussion of the looking-glass self in *Human Nature* (pp. 230–37). Pride and vanity represent the eclipse of being by (the preoccupation with) seeming. Consequently, "a man may be very self-conceited and yet not know his own good qualities. Self-knowledge, whether of good or bad, is equally hard to acquire" (*Journal* V. 11 [5/7/1897–3/21/1897] 5/7/1896, p. 18). While pride is a form of self-approval characterizing "the more rigid or self-sufficient sort of minds," the "proud man is not *immediately* dependent upon what others think" (1902, rev. ed. 1922, p. 232). The word "vanity," on the other hand, "indicates a weak or hollow appearance of worth put on in the endeavor to impress others, or the state of feeling that goes with it" (p. 234). The vain person is preoccupied with his own image in another's mind and is "frequently tortured by ground-less imaginings that some one has misunderstood him, slighted him, insulted him, or otherwise mistreated his social effigy" (p. 235). This subtheme of the looking-glass self also derives from Cooley's inner work and his reading of the essay tradition, especially the French moralists, such as La Rochefoucauld with his cynical observations of life around him, especially those concerning vanity and pride. This is integral to his thinking on the self, as is attested to by the following journal entry, containing an observation of his infant daughter "M" (Margaret), which suggests a reflection on vanity:

> M., one month old, has begun to stare at the eyes of her mother and nurse. The latter has glasses which she sometimes wears: these are said to be an object of particular interest to the baby.
>
> One thing about nursing a project and saying nothing to anyone about it, keeping it hid and private, is that it becomes identified with one's feeling of self-reverence and independence. . . .
>
> Vanity—pride—self-reverence are forms of self-valuation, the first having most immediate regard to what others think, the second also being based on opinion but stabler, depending more on the actual possession of the thing prized. The third rests upon a private judgment and is more truly individual than either of the others. . . . Vanity is vulgar and weak, pride strong but not truly noble, self-reverence the very kernel of lofty character. . . .

> The Self is very much indeed like a musical instrument upon which we do not know how to play. We want to give forth music; it is life and joy to do so; but another must draw the bow. (*Journal* V. 12 [5/2/1897–7/31/1898] 8/29/1897, p. 31)

Evidently the issue of development of the self is dialectically connected to the one of development of character and consciousness. Inasmuch as the difference between self-reverence and pride here verges on hairsplitting, Cooley succumbs to his own vanity (the "project" in the quote will be his much celebrated *Human Nature and the Social Order*). He conceives of his project in terms similar to those creative writers use to refer to the gestation and birth of their work. However, to recognize that the intimate record of his journal also reveals the faults of the man himself certainly does not gainsay the existential or intellectual results of that work. Moreover, Cooley is not an outwardly vain person. Quite the opposite, he is shy and self-effacing; but he recognizes, as certain mystical traditions do, that vanity is the fellow traveler of the human self. Like Thoreau, whom he admires, Cooley hearkens to the beat of a different drummer, as revealed in his summary judgment on the issue of vanity as it bears on the social self:[9]

> Vanity is a partly social passion. One strives for the show of a social self, rather than for the real thing. He wants to be something in another's mind for the sake of that being. It is selfish in that the self is willing to impose itself on the world at a false valuation. The truly social mind is one who values others' judgments, but values truth and reality more. He needs to be and cannot for a moment be satisfied with seeming. His sympathy can work without recognition. The vain man may be described as pseudo-social. (*Journal* V. 11 [5/7/1896–3/12/1897] 4/1/1897, p. 78)

How to *be* is critical for Cooley. The above hints at the transcendental priorities that enable him to establish a kind of aesthetic and intellectual, indeed, an emotional distance from his subject, society grounded in social interaction, for in the frequent practice of observing oneself and society one acquires the ability to observe nonjudgmentally, and hence at the proper distance. The difference between being and seeming is underscored in *Human Nature and the Social Order* (1902, rev. ed. 1922, p. 236), where he says that the "self-respecting man" who values others' judgments "will not submit to influences not in line with his development" and "always feels the need to *be,* and cannot be guilty of that separation between being and seeming that constitutes affectation." In contrast to the positivist apotheosis of transcendental reason, or scientific rationality, Cooley posits an aesthetic arbiter of valuation. He espouses the "higher" spiritual values counterpoised against vanity and pride in the person and societally against institutions. This prioritization runs throughout his work and energizes, for example, his approach to pecuniary valuation or economic sociology.

In sum, pride and vanity are, like egotism, more complex than common sense acknowledges, for they reflect self-reliance and self-sufficiency as well as rigidity and weakness. "Pride is the form social self-approval takes in the more rigid or self-sufficient sort of minds," says Cooley (p. 234). It implies a more stable and consistent character than vanity, which is indicative of a lack of substance. Vanity "will swallow any shining bait" (ibid.). It is the proverbial mirror on the wall and is exemplified by an exaggerated and morbid form of the internal accounting or considering of the looking-glass self. The vain individual is "so taken up with his own image in the other's mind that he is hypnotized by it" (ibid.). In contradistinction is the "self-respecting man [who] values others' judgments and occupies his mind with them a great deal, but . . . keeps his head, . . . discriminates and selects, considers all suggestions with a view to his character, and will not submit to influences not in the line of his development" (p. 236).

Moving to the etiquette of the looking-glass self, Cooley suggests that "common sense approves a just mingling of deference and self-poise in the attitude of one man toward others" (p. 237). Honor is a finer kind of self-respect and represents something one feels regarding himself or herself and/or what others think of him or her: one's honor as subjectively felt or as perceived in others' minds are two aspects of the same thing and thus join the private and public aspects of self. Goethe's use of "self-reverence" and Emerson's use of self-reliance as desirable ideals brings us into "the imagined presence of masters and heroes to whom they refer their own life for comment and improvement" (p. 242). Here we enter the subject, as discussed below in chapter 4, of the essay tradition, of representative men (transcendental mediators), a notion that Cooley derived from Emerson. I underscore the importance of this Emersonian idea for Cooley's intellectual membership in the essay tradition, that is, his own self-defined literary reference group and his participation in the Great Conversation that the moralists and essayists pursued.

In *Human Nature and the Social Order* Cooley states that "every outreaching person has masters in whose imagined presence he drops resistance and becomes like clay in the hands of the potter" (p. 243). In connection with this allusion Cooley discusses humility and its relation to character, spirituality, and the inner life. In the social world, humility should connote self-respect or the deference of one's evolving character in the presence of that or of one embodying one's ideals. Humility, if joined to high ideals, "to an ideal personality developed in one's mind . . . is a submission to external rule which is designed to leave the will free for what are regarded as its higher functions" (pp. 244–45).

As Cooley suggests, there is no getting away from the self. Indeed, self-remembering is the only way out "for the mortifications and uncertainties of the social self . . . not the negative one of merely secluding or diminishing the 'I'" (pp. 253–54). No, it is "the positive one of transforming it." The trick is to remember oneself enough to discern its appropriativeness and its ideational and sentimental identifications, so that we can then free ourselves to live in the larger life. This is indeed the lesson of representative men: "So if one, turning the leaves of history, could evoke the real selves of all the men of thought, what a strange procession they would be!—outlandish theories, unintelligible and forgotten creeds, hypotheses once despised but now long established, or *vice versa*—all conceived eagerly, jealously, devotedly, as the very heart of the self" (pp. 254–55). Thus persons of grand ambition "lie open to disorders of self-feeling, because they necessarily build up in their minds a self-image which no ordinary environment can understand or corroborate." They seek surcease of their torment by "cultivating in imagination the approval of some higher tribunal" (p. 258), which I speak of in relation to Cooley's membership in the essay tradition, his literary reference group, or a "society of men speaking across the ages." Such figures transcend the social self, but remain touchstones for society and its members. As Emerson puts it, "He is great who is what he is from nature, and who never reminds us of others. But he must be related to us, and our life receive from him some promise of explanation" (Emerson, 1929, I, p. 328). Such characters are subject to the disquietude plaguing all of us. As Schwartz says in reference to Emerson's and Cooley's democratic conception of the hero—representative men—they provide us with models of what society represents in order that we may visualize or imagine it if we wish to improve it.

Representative men transcend conformity (the maintenance of group standards) inasmuch as they avoid accepted standards and adopt those that are comparatively remote and unusual. Nonconformity is a remoter conformity and constructive nonconformity is marked by the selectivity of remoter relations

(pp. 302–3). Consequently, there is no line between conformity and nonconformity; they are complementary phases of human activity. Nonconformity, or
"creative impatience," represents the "full and demanding" outlet for creative
energy (p. 303). The nonconformist emulates hidden masters, or masters known
through books. The hero-worship of youth has its place in that "plastic" period
in the formation of character. Even science has its hero-worship as a means of
inspiring creative work. As it becomes more imaginative it becomes a kind of
religion (1902, rev. ed. 1922, p. 314). Thus the ideal personages of religion are
fundamentally the same as other personal ideas.

Following the above, "all leadership takes place through the communication
of ideas to the minds of others, and unless the ideas are so presented as to be
congenial to those other minds, they will evidently be rejected" (p. 328). Leaders
are symbols, and as personal ideas they are *perceived* as godlike, as demigods for
the "idealizing tendency" (p. 341). They offer a blank slate to the imagination,
"whose very blankness or inertness insures the great advantage that it cannot
repudiate the qualities attributed to it" (p. 346). This is frequently conveyed by
writers and artists through a sense of mystery in their work, which serves as an
expression of personality (p. 348).

Leadership, more than simple nonconformity and unconventionality, actually appeals to these forces. Thus "all leadership has an aspect of sympathy
and conformity . . . so that every leader must be a follower in the sense that
he shares the general current of life. He leads by appealing to our own tendency, not by imposing something external on us" (p. 354). Great men express
the social conditions under which they operate.

Thus, Cooley's discussion of the self incorporates much of his thinking on
the development of character and the cultivation of one's inner life. As we have
seen, much of this material derives from his ruminations on these matters in
his personal journal. In this light, the statement by a scholar of Cooley's work
(Schubert, 1998, p. 7) that in the early years following the turn of the century
"Cooley finally overcame transcendentalism by finding his own path toward
self-fulfillment" and beyond his father's utilitarianism, in a "communally ori-
ented, sociocultural republican tradition" manifested in his sociological and so-
ciopsychological theory, is utterly simplistic. This is not to say that there is no
maturation process occurring in Cooley, or that his sociological interests do not
change, or even that he did not outgrow Emerson as well as seeking a path independent of his father's influence and ideas. Rather, it does insist that Cooley

abided by the aim of seeking the "higher life" and spirituality through inner work. As his writing on egotism, vanity, pride, and humility demonstrates, Cooley saw no *intellectual* contradiction between the foundations of the self in communicative interaction and the pursuit of one's spiritual aims. Since the self is the focal point of our mundane pursuits, it is a locus of our mental disquietude and as such gives us material on which to focus our inner work. Thus,

> As social beings we live with our eyes upon our reflection, but have no assurance of the tranquility of the waters in which we see it. . . . If a person of energetic and fine-strung temperament is neither vain nor proud, and lives equably without suffering seriously from mortification, jealousy and the like; it is because he has in some way learned to discipline and control his self-feeling, and thus to escape the pains to which it makes him liable. . . . [T]he literature of the inner life is very largely a record of the struggle with the inordinate passions of the social self. (pp. 247–48)

The aims of character development, cultivating the inner life, and spiritual seeking remained with Cooley throughout his life, as evidenced in his personal journal (see Jacobs, 1976) as well as his published work; what we see changing is his aesthetic priorities, namely the movement from the oratorical to the literary or writing self, which I discuss in chapters 4 and 5. Cooley's alleged substitution of a maturer sociological vision for the transcendental philosophical one, alluded to by Hans-Joachim Schubert, is an overly rationalistic interpretation of both Cooley's life and his work. Broader familiarity with the belletristic sources of Cooley's intellectual inspiration not only places a wider frame around his perspective but provides more insight into the figure-ground relationships within it. Moreover, in assuming that Cooley's Emersonianism was succeeded by his sociology, the different orders of facts in his biography and his sociology are confused. The real successor to Emerson is Walter Pater, but chiefly in the sense that the latter served as a literary reference point. And what of Montaigne, Goethe, Shakespeare, La Rochefoucauld, among others who remained as mental companions? Does any linear assessment of Cooley's development do justice to his thought? Outside of this frame, Cooley does not simply forsake one thinker for another or for "sociology." A glance at his last book, *Life and the Student* (1927), easily confirms this, for it arrays and juxtaposes *all* of his focal concerns and interests. In this regard, Cooley reminds us that for him, and, perhaps ourselves, "as processes of mind . . . science and art are much the same; both occupy themselves with a precise study of facts; in both man seeks to interpret and reconstruct nature after patterns of his own; both, in the pursuit of truth, rise above the tumult of the hour to serene and lasting truths" (1927, p. 144). Now, descending from these Olympian heights, I turn to the influence of pragmatism on Cooley's approach to human nature and the self.

The Pragmatic Anchorage

An acknowledged catalyst of Cooley's conceptions of human nature and the self is pragmatism and the work of James Mark Baldwin, especially pragmatism's social scientific implications in the work of William James and John Dewey, and Baldwin's somewhat cumbersome scheme of the social psychological processes of the formation of the self. Thus, Cooley informs us that the "idea that social persons are not mutually exclusive but composed largely of common elements is implied in Professor William James's doctrine of the Social Self and set forth at more length in Professor James Mark Baldwin's Social and Ethical Interpretations of Mental Development." He adds, "Like other students of social psychology I have received much instruction and even more helpful provocation from the latter brilliant and original work. To Professor James my obligation is perhaps greater still" (Cooley, 1902, rev. ed. 1922, p. 125 ff.).

Pragmatism's conception of action unmoored from instinct, that is, from biological determinism and from the biologistic rooting of society in the Spencerian evolutionary meshes, supplies a philosophical grounding for Cooley. Pragmatism's efficacy in this regard is both philosophical and rhetorical, for its conception of action and of language and thought as action weds its perspective to common sense and the social world. Moreover, James's notion of the self directly inspires Cooley's own formulation. I take this up following my discussion of the pragmatists' conception of action.

A young instructor, Cooley attended John Dewey's lectures on political philosophy in 1893–94 at Michigan (Cooley, 1928 in 1930, p. 6). At that time Mead, an instructor in psychology, was also at Michigan. Apparently the two were not in contact with each other; at least, there is no evidence that they did sustain any kind of relationship (Joas, 1985, p. 219 f.). C. Wright Mills in his study of the pragmatic movement (1964, pp. 296–97) notes that both William James and George Herbert Mead deeply influenced Dewey in the derivation of the "psyche."[10] However, while Cooley was familiar with James's psychology, he stated that Dewey left "a lasting mark, but rather by his personality . . . than by his lectures." He continued: "We believed there was something highly original in his philosophy, but had no definite idea as to what it was. The chief thing I now recall from his lectures is a criticism of Spencer, in which Dewey maintained that society was an organism in a deeper sense than Spencer had perceived and that language was its 'sensorium.' I had already arrived at a somewhat similar view" (1928 in 1930, p. 6).[11]

In this reflection toward the end of Cooley's life, it is possibly the case that time had erased the (other) specific sources of Dewey's influence on him; but considering that at that time Dewey was also in his formative period, he also was probably working through and externalizing the impact of James and the influence of Mead. In other words, Cooley was breathing in the pragmatic ideas then in the wind. The intense but often diffuse conversational atmosphere of academic discourse must have had a considerable effect, especially at a time when an intellectual movement such as pragmatism was at the point of prose-lytizing. Thus the atmosphere at Michigan must have been highly charged and still somewhat inchoate with respect to an exact understanding of the tenets of pragmatism.

William James is the chief mediating influence on Cooley's formulation of the self, indirectly via Dewey and directly through Cooley's reading of his psychology and its pragmatic foundations. It is Dewey's conception of the unity or interchangeability of perspectives of society and the individual, how-ever, that is more thoroughly amenable to Cooley's entire perspective, since Dewey's own background is heavily influenced by transcendental idealism and the "hermeneutical circle," wherein "society is treated here as an artifact produced by individuals' interpretative activities, while these activities are accounted for as fundamentally social in their origin and form" (Shalin, 1990, p. 11).

In looking through the detailed notes Cooley took on Dewey's lectures in 1893,[12] we encounter in these lectures—largely devoted to the subjects of sovereignty, law, and the state—some nascent themes Cooley develops as he simultaneously disentangles himself from Spencer and formulates his conception of the social: the meaning and properties of the social organism, the relationship between the individual and society, and language, the self, and social consciousness. Revealed here is how Dewey assists Cooley in developing his ideas. Dorothy Ross also credits Cooley's notes with providing "a revealing record of how Dewey drew together the resources of individualist and organicist traditions in an effort to socialize liberalism" (1991, p. 168). Clearly, it was a formative period for both men.

It is important to note that Dewey stresses language as a key factor in his demurral of Spencer's rejection of the idea of the social sensorium—the sentient aspect of society. In following Dewey's conception of language as the sensorium mediating the realm of the individual and society, we can see how this perspective aided Cooley in constructing a view of social organization and process based upon communication.

On the second page of Cooley's notes we hear Dewey ask, "Has society such unity of activity and self-conscious direction that it may properly be termed an organism?" The answer is, "What is, in society, the principle of totality is sovereignty. . . . The particular individuals form the various organs by which wholeness or totality is maintained." Anticipating terms Cooley uses eight years later in *Human Nature and the Social Order* we hear the transcribed Dewey say, "Totality & unity and individuality are two sides of the same thing." Much further along, Dewey shuttles back and forth between his ideas of individual and social consciousness and his notions of sovereignty, law and government.[13]

Individual consciousness is conceived as "the tension in this circuit between what the individual Organ would do if left to itself and the way in which various responses modify its action" (p. 78). Here consciousness of the individual "relate[s] directly to his own activity or to this as reflected back to him through the way in which it coordinates with the activity of others" (p. 79). Thus the individual's "consciousness is part of a social consciousness. The individual's consciousness always represents a balance between the resistance which the Ind[ividual] meets from others and the reinforcement which he secures from them" (p. 80). Here we can see how Dewey's conception of action articulates with Cooley's idea of sympathy and feeds into the notion of the looking-glass self, and how Cooley transforms resistance and reinforcement into the self's positive and negative affect.

Of Dewey's conception of language as the social sensorium, Cooley's notes tell us: "The significance of the sensorium is not that it is something outside to which the individual Organ renders up its own value and welfare but it is the system of co-ordinated activities which mediate the activity of the individual Organ, which determine the form in which its activity shall return back to it" (p. 78). In terms later taken up by Mead, Dewey tells us that the "meaning of any organic action whatever is constituted by the return into it of the other activities which it arouses" (p. 76). Thus the question of whether there is a social sensorium "is not the question whether there is a particular structure called society which is conscious of itself, by itself, apart from individuals." Rather "it is the question whether there is any mechanism by which the activity of the whole is made available to the individual; and the individual's activity, in turn, co-ordinated with that of the whole" (pp. 74, 75). Finally, "the development of the Sensorium as a mechanism is the development of language as an institution" (pp. 82–83). As we shall see in the following chapter, this focus on language articulates well with Cooley's use of communication as a building block of social organization.

James is credited with the development and popularization of the early pragmatists, especially C. S. Peirce. Peirce, an academic outsider, laid the foundations of pragmatism, but in an esoteric and abstruse manner. His limited audience and marginal academic status may have stalled the legitimacy of pragmatism in its early stages.

Utilizing Mead's notion of the generalized other as a nexus between mind and its social context, C. Wright Mills suggests that the form and content of an intellectual's work may be analyzed from the standpoint of the sociology of knowledge. In other words, the content of ideas may be traced to thought, and, in turn, thought, or "the mental," may follow the pattern of internal conversation constituting the generalized other of the thinker. In his terms, "The generalized other is the internalized audience with which the thinker converses: a focalized and abstracted organization of attitudes of those implicated in the social field of behavior and experience. . . . I do not believe . . . that the generalized other incorporates 'the whole society,' but rather that it stands for selected social segments" (Mills, 1939 in 1963, pp. 426, 427 ff.). Thus the intellectual's, like anyone else's, generalized other reflects the individual's variegated pattern (as opposed to Mead's monolithic conception) of group memberships and reference groups. So-called categorical imperatives and rules of logic are really the internalized norms of intellectual discourse, or the thinker's internalized spectators and reference groups. Mills applies this approach to the study of the pragmatic movement and shows how pragmatism may be traced from the early inner circle of the Metaphysical Club, and Peirce, whose esoteric work reflected his marginal academic position and difficulties in getting his work published, that is, the absence of a following (1964, pp. 141–42). Similarly, I discuss Cooley's literary reference group or "invisible college" of essayists below, in chapter 3.

James takes Peirce's view of the public nature of truth and thought as action and habit, and transforms it into a doctrine more congenial to a wider audience constituted of the liberal middle class. James's doctrine emphasizes four elements of pragmatism, which Mills stresses as relevant to a vocabulary of social practice, including his: (a) category of action kept within its human locus; (b) elevating of common sense to the status of philosophical consideration; (c) equating expediency as a claim on reality, with truth; and (d) use of a commercial vocabulary connoting his sensitivity to his popular audiences (pp. 235–40).

Mills says that for Peirce the outsider "pragmatism was the slogan for a sect. . . . Peirce called it 'Pragmaticism,' a name that was so ugly no one would kidnap it." On the other hand, "For James, 'the beloved Harvard professor,' living in the midst of many social and intellectual currents, pragmatism was to serve as 'church' for everyone" (p. 223). While action for Peirce ultimately ends up cosmologically, in James "it is kept within the human locus" (p. 235). James makes epistemological criteria plebeian and thereby relativizes science and philosophy by common sense.[14] Hence "he attempts to bring the street perspective into the classroom, or to find a *modus vivendi* for it" (p. 238).[15] The explanation for this rests in James's sensitivity to his popular audiences—not so much out of a desire to pander to them as to communicate *with* them. This current manifests itself clearly in Cooley's program for social science methodology, which locates truth in the meaning and commonsense experience of the actor (1926 in 1930). Hence "pragmatism is a side window opening out on human action" (Mills, 1964, p. 236). Whereas Spencer erected a new cosmology on the ruins of theology, James's solution was humanistic, stated in terms that were not ontological but experiential and psychological (p. 244).

The pragmatists' conception of action, as James outlines it, means "action in the widest sense," that is "I mean speech, I mean writing, I mean yeses and nos, and tendencies 'from' things and tendencies 'toward' things, and emotional determinations; and I mean them in the future as well as in the immediate present" (quoted in Mills, 1964, p. 235). This represents a conception of human nature as open and plastic. Although James used the term "instinct" he did so ambiguously and focused on habit and plasticity as its substrate. Thus,

> The habits to which there is an innate tendency are called instincts; some of those due to education would by most persons be called acts of reason. The laws of nature are nothing but the immutable habits which the elementary sorts of

matter follow in their action and reactions upon each other. In the organic world however, the habits are more variable than this. Even instincts vary from one individual to another of a kind; and are modified in the same individual . . . to suit the exigencies of the case [and] the phenomena of habit in living things are due to the plasticity of the organic materials of which their bodies are composed. (James, 1890, I, pp. 104–5)

Now, having turned the tables on instinct, James states that man's behavioral versatility evinces "a tendency to do more things than he has ready-made arrangements for in his nerve centers" (James, 1963 [1892], p. 135). While most of the behavior of other animals is automatic, the number of human performances "is so enormous that most of them must be the fruit of painful study" (ibid.). Habit is "the enormous fly-wheel of society, its most precious and conservative agent. It alone is what keeps us all within bounds of ordinance, and saves the children of fortune from the envious uprisings of the poor. It keeps different social strata from mixing" (James, 1890, I, p. 21).

The pragmatic perspective conceives of human action unmoored from instinct, with habit accounting for human behavior's stability. The view is adopted, as Mills indicates in Dewey's case, that human nature is plastic, thus liberating pragmatism from biological determinism. On the other hand, human nature is grounded in habit, which serves as a "lag" that sets problems at the same time allowing and accounting for adaptability (Mills, 1964, pp. 449–54). As we have seen, this rounded conception of human nature is a springboard for Cooley's conspectus of the self and social organization.

In addition, it is William James's conception of the self—that is, his psychology—that has a direct bearing on Cooley's thinking. It might be worthwhile commenting here that pragmatism's potency was then and is now not so much in its systematic organization as in its flexibility and capacity for straddling—mediating—disciplines, perspectives and philosophical boundaries. As William Barrett says of William James, philosophers acknowledge James's genius "but are embarrassed by his extremes: by the unashamedly personal tone of his philosophizing, his willingness to give psychology the final voice over logic where the two seem in conflict, and his belief in the revelatory value of religious experience" (1958, pp. 18–19). Similarly, Mills calls pragmatism James's "seat on a number of fences." Its "'cash value' . . . for James is its openness, its meditative character" (1964, p. 225).[16]

James's notion of the self is pertinent to Cooley in three respects: it is a social self reflecting one's group memberhips; it is a *reflexive* self, that is, a self-apprehending self; and it is an appropriative self. For James the self is duplex, both subject and object—respectively the "I" and the "me"—partly knower and partly known. Both are defined in terms of appropriativeness. The "I" is "that which at any given moment *is* conscious, whereas the Me is only one of the things which it is conscious *of*. In other words, it is the thinker "which appropriates the me" (James, 1963 [1892], pp. 182, 188). The Me is "*in its widest possible sense . . . the sum total of all*" that a man "*CAN call his,* not only his body and his psychic powers, but his clothes and his house, his wife and children, his ancestors and friends, his reputation and works, his lands and horses, and yacht and bank account [James's italics]" (1963 [1892], p. 167).

The Me is divided into three parts: its constituents (the material, social, and spiritual Mes); the feelings and emotions aroused by its constituents ("self-appreciation," that is, self-complacency and/or dissatisfaction); and the acts that are prompted by the emotions (self-seeking and preservation) (pp. 167, 170).

The material Me consists of one's possessions (human and material in the widest sense) and bodily aspects. The spiritual Me consists of "the entire collection of my states of consciousness, my psychic faculties and dispositions taken concretely: and the more "active-feeling" states of consciousness. It is "the core and nucleus of our self" (p. 170). The social Me, or social self, is the recognition one "gets from his mates. We are not only gregarious animals . . . but we have an innate propensity to get ourselves noticed, and noticed favorably by our kind. . . . Properly speaking, a man has as many social selves as there are individuals who carry an image of him in their mind" (pp. 168–69). Thus, "To wound any one of these images is to wound him." Here, as we shall see, is the crux of the relevance of James's notion for Cooley, for it contains all of the elements, ranging from the "personal idea" to the intrinsic socialized component of feeling, of the looking-glass self. Finally, James caps his conception, noting that "as the individuals who carry the images fall naturally into classes, we may practically say that he has as many social selves as there are *distinct* groups of persons about whose opinion he cares." Moreover, "He generally shows a different side of himself to each of these different groups," and "there results what practically is a division of man into several selves" (p. 169). But here too the appropriative aspect is seen, for "A man's *fame,* good or bad, and his *honor* or dishonor, are names for one of his social selves" (ibid.). It is tempting to consider what Cooley and Mead each emphasizes from James: Cooley the appropriative self, with the "Me" understood and serving as the contextual background for his looking-glass self; Mead the logical-lexical equation representing the spontaneous subject, the "acting" "I" being apprehended and converted into the "Me" object. One dwells more on the *feelings* of possession or even possessiveness and the *identification* of the self with all that it lays claim to; the other focuses on the properties of language and its constitutive connections with thought and mind. A noteworthy consideration is Cooley's reservation about James's perspective being "intensely individualistic." Despite James's "insight into the social nature of the self, he did not develop this into a really organic conception of the relation of the individual to the social whole." In other words, James "saw men as separate individuals, not as, in any intelligible sense, members of one another." Accordingly, his "conceptions are intensely individualistic, or, if you please, mystically social, but not organically or intelligibly so." Therefore, "a social, or perhaps I should say a sociological pragmatism remains to be worked out" (*Journal* V. 22 [4/20/19–5/25/25] 3/25/21, pp. 47–48). Below I suggest that this individualistic focus also applies to Mead, although certainly not in the atomistic sense with which it applies to James.

James Mark Baldwin's Unwieldy Adumbration of the Social Self

James Mark Baldwin (1861–1934), who was largely influenced by Tarde, the Hegelians (especially Royce), and the pragmatists (chiefly James), sought to delineate the process of mental development in the child vis-à-vis imitation and suggestion against the background of the "recapitulation hypothesis," that is, that the development of the individual represents a recapitulation of the evolution of the race. Predictably, the vocabulary of imitation makes his formulations awkward, but his insight into the development of the self is nevertheless viable and instructive for Cooley, for he rests his notion of the self and its development on sympathy.

Starting with the premise that sympathy "may be called the imitative emotion *par excellence*," Baldwin (1895, pp. 18–19, 333–39) posits four stages in the child's experience of persons: (1) objective, (2) projective, (3) subjective, and (4) ejective. In the first persons are simply objects, "part of the material going on to be presented, mainly sensations which stand out strong" (p. 18). The second phase marks the beginnings of a sense of self wherein the child begins to make distinctions between persons and things. Here sympathy comes into play since other persons are "very peculiar objects, very interesting, very active, very arbitrary, very portentous of pleasure or pain." As such persons and their visible emotions become "copies" associated with "memory copies" of the child's own personal emotions or duplicates in the child who sees other persons as objects projected out (pp. 18, 333–35). In this second stage another person "stands for a group of experiences quite unstable in its historical meaning" (pp. 335–36). The child is now able to distinguish between "agencies" (self-directing objects) and objects, persons and things (pp. 124–25, 335). This process begins as early as the second month. By about the seventh month the child "begins to be dissatisfied with 'projects,' with contemplation, and so starts on his career of imitation. And of course he imitates persons" (p. 336). This culminates in a cleavage of the child's experience marked by volition and a separating off of the subjective. It appears with a new sense of "agency" or power over his own actions. The attributes that made other personal bodies different from things "are now attached to his own body . . ." (p. 337). In other words he perceives his own responses to projected persons and this gives him light upon himself as subject (p. 18). Lastly: "The child's subject sense goes out by a kind of return dialectic . . . to illuminate these other persons. The project of the earlier [second] period is now clothed . . . with the raiment of selfhood." The projective becomes ejective,

> that is, other people's bodies, says the child to himself, have experiences *in them* much as mine has. They are also *me's*: let them be assimilated to my *me* copy . . . the ejective or social self is born. The ego and the alter are thus born together. Both are crude and unreflective, largely organic, an aggregate of sensations. . . . And the two get purified and clarified together by this twofold reaction between project and subject, and between subject and eject. My sense of myself grows by imitation of you, and my sense of yourself grows in terms of my sense of myself. Both *ego* and *alter* are thus essentially social; each is a socius and each is an imitative creation. (p. 338)

Here we find the element of reflexivity couched in terms of imitation used to derive a model of social interaction, and thence, a conception of self. In

Giddings we saw a notion of reflexivity built on imitation regressed back to the imitative conception of social organization in which self must at most only be implicit or short-circuited. Although Baldwin does not develop a model of social organization, his approach is open-ended and essentially the same as James's social Me. While Baldwin sees sympathy as the imitative emotion par excellence, he stipulates that sympathy shows "the 'circular' form of reaction. The motor attitude seen, we may say, is itself the copy which tends to bring about its own duplication in the person seeing it. And all emotion has the same origin as this" (1894, p. 334).

On the other hand, Giddings, as we know, takes "reflective sympathy" and derives from it feelings such as affection, desire for recognition, and so on, and leapfrogs to the collective behavior model of society based on imitation, that is, like-mindedness expanded to "consciousness of kind." It is Baldwin's reasoning, not his language, that instructs Cooley.

Analyzing the Ambivalent Image of Cooley in the Sociological Canon

Looking at contemporary assessments of symbolic interaction and the self, one encounters a paradox: the accounts frequently credit Cooley as much as they do G. H. Mead with founding the tradition and with formulating a pathbreaking conception of the self, but on the heels of this they allege that Cooley's notion of the social self is solipsistic, that is, it is conceived as a product of the individual mind and not directly derived from the social process. Furthermore, Cooley's work is long on observational but short on theoretical acuity (Stone and Far-berman, 1970, p. 370). In addition, some accounts credit Cooley with being the first to develop a theory of the self but qualify this recognition, as Joas does, by stating that his formulation lodged the self emotionally rather than cognitively and lacked the logical rigor of Mead's conception (1993, p. 23).

In addition, having recited Cooley's many pathbreaking contributions (among them his unique reflexively intersubjective grounding of the self in emotion as much as cognition, his contribution to qualitative methodology, his appreciation of language as fundamental to the development of self and society, the formulation of the primary group), these accounts announce that he nevertheless failed to appreciate the significance of his own theory (Prus, 1996, p. 51),[17] and that finally, despite the fecundity of his social psychology and the notion of the primary group Cooley, in keeping with the above, lacked a tight theoretical enunciation of the social comparable to his recognition of the individual as given (Parsons, 1968).[18]

In short, the paradox lies in the juxtaposition of recognition of Cooley's extraordinary insight and conceptual creativity in his formulation of the social—the self, its anchorage in social process, the group, social organization, and their communicative anchorage—with a criticism of his lack of theoretical sophistication. I submit that the origin of such grudging acceptance and admiration stems from three sources: (a) the fact that Mead's devastating sociological obituary (1930) and other writing established a precedent for the ensuing ambivalence toward him and assured Mead the leading position in the tradition following him (Mead, 1930 in 1964; Mead, 1962 [1934], pp. 173, 224 n.); (b) Cooley's stylistic failure to conform to academic discursiveness, that is, his literariness; and (c) Cooley's disadvantageous location outside the pale of the University of Chicago. Here I will chiefly discuss Mead's role because, combined with the facts that he was at Chicago, trained key figures in the symbolic interactionist tradition, and also hewed to a "discursive" style of writing and inquiry, his influence clearly was regnant, and his views on Cooley were passed on to his students, who, not questioning them, perpetuated the myth of the inferiority of Cooley's ideas to Mead's.

Mead's commemorative article (1930) written soon after Cooley's death is the most significant influence on these views. It underscores his judgment of Cooley's thinking as "mentalistic," or as representing mind as the locus of both the individual and society. Conceding that Cooley's virtue is "his freedom to find in consciousness a social process going on, within which the self and others arise," by the same token, this consciousness precedes observable conduct: "for Cooley selves and others lie inside of the consciousness of ordinary psychology, and yet they also are the 'solid facts' of sociology, that is, they are the field of the external social organism" (1930 in 1964, pp. 300, 302).[19] In other words, the inner mental world of the individual is simultaneously, and contradictorily, the primary experiential source of self and society. Thus, according to Mead, in Cooley's perspective there is no difference between inner and outer. All is subsumed by the individual's consciousness without Cooley having derived it from the train of observable interactional behavior. Thus, "his method was that of an introspection which recognized the mind as the *locus* of the selves that act upon each other, but the methodological problem of the objectification of this mind he pushed aside as metaphysical" (p. 304).

Mead asserts that consciousness depends on mind, which arises out of the *behavioral-gestural interaction* constituting the observable field of individuals, whereas: "The crucial point . . . is found in Cooley's assumption that the form which the self takes in the experience of the individual is that of the imaginative ideas other have of him. And the others are the imaginative ideas which he entertains of them" (ibid.). Mead thinks this amounts to another contradiction in Cooley's thinking, for it presupposes a kind of psychological parallelism. In other words, without having satisfactorily established the social "out-there," our self-concepts, conceived by Cooley as the fruit of our internal mental process "in-here," are baldly posited as they stand on other people's images (*their* "imaginative" ideas) and opinions of us. The key question this poses then, is: "Are selves psychical, or do they belong to an objective phase of experience [that is, the behavioral-gestural field] which we set off against a psychical phase?" His answer is that, contrary to Cooley, selves belong to the same objective experience, shaped in the process of action that "we use to test all *scientific hypotheses* [my italics]" (p. 304). That process does not originate in the mind of the individual but in the other's response to us, which, then and only then, figures in our capacity to reflect and mentally rehearse our actions before acting, thereby creating both mind as the theater for the rehearsal of future action and the social action process constituting it. The action process is "objective" (empirically or observably real) because it is initiated in the observably "objective," gestural interplay of people, out of which meaning, mind, and consciousness arise. As I discuss below, Mead's conception of the social and the self, while plausible, is a *monovalent* one, which runs into the dilemma of accounting for and explaining societal differentiation in the modern urban, industrial world.

Mead clearly misrepresents Cooley here. Cooley is not simply saying that we are that as we are addressed, or, as exactly what others imagine us to be. Our self-images are *not* carbon copies of others' images and opinions of us. Nevertheless, Mead would have us believe Cooley sees one's self-image as identical to, or at least directly dependent upon, the image held by the other. Demurring to Mead's contention, Cooley is saying our selves are a *response*—an emotional as much as a cognitive one at that—to how we imagine, that is, *perceive* ourselves *appearing* to others, and to our imagination of their opinion, evaluation, imputed judgment, and feelings about that appearance. Mead is guilty of the error Reitzes has found in the interpretation by many introductory text treatments of Cooley's notion of the self, that is, an oversocialized interpretation. This flawed understanding fails to grasp Cooley's notion as including "the active role of the individual in interpreting the perceived responses of others," the selective application and assessments of which responses of others are deemed important, and the control and manipulation of the responses of others to create one's self-conception (Reitzes, 1980, pp. 631–37). In other words, Mead, as later misinterpretations would, mistakenly reduced Cooley's conception to a one-way internalization of the perceptions of others.

Developmentally, according to Mead, the human organism assumes the "attitude," or takes the role, of the other, whom it initially addresses by vocal gesture, thereby "arousing in ourselves those responses we call out in other persons so that we are taking the attitudes of other persons into our own conduct" (1962 [1934], p. 69). This is Mead's way of saying that the human organism *empathizes* with the response of the other, and, via its linguistic capacity, thereby reflects upon its own anticipated action. Mead says that Cooley has not sought the reality of the self in the similar "dim beginnings of human behavior" (p. 306). Therefore, "the *locus* of society is not in the mind, in the sense in which Cooley uses the term" (p. 305). He concludes that this failure "commits him to *a conception of society which is mental rather than scientific* [my italics]" (p. 306).

In short, contrary to what might be expected in this intellectual obituary, the essay may be read as a testimonial to Mead's own thinking; nowhere in this *commemorative* essay does Mead explicitly acknowledge Cooley, who died scarcely a year before its publication, as a tangible influence on his own work. Now, in what appears as a grudging concession to propriety, only the essay's last paragraph faintly hints that this might be so: "But I am unwilling to conclude a discussion of Cooley's social psychology upon a note of criticism. His successful establishment of the self and the others upon the same plane of reality in experience and his impressive study of society as the outgrowth of the association and co-operation of the primary group in its face-to-face organization are positive accomplishments for which we are profoundly indebted to his insight and constructive thought" (p. 307). Presumably the primary group is sufficiently "objective" to merit Mead's approval. After discussing the purported mentalism of his "non-cognitive," affectively based conception of self, I will take up the matter of the *presumed*, nonobservable—that is, not empirically ascertainable—phenomena Cooley bases his formulation on.

That Cooley's conception of the self is literally grounded in the opinions of others, as Mead says, derives from his "mentalistic" view of society as existing entirely in the mind of the individual. It is from this premise that Mead derives the label of solipsism he affixes to Cooley's thought. In *Mind, Self, and Society* (1934) Mead states that "Cooley and James . . . endeavor to find the basis of the self in reflexive affective experiences, i.e., experiences involving 'self-feeling'; but the theory that the nature of the self is to be found in such experiences does not account for the origin of the self, or of the self-feeling which is supposed to characterize such experiences" because such feeling alone does not require that the "individual take the attitudes of others toward himself," and without doing so one "cannot develop a self." Rather the "essence of the self . . . is cognitive" (1934, p. 173). In addition to partially grounding the self in feeling, Cooley's "mentalistic" social psychology is founded on the assumption that the content of experience "is entirely individual." Moreover, "all social interactions depend upon the imaginations of the individuals involved." Thus, "Cooley's social psychology, as found in his *Human Nature and the Social Order*, is inevitably introspective, and his psychological method carries with it the implication of complete solipsism: society really has no existence except in the individual's mind." Cooley thus is committed "to a subjectivistic, rather than an objectivistic and naturalistic, metaphysical position" (p. 224 n).

It is clear from the foregoing that Mead distorts and oversimplifies Cooley's position, whittling it down to a cliché, and, by omission, does not recognize how Cooley intersubjectively roots the self in reflexivity via sympathy, the imaginary playmate (also used by Mead in deriving the intersubjective basis for the self), and the communicative-conversational matrix formed by the social and situational contexts essential to the development of the self. Clearly these include feeling, and verbal and visual cognition. Mead talks in absolutes: in the first instance he makes it appear as though Cooley and James ground the self solely in self-feeling, without cognition. While Cooley states that self-feeling is rooted in human nature in an inchoate form, it requires social experience to develop it.[20] Clearly, the three elements of Cooley's looking-glass self *integrate* feeling, appearance, and cognitive thought. Mead, however, excludes, whether by logic or inattention, any other elements before or after the self arises.

The cognitive basis of the self is a keystone of Mead's argument, for meaning and the mind arise from the organism's gestural interaction with the other. For Mead, "observable" interaction initially is largely, and emphatically, vocal, and when reflected on and made symbolic, remains *verbally* symbolic, hence cognitive. But even here Mead's view is excessively narrow. Cognition means *knowing,* which, for Mead means verbal knowing. Is not feeling a way of knowing, and are not nonverbal appearance and other sensory experiences—which, having traversed the uniquely flexible sensory motor apparatus (the nervous system) Mead attributes to the human organism's capacity to construct its "objective" environment—aspects of knowing, that is, of cognition? So fixed on *verbal* cognition is Mead's notion of the self, that feeling is scarcely mentioned, and, for all intents and purposes, does not figure in it at all (Scheff, 2003, p. 2). By itself, this emphasis, serving as a basis for Mead's critique, is fateful for Cooley's reputation. As Sheldon Stryker puts it, "Cooley's somewhat more affective orientation has long been neglected by symbolic interactionists relative to Mead's more cognitive emphasis" (1980, p. 6).

The fixation on verbally cognitive discourse reveals, as Stone calls it, Mead's "discursive bias," which excludes *appearance,* that is, those cues to identification "communicated by such non-verbal symbols as gestures, grooming, clothing, location, and the like" (Stone, 1962, p. 90). Under this aegis, much of Cooley's emphasis on personal impressions and ideas, personal symbols and imagination, all them consisting of, perhaps in large or largest part, nonverbal elements, would not be viewed as properly relevant. Mead shoves it all into the dustbin of the "mental." This is a critical point, for these notions, all of which depend upon appearance in one way or other, are building blocks of Cooley's idea of the self. Indeed, the nonlinguistic elements of the transmission of the sense of self are critical ones (Meltzer, Petras, and Reynolds, 1975, p. 14). As we know, appearance occupies a central position in Cooley's description of the looking-glass self. In line with his own frequent allusions to the behavioristic account of the conditioned reflex, the effect of Mead's criticism is to, indeed, condition readers to narrowly label Cooley's (and James's) accounts of the self as mentalistic and freighted with bald, unreflectively derived, hence, *unsocialized* feeling. But this, among Mead's other charges, inaccurately characterizes Cooley's thought.

Let us remember that the looking-glass self, emphasizing imagination, appearance, and feeling, is constructed from a key building block of Cooley's conception of the social and of the self—*sympathy*. Sympathy is a foundation, whether acknowledged or not, deriving from Adam Smith and the Scottish moralists, of Mead's and Cooley's thinking on mind, self, and society. Here too, verbal *and* visual thought and feeling are intrinsic to the sympathetic integument of social process and organization (Joas, 1985, p. 47; Dingwall, 2001, pp. 239, 241; Stryker, 1980, p. 5, Shott, 1976; Truzzi, 1966).

Concerning Mead's charge of "mentalism," or "solipsism," to the extent that our observations (including our scientific ones) of ourselves or of others are always compromised, or at least influenced, by our perceptions, Mead is correct in saying that Cooley, he, and anyone else is a solipsist! As posted at the head of this chapter, Cooley states that we—social scientists as well as ordinary folks—cannot know anyone directly, except as imaginative ideas in the mind. Mead demurs and says that selves are "objective" realities that can be known directly, as though selves—or their owners or others—are not perceptually filtered and refracted. Cooley tells us that "The intimate grasp of any *social fact* will be found to require that we divine what men think of one another [my italics]" (1902, rev. ed. 1922, p. 122). By "divine" he refers to plumbing our own and others' perceptions through sympathetic introspection; by "social fact," he is referring to what Mead's student, the symbolic interactionist Herbert Blumer, calls the "obdurate character of the empirical world" (Blumer, 1969, p. 23). I do not think Mead is warranted in labeling Cooley's perspective solipsistic—that term denotes a solely monadic consciousness. Cooley is not solipsistic in his recognition of the fact, as relevant to the scientific as it is to the everyday world, that our knowledge of ourselves and of the world is mediated by perception. While it is true that he was a ruminative, introspective romantic, we need to be clear and careful in our assessment of his ideas before making sweeping generalizations. Nevertheless, Mead's application of the term "solipsism" has become an unshakable epithet applied to Cooley's thinking.

Is Mead's derivation of the self and its social context more "scientific" than Cooley's? In other words, is it more empirically grounded? Consider what Holstein and Gubrium's recent appraisal of classical and current treatments of the self tells us about Cooley's formulation of the "empirical self":

He throws his lot in with the scientific method, in particular, with what "can be apprehended or verified by ordinary observation." *While Cooley's subsequent development of introspection is scientifically suspect, he nonetheless intends to proceed empirically,* in relation to concrete experiences. His systematic observations of his two children's self-references at play are exemplary [my italics]. (2000, p. 5)

Notice here how Cooley's purported introspectionism, juxtaposed with the lauding of his empiricism, appears gratuitous, as, indeed, it is, given the fact that little or no verification of it is given in Holstein and Gubrium's treatment of him. My discussions of Cooley's supposed mentalism, his imaginative emphasis (as opposed to a verbal-cognitive one), the identity of self-image with other's opinions, and his purported solipsism, have, in part, refuted the charges of mentalism and introspectionism, at least as far as his recognition of the ubiquity of perceptual distortion of social scientific, as well everyday knowledge, is concerned. This, however, does not address Mead's confidence in the scientific validity of his own theorizing. I contend that Mead used the behaviorist point of view as both legitimation and foil for deriving meaning and mind, that is, internal mental processes.

In his tracing of a linear progression toward the development of meaning, the mind, and self, we can see the operation of Mead's discursive reasoning and writing style. His formulation of the self is built up step by step from the transformation of the external conversation of vocal gestures to the internalized gesture, or the significant symbol, conscious meaning, and mind. Mead begins with the derivation of meaning from the conversation of nonsignificant gestures. Then he moves on to the derivation of *conscious* meaning from the social (interpersonal) process, relating the adjustive responses of the individual to the other's response to the individual's vocal gesture. From there he turns to the individual's entertainment of the anticipated response by the other via the internal conversation of significant symbols to his or her anticipated gesture (that is, the fully reflective self-indicative mental response to others' responses to one's gestures, and to one's own *anticipated* gestures lying at the base of conscious meaning). All of these steps provide a basis for role-taking and the formation of mind and self (1934, pp. 14, 45–48, 63–82; 1913 in 1964; 1922 in 1964; 1924–25 in 1964). By "linear" I am referring to reasoning that creates an impression of an inexorably forward trajectory of the behavioral-mental sequence resting upon the verbal gesture. In this fashion Mead breaks the interaction process down into segments.

To legitimate the claim that in "social psychology we get at the social process from the inside as well as from the outside," the discursive approach serves Mead in establishing what he calls a "social behaviorist," and a more "scientific," or empirical, account of mind and self. Since behaviorism represents the study of only that which is observable, for Mead "social psychology is behavioristic in the sense of starting off with an observable entity" (p. 7). The so-called observable sequence begins with the vocal gesture, followed by the significant gesture and the derivation of meaning, mind, and self. The meaning of behaviorism is thereby stretched, albeit for the purposes of using it as a foil: it is claimed that social behavior is objectively, that is, empirically, observable from an expanded behaviorist standpoint. Cloaking his conception of mind and self and their encompassing internal processes in the behaviorist mantle, Mead rationalizes their palpably observable nature.

Cooley is neither taken in by behaviorism nor attracted by its legitimacy. Content with explaining the human self and behavior through sympathetic introspection, in language similar to but in significant ways different from Mead's, he says:

> Outside and inside in human life mutually complement and interpret each other. Thought and action, sympathy with others' ideas and feelings, observation of their behavior, go to build up a competent intelligence. "Behaviorism" as a thing by itself, apart from sympathetic observation of the mind, is particularism, the isolation of an aspect of life. It is as barren as mere introspection, and for essentially the same reason. (*Journal* V. 22 [4/20/1919–5/25/1925] 7/30/1922, p. 81)

On the same page of his journal Cooley expatiates further on behaviorism, keeping it in quotation marks, thereby conveying that its value is metaphorical: "'Behaviorism' is a trait of the best literature," appealing "to conceptions of actual conduct, rather than to conventional notions." It "puts everything to the test of life, is pragmatic if you please." Note how Cooley *equates* behaviorism with introspection: both are particularistic, and both shear life of its nuanced complexity. The extremes of subjectivity and objectivity, introspection and behaviorism, as polar opposites along the continuum of individualism, admit of no sympathetic understanding. We know that Cooley already has converted introspection into the instrument of intersubjectivity and a tool to study the social world—sympathetic introspection. In addition, he nonplusses us by playfully turning "behaviorism" into a gadget, thus crafting a sobering perspective by incongruity.

How clearly Cooley reveals the meaning of Mead's behavioristic shroud! Mead, a pragmatist, slyly uses the perspective as a way of arriving at exactly the point where Cooley begins, whereas Cooley, even more the pragmatist than Mead, in his demure yet unaffected way, *paints* with "behaviorism," that is, plays with it and makes it work for him. For Cooley the word is a literary medium—a pigment—whereas for Mead it is a stratagem, a Trojan horse enabling him to breach the walled city of Science.

Despite the fact that Mead's thought on the self parallels Cooley's, in *Mind, Self, and Society* he explicitly treats sympathy as an afterthought. The more academic Mead prefers "role taking," whereas the more aesthetically grounded Cooley prefers sympathy. Thus "sympathy" reflects a different order of knowledge usually encompassed by poetry and literature. In this case, the choice of terms might appear to be simply semantic, but it is a difference pointing in the direction of divergent sensibilities. Joas grasps this when he says, "The ability to sympathize may of course be unequally distributed: it is, above all, attributed to poets. Indeed, it is only in the literary and, admittedly, not in the philosophical strands of the above traditions [the Scottish moralists, e.g., Adam Smith] that we encounter the ego actually evolving from such acts of putting oneself in the other person's shoes, and thus only in literature does 'sympathy' play a constitutive role for the ego as actor" (1996, p. 186).

I contend that the key issue differentiating Mead's from Cooley's approach is one of *style.* In fact, as noted above, Mead is making a false contrast, for both he and Cooley had arrived at the same point using different imagery and writing styles. In constructing his own formulations, and in his criticism of Cooley, Mead pitches his arguments to an audience of academic psychologists, philosophers, and sociologists, many of whom value "scientific" thinking and reasoning. Their penchant is to establish one's findings and formulations as empirically "real," and to uphold "the conventional distinction between fiction and non-fiction, relegating textuality, literarity and metaphoricity to fiction" (İlter, 1995, p. 11).[21]

It is for this reason too, that Mead stretches the meaning of terms like "nature," as when he says that "the social process, through communication . . . is responsible for the appearance of a whole set of new objects in nature . . . (objects, namely of 'common sense')" (1930, p. 79). Hyperbolically, Mead tells us: "Certain objects . . . exist for us because of the character of the organism." In this case, what are "nature," "objects," and "common sense"? From the same scientistic vantage point, can't we conceive the material and symbolic "objects" created by humans in the social process as artifactual or unnatural, that is, as crafted and contrived, as opposed to empirically given, outside of human activity? But Mead is endeavoring to extend radical empiricism's meaning to include social objects by using its own precepts to do so.

He boldly asserts: "the organism ['naturally'] determines the environment as fully as the environment determines the organism" (p. 129). Thus, "If an animal that can digest grass, such as an ox, comes into the world, then grass becomes food. The object did not exist before, that is, grass as food." Outside of being part of it, is the organism actually *determining* the environment? By one set of criteria—Mead's—yes, for the biological makeup of the organism *frames* the environment, or part of it for itself. But in another sense, no, if one allows species creation by natural selection, in which case Mead is telling us that the chicken precedes the egg; the idea that nonhuman organisms determine their environment is absurdly contradictory.

Mead extends the same reasoning to the more supple and versatile structure and functioning of the human nervous system, and makes it appear as if all of the aforementioned complexities of the derivation of meaning from a process he calls social are "natural." He states that "in the central nervous system one can find, or at least justifiably assume . . . the mechanism of just such complexities of response, as we have been discussing," namely the derivation of conscious meaning from a social process comprising human communication (p. 127). On the other hand, "there is nothing in the mechanical, electrical, and physical activity that goes on in the nerve which answers to what we term an idea." Rather, the central nervous system coordinates the various processes carried out by the body, which are called consciousness (pp. 127–28). In this case, "environment thus arises for . . . [the] human organism through the selective power of an attention that is determined by its impulses that are seeking expression" wherein the "consciousness of the organism consists in the fact that its future conduct outlines and defines its objects." He concludes that "imagery is for the percipient as objective as the so-called sense object (Mead, 1924–25 in 1964, p. 272), thus coming around to the same place Cooley begins—consciousness, the mind, and the imagination! What this amounts to is to say that the mind and society, both containing images or social constructs, constitute that part of nature falling under the aegis of the behavioral sciences, and are as "natural" as those phenomena studied by the natural sciences.

Mead's thinking, conceiving the social construction of the environment, is intriguing, but his leap from the prehuman to the human construction of the environment is based on a faulty premise regarding the creation of the environment by *all* organisms. It is really a form of backward reasoning, which actually reifies the prehuman determination of the environment by the assumption of the social construction of the life world. Put another way, "Mead wants to claim that sociality in a certain sense is a property of all beings, inorganic as well as organic" (Wilson and Dixon, 2004, p. 80). On the face of it, is his conclusion more "scientific" or plausible than Cooley's imagining of imaginations?

I conclude that Mead's thinking and use of terms such as "nature," and his derivation of consciousness and human objects, is no more valid than is Cooley's qualified use of the terms "instinct," "sympathetic introspection," "mind," and so on. While he uses "social behaviorism," "nature" and "science" as foils for his own creativity, he does not state that it *appears as if* the organism creates its environment in the sense of what Simmel calls "more life," or that language and other human symbolic and material "objects" acquire a facticity along the lines of what Simmel calls "more-than-life," to the point that they appear *as if* they are, in effect, part of nature (Simmel, 1971 [1918] pp. 368–73). I say "as if" because Mead subscribes to empiricism, and cloaking his assumptions in scientific garb enables him to store the "objects" *he* creates inside a vault of stark empirical reality. This may be viewed as a stylistic preference. In this fashion Mead tries to have it both ways: he wishes to be "scientific" and he can take an innovative and imaginatively incongruous "behaviorist" stance toward mind. In other respects his thinking might, indeed, be construed as poetic, or artistic. As Green tells us: "Whereas science seeks a conceptual interlock with real objects and events, as proven by empirical entry into the world, art uses worldly material to create objects and events that are simultaneously inside and outside of everyday reality; of the world, yet somehow at odds or in tension with it" (1988, p. 25). For Cooley the symbol is not an analytic end in itself, but a palimpsest upon which he can rewrite social process, and in this way he is not a mere symbolic *interactionist,* rather a symbolic *pro*actionist. Thus as he would have it, with respect to representative men as social types, the social process is intrinsically creative: "What we need is a good symbol to help us think and feel; and so starting with an actual personality which more or less meets this need, we gradually improve upon it by a process of unconscious adaptation that omits the inessential and adds whatever is necessary to round out the ideal. Thus the human mind working through tradition is an artist, and creates types which go beyond nature" (1918, p. 116). Cooley was more inclined to take a riskier path, openly and avowedly placing artistic insight on a par with scientific discourse. This makes him vulnerable in a profession increasingly concerned about its scientific validity.

As Hans-Joachim Schubert tells us, Mead's contention that Cooley is a mentalist actually distorts Cooley's understanding of mind and imagination by taking them out of context, and, as I have noted, misconstrues the place of personal ideas and imagination in his notion of the looking-glass self (Schubert, 1998, pp. 20–21). Cooley's statements like "the immediate social reality is the personal idea," "society . . . is a relation among personal ideas," "society exists in my mind as the contact and reciprocal influence of certain ideas," and "the imaginations people have of each other are *the solid* facts of society" are shorn of the social and communicative contexts Cooley assures us they are embedded in. Thus Cooley also informs us that "I do not mean merely that society must be studied by the imagination . . . but that the object of study is primarily an imaginative idea or group of ideas in the mind, that we have to imagine imaginations," that is, as social and individual constructions (1902, rev. ed. 1922, pp. 121–22). As a result, Cooley articulates his concepts in a spirit akin, although admittedly not identical, to Mead's.

There is little cause for doubt concerning Cooley's understanding of the incarnation of the so-called realities of meaning and the self in an "objective" social process, but for Cooley objectivity is more or less negotiated in the conversational sphere of science, much as reality is negotiated in other forms of discourse. Objectivity is not fetishized by Cooley, who in his journal quotes Goethe as speaking of "stiff realism and stagnating objectivity" followed by the wish to "'bring nature within reach of the imagination'" (*Journal* V. 11 [5/7/1896–3/12/1897] 5/7/1896, pp. 9, 10). Hence, Schubert concludes that for Cooley imagination "is not a force isolated from the empirical world, but, rather, a practical 'intercourse,' an intersubjective 'communication'" (1998, p. 21). Thus, with respect to the self and the anchorage of the "I" in social reality, Cooley, taking the observational stance, informs us that "the 'I' of common speech has a meaning which includes some sort of reference to other persons" and "is involved in the very fact that the word and the ideas it stands for are phenomena of language and the communicative life" (1902, rev. ed. 1922, p. 180). In other words, they are socially grounded!

Finally, it bears repeating that Cooley's notions of sympathy and the self, with their partial derivation from Adam Smith, share with the latter the stance of the scientific observer. Indeed, the notions of sympathy and of the impartial spectator prefigure and no doubt are ancestral to Mead's, Cooley's, James's, and Baldwin's conceptions of a self framed by the phenomena of sympathy and reflexivity. Viewed in this light, Smith's ideas were devised in the spirit of scientific objectivity (Shott, 1976; Costelloe, 1997; Miller and Dingwall, 1997). In this respect, Mead inaccurately characterizes Cooley's method as introspection. It is *sympathetic* introspection, which Cooley, in line with a keen awareness of the difference between the methodological requirements of psychology and sociology, sharply differentiates from psychological introspection. I take this matter up below in the chapter discussing Cooley's methodology. As H. T. Buckle, a mid-nineteenth-century historian, noted of Smith: "In the *Moral Sentiments,* he investigates the sympathetic part of human nature; in the *Wealth of Nations,* he investigates its selfish part. And as all of us are sympathetic as well as selfish . . . and as this classification is a primary and exhaustive division of our motives to action, it is evident, that if Adam Smith had completely accomplished his vast design, he would at once have raised the study of human nature to a science" (quoted in Raphael and Macfie, 1976, p. 21).[22] As Albert Saloman suggests, "Smith laid the foundations for an empirical science of society" (quoted in Costelloe, 1997, p. 94). While Mead, in effect, derives sympathy, or empathy, as role-taking from the gestural interchange, Cooley proceeds directly with sympathy. Whether this is more or less scientific, I cannot say, but it is clear that Mead's formulation of the self probably was influenced by Smith's notions of sympathy and the impartial spectator (Costelloe, 1997; Joas, 1985, p. 47). Mead had a different scientific agenda, one stemming from and attuned to behavioral psychology, and so he chose that idiom to frame his inquiry. I must conclude that his criticism reflects an idiomatic or, with respect to his view of Cooley, a stylistically censorious mien more than a valid sociological one. Unfortunately, for reasons of style, geographic and institutional location, and professional choice, Cooley took second place.

A footnote in Prus's treatment of the classical roots of symbolic interactionism clarifies the reasons for the ambiguous place held by Cooley in the sociological canon. We are told that "Cooley's contributions would likely have been much more consequential had he been located at the University of Chicago" instead of Michigan. Furthermore, "while Mead read and incorporated aspects of Cooley's thought into his own work and Cooley served as a literary inspiration of sorts for the students at Chicago who played such an important role in the developing the ethnographic tradition, much of Cooley's potential may have gone unrealized by virtue of his location" (1996, p. 63 n). While Cooley's location is underscored as the major block to his influence, noteworthy are the observations concerning the "second generation" students of Mead, such as Herbert Blumer and Everett C. Hughes, who formed, promulgated, and passed on the symbolic interactionist tradition and its associated emphasis on ethnographic methods (Colomy and Brown, 1995).[23] Let us not forget that Cooley's literariness was admired, and most importantly that his contribution was integral to Mead's formulation of the self. These latter elements play a key role in Mead's ambivalence toward Cooley.

Could it be that Mead, having based his own thinking on Cooley's formulations, felt it necessary to criticize them to prevent them from overshadowing his own? My answer is a qualified yes. Mead's competitiveness is plausible since Cooley's work on the self, antedating his own, was recognized as truly original. Possibly the rivalry was subconscious, a variety of Bloom's "anxiety of influence," the attempt to defend intellectual autonomy by disavowing the influence of a precursor. Perhaps I am being ungenerous here, for on the face of it, Mead, a philosopher, was simply trying to "solve a whole series of epistemological and psychological problems by unraveling the implications of social behavior" (Miller, 1973, p. xx). But to repeat, in order to do this he conceived self and society as plausibly consistent with behaviorist and positivist premises; this brings me back to my suspicions concerning rivalry with Cooley, for in any event he needed to dispense with Cooley's thinking to remain consistent with his own investment in the positivist approach.

There is one remaining sociological issue: Mead's derivation of mind, self, and society ultimately results in a conception of the social that rests on interacting *individuals,* and thereby in a monolithic conception of the group, institutions, and society. This is ironic on two counts: his inheritance of Adam Smith's ideas of sociality derived from sympathy and the impartial spectator, and his attribution of solipsism to Cooley. In the first case the irony is that Mead also took on Smith's emphasis on "civil society as a collection of interacting individuals" (Fourcade-Gourinchas, 2001, p. 414). Herbert Blumer, who systematizes

Mead's emphasis, tells us that "social action is lodged in acting *individuals* who fit their respective lines of action to one another through a process of interpretation; group action is the collective action of such *individuals* [my italics]" (1969, p. 84). In a sense Mead's, and later Blumer's, reference point remains the individual, with a notion of the group scarcely developed beyond the generalized other—which is, after all, a monolithic "imaginative" conception of the group and society. There is no solid conception of groups, institutions, and society in their own right, that is, as social entities with features and characteristics of their own, even in the section of *Mind, Self and Society* entitled "Society" (1962 [1934], pp. 227–336). Indeed, Turner includes Blumer among other symbolic interactionists as representing "micro-reductionism" (1995, p. 182).[24]

Mead's opening premise that human society could not exist without minds and selves is not one I can disagree with, but there is scarcely any development beyond this of a conception of groups, institutions, and society. There is no conception of societal and group entities sui generis. When contrasted with Durkheim's "sociologistic" conception of the group and society as sui generis realities, this perhaps appears advantageous, considering that Durkheim's notion is a type of conceit, or reification, defining the social Absolute that places "some individuals in an unjustified position of privilege" (Infantino, 1998, p. 76). On the other hand, Mead's conception of the social finally reduces to the distributive side of the same thing—methodological individualism. Mead's notion of the social, or what he calls the "social" aspect of human society, is "simply the social aspect of the selves of all individual members taken collectively." How different is this from Spencer's liberal utilitarian assumption? Thus Mead defines society as follows: "human society as whole . . . is nothing but the sum-total of the social experiences of all of its individual members ([1962] 1934, p. 321). An institution, for example, is simply and naively defined as "a common response on the part of all members of the community to a particular situation" (p. 261). What does this tell us about a complex modern society such as the one Mead lived in? How is societal *differentiation* in all its aspects to be explained when, at best, difference might be viewed as deviation, or as reducible to individual differences? Mead simply follows Comte (although he does not say so) in stating that the family, being the basis of species reproduction, is the fundamental "unit of human social organization" upon which all complex social organizations such as the clan, tribe, and state are based ([1962] 1934, p. 229).

Symbolic interactionists largely build on Mead's conception of the social, which is, when all is said and done, naively circumscribed by the interaction of individuals. Cooley's criticism of James applies more pointedly to Mead: "Wm. James had a social spirit, which, however, did not . . . give rise to a sense of organic social wholes" (*Journal* V. 22 [4/20/19–5/25/25] 3/8/21, p. 46). Mead naively asks how order and structure in society can be maintained while bringing about change when such change would seem to destroy the given order (1936, pp. 361–62). Such questions assume the quality of ultimatums because Mead's notion is not framed from the standpoint of a social matrix recognized as a supraindividual or collective reality containing different or conflicting levels of generality and complexity. Yes, the *generalized* other is a conception of the society at large, but Mead construes it as the *individual*'s conception of a monolithic community—that is, "the organized community which gives to the individual his unity of self . . . , the generalized other is the attitude of the whole community" (1934, p. 154). This perspective cannot account for diversity and conflict between and within groups, institutions, and society (Lee, 1966).[25] Multivalence was sacrificed in Mead's dismissal of James's social self, whereas for Cooley it was retained. For the time being, note Cooley's simile of the cornfield, suggesting that the group and individual perspectives are vantage points, allows him to move flexibly between and within the realms of interpersonal interaction, groups, institutions and society.[26]

Metaphor and analogy have a place in social science, not to conceal a lack of an exacting descriptive or analytic frame, but because they enhance descriptive and theoretical accuracy. Unlike Mead's, Cooley's organic view leaves him free to explore the self and social organization without reifying one as the other. He sees society, groups, institutions, and the individual as distinct levels of social generality with properties of their own, yet somehow interchangeably offering better perspective. Cooley's conception of social organization, building on and cohering by communication, again establishes the matrix out of which the individual and the social can be differentiated. It is to that conception that I now turn.

CHAPTER THREE

COMMUNICATION WRIT LARGE

Cooley's Concept of Social Organization

> The view that popular rule is in its nature unsuited to foster genius rests chiefly on the dead-level theory. Equality not distinction is said to be the passion of the masses, diffusion not concentration. . . . "In modern society," said de Tocqueville, the chief begetter of this doctrine, "everything threatens to become so much alike that the peculiar characteristics of each individual will soon be entirely lost in the general aspect of the world." Shall we agree with this or maintain with Plato that a democracy will have the greatest variety of human nature? . . . Certainly America is a rather convincing proof that democracy does not necessarily suppress salient personality. . . . The "individualism" of our social system is a commonplace of contemporary writers. Nowhere else, not even in England, I suppose, is there more respect for non-conformity or more disposition to assert it. In our intensely competitive life men learn to value character above similarity.
>
> CHARLES HORTON COOLEY, *Social Organization*

Cooley opens his treatment of social organization (1909) with a premise identical to the one initiating his earlier work: "Self and society go together, as phases of a common whole. I am aware of the social groups in which I live as immediately and authentically as I am aware of myself" (pp. 8–9). He follows this immediately by launching into social organization as a whole—the "social organism"—"a vital unity in human life" representing "social consciousness" manifested "either in a particular mind or as a coöperative activity of many minds." The unity of social organization—the social organism—"consists not in agreement but in organization, in the fact of reciprocal influence or causation among its parts, by virtue of which everything that takes place in it is connected with everything else, and so is an outcome of the whole" (p. 4). Thus there are three aspects of consciousness all linked by the connective tissue of communication: "self-consciousness, or what I think of myself; social consciousness (in its individual aspect), or what I think of other people; and public consciousness, or a collective view of the foregoing as organized in a communicating group" (p. 12). Social consciousness entails the "mutual understanding of one another's point of view on the part of individuals or groups concerned as naturally results from discussion" (pp. 9–10). The latter manifestation is public opinion. As an organic unity it is not one of agreement but of organization. As such, it embraces a unity consisting of "a differentiated and coöperative life" (p.11). This is a key premise uniting Cooley's abstract approach to social organization with his view on democracy. Both are unities cohering by differentiation.

In the first five chapters of a later book, *Social Process* (1918, pp. 3–51), Cooley depicts the growth of society and social organization in terms reminiscent of Ward's notion of sympodial growth. Cooley calls it the "tentative method," a method of trial and error, "the pragmatic method, the growth of that which 'works' or functions. . . . [I]t is a process of experiment which is not necessarily conscious" (p. 8). Hence the growth of social forms is analogous to that of the wild grapevine; "intelligence may have a part in this or it may not" (p. 9). His illustration is pragmatic: it is the drift of a man's career, not zoology. Thus "a political party, a business enterprise, a social settlement, a church, a nation, develops by means of a mixture of foresight and unforeseen experience" (p. 11).

Organization is a process of "adaptive working" since a system of coordinated activities emerges; that is to say, a social form endures if it "works" or has some kind of existential value. Still, organization is more unconscious than we perceive. Because we engage in activity as a cooperative project we suppose that this is the result of a plan, "but . . . organization is something far more extended than consciousness" (p. 20). Social processes are hardly planned. Consciousness is at work in them "but seldom consciousness of anything more than some immediate object, some detail that contributes to the whole without the actor being aware of it" (p. 21). The large movements of history testify to this.

The social organism coheres by communicating. On the societal level this is exemplified in public opinion to the extent the society is more or less aware of itself (1909, p. 10). The unity, however, is not of agreement but organization, of interaction and mutual influence. The result is a unity consisting of a differentiated and cooperative life. Hence, "visible society is, indeed, literally, a work of art, slow but mostly subconsciousness in its production—as great art often is—full of grotesque and wayward traits, but yet of inexhaustible beauty and fascination" (p. 21). *This* is social organization, the "larger mind" that consciously and unconsciously is "continually building itself up into wholes—fashions, traditions, institutions, tendencies, and the like—which spread and diversify like the branches of a tree, and so generate an ever higher and more various structure of differentiated thought and symbols" (p. 21). No more vivid imagery could convey the analogy of society-as-artwork.[1]

Finally, so far as the moral view is concerned, "it should be the result if this organic view of mind to make the whole teaching and practice of righteousness more rational and effectual by bringing it closer to fact" (1909, p. 13). Thus the organic view "calls for social knowledge as the basis of morality" (p. 210). In contrast, impractical standards have the same ill effect as unenforceable law since we are lulled into divorcing theory from practice, and therefore, the individual from the moral ideal. What "righteousness," "practical standards," "rational," and "effectual" are appear to be subsumed under the aegis of "sympathetic reform" in the sprit of relativism.

The Primary Group

It is ironic that one of the notions for which Cooley is principally known was written as an afterthought in *Social Organization* (1909, pp. 23–50). In his essay "The Development of Sociology at Michigan," he informs us that "since the matter in that book on Primary Groups has attracted much interest, it may be worth while to recall that this matter, although it appears early in the book, was the very last part to be conceived and written, not appearing in the earliest draft at all. When I had this draft before me there appeared to be a hole in my exposition which I was impelled to fill up" (1928 in 1930, pp. 11–12).

As Dorothy Ross characterizes it, that first draft started with his psychological theory of organic human nature and went directly to his liberal exceptionalist analysis of American society. "Only afterward," she writes, "did he realize that there was a missing link in his argument" (1991, p. 245). In a sense, the development of the concept illustrates Cooley's notion of the tentative method as it applies to his work. It also sheds light on aspects of the accreditation of knowledge—in this case working in Cooley's favor—in the discipline.

Cooley's biographer Edward C. Jandy observes that Cooley's disclosure leaves us at a loss to "explain where he drew his inspiration for the concept"

(1942, p. 179). He informs us that Cooley had read Small and Vincent's text *Introduction to the Study of Society,* published in 1894, which had a chapter titled "The Primary Social Group," and that Cooley's earliest direct references to the matter appear in journal entries in 1908 in regard to primary ideals. He states that it "is extremely likely that the mere label of primary group came as a suggestion from Small and Vincent," and he probably "was as much influenced by Sumner and others in his discussion of primary groups and ideals" (p. 180). Jandy asserts that anyone reading "Small and Vincent's and Cooley's discussion of this subject can scarcely fail to note that, outside of the label and one or two suggestions about the psychological bonds connecting individuals in these groups, there is no further parallel in the two treatments" (ibid.) Moreover, finding the gap in *Social Organization* before its publication, Cooley "found a few comments on primary groups in his Journals and notes" and used them to fill the gap "without mentioning where the label . . . came from" (p. 181). Jandy concludes: "diffusion, not independent origin of the term, is the more probable explanation" (p. 181).

The "independent origin" Jandy refers to is the implication made by Floyd N. House in 1929 in *The Range of Social Theory* that Cooley was not the originator of the concept because he did not mention the Small and Vincent text in *Social Organization* in his discussion of primary groups. House also noted that in the same year of the appearance of *Social Organization* (1909), Helen Bosenquet's *The Family* came out in print, which treated the family as a social unit of interacting personalities, and Cooley failed to mention that work as well. As to the latter work, Jandy states that Cooley had not heard of Bosenquet's work and that House had forgotten "Cooley already had a rich background of child study behind him," including his formulation of the genesis of the self.[2]

I am inclined to agree with Jandy's argument. Of greatest importance is that "Cooley gave the concept meaningful content" (p. 181). As I discuss in the following chapter concerning the literary influences on Cooley's work, the provenance of the *term* is *intertextual,* that is, a product of Cooley being *at* an intersecting point of textual contact, while the significance given to the term can be largely credited *to* Cooley. By the time Jandy's biography had been written, Cooley's treatment—and it was his treatment that indisputably held sway—had stimulated much discussion and use of the notion, including the development of other formulations (such as the secondary group).

Cooley's concept is pivotal because of the place primary groups occupy in society as incubators of human development and social nurturance, and as sources of values. They appear in all societies, and are ubiquitous, adaptable, persistent, and capable of being transformed under conditions of social change. Through primary relations "mankind realizes itself . . . and from the experience forms standards of what it is to expect from more elaborate association" (1909, p. 32). Thus, as Dorothy Ross suggests, the primary group "was fashioned as the linchpin of the whole" (1991, p. 245). The notion is fundamental to Cooley's treatment of democracy and commences his dialogue with de Tocqueville on that subject, by noting that the primary group is the building block of community, and agreeing with de Tocqueville's statement that "the commune seems to come directly from the hand of God" (1909, p. 27).

The crucible for the social transmission of morality is the primary group: it is the cradle of the self and of "primary ideals." Primary groups are "those characterized by intimate face-to-face association and cooperation" (1909, p. 23). The primary group supplies the foundation of Cooley's faith in democracy. Noting its universality as well as the contemporary dissolution of the neighborhood by "the growth of an intricate mesh of wider contacts," Cooley boils its essential character down to "a certain intimacy and fusion of personalities" (p. 26), for "it is a 'we'; it involves the sort of sympathy and mutual identification for which 'we' is the natural expression" (p. 23). Its new forms are outcroppings such as clubs and fraternal organizations as well as primary relationships formed within occupational contexts. The primary group is fundamental as a socializing agency ("in forming the social nature and ideals of the individual"). While it fuses personalities into a whole, this unity is not simply of harmony and love but is rather of antagonistic cooperation—"a differentiated and competitive unity, admitting of self-assertion and various appropriative passions" (ibid.).

Human nature is nurtured in the primary group, but Cooley does not explicitly discuss the effects of the feedback of secondary influences on primary groups—for example, in occupational settings—except in some pungent insights into university bureaucracy and administrators in his diaries and *Life and the Student* (1927). On the other hand, while the notion of "secondary group" is not his formulation, he is clearly aware of the nature and existence of such associations. In his essay "Personal Competition" (1899 in 1930, pp. 185–86, 221) he states that "the fact that definite associations are more numerous and more specialized than they have been in the past increases the impersonal tendency. . . . [T]he increased facility of association effected by modern communication, brings it to pass that the modern man shares in many associations, each one of which is narrowly restricted in its aim, and of course feels a personal responsibility for each in inverse ratio to their number." In the same place he notes that "the large, complex and shifting groups that carry on commercial and political life cannot so readily be made social, in the higher sense , as a small, stable and presumably congenial group like the family" (p. 212).

The primary group instills in us ideals, standards, and expectations of what one is to expect from more elaborate association. While the primary group is universal, the primary ideal is not articulated by children and savages. Nevertheless "they have it . . . they see it; they see themselves and their fellows as an indivisible, though various, 'we,' and they desire this 'we' to be harmonious, happy and successful," and thus incorporate and amalgamate this inchoate feeling—that of "a moral whole or community"—into and with the self. It is within the primary group that "individual minds are merged and the higher capacities of the members find total and adequate expression" (p. 33). The desire for moral unity is "the mother . . . of all social ideals" (p. 35). Freedom, democracy, justice, avarice, truculence, loyalty, the service ideal—all are fostered in primary groups. One reason we never live up to the more laudable primary ideals is that "our higher nature has but an imperfect and transient mastery over our lower"; beyond that "the cause of failure is seen to be the difficulty of organization," as in the case of institutions that brutalize or ossify the individual so that primary idealism is all but obliterated (p. 53). While "explicit democracy—deciding by popular vote and the like—is not a primary ideal, freedom, "natural freedom" or natural rights to freedom, is (pp. 46–48).

Cooley clearly is a pioneer in his discussion of the genesis of values in primary groups and in communication. Hans Joas's recent discussion of the birth of values among sociologists, for all its erudition concerning the pathbreaking attempts of the pragmatists James and Dewey, especially his appreciation of the latter's account of how the derivation of value from "the unlimited nature of everyday communication and its institutionalization in the form of the procedures and institutions of democratic society become the highest ideal," is strangely bereft—considering the comprehensive sweep of his earlier writing on American pragmatist-based sociology—of any discussion of Cooley (2000, p. 119). Cooley, as we know, initially derives value from primary ideals, and, secondly, derives and justifies democratic principles, as I am about to point out, in his limning of the role of communication as the integument of societal organization. Moreover, Joas's praise of Dewey's recognition of "the religious values implicit in our common life" and his understanding of their close kinship with the aesthetic dimension of quotidian aspects of social life (Dewey "sees the genesis of values as the creative work of our imagination") (2000, pp. 119, 115), transparently neglects Cooley's more sociologically developed conspectus of values, including his sociological aestheticism, which conceives society as a work of art. Cooley's analysis of pecuniary valuation (see chapter 7) further develops his initial derivation of values and employs it in a sophisticated critique of neoclassical economics. Joas's omission is perplexing given his erudition concerning, and greater sensitivity to, the very issues I focus on here as contributing to the eliding of Cooley in the sociological canon.

Communication and Democratic Togetherness

One recent commentator on Cooley (Simonson, 1996) claims that his notion of the primary group idealizes "*Gemeinschaft* relations of family and place as models" and highlights "the moral ideals or ends served by small communities" while tying those ends "to grander religious and political projects" (p. 329). In this light, communication occupies the master status as the process connecting primary groups and their ideals with other phases of social organization such as public opinion, sentiment, classes, and institutions. Communication thus is the vehicle for the radiation outward of primary group ideals. This outward extension of the primary group and its ideals marks Cooley's nostalgic pinning of "communication hope" or the ideal of democratic togetherness onto social organization. Simonson's analysis is reminiscent of Parson's reservation concerning Cooley's "bias" towards primary and against secondary relations (1968, p. 63).

Communication media (speech, printing, the telegraph, the telephone, railways) form an organic whole. As "truly the outside or visible structure of thought," it is "as much cause as effect . . . of the conscious life of men" (p. 64). Writing made history possible; printing means democracy since it brings knowledge within the grasp of the common people (pp. 74, 75). The arts considered as communication "communicate matter that could not go by any other road" (p. 77). The rapid expansion and differentiation of communication make possible the organization of society on the basis of the higher human faculties. As far as newspapers are concerned, however, they might best be described as "organized gossip" (p. 84), a notion Robert E. Park borrows in his classic essay on the culture of the city.[3]

From the standpoint of politics "communication makes possible public opinion, which, when organized, is democracy. While our government as constituted was not designed to be democratic, modern communications appear to be fostering the growth of democracy everywhere (Cooley, 1909, p. 85). Human nature, desiring the good, is receptive to the democratic ideas brought to it by communication (p. 88). The enlargement of human nature in this fashion affects sentiment and augments sympathy between groups and nations (pp. 88–90). This enlargement of life is attended by greater differentiation and thus greater individuality. Individuality can be the result of isolation or of choice: modern conditions reduce isolation and augment choice. The contrast may be seen in the local individuality of neighborhood dialects in the former, and the specialization of the city vis-à-vis the cultivation of specialized forms of art, knowledge, or conduct. While this enlargement is generally beneficial, its ill effects are superficiality and strain à la the hurried life, the "habit of intention," ennui, and so on. This is manifested in popular literature, which is written for those who "run as they read" (p. 100).

The most dramatic result of this enlargement of communication and consciousness is the growth of public opinion and the expansion of fellow-feeling—the extension of primary ideals. Hence the sway of democracy is widened. Public opinion is not an aggregate of separate individuals but an organization, a cooperative product of communication and reciprocal influence (p. 121). However, public opinion does not merely express a mean between higher and lower intelligence in society: rather it is representative inasmuch as its actors (like elected legislators) express society's constituencies. We witness also specialized opinion as in the case of occupational groups, but these nevertheless share in the general spirit.

Public opinion is a latent authority; it stimulates the organization of groups, and the press exploits this. Enthusiasm seeks an outlet; ambition and pecuniary interest "are enlisted to gratify the demand." Leadership and organization are mobilized and this raises ethical standards (as among professional groups). Thus "the public mind, like a careful farmer, moves about its domain, hoeing weeds, mending fences and otherwise setting things to rights, undeterred by the fact that the work will not stay done." Herein lies moral unity in diversity (p. 133).

As public opinion does not seek a dead level, the dead level theory is equally inapplicable to the question of creative production in a democracy: Democracy does not suppress "salient personality" (creativity) but only makes for a "larger theater of success" (pp. 159, 161). The conviction that the mass will submerge the individual rests on the spurious assumption that one aspect of society will remain stationary while another grows. More likely literary and artistic weakness is a sign of the "spiritual disorganization incident to a time of rather sudden transition" (p. 162). Old social forms are disintegrating, leaving a vacuum of discipline such that "our life remains somewhat inarticulate." This is evinced by a lack of "mature culture groups" (p. 163). High culture in the Old World was a class culture, and our new immigrant culture has left this behind, along with the visible monuments of culture left from the past. This is augmented by the leveling effects of commercialism. America is thus too transient and restless to favor the rapid crystallization of a new artistic culture (p. 169); its pace is more suited to the production of mediocre goods on a vast scale. The confusion leaves the modern artist with too much choice. It would seem that nine years later, in *Social Process*, Cooley is about to recant his dourness when he tells us "in these noisy and unrestful times people flock to the motion-picture shows, or buy cheap fiction, in an eager quest for the ideal. How idle it is to deprecate, justly or otherwise, the poor taste of the masses, as if art were a matter of mere refinement, and not of urgent need." But, "I cannot imagine any broad and rich growth of democracy without a corresponding development of popular art, and one of the many indications that our democracy is as yet immature and superficial is its failure to achieve such a development" (1918, pp. 411–12). Here Cooley pursues his dialog with de Tocqueville. On the one hand he disagrees with him about the conformity produced by the alleged tyranny of the majority—the "dead level" theory Cooley refers to in the epigraph to this chapter. On the other hand he concurs with de Tocqueville when it comes to popular art and taste, and on this matter Cooley remains consistent, disagreeing with de Tocqueville when it comes to the general viability and vibrancy of American democracy and agreeing with him on the proliferation of the commonplace in the arts in America.

This is perhaps more Cooley's issue—actually a predicament shared by most sociologists of his time who espoused one version or revision or another of the American exceptionalist ethos—than a predicament of the arts in his time. Broadly speaking, the very things Cooley feels shackles artistic culture—

commercialism, materialism, heterogeneity, even the violence and destruction of World War I, crass and banal as they are, inspired artists and art movements here and abroad: Homer, Eakins, Sargent, Hunt, Prendergast, and Whistler in the United States, the Dadaists (and later the surrealists), expressionists, and futurists in Europe, to name a few. As for music, I wonder how he perceived jazz; I suspect he saw, or would have seen, it as a vulgar expression of black people—given, as I say below, his unfortunate sharing of the belief in their inferiority and his somewhat effete artistic preferences. At bottom, the alleged lack of community and its related institutions (such as criticism) is more an idea Cooley picks up from his reading and selective tastes. The exceptions he lists—Thoreau and Whitman—testify to this in a significant way. Nor is he really in a position to judge the press. It would be up to the Chicago School (in Thomas and Znaniecki's *The Polish Peasant in Europe and America* [1958]) to discover the immigrant press, for example, a product of the very fragmentation he decries (Park, 1922). On the other hand, my criticism is somewhat tempered by the fact that in the chapters on sentiment (pp. 177–205), for example, he moves into the productive implications of its diversification.

Sentiment is socialized feeling, feeling that "has been raised by thought and intercourse out of its merely instinctive state" (p. 177). Reminding us of Simmel's allusion to urban reserve, Cooley observes that the demands on feeling made by modern life give rise "to the need and practice of more economy" as typified by the city man. This diversification is accompanied by an accentuated humanism, a widening of sympathy and consciousness of unity that impel social classes to seek to understand each other (pp. 180–81). It thus makes possible more freedom to seek the truth. The result is an enlargement of consciousness despite and through opposition, and the growth of a new idealism, a further extension of primary ideals. The most urgent need of the time is for a new consciousness of "the rules of the game," for new ideals and popular ethics, for the social "I" to assert itself.

Institutions versus the Creative Potential of Tradition

While Cooley's material on public opinion, democracy, and sentiment evince a general optimism, his writings on institutions are more skeptical, reflecting the nonconformist individualism of Thoreau and Emerson, his transcendental forebears. Institutions mark "a definite and established phase of the public mind." As such they do not differ ultimately from public opinion, but because of their permanence and the visible customs and symbols with which they are cloaked they have a distinct and independent existence. Their moral and material accoutrements make them distinct products of human invention. They are crystallized organization, and exist in the individual "as a habit of mind and of action, largely unconscious because largely common to all the group" (p. 314).

An institution is a mature, specialized, and rigid part of the social structure but while it consists of persons, "each one enters into it with a trained and specialized part of himself" (p. 319). And here is a clue to Cooley's detachment: "A man is no man at all if he is merely a piece of an institution; he must stand also for human nature, for the instinctive, the plastic and the ideal" (ibid.). Human nature, the "I," is thus set against institutions, especially as in the case of youthful discontent with the establishment. It is through the interaction of personality and institution, that progress comes. Solidarity exists, not in mere likeness, but as much through the reciprocal struggle of discordant powers (p. 330). Here Cooley's thinking sounds strikingly like Durkheim's: "A social group in which there is fundamental harmony of forces resulting in effective cooperation may be said . . . to be *solidaire,* to adopt a French word much used in this connection" (p. 330).

He analyzes tradition similarly. Reflecting on Tarde's distinction between "custom imitation" and "fashion imitation," Cooley transposes this to tradition versus convention and thus to the contrast of traditional and modern society, the one coming down from the past, the other arriving from our contemporaries (pp. 335–36). They are not, however, mutually exclusive: a traditional usage is conventional within the group where it prevails; and conventions must also be traditions, as in the case of new fashions, which are adaptations of old ones (pp. 337–38). The difference is simply that one convention is more extended than the other. Both "are aspects of the transmission of thought and of the unity of social groups that results from it." The historical phase of the matter is traditional, the contemporary conventional (p. 338). In modern society, which is bound together by "facile communication," people are not less bound by the past; tradition is just more intricate and so spread out that it is hardly noticed. It is more "lateral," so that "influences seem to come in sidewise and fashion rules over custom." Through communication the known past becomes accessible anywhere, "and instead of the cult of immediate ancestors we have a long-armed, selective appropriation of whatever traditional ideas suit our tastes" (p. 339).

Cooley is viewed by one present-day scholar as unique among the founders of sociology in the United States, for he has not dichotomized tradition and modernity; instead, he suggests that tradition has a modern utility as a "set of resources" expressing the reality of modern life; it is thus not "blind generic force, but the conscious product of human intelligence and will" (Clark, 1994, pp. 279, 280). In this respect Cooley's view resembles the view of culture and tradition enunciated by Fernando Ortiz, the dean of Cuban anthropology, who coined the term "transculturation" to refer to the manifold "loss or uprooting of a previous culture" and "the consequent creation of new cultural phenomena" out of the elemental agent-centered combining, layering, discarding, and synthesizing of successive waves of the old cultures and traditions in multiculturally formed societies (Ortiz, 1947, pp. 102–3).

When society becomes too mechanical its manifestations are variously known as institutions, formalism, traditionalism, conventionalism, ritualism, bureaucracy, and the like. Cooley prefers "formalism," which denotes the failure of organization to express human nature, the substitution of the outer for the inner—"it is psychically cheap" (1909, p. 343). Formalism starves the higher life of personality (the "I") and leaves a legacy of apathy, self-complacency, etc. Here he suggests a metaphor akin to Weber's in asserting that formalism "confines the individual mind as in a narrow cage" (ibid.). Intolerance is the companion of formalism, since to the closed mind grasped by a fixed system of thought "anything that departs from that system must appear irrational and absurd" (p. 344).

Despite the rigidity of this dead mechanism, its apparent opposite, disorganization or disintegration, is closely akin to it: "One is mechanism supreme, the other mechanism going to pieces" (p. 347). Here general order and discipline are lacking; individuals and groups work at cross-purposes. The frequent appearance of great personalities during such times, however, contradicts the assumption that the healthy development of individuals must coincide with that of institutions. Enlisting only segmental aspects of the individual, formalism takes hold only from the outside, as in the case of the declining Roman Empire when it was most rigid and "the people became unpatriotic, disorderly and sensual" (p. 349).

The Reluctant Critic: Social Problems

What we have here is in essence an analysis of the decadence of institutions and of society. Cooley would have objected to this as a general description of the United States, for typical of his Progressive exceptionalist thinking he is a Pollyanna in his approach to democracy. We see how this appears in his discussion of communication and primary ideals. Nonetheless, a certain ambivalence seeps through that still typifies the Progressive spirit, for on the one hand he describes the absence of an integrated high culture, while on the other he wishes to retain the democratic model. Like Veblen he might deplore the conspicuous consumption of European art by J. P. Morgan, little realizing despite his antipathy to commercialism that this is the very product of the capitalistic democracy he has such high hopes for. Like many Progressive thinkers he is caught between his scorn for the evils of capitalism and those primary ideals vaunted by it, not realizing that their common ancestor produces both out of structural necessity. So Cooley attributes society's vices to the dislocations of change, seeking its virtues in the same cornucopia. Society as a work of art is also a Pandora's box!

Democracy in Cooley's time is simply a disordered ship: it wants a captainship of ideals to restore a "higher discipline": "Old institutions are passing away and better ones, we hope, are preparing to take their place, but in the meantime there is a lack of that higher discipline which prints the good of the whole upon the heart of the member" (pp. 351–52). In a spirit akin to Durkheim's attribution of anomie to the evaporation of regulation of the individual's passions occasioned by social change, Cooley tells us that

> in our own time there is for many persons, if not most, no authoritative canon of life, and for better or worse we are ruled by native impulse and by that private reason which may be so weak when detached from a rational whole. The higher morality, if it is to be attained at all, must be specially sought out; and of the few who can do this a large part exhaust their energy in thinking and do not practice with any heartiness the truths they perceive.
>
> We find, then that people have to make up their own minds upon their duties as wives, husbands, mothers and daughters; upon commercial obligation and citizenship; upon the universe and the nature and authority of God. Inevitably many of us make a poor business of it. It is too much. It is as if each one should sit down to invent a language for himself. . . . That great traditions should rapidly

go to pieces may be a necessary phase of evolution and a disguised blessing, but
the present effect is largely distraction and demoralization. (pp. 351–52)

Disguised blessing indeed. Democratic modernity is a cloud with a silver lin-
ing, for the gloomy loss of tradition has promised the vitality, the primary ideals of the frontier—plain dealing, love of character and force, kindness, hope,
and courage. Thus "alongside of an extravagant growth of sensuality, pride and
caprice, we have about us a general cult of childhood and womanhood, a vast
philanthropy, and an interest in everything relating to the welfare of the masses
of the people" (p. 355).

   These words represent the ambiguities, ambivalence, and contradictions
Cooley is heir to. Speaking of disorganization within the family, he has mixed
feelings about the declining birth rate among the comfortable classes, "the lack
of discipline and respect among children," a growing independence of women
accompanied by alleged neglect of the family, and an increase of divorce. On the
one hand, this represents "a higher life at the cost of incidental demoralization";
on the other the modern democratic family is more aptly described as "anarchy"
(pp. 361, 368). He applauds the aggressive idealism of women in the career world
but confines the work of women in "independent careers" to "much-needed social service—education and philanthropy" as the organization of the "maternal
instinct" on a vast scale. Hence, "the masculine element . . . on the whole more
rational and stable, should be the main source of government, keeping in order
the emotionality more commonly dominant in women" (p. 364); "the emancipation of women comes chiefly from male initiative." Lauding the emergence
of "free marriage," that is, marriage for love, on one page, he regrets the increase
of divorce born of it, on the next: "And while freedom in well ordered minds
tends toward responsibility . . . it is likely to become an impulsiveness which
is displayed equally in contracting and in breaking off marriage without good
cause" (p. 366). Children sharing in the democracy of the new family is fine,
"but where this ideal is not reached, there is apt to be a somewhat disastrous
failure which makes one regret the [loss of] autocratic and original order" (pp.
361–62). So the association of parenthood with divinity of the old days could
stand us in good stead today, when parents "might receive a reverence not dependent upon their personality." They are "likely to be better loved if they
exact respect—just as an officer is better loved who enforces discipline and is
not too familiar with his soldiers" (p. 362). Traditional marriage too has its

uses in holding the family together. The modern democratic family succumbs to anarchy because it lacks a constitution and laws "prescribing the rights and duties of the various members" (p. 368). Now the situation of captain and ship resembles a mutiny on a private vessel (p. 369)! Yet Cooley ends the discussion on a note complimentary to women. The evils of divorce are "associated with the beneficent rise in the standing of women," permitting them to revolt against the abuses of marital power. Like the right of workers to strike, it "does most of its good without overt exercise" (p. 371).

He is less equivocal in his assessment of formalism and disorganization in religion and education, where "piracy" also prevails. The root problem of the church lies in the severance of the institution from human communication, community, and influence: its symbols have become bereft of meaning. Here he applauds the anarchic religion of Emerson, who "saw the necessity of institutions, but was inclined by temperament and experience to distrust them" (p. 374). Religious symbols have persisted beyond their function because of their affinity for imitation and repetition, so that all that is inert and mechanical clings to them (p. 376). Jesus had not system but "an intuition and expression of higher sentiments" (p. 377). Formulas must not be exchanged for principles.

Schools have extended their system rather than their vital energy. Routine methods prevail, "turning out cheap work in large quantities" (p. 345). In higher education there is a mixture of new materials, "imperfectly integrated, with fragments of a decadent system" (p. 388). While the decline of classical education may be a good thing, a new type of culture may be arising in the form of a large study of the principles of human life and of their expression in history, art, philanthropy, and religion (p. 389). Sociology will be a part of this.

Competition, Social Class, and Race

Cooley's approach to masses, classes, poverty, and deviance reflects the contradictions mentioned earlier. He disagrees with the view that democratic society is simply the rule of the crowd, and with the aforementioned "dead-level" theory of de Tocqueville, contending that the processes uniting modern society into denser wholes also bring discipline, that public opinion occasions judgment and social control. Moreover, the crowd mind does not characterize the urban milieu. He contends that this approach comes from writers generalizing from French history (among them Gustave Le Bon and Scipio Sighele) and even here they are mistaken in their zeal to correct the faults they exaggerate (pp. 149–55). Likewise, the *masses* themselves are more typically original in sentiment, and superior in this respect to the more privileged *classes*. This is supported by the fact that radical movements aiming to extend higher sentiment have been inspired by the common people, who "live more in the central current of human experiences than men of wealth or distinction" (p. 136). The upper classes are too identified with the formalism of institutions to exhibit the critical shrewdness of plainer men (pp. 140–42).

Cooley's work on class extends back to his early material on competition (1899 in 1930, pp. 163–226). There he asserts the intrinsic value of competition to "assign each individual his place" (p. 164): it is the only alternative to status as an ordering principle in society. Until the time is reached that a higher principle of rationality will assign roles, selection will have to be competitive (p. 181).[4] Thus in a journal entry about a decade earlier he states that "all men are constituted into a detective agency, to discover what you are good for" (unnumbered [1889–1891], p. 27). After all, "society is a vast machine the purpose of which is to organize goodness and power" (ibid.). As for his own part in it, this would entail viewing life "as a game for the exercise of truth and justice. . . . Everyday's work should be a practicing of virtue and a weaving of it into character" (pp. 43–44). Clearly, these thoughts stem from Emerson's formula wherein human beings and language are transcendental mediators of the oversoul. Now competition has become the social mediating principle.

Competition presupposes sympathy among competitors (pp. 210–11). While competition is itself amoral, the competitive struggle is a training ground in moral qualities, since it reinforces sympathy. Success "is a matter of effective participation in the social process" (p. 89). Is Cooley making a statement of value, of fact, or of fact based upon value, that is, a restatement of the self-fulfilling prophecy of the Protestant success ethic? For example, one would expect a definition of success to refer to simple preeminence in the struggle for scarce goals, but Cooley in *Social Process* (1918, pp. 88–89) defines it in terms of *his* ideals, namely "self-development in social service," a principle that a businessman may share in ideology but not in an unguarded moment or in practice. If success is effective participation in the social process, then one is able to comprehend Cooley's inclusion of sympathy as the sine qua non of competition. Such a fusion of value and fact appears in the guise of a cliché, as when he says: "Modern conditions are more and more requiring that every man be a man of the world" (1918, p. 95). This is a restatement of his earlier observation (1899 in 1930, p. 192) that "Every successful mechanic, in a free society, becomes more or less a man of the world; he knows the minds of many men, learns to make his way among strangers, and to fall upon his feet when he is thrown off them by one of the frequent displacements incident to social change. In order "to succeed one must understand opposing forces, and understanding is the beginning of sympathy" (p. 211). This entails savoir faire, (sympathetic insight into human nature . . . steadied by a natural coolness or phlegm" necessary for "dealing with the infinitely variegated forces of the social environment" (1899 in 1930, p. 190). Cooley is subtle enough, and sufficiently identified with intellectual values to recall his own retiring self, his sickly adolescence, and the sensitive personalities of mentors such as Thoreau to say: "there are many who cannot endure with equanimity the rough-and-tumble of ordinary competition, and need, if possible, to seclude themselves from it" (pp. 94–95). Thus he pays heed as much to his devil as his angel, juxtaposing his obvious weaknesses with his obvious strengths. Cooley's banality is more inspired by his ideals (his angel), his consciousness by a devil of a conscience! Each insight seems to be the outcome of a struggle. Notice, for example, some concluding lines of the chapter "Success and Morality" in *Social Process*. Contemplating the question whether might should make right he asks if the good should also be the strong:

> If we accept the idea that life is progress, it is easy to see that no such coincidence is to be expected. If we are moving onward and upward by the formation of higher ideals and the struggle to attain them, then our conscience will always be going out from discrediting the actual forms of power. . . . Right appeals to our conscience somewhat as the child does, precisely because it is not might, but needs our championship and protection in order that it may live and grow. As time goes on it acquires might and gradually becomes established and institutional, by which time it has ceased to be right in the most vital sense, and something has taking its place. In this way right is might in the making, while might is right in its old age. . . . The tendency of every form of settled power—ruling classes, the creeds of the church, the formulas of the law, the dogmas of the lecture room, business customs—is bound to be at variance with our ideal. . . .
>
> This way of stating the case would seem to indicate that it is right that precedes and makes might, that a thing comes to power because it appeals to conscience.

But it is equally true that might makes right, because ruling conditions help to form our conscience. (1918, pp. 109–10)

Cooley's ideas about competition represent the continuity of his thought with that of his father, the eminent jurist Thomas McIntyre Cooley (1824–98). His extolling of primary ideals that circulate through and integrate society and self via sympathy and communication envisions a "'democracy of sentiment' in lieu of an oligarchy of property, a society governed by 'self expression' rather than 'self interest,'" representing, as we shall see, a critique of the pecuniary values of American capitalism (Sklansky, 2000, p. 92). Cooley views competition as "the only constructive principle" or alternative to status or inheritance (1899 in 1930, p. 166). Just as his father's development of a rationale for the regulatory state serves as a counterbalance to his recognition of cooperate property rights, so Charles Horton Cooley's collective ideal of the communicatively cemented (via public opinion) democracy is tempered by an ideal of service, which, as noted below, is the antidote to hostility between classes.

Cooley's notion of competition as a social selection process assigning roles within the division of labor hearkens back to his Emersonian transcendentalism, wherein the oversoul is translated into societal terms, and it also reflects the idea of the invisible hand, inherited from Adam Smith, which underscores the belief in the wisdom and self-regulating character of the market. On the other hand, as he points out in his essay on competition, "social selection can never be the simple act of a presiding intelligence" (p. 181). Rather, the competitive process "in its highest form . . . [is] an amicable testing and comparison of powers, with a view to securing the happiness of all, by helping each to find his own peculiar and appropriate work" (p. 182). Like his father, Cooley champions regulation. He tells us (1918, p. 384) that "While there is a great deal of truth in the idea of the involuntary beneficence of economic competition, it is certain that under the too great sway of this idea natural resources are wasted, children stunted and deprived of opportunity, women exploited, and the unrighteous allowed to thrive." He advocates "rational control" embodying high standards of service.

Defining class as "any persistent social group, other than the family, existing within a larger group (1909, p. 209), Cooley distinguishes three types of class divisions: occupation, income, and cultural (refinement) (p. 348). The fact that he finds little alignment of the three strains the plausibility of his conceptualization of class, although the balance of the text indicates that he held wealth to be the key variable (p. 250), as indeed does his derivation of the caste principle.

When a class is strictly hereditary, Cooley says, it is a caste (p. 211). Hereditary distinctions begin in a selective struggle such as military and commercial competition and generally are never so rigid as not to be modified by these processes. The psychological source of the inheritance principle lies in the effort to secure for one's children the desirable things one has inherited and enjoyed for oneself. The principle thus stems from human nature and the moral unity of the family. Wealth is transmissible and convertible into educational, business, professional, and cultural opportunity (pp. 211–12). The inheritance principle does not involve capacity or aptitude, although differentials in these areas do exist.

There are three conditions influencing the caste principle: (1) the heterogeneity or homogeneity of the population; (2) the rate of social change; and (3) the state of communication or enlightenment in the population. Hence, "unlikeness in the constituents, a settled system and a low state of communication and enlightenment favor the growth of caste, and *vice versa*" (p. 217). It is under the heading of caste that Cooley discusses race. In applying this principle to the United States, Cooley acknowledges that there might be differences in racial capacity between blacks and whites, but he still condemns caste on account of "caste arrogance which does not recognize in the Negro a spiritual brotherhood underlying all race difference and possible 'inferiority'" (p. 219). The practical question, then, is "not that of abolishing castes but of securing just and kindly relations between them, of reconciling the fact of caste with ideals of freedom and right" (p. 220). The persistence of the race caste in the United States "illustrates the impotence of democratic traditions" (p. 218). The caste nature of the social division among whites and blacks consists in the feeling that "the Negro must be held apart and subordinate not merely as an individual . . . but as a race, a social whole." Many Negroes are equal or even superior to the majority of whites, but this offers no justification to adherents of the view to "make it expedient to treat them apart from the mass of the race" (ibid.). This would be a sound argument if the races would be recognized as "distinct organisms" (p. 219).

In step with the liberal exceptionalism of his peers, Cooley cannot go much further when it comes to the matter of race than hoping that "the diffusion of intelligence, rapid communication, the mobilization of wealth by means of money . . . mark the ascendancy of the human mind over material and biological conditions." These nostrums of modernity are sufficiently vague to harness liberal exceptionalist hopes of deliverance from the most vexing of social issues—the dilemma of race. From Cooley's standpoint this refers to his simultaneous belief in the *humanity* of blacks and his doubts concerning their innate capacities. Thus his stated belief that the growth of dissemination of knowledge will conquer all obstacles, be they technical, social, or constitutional impediments to progress, is a way of sweeping his contradictory beliefs about the race issue under the table. His recognition of the humanity of blacks prompts him to insist that they cannot be denied their humanity. Once again invoking the panoply of the Enlightenment heritage, Cooley proclaims: "The idea that he is fundamentally a man like the rest of us cannot and should not be kept from the Negro any more than from other lowly orders of people. Since, religion and the democratic spirit all give him a right to it" (p. 220).

Almost a decade later, in a discussion of the ramifications of the higher birth rates of Southern blacks in *Social Process* he observes that "if social reforms were rapidly introduced lowering the death-rate of colored children to that of the whites," the latter would overwhelmingly be outnumbered, and Cooley wonders "whether we might not make a . . . mistake by pushing improvements in the care and feeding of infants without at the same time pushing eugenic measures aimed at raising the standards of heredity in the infants born" (1918, p. 232). Is this consistent with his earlier plea not to deny the black his or her humanity?

In the lecture notes of 1902 under the headings "ASSIMILATION OF FOREIGN ELEMENT IN OUR POPULATION . . . THE MAIN OBSTACLES TO ASSIMILATION ARE", Cooley hews to an essentialist phenotypic paradigm (Omi and Winant, 1994, pp. 54–55):

> RACE DIFFERENCES—where there are distinct races, this perhaps is the most serious obstacle of all. The older immigrant, especially the German, was of a people practically the same as the Anglo-Saxon stock that was here already. And much the same regards the Irish. [As a] race they are now believed to be for the most part not very divergent from the Teutonic people. The idea that they are a wholly distinct race is not so much in vogue now as it once was. In the case of the Chinese we had a totally distinct race, and they probably never would have assimilated with the native population. (p. 127)

Many years later he opines in his journal that "I do not believe in the natural equality of the races. It is true that we cannot separate and measure potential ability apart from social heritage: we have no precise knowledge one apart from the other. But taking them together it seems to me that the different behavior of race groups in past history and at the present time points strongly to deep-seated differences among them" (V. 22 [4/20/19–5/25/25] 9/28/25, p. 134). Consistent with his repugnance to "caste arrogance," he exclaims some five months earlier, "What is this 'instinctive race antagonism'?" He mentions that he has known "hundreds of students from Japan, China, India, etc., also Jews and Negroes, but have never perceived anything of the sort. They are just *people*, like the rest of us—the same human nature with interesting differences of culture and viewpoint" (4/30/25, p. 69). He goes on to explain racial antagonism as the psychological effect of differences in color and physiognomy. Moreover, "There may be, probably are, differences in the degree and type of mental capacity, but these are obscure and certainly less than may be observed between individuals of the same race" (p. 70).

Obviously he does not care for caste, but he cannot escape the widespread belief in color differences. Thus, early in *Social Organization* (1909, p. 44), in discussing the incubation of the primary ideal of justice, freedom, and equality in children's play groups he informs us that "no doubt American boys have more of the spirit and practice of this sort of organization than those of any other country, except possibly England . . . [and] *it is doubtful if there is any great difference among the white people in* [this] *regard* [my italics]."

There is no avoiding Cooley's racism here. While recognizing the common humanity of all races, he is unwilling to surrender his belief in deeper differences beneath social veneer. Cooley's humanism is at odds with the received ideas of American racial conventions and morals, which to some extent he shares, and which, to be sure, reflect local and regional differences, but nonetheless hold remarkable consistency with respect to color. Thus Page in his 1940 treatment of some of the American founders' views on class, writes, in this case of Ward, Cooley, and Ross as "ardent exponents of a broad democracy," that they are all of the Middle West and share in that region's credo—quoting Odum and Moore (1938)—"'All men are equal (except the Mexican, [and the] Negro) economically and socially'" (Page, 1969 [1940], p. 23). These beliefs and values still hold sway and are fixed by the same normative mordant which still supplies anchorage for their application under beliefs in hegemonic whiteness to the recent waves of immigrants from the Caribbean, Asia, South and Central America, and Europe.

Speaking of the sociologists of Cooley's generation who ignored W. E. B. Du Bois's work, although not mentioning Cooley (who does not refer to Du Bois in his work), Dan S. Green and Edwin D. Driver note that this conspiracy of silence on the part of "the white sociological fraternity" represented a commitment to "a caste-like system premised on white superiority–black inferiority, and to an ideology comprising social Darwinism, manifest destiny, and racism during the era 1896–1910" (1978, p. 47). While Cooley was neither a social Darwinist nor an advocate of manifest destiny, he did share, as I have discussed above, racist premises, that is, belief in black inferiority common among liberals of his time.

With the growth of freedom, competition ensues and the class system opens, although competition has its negative features—principally, the waste of energy and a tendency to anarchy (1909, p. 240). As to the matter of class consciousness, Cooley hopes it will never deepen to the point of antagonism, since a class war would be a calamity (p. 241). In fact there is a lack of unity and spirit within all classes, largely owing to the lack of pride in craftsmanship. Class organization would cultivate freedom for social mobility and allow people to remain in a stratum yet avail themselves of "comfort, culture and good surroundings" for their families (pp. 245–46). Cooley thus admires the so-called service ideal of the upper classes (pp. 235–37). Still, he posits the existence of class antagonism, for class feeling is likely to be better where the ideal of equality "is strong but has no regular and hopeful methods of asserting itself" (pp. 301–2). This is, however, more a European than an American manifestation, as in Germany, "where there is a fierce democratic propaganda on the one hand, and a stone wall of military and aristocratic institutions on the other" (p. 302).

The "illpaid classes" need class consciousness to offset the pressure of other classes; and this is as much a need for the rest of society (p. 284). The principal expression of class consciousness in the "hand-working classes" are labor unions and the wider movement of socialism. The unions have arisen out of self-defense; they have been valuable in bargaining and influencing legislation as well as having promoted fellowship and we-feeling. Cooley underlines the value of the union in making the worker part of a whole, "one of a fellowship" (p. 287). It supplies training in democratic organization, and so promotes a common standard of conduct for all. This class consciousness, however, does not extend to hostility toward the state. Agreeing with de Tocqueville "that in the United States there was no proletariat," defining that class as one "regarding the law as their natural enemy," Cooley lodges the reason in the fact that "where the state is directly and obviously founded upon the thought of the people it is impossible to get up much fundamental antagonism to it; the energies of discontent are absorbed by moderate agitation" (1909, pp. 116, 117).

Concerning the state, Cooley notes "a tendency toward extension of state functions which after all is perhaps no more than symmetrical in view of the general expansion of larger structures in every sphere." This is chiefly a response to the need to control "the exorbitant power of private economic associations, and the need of meeting novel problems arising from life in great cities" (1909, p. 410). This, of course, stems from Cooley's advocacy of state regulation of competition. The key danger, however, as with institutions in general, lies in the tendency toward formalism; but Cooley is not worried about this. As for socialism, state monopoly on the federal level is prone to this defect, but municipal socialism, on the other hand, permits "diversity, experiment and comparison"—none of the deadening uniformity "and obliteration of alternatives involved in the blanket socialism of the central state" (p. 408). Thus Cooley comes once again to the same conclusion as Durkheim, who sees the increased scale of state development as commensurate with, that is, natural to, the development of a modern differentiated urban society (Durkheim, 1933, pp. 219–26, 291–97). Yet its force—its rigidity—if not its scale, must be limited. The brake on governmental rigidity is public opinion. Socialism is fine, but only as one of many local pluralistic discourses, not as *the* discourse legitimizing and undergirding the state.

Ultimately the ties that bind—principally based on communication—are those that heal societal maladies. Communication is both the societal integument and balm. It is quintessentially social. Is this any surprise? The symbolic interactionist school rests upon this base, but what are not customarily adduced are the *non*-academic origins of this assumption. In chapters 4 and 5 I uncover this infrastructure of Cooley's thought in discussing the essay tradition.

Cooley's rooting of democracy in primary ideals marks his exceptionalism as a romantic liberal type, for the United States is not bound to the "class culture" of the Old World. He tells us "that our time has . . . cast off all sorts of structure" (1909, p. 176). Thus the progressive creation of society inspires the efflorescence of new forms via the tentative method. Ross analyzes American social science as exemplifying revisionist exceptionalism, characterizing his vision of the democratic ethos as one wherein

> Cooley was convinced that the United States would . . . retain the lineaments of
> democracy that were set out in her original institutions. . . . Cooley characterized
> these institutions by playing off American realities against Europe on the one
> hand and the democratic ideal on the other. As against the ideal, he found much
> wanting, but as against Europe, he slipped into the idealized vision of American
> exceptionalism. The American reality was at once ideal and less than ideal and
> the disparity drove him to nuanced exceptionlist analyses of political and social
> institutions. (1991, p. 246)

Thus Cooley's saving grace may be constructed, as Ross suggests, as a more subtle analysis of institutions that allowed him to see the emperor's clothes despite his idealism. This ability stems from his broad reading in the essay tradition, which humanized and tempered what otherwise might have been scolding criticism of bad popular taste on the one hand or fawning admiration of patrician conventions on the other. So, while Cooley for the most part did not care for the grosser forms of racism and anti-Negro sentiment, yet accepted the more polite skepticism about African Americans' capacities for achievement, he could broadly appreciate ethnic and immigrant diversity and reject anti-Semitism at a time when it was frequently tolerated.

No doubt some of Cooley's liberal tolerance stems from the family values he inherited from his father, whose beliefs in equality called for the abolition of slavery. Yet, as I have just said, it stems too from Cooley's subscription to the humanist sensibility of the essay tradition. On the one hand, as his biographer Jandy informs us, he could be "singularly innocent of 'how the other half lives,'" yet make forays into the Jewish ghetto of the Lower East Side. (I discuss Cooley's ethnographic bent, in chapter 6, as deriving from his reading of the essayists as that influenced his methodological credo.) For the most part the common "concern over problems of alcoholism, poverty, degeneracy, bad housing, and crime was hardly suitable to a mind theoretically and synthetically inclined" (Jandy, 1942, p. 54), but he did not allow this, for example, to deter him from visiting Hull House. This "theoretically and synthetically inclined" mind was too appreciative of the give and take of the essayists' conversational bent to allow even his own disposition to get the better of his sociological good sense, and it is to the essayistic underpinnings of Cooley's sociology that I now turn.

CHAPTER FOUR

COOLEY AND THE ESSAY TRADITION, PART I

The Influences of Montaigne and Emerson

What I learn from the history of thought is that there is a larger society of men who live for the ages as well as for the hours and, by virtue of their representative minds, speak to one another from century to century. Of these I imagine that I am one: at any rate I can hear what they say, whether I myself am audible or not.

CHARLES HORTON COOLEY, Journal, August 6, 1918

Among my many borrowings I take delight in being able to conceal the occasional one, masking it and distorting it to serve a new purpose. At the risk of letting people say that it is because I failed to understand any of the meanings in context, I give that one some peculiar slant with my own hand, so that they may all be less purely and simply someone else's. But those others put their larcenies on parade and into their accounts, thereby acquiring a better claim in law than I do! Followers of Nature like me reckon that, in honour, invention takes incomparably higher precedence over quotation.

MICHEL EYQUEM DE MONTAIGNE, "On Physiognomy"

Having surveyed Cooley's pathbreaking contributions to the formulation of the social, his development of the theory of the social self, and his ideas concerning social organization, we stand on the threshold of a probe into the deeper comprehension of his intellect and method along the line formed by the meeting of sociology and literature. Advancing toward this horizon, new questions arise concerning these two realms and Cooley's place in them. Among these are issues of style and genre. We know, for example, that style is so important to the literary field that it looms as a preoccupation, which appears trivial to natural and social scientists. Style merges with content in literature and literary studies, to a degree that is inconceivable to us; yet, as we learned in chapter 2, style counts, if only as a negative element. In other words, while matters of style may be inexplicit to social scientists, deviations from accepted norms of writing and of investigation have consequences. Thus, my interpretation of Mead's critique of Cooley and the consequent lessening of Cooley's prestige in comparison to his, is that it is essentially based on Cooley's literary style, which Mead successfully, though not explicitly in stylistic terms, disparaged. Style is a *concrete* concern for Cooley. Indeed, it is a preoccupation with him, and I will discuss it at length in the second part (chapter 5) of my treatment of Cooley as a member of the essay tradition, specifically in relation to the shift in his identity as a writer from the oratorical self and fealty to Emerson to his embracing the literary self and subscribing to the sensibility of the Victorian essayist, Walter Pater.

I have identified the literary elements of Cooley's creativity in his writing and thinking as contributing to his uniqueness, and, ironically, in some respects, to his relative lack of recognition as a stylistic nonconformist. But aside from simply assigning him to the catchall category of literature, there remains the question what branches or genres of literature he participated in, and, in turn, which influenced him. We know, for example, that Emerson's transcendentalism played a prominent role in the crafting of his ideas. Until now, however, there has been little available beyond loose generalizations to help us to see how Emerson's work is incarnated in his ideas. The same goes for the myriad of personages alluded to, but seldom analyzed, by secondary accounts.

In sum, Cooley's avowal of Emerson's influence upon him, and that of other literary figures, leaves open the matter of *how* they impressed him and shaped his ideas. Summarizing glosses will not suffice to explicate them. The paucity and clumsiness of sociologists' analyses of the literary influences on Cooley have handicapped thorough comprehension of his work, and, consequently, impaired its standing in the sociological canon. This points to work that needs to be done if we wish to improve our understanding.

Below I explore the central features of the essay writing tradition, which is autobiographical in focus, often fragmentary in form, and conversational in tone. In the order in which I discuss them, the key figures representing these elements in Cooley's published and unpublished writing are the subjects of this and the following chapter—Michel Eyquem de Montaigne (1533–92), Ralph

Waldo Emerson (1803–82), and Walter Pater (1839–94). They play a critical role in Cooley's development as a writer and sociologist, because he identifies with their thinking and writing styles. They do this not as isolated, disparate figures but as sharing the culture of the essay, and thus influence Cooley (who considers himself a participating member of this tradition) in an interrelated manner. Cooley frequently talks about them according to his assessments of their writing styles and genres. I thus characterize them as Cooley's *genre matrix*, and in some places, showing the kinship of this notion with sociological studies of influence, I call them his "invisible college" (Crane, 1972). While figures such as Goethe, Thoreau, Lamb, Shakespeare, and others also are notable influences on Cooley, the writings of Montaigne, Emerson, and Pater are the cardinal points of reference in this study, a configuration evincing the tenets of writing style within the tradition Cooley subscribes to, and playing an important role in the development of his authorial personality. Montaigne is the founder of the essay tradition, which encompasses a conversational style of discourse and an auto- or self-referential and autobiographical reference point, and supplies Cooley both with an orientation to, and with writing strategies focused on, the self.

Identifying the essay tradition as such perhaps overly concretizes, or reifies, what otherwise might loosely be called a congeries of genres or styles, but this shadowy terminology aids little in clarifying what turn out to be more concrete norms of style and composition shared by the tradition's founders, exemplars, critics, commentators, and readership. This is the tradition that prompts Cooley to live and write by his scholarly lights, whose truths he seeks to uncover by discovering himself through the practice of writing, and it defines, shapes, and supplies his implements for examining the social world, as well as philosophical and spiritual ones for elucidating its secrets. The essay tradition and literary aestheticism add substance and texture to the otherwise stark answer that it is literature that supplies the key to Cooley's prescience and his nonconformity with positivism, to his emphasis on style, and even to his views on communication, the self, and the creative potential of social process and social organization.

Employing analysis of influence and "intertextuality," I shall trace the thematic patterns of his thought and his work; I will then elucidate the nexus between genre and content of the essay tradition, which was established by Montaigne, whom both Emerson and Cooley read and discussed. Montaigne is as vibrant now as in his own time. The essay seems recently to have imparted its signal features to other writing genres and to media such as theater and film. Montaigne named it, mapped its contours, established many of its norms, and, at the same time, by his example, ensured its viability over the past four hundred fifty years! He is thus a literary analog to Comte, yet unlike the latter is not regarded as obsolete. This is owing to the versatility and flexibility of the essay, from its "intertextual" quality. The question of how Montaigne, one literary personality among others, influenced Cooley demonstrates the mechanics of influence and intertextual interaction and their role in the shaping of the essay tradition.

Ascertaining Influence and Intertextuality in the Examination of Cooley's Work

Within the realm of the social sciences the question of influence appears clear-cut, since we can trace influence through avowed point of view, lines of inquiry, literature reviews, and footnote and referencing analysis; but in Cooley's case this places us back on square one in tracing influence, for in literature and the arts lie traditions, methods of analysis, and evaluations of quality unfamiliar to sociologists. Some discussion of literary/textual influence and impact is therefore in order.

The notions of influence and intertextuality, deriving from literary criticism and theory, assist in placing Cooley and in tracing the lines of force shaping his thought. The two notions are often viewed as rival conceptions in the analysis of literary works, the former being agent- or author-centered, while the latter, associated with postmodernism, ignoring the author, focuses exclusively on the crossing or dissemination of texts (Clayton and Rothstein, 1991, p. 4). In the actual practice of contemporary literary critics, the methods often are complementary (Clayton and Rothsein, 1991, pp. 10–11; Friedman, 1991). They *are* methods of assigning the impact of personages and textual materials on a writer that are analogous to the empirical imputation of causality in the natural and social world. But they differ importantly with respect, in the case of influence, in choosing to emphasize the author's or mentor's ideas, and in that of intertextuality, in the ascertaining of the impact of texts, text fragments, and their motifs on other texts or authors.

Influence aids in the analysis of Cooley's sentiments and attitudes toward his precursors (Emerson, Montaigne, and Walter Pater) and their articulation with his own concepts. Influence helps tease out the entanglement of Cooley's intellect and sentiments with his adaptation and use, beginning with Montaigne, of metaphors of the cross-historical conversation of the essayists, his own adoption of the Emersonian notion of representative men and his donning of the "oratorical self," and later, his adaptation of Pater's literary aestheticism, which encompasses style and authorial personality.

Referring to the impact of precursor texts and authors on literary work, Harold Bloom, a leading scholar of the notion of influence, stipulates that the manifestation of this impact takes the form of a creative distortion, a misreading or "misprision" of precursor texts on the parts of authors. Thus, "influence . . . always proceeds by a misreading of the prior poet, an act of creative correction that is actually and necessarily a misinterpretation" (1997 [1973], p. 30). The misreading entails a denial of the precursor's influence. As Bloom characterizes it, "Every major aesthetic consciousness seems peculiarly more gifted at denying obligations as the hungry generations go on treading one another down (p. 6). This denial occasions anxiety: "What writers may experience as anxiety, and what their works are compelled to manifest, are the *consequence* of poetic misprision, rather than the *cause* of it." Finally, the misreading "is almost certain to be ambivalent, though the ambivalence may be veiled" (p. xxiii). Thus the mechanics of influence operates within the parameters of a psychic matrix (originally delineated by Freud) akin to the struggle between father and son within the family. As Bloom tells us, "'Influence' is a metaphor, one that implicates a matrix of relationships—imagistic, temporal, spiritual, psychological" (p. xxiii). Moreover, poetic influence "is necessarily the study of the life-cycle of the poet-as-poet," and is "akin to what Freud called the family romance" (7–8). In this work I borrow Bloom's notion in my treatment of Cooley's passage from the oratorical to the literary self.

While one may take for granted the potency of the percursor's ideas on the writer, influence—as Bloom himself implies—is not a one-way process. It may involve a rich array of responses and reactions on the parts of those being influenced as readers, which thereby *decenter* the literary text. As a result, the *meaning* of the text is clearly produced by the reader as much, perhaps more than, by the writer. From this standpoint, looking at the matter broadly in terms of the dissemination of texts in society, it is plausible to think of their production itself shared by readers and writers. Moreover, as I discuss below, such decentering when taken to its limits can detach texts and textual fragments from the agents producing them and permit us to conceive of their movement and interrelations independently of the agent-producers. This brings us into the realm of inter-textuality. With respect to the decentering of texts the art historian Michael Baxandall elaborates on a variety of responses made by the writer or artist as he or she responds to and appropriates the precursor:

> If one says that X influenced Y it does seem that one is saying that X did some-thing to Y rather than that Y did something to X. But in the consideration of good pictures and painters the second is always the more lively reality. . . . If we think of Y rather than X as the agent, the vocabulary is much richer and more attractively diversified: draw on, resort to, avail oneself of, appropriate from, have recourse to, adapt, misunderstand, refer to, pick up, take on, engage with, react to, quote, differentiate oneself from, assimilate oneself to, assimilate, align oneself with, copy, address, paraphrase, absorb, make a variation on, revive, continue, remodel, ape, emulate, travesty, parody, extract from, distort, attend to, resist, simplify, reconstitute, elaborate on, develop, face up to, master, subvert, perpet-uate, reduce, promote, respond to, transform, tackle . . . —everyone will be able to think of others. Most of these relations just cannot be stated the other way round—in terms of X acting on Y rather than Y acting on X. (quoted in Clayton and Rothstein, 1991, pp. 6–7)

Broadening "influence" to encompass the reader's response of course extends its purview beyond the limits of poetry. In addition to expanding the boundaries of genre and even art form, the pathways of social and political texts have been opened and brought closer to home by those seeking to enlarge the canon in demanding a place for other quasi-textual social influences. Indeed, a number of literary critics speaking on behalf of women, racial and ethnic minorities, and gays have preferred to retain the notion while making it more inclusive (Clayton and Rothstein, 1991, pp. 9–11).

In the manner in which their work is appropriated by him, the three literary influences treated here are not fully accounted for, either by Cooley himself, or by scholars analyzing his work. This is partly because an author is never fully aware how influences operate on him or her; it is also attributable to the lack of familiarity on the part of sociologists with literary figures and methods of liter-ary criticism. Cooley's incomplete awareness perhaps represents Bloom's anxi-ety of influence—an unwillingness to see the extent of a precursor's influence. To some degree the pattern of his selective acknowledgment of his precursors also reflects the nonconscious absorption of textual materials—intertextuality. Here the emphasis shifts to the *textual* affinities and resemblances between writings and their precursors.

"Intertextuality" serves, as it were, as a first tack in identifying, say, Cooley's absorption and adaptation of textual materials, particularly from the essay tradition, exhibiting the hallmarks of a genre he clearly identifies with but which is not readily identifiable by sociologists unfamiliar with it. In addition, it is evident that the essayists, including Cooley himself and those he read, objectified the issue in their writing, referring to the impact of texts and textual fragments as part of a dynamic field of intertextual interaction. Intertextuality, the bearing of texts on other texts, is a deconstructionist concept of literary analysis originated by Julia Kristeva, and developed by Roland Barthes, Jacques Derrida, Paul de Man, Michel Foucault, and others. These writers suppose that a literary text itself represents a reconstituted incorporation or reincarnation of multifarious texts including anonymous oral (spoken), graphic, and other cultural elements as well as written ones. As Kristeva (1980, p. 36) puts it, a text is a *"productivity*, and this means . . . that its relationship to the language in which it is situated is redistributive . . . and . . . in the space of a given text, several utterances, taken from other texts, intersect and neutralize one another." Thus, "any text is constructed as a mosaic of quotations; any text is the absorption and transformation of another" (p. 66). In view of this, the "writer's interlocutor, then is the writer himself, but as reader of another text. The one who writes is the same as the one who reads. Since his interlocutor is a text, *he himself is no more than a text rereading itself as it rewrites itself* [my italics]" (pp. 86–87).

The theorists of intertextuality view the author/reader, as Barthes puts it, as "the space on which all of the quotations that make up a writing are inscribed." While much of this melange is identifiable, none of it can be as definitively ascribed to personal agency as the proponents of literary influence would have it. The author/reader "'cannot any longer be personal; the reader is without history, biography, psychology; he is simply that *someone* who holds together in a single field all the traces by which the written text is constituted'" (quoted in Clayton and Rothstein, 1991, p. 21). In effect, as Derrida epigrammatically puts it, "*Il n'y a pas de hors-texte*"—there is nothing outside the text. Put another way, reason, the instrumentality of agency, "is necessarily burdened with language and cannot achieve pure, self-authenticating truth." Thus, there is "no possibility of an unmediated access to reality" and reason "then cannot dispel the opacity of intertextuality" (Smart, 1996, p. 402).

As a tent of postmodernism, intertextuality admits of neither authorial nor textual provenance. Thus, "every text is related to every other text, and this makes for 'intertextuality.'" Every text, according to Barthes, "being itself the intertext of another text, belongs to the intertextual" (quoted in Rosenau, 1992, p. 36). The mechanics of intertextuality presuppose the dissemination of texts to the reader. In effect, the vaporization of agency thereby "distance[s] intertextuality from most theories of influence" (Clayton and Rothstein, 1991, p. 22).[1] The uncertainty stemming from the textual circularity of intertextuality can curtail the concept's effectiveness as a tool of analysis (pp. 22–23). On the other hand, the notion usefully points to the multivalent elements constituting texts and their ingredients, that is, to their "polysemy," and this, as we shall see, is a key ingredient in both the essay and in society. It becomes more apparent with respect to the essay genre as founded by Montaigne.

Beyond evoking its ubiquity, considering its decentering effect on both author and text, how should the notion of intertextuality be used? The deconstructionists tend to focus more on what a text under review does *not* say than on what it explicitly says. This brings the discourse within the orbit of critique and so allows the concept to escape from the mists of ethereal indeterminacy. In any case, from the standpoint of analytic practice, intertextuality and influence converge at the crossroads of textual affinity and the felt impact of precursor authors—that is, authors about whom writers form impressions (a key idea for Walter Pater, whom Cooley admired; or "personal ideas," as Cooley would say). Hence, despite their apparent inconsistencies, the two notions complement each other. Herein influence is used to analyze Cooley's subscription to, use of, and conscious and unconscious identification with the associated ideas and members of his literary reference group, the precursors of his own work. The notion of influence is especially useful in making sense of the manner in which Cooley subscribes to, emulates, critiques, employs, adapts and modifies, and occasionally distances himself from these figures and their ideas.

On the other hand, the essay tradition, which exerts the most powerful influence on Cooley, also represents a literary watershed with its self-referentiality and its objectification of the intertextual, somewhat billiardlike collision, mutual osmosis, or even mating of texts, and their consequent change, growth, or propulsion in one direction or another. The essay represents an increase in scale in the referencing and dissemination of other texts, and a heightened auto-biographical awareness (Gebauer and Wulf, 1992, pp. 62–63, 94–103). Cooley's appreciation of "fragmentary writing," his autobiographical focus, and his su-perimposition of literary aestheticism onto sociology, are clarified from the standpoints of intertextual affinity and the influence of precursor authors and texts as applied to the essay tradition. Both types of analysis "have not been and cannot be kept pure, untainted by each other" (Friedman, 1991, p. 154),[7] and therefore will be intermeshed. In any case, my focus on Cooley as a reader and writer establishes a point where influence and intertextuality converge on the reading subject.

The Compatibility of Montaigne's Essayistic Action with Cooley's Sociology

The reasons for Montaigne's importance in literary history also apply to his significance for Cooley; he established the quintessential features of the essay tradition, particularly its autobiographical discursiveness and its fragmentary format. This tradition and its attributes are real for Cooley, who conceives of the essay and its practitioners as true to Montaigne's conception of the essay as conversation. This motif is central to the development of Cooley's notion of the self, for he conceives of himself as a participant in the essayists' "great conversation." Indeed, it can be argued it underlies Cooley's insistence on com-munication as the integument of society, that is, of his conception of the social.

Cooley began to read Montaigne much earlier than his fiftieth year and finally fulfilled his dream of publishing a book (*Life and the Student* [1927]) of such quintessential "fragmentary writing," as he calls the prose of the diary and essay traditions, at the end of his life. Throughout his life he asserted the pungent character of the creativity inspiring art and science. As he implies in his journal, the creative source itself is emotionally freighted: "The creative ac-tivity of the mind is like that of the sexual instinct; now a need, a passion, a joy, now a disgust to think of" (*Journal* V. 18 [9/9/1904–2/11/1908] 3/31/1907, p. 112). This unity, he contends, springs from deep within the writer in the embroiling struggle resulting in the parturition of ideas, and, among the belletrists, results in the emergence of a truth akin to scientific truth. As he puts it, "Productive thought is a strenuous and costly function. It springs from struggle and is com-monly instigated by a purpose, which, however, may be the purpose to build scientific or artistic truth. The fragmentary thinkers are no exception. Emerson and Montaigne were striving men who would not have had these thoughts without the purpose to utter them" (1927, p. 80).

Following Montaigne's lead, the struggle is one for self-knowledge. In Cooley's published and unpublished writing, Montaigne is a presence and serves to define his genre, as he does for many essay writers. Mere mention of this does not sufficiently explicate the essential features of Montaigne's thought and of the tradition it establishes, for the essay encapsulates a distinct form of intellectual practice. Rather than calling his own works treatises, discussions, or letters, Montaigne dubs them "essays," which "may mean 'assays,' weighings and testings; or more probably, 'attempts.' More probably the latter because they follow no systematic scheme, such as they would have if they were really weighing facts and opinions" (Highet, 1949, pp. 191–92). Montaigne's *Essays,* with their lack of system, or fragmentariness, follow the humanist tradition of Erasmus, whose *Adages* had 120 editions between 1500 and 1570. Montaigne also is steeped in classical, especially Latin, texts, which are frequently quoted, alluded to, or paraphrased and disguised in the *Essays*. An important element distinguishing the *Essays* (completed between 1580 and 1588) is the subjective factor, "which makes them vehicles for Montaigne's own autobiography." He proclaims: "I examine nothing, I study nothing, but me" (Montaigne, 1991, p. 424). Thus, "At one time or another he tells us nearly everything about himself: his height, his health, his education, funny things he has seen, a ghost-story he has just heard, the fact that he seldom dreams, etc. This gives the *Essays* an intensely real, vivid, individual style; we hear him talking, more to himself than to us. He begins where he likes, ends where he likes, and is content to come to no conclusion, or several, or half a one" (Highet, 1949, p. 192). How congenial to Cooley, who considers sociology "systematic autobiography." Auerbach (1953, pp. 258–59), certainly not a postmodernist, observes that the *Essays'* spontaneous quality is enhanced by their fragmentariness, and that in turn, this fragmentariness is a hallmark of their vividness and conversational, everyday quality. Thus they

> are neither an autobiography nor a diary. They are based on no artfully contrived plan and do not follow chronological order. They follow chance. . . . He follows his own inner rhythm, which, though constantly induced and maintained by things, is not bound to them, but freely skips from one to another. . . . Montaigne is something new. The flavor of the personal, and indeed of a single individual,

is present much more strikingly, and the manner of expression is much more spontaneous and closer to everyday spoken discourse, although no dialogue is involved.

In this case knowledge is "autoreferential, autopoietic, and mimetic." It "establishes reference between itself and other knowledge via language, perception, and imagination, and it constitutes itself out of this relation of reference." Language, perception, and imagination: words are social things, sociality is discursive, the essayistic writing act nudges against everyday spoken discourse—all of these connections intersect in the writer writing, and, as forms of action, are recursively reflexive, conducing toward the processes of self-formation.

The fragmentariness of the writing, among the conditions of reference in the *Essays*, is "bound to the excerptlike character of perception and an awareness of the temporality of perception" (Gebauer and Wulf, 1995, p. 97).[3] Cooley called this "writing *stellen-weisse*." The fragmentary quality of his text, coupled with his confessed—indeed, proclaimed and sometimes wickedly saucy—forgetfulness, squarely places Montaigne in the present tense, which prompts him to release himself to the process wherein, nudged by his impulses and feelings, "images, thoughts and statements immediately supplied by the imagination then become the reference point for the further production of the text" (p. 98).[4] Fragmentariness thus in a sense replicates the flow of everyday life.

Montaigne's *Essays* are a watershed in the history of writing also with respect to the evolution of the role of the reader in the formulation of the text, and, consequently, of the increase in textual density and layering resulting from the spread of print media, the proliferation and increased dissemination of texts (p. 62). The reader is drawn into a textual matrix wherein his or her own mimetic faculties are evoked and challenged so that there are many vantage points for writer, text, and reader. Here, the essay moves even closer as both a depicter and replica of the multifarious social process, and here Montaigne, adumbrating the recent shift in emphasis away from the author toward the reader, toward heightening of polysemy—the multiplicity of meanings of a signifier (Rosenau, 1992, pp. 25–41)—brings the voices of the everyday world into his text. In this respect, in the looking-glass held up to the reader by Montaigne's *Essais*, "the reader is personified, not only through Montaigne's often ironic, second-person asides, but through the writer's self-personification as a reader of other texts and of his own" (Cave, 1982, p. 154). Thus we see how the interactional quality of writing and the essay is objectified. We also see how writing is multivalent, going beyond the unidirectional focus upon the writer, to the multidirectional and multiperspectival inclusion of the reader. *Inter*-textual means interactional! Montaigne appears to playfully disguise his references to other texts as he "takes up thoughts and insights without identifying their origin or context. He even attempts to conceal the origin of his own thoughts by omitting possible clues or leading readers astray, consciously putting them off on the wrong track" (Gebauer and Wulf, 1992, p. 94). Indeed, Montaigne's frequent disguising of his references compels the reader "to discover the mimetic references to prior texts woven into the text by the author, to follow the traces of the transformation process undertaken by the author, and to find literary appeal in this activity" (ibid.). On the other hand, he has no qualms about letting the reader in on his tactics. Such is the case with the quote from the essay "On Physiognomy" which opens this chapter, where the masking of the appropriation of other texts is alternately removed and replaced as a contrivance. In this way, the reader becomes an ally of the writer in the latter's textual guerrilla warfare. Montaigne makes us confederates in alliances and misalliances, all cloaked in the garb of writing. Thus, social geometry qua Simmel intrudes here: the reader becomes the *tertius gaudens*, the one who enjoys.

The reader is now actively inserted into the process of *creation* of the text as a result of having his or her interpretive process conceived of as constitutive of the text's meaning. This is what Barthes calls the "writerly text" because "To interpret a text is not to [merely] give it . . . meaning, but on the contrary to appreciate what *plural* constitutes it" (Barthes, 1974, p. 5). Thus, the literary text "in common with the reader's reading give rise to a new *intertextuality*, which endures as a model for many authors into our own times" (Gebauer and Wulf, 1995, pp. 98–99). This results in the objectification of intertextuality, because Montaigne's pranks are either confessed or revealed through the act of reading.[5] Conceived in this way, it is clear that Montaigne views writing as more than a one-way social act, that is, as more than the effort of the author to inform or persuade readers; rather, it is a means of *interacting* with them, of engaging in a dialogic process of conversation with them. As Cooley says, "the spontaneous reader will love the spontaneous writer" (*Journal* V. 19 [2/16/1908–1/1/1910] 11/26/1908, p. 29). In addition, as Cooley demonstrates, writing is the instrument for engaging in a conversation extending beyond the historical epoch one lives in; it is a conversation "across the ages." Thus it necessarily includes the reader. This being the case, it is easy to conceive the essay's conversational quality as embracing other processes familiar to sociologists, such as the creation of selves.

Montaigne's pulling the reader in as a participating agent in the text objectifies the self-other dialectic and communication as constitutive of the text (Bauschatz, 1980). In the process of establishing the writer as subject, the reader is coaxed into constituting himself or herself as the subject through the act of reading (Cave, 1982, p. 159). Montaigne is unique to his epoch in this respect, for the objective of the *Essays* is the joint enterprise of the development of self-knowledge via writing and reading. For this reason, the Montaignean essay has been called the "reflective text" (Bensmaïa, 1987, passim).[6] Reading Montaigne draws one both into Montaigne's arena, and, more or less consciously, into the orbit of self-reflection. Apart from the matter of writing's personal effects upon him, how could Cooley, prompted by Montaigne's engaging patter, fail to conceive of the processes of reflective emergence of the self? While the notion of the looking-glass self is not directly traceable to Montaigne, one can be sure that Cooley, so inspired by the ambience of the essayists—as he was more directly by the moralist Adam Smith—could not have done anything but create vivid imagery to convey this idea.

As the culmination of an evolution of the conjoined roles of writer and reader, the *authorial personality*, a self, is the central agent and object of this genre. Montaigne marks the advent of literary subjectivism, wherein personal style is expressed through the appeal to the authority of ancient authors, thereby making a historical detour to modernity around such repressive forces of feudalism as ecclesiastical authority, the constricting social structure of small states and the guilds, inherited privilege, and philosophical dogma (Highet, 1949, p. 193). Such an insertion of the personal element into style and its apotheosis in and through the *Essays* represents Montaigne's appropriation of his own freedom and marks him as a skeptic. Personal style, deriving from the authorial personality, as we know, is a hallmark of Cooley's thought. This draws us into the exploration of the self, an arena where Cooley distinguishes himself as both a sociological writer and reader.

Montaigne succeeds in creating a multicentered world through autobiography, that is, through shuttling back and forth between self and other, thereby making intertextuality an explicit, conscious writing strategy. Implicit in this process is the decentered view of society and the individual via the intersubjective, reflexive constitution of the self, which later marks Cooley's originality in sociology. For example, in the essay, "On Experience," Montaigne tells us: "This application which I have long devoted to studying myself also trains me to judge passably well of others. . . . By having trained myself since boyhood to see my life reflected in other people's I have acquired a studious tendency to do so; when I give my mind to it, few things around me which help me to achieve it escape my attention: looks, temperaments, speech, I study the lot for what I should avoid or what I should imitate" (1991 [1587–88], p. 1221). "By having trained myself . . . to see my life reflected in other people's" jumps off the page at us. Once again the quintessentially social self comes into the foreground. Once again we are reminded of the confluence of these ideas and influences in Cooley's conception of personal ideas as they figure in an intrinsically reflective social process. Looks, temperaments, and speech—these are the stuff of the personal impressions Cooley speaks of so vividly as comprising personal symbols in *Human Nature and the Social Order*. "I study the lot for what I should avoid or what I should imitate" reminds us again of the affective and judgmental elements of the looking-glass self, and acquiring "a studious tendency" draws us into our friend Cooley's demeanor as a quiet observer of the life around him.

As two scholars tell us, Montaigne's "rolling about in the self, is . . . the most intense form of life." Thus, "where the I finds reflections of the Other in itself . . . it is constantly being thrown back on itself, without ever achieving unity, for its movements are polycentric" (Gebauer and Wulf, 1995, p. 96). How much more sociological can literature get! Here again we have the processes of the self occupying center stage, and—equally significant—coming out of the consideration of the essay's multiperspectival quality is a *multivalent* self. As Montaigne so trenchantly demonstrates, polysemy is thus not merely a postmodern gimmick confined to textual analysis. Nor is this is another way of faddishly identifying him as a proto–postmodernist. Here postmodernism, in fact, has nothing to do with the realization that the self is quintessentially a literary-social product. Polysemy has always typified the essay tradition; the self always has been social; and both have always evinced and reflected a multivalent and multifaceted social world.

For those who might criticize Montaigne's subjective bias, he tells us, in "On Repenting," that "If all complain that I talk too much about myself, I complain that they never even think about their own selves" (1991, p. 908). He is goading us to reflect. The autobiographical emphasis (his self-observation) and his frequent movement back and forth between self and other thus validate *subjectivity* as a basis for understanding. In this respect, Montaigne's autobiographical approach to understanding experience is, as Eric Auerbach calls it, an "experimental method," and thus is scientific (Auerbach, 1953, pp. 255–56). It anticipates Cooley's use of his journal, including his observations of his children, to explore the contours of the looking-glass self—that is, his and others' looking-glass selves! As is evident, Cooley's, and Montaigne's, method is auto-experimental, for the act of personal writing serves as a mechanism of personal growth and evolution. And as an approach that blurs the division between objectivity and subjectivity, feeling is placed at the center of the textual moment as part of the matter to be dissected, which later appears in Cooley's formulation of the self and in his joining of sympathy with observation as a sociological method—"sympathetic introspection" (Cooley, 1926 in 1930, pp. 289–309).

Cooley Enters the Essayists' Great Conversation and Addresses Montaigne

Intellectually Cooley anchors himself among the essayists through the construction of a literary reference group, among whom he characterizes himself as conversing. Cooley visualizes this "invisible college," his genre matrix (Crane, 1972; Jacobs, 1976, pp. 155–253), in terms familiar to the essay tradition. He conceives of himself as a member of "a larger society of men who live for the ages as well as for the hours, and, by virtue of their *representative minds*, speak to one another from century to century" [my italics] (*Journal* V. 21 [1913–19] 8/6/17, p. 161). In a number of places Cooley conceives of himself and other essayists as representative men (a theme borrowed from Emerson) who are sub specie aeternitatis—under the aspect of eternity (*Journal* V. 22 [1919–25] 8/16/18, p. 42; V. 23 [6/6/25–10/4/28] 9/16/25, 12/6/26, pp. 7, 46). Toward the end of his life, he expands the orbit of the sub specie to include the social heritage and all who share it, owing to the fact that "man became an imaginative and creative animal and began to hand on a social heritage" and "at the same time transcended in a manner his individual mortality and began to dwell in an immortal whole."[7] Thus it "requires no special effort, no peculiar virtue, to live for eternal things; we are by nature of them" (*Journal* V. 23 [6/6/25–10/4/28] 12/6/26,

p. 45). Immediately afterward, in *Life and the Student*, where these passages appear almost verbatim, a clarification of their significance follows which helps us understand Cooley's use of the term "sub specie aeternitatis": "How should I who read Marcus Aurelius and Dante and Goethe not live in the same life in which they lived?" (1927, p. 239). For Cooley the essay tradition is a living social entity fed by those participating in it in any historical age. Consistent with his perspective on the relation between the individual and society, this tradition, as part of the social heritage communicatively mediates the transcendental realm to the individual. Cooley is suggesting that the eternal-transcendental is intellectually attainable by virtue of our participation in society, especially through creative activity emphasizing the imagination.

One might say that Cooley posits a seminal relationship between mundane society and the transcendental. Here he is synthesizing the insights attained by Durkheim and Simmel; the first in terms of the direct derivation of the notion of the sacred (namely, sacred force and idea of the soul) from the social; and the latter from his notion of the transcendent character of life (Durkheim, 1995 [1912]; Simmel, 1971 [1918]). Cooley's approach comes closer to Simmel's, for rather than bluntly viewing the sacred as a proxy of the social as Durkheim does, Cooley and Simmel derive the transcendental from the *creativity* of the human life process itself. Moreover, each conceives of this process as imaginative, and so both include a quintessential aesthetic element. Because of its stylistic similarity to Cooley's, Simmel's idea of the transcendent merits a brief summary. He contends that life is "the movement which at every moment draws something into itself . . . in order to transform it into life" and so can only exist by virtue of being more-life because life "is always more life than there is room for the form allotted by and grown out of it" (1971 [1918], pp. 369–70). Indeed, the perceptions of birth and death are "events attached to the subjective life and transcend it, toward above and toward below, so to speak" (p. 369). Moreover, in the case of creativity, "imagination produces content that has its own sense, . . . a certain validity or permanency that is independent of it being produced and borne by life," and this "transcendence into the level of objective content . . . constitute[s] more-than-life" (p. 371). Finally, transcendence reveals itself "where the process knows itself from the start as transcendent and feels the will of the transcendent object to be its ultimate own" (p. 373).

How strikingly close to Cooley this is. In *Life and the Student* (1927, p. 238) he muses:

Man lives both in that which is sensuously present—the sunshine, the walk, the bath, the food—and in his plans and ideals. So he lives both in activities that have little common meaning—chiefly these same sensuous affairs—and in the social imaginations and strivings that are even more himself. His life is sensuous and ideal, private and social, transitory and immortal. When he needs a larger world it begins to appear, because those powers that create the need also satisfy it. Sensuous man does not need a future, imaginative man can make one. Without imagination there is no fear of death, with it we may live above that fear in a greater life.

Beyond simply deriving one from the other, or contrasting them, Cooley implies a dialectical relationship—a creative tension—between the transcendental and the mundane, wherein they may nourish or occasionally clash with each other, thus bringing us back to the matter of conscious or imaginative participation in the transcendental realm. In focusing on the imagination, Cooley, like Simmel, stresses the aesthetic dimension. This, in turn, elucidates Cooley's stress on living and working, that is, creating sub specie aeternitatis, the arena of communication with representative men, who are types representing social ideals and at the same time serve as transcendental mediators, exemplars, or mentors for the individual. It is from them that we derive the standards by which we may judge our craftsmanship. Elucidating this connection with respect to art and the artist, Cooley tells us: "Among the followers of any art there is a society, mostly second-rate, of the present place and hour, and a higher society of the masters of all time. The artist needs both, but only the latter can lift him above mediocrity. An artist should see his work as nearly *sub specie aeternitatis* as he can" (pp. 136–37).

Indeed, his modesty notwithstanding, Cooley sees it as his function to understand poets and prophets (*Journal* V. 15 [12/24/01–9/12/02] 2/8/02, p. 20), for in aspiring to live in the minds of the wise (*Journal* V. 14 [1/2/00–12/20/01] 9/13/01, 10/22/01, pp. 69, 71), he is convinced that popularity (vogue) must be forsaken and that he "must refuse intimacy with any who may impose themselves upon him to his detriment." To be a part of "a larger moment of thought flowing on" after his death, he has to "write for criticism as remote as Dante" (*Journal* V. 18b [2/16/08–1/1/10] 12/12/09, p. 75; V. 19 [2/6/10–10/15/11] 12/10/11, p. 54). This must be a high tribunal: the writer must entertain only "the higher views of select persons" (*Journal* V. 14 [1/2/00–12/20/01] 12/20/01, p. 85). The following year (1902) these thoughts appear in his first book, *Human Nature and the Social Order:*

> Persons of great ambitions, or of peculiar aims of any sort, lie open to disorders of self-feeling, because they necessarily build up in their minds a self-image which no ordinary social environment can understand or corroborate, and which must be maintained by hardening themselves against immediate influences, enduring or repressing pains of present depreciation, *and cultivating in imagination the approval of some higher tribunal.* If the man succeeds in becoming indifferent to the opinions of his neighbors he runs into another danger, that of a distorted and extravagant self of the pride sort . . . he has perhaps lost that wholesome deference to some social tribunal that a man cannot dispense with and remain quite sane [my italics]. (1902, rev. ed. 1922, p. 258)[8]

An earlier journal entry brackets this statement in *Human Nature,* noting that any book he would write must be judged by a "conclave of wise spirits of the past" (*Journal* V. 10, [7/21/95–4/26/96] 7/21/95, p. 39). Having established himself as a stylist in his writing, the mature Cooley states, "My art is a peculiar kind of art, seeking a somewhat peculiar type of beauty, not one of the popularly recognized branches" (*Journal* V. 13 [8/8/98–4/26/99] 10/25/98, p. 21). Thus his aesthetic conception of his vocation as a sociologist is not a passing fancy of youth but a conviction tied to the sense of self that sets him apart from mundane academic thinkers.

Like Montaigne, Cooley professes the consubstantiality of himself and his writing, or as he says, "I am to conceive all my work as a kind of autobiography.[9] If it is not a confession, like parts of Human Nature [*Human Nature and the Social Order*], it is an imaginative extension of my experience to embrace others in whom I am interested." Thus, the "reality of the whole depends on it being *mine—my life.* It all springs from an experience in which I am heartily implicated. If I cease to be this I cease to write anything vital." Cooley blurs the lines separating his literary and quotidian selves, and like Montaigne makes his self a foil for the analysis of experience: "Under this conception the books I plan are all chapters of one book, an inward account of my life in this place and time—referred, as my nature demands, to lasting principles." In this respect, "My several books . . . stand for necessary phases of my life and thought" (*Journal* V. 19 (1910–11) 2/9/10, 6/19/10, pp. 2, 25). Indeed, Cooley, testing the limits of objective social science, asserts that "a true sociology is systematic autobiography" (*Journal* V. 15 [12/24/01–9/12/02] 5/n.d./02, p. 38). With this declaration holding to the norms of the tradition, he places himself squarely among the essayists.

Cooley cannot include himself among systemic academic thinkers, whose sensibilities he finds alien to his own. He prefers the autobiographical humanist approach of the essayists who "see directly": "Nearly all writers with any tendency toward system observe only within certain limits set by their systematic preconceptions—not simply, impulsively, humanly. The superiority of unharnessed spirits, liked Montaigne and Emerson, is that they see directly, naïvely, like children" (*Journal* V. 17 [7/8/03–8/28/04] 8/23/03, p. 19).

The attribution of eidetic perception to the essayists is Cooley's means of getting to the heart of the matter concerning accurate understanding of the human condition. In endorsing the earthiness of everyday conversation and the facts of daily life, as Montaigne himself often does, Cooley seizes the opportunity to draw on commonplace facts as his data for the analysis of the self and society. In this regard, he declares epigrammatically: "To know men perhaps the surest way is to have simple and necessary relations with them" (*Journal* V. 16 [9/19/02–7/17/03] 11/23/02, p. 30).[10] The sensibility and imaginative world of the child is a device by which Cooley seeks to gain leverage for a humanistic approach to sociological understanding, as well as a substantive issue in its own right. The imaginary world of children thus serves as both method and subject of his analysis, with Montaigne's reflexivity acting as a lever for his analysis of the self.

Peak-a-Boo I See Me: Montaigne in the Formulation of the Looking-Glass Self

Montaigne appears in Cooley's first and last books, *Human Nature and the Social Order* (1902, rev. ed., 1922) and *Life and the Student* (1927), and thus, has, in a sense, the first and last words in Cooley's published writings. In Chapter III, "Sociability and Personal Ideas," in *Human Nature and the Social Order,* where Cooley lays the groundwork for the looking-glass self, which appears two chapters later, he delivers a paean to Montaigne. Quoting from the essay "On Vanity," he asserts that the Frenchman and the members of the diary tradition epitomize the communicative element in human nature:

Montaigne, who understood human nature as well, perhaps, as anyone who ever lived, remarks: "There is no pleasure to me without communication: there is not so much as a sprightly thought comes into my mind that it does not grieve me to have produced alone, and that I have no one to tell it to." And it was doubtless because he had many such thoughts which no one was at hand to appreciate, that he took to writing essays. The uncomprehended of all times and peoples have kept diaries for the same reason. So, in general, a true creative impulse in literature or art is, in one aspect, an expression of this simple, childlike need to think aloud or to somebody; to define and vivify thought by imparting it to an imaginary companion; by developing that communicative element which belongs to its very nature, and without which it cannot live and grow. (p. 92)

Doubtless Cooley, stimulated by Montaigne's characterization of his own intellectual activity as conversation, his reflections on his own reclusive nature, his observations of his children entered into his journal, and his ongoing dialogues with and ruminations on his precursors within the essay tradition, develops the imaginary playmate as a building block for the construction of the looking-glass self. How this occurs is through conversation, and it becomes a habit persisting through adulthood, albeit "something more elaborate, reticent, and sophisticated," such that "the mind lives in perpetual conversation" (pp. 89–90). Thus, given the vividness of his own interlocutors, Cooley tells us, "It is worth noting here that there is no separation between real and imaginary persons; indeed, to be imagined is to become real, in a social sense" (p. 95). Out of impressions of the other's physiognomy, mannerisms, or traits serving as personal symbols (p. 106), and the feelings evoked by them, the person becomes further concretized as the personal idea. In other words, as Cooley explains in connection with judgments of personal character: "The symbol before us reminds us of some other symbol resembling it, and this brings with it a whole group of ideas which constitutes our personal impression of the new man" (p. 106). Cooley adds, in terms significant for the discussion of style below, that "[t]hese visible and audible signs of personality . . . are also a chief basis of the communication of impressions in art and literature" (p. 107). Social reality is thus constituted of these impressions and "*[t]he immediate social reality is the personal idea. . . .* Society, then, in its immediate aspect, *is a relation among personal ideas*" (p. 119). And here too, personal impressions are of the same quality as literary ones.

Here Cooley has established the architecture of the self as a mental-social complex on a semiotic foundation: persons are symbols. He is now free, as we have seen, to explore its study through imagination: "the imaginations which people have of one another are the *solid facts* of society . . . and . . . to observe and interpret these must be a chief aim of sociology" (p. 121). The close connection between appearance and the visual symbol is no doubt inspired by Cooley's immersion in the essay tradition as it wends its way from Montaigne through the moralists. Why not conceive of persons as symbols—not in the charismatic sense, but more mundanely, as Montaigne and the essayists do!

The imaginative foundation of the self in conversation with others calls to mind the essay genre's basis in conversation, but it also invokes the emphasis on another exemplar of Cooley's, Walter Pater, a Victorian literary figure and essayist who rested his aesthetic literary philosophy on the "impression" or the writer's perceptual construct of reality. As we shall see, Pater's aestheticism serves as a basis for Cooley's own aesthetic construction of society and social process. Moreover, Cooley includes the element of feeling in his approach, and this comes directly from the essayists. Conventional wisdom concerning Cooley's emphasis on feeling suggests that it derives from a literary context, but this is a half-truth reflecting a stereotype that artistic and literary views are intrinsically expressive and emotionally freighted. In the cases of Montaigne and Walter Pater, feeling is an observed constituent of experience, aesthetic and otherwise, and a necessary condition of knowledge and judgment (Donoghue, 1995, pp. 144, 205–6). Literariness by itself does not explain Cooley's emphasis on feeling. Feeling serves as an indicator, even an arbiter, of truth in this genre. It is appropriate that Cooley's emotionally constituted self is now achieving belated recognition for its originality, and perhaps will continue to do so via the emergence of ethnography as a literary genre (Stryker, 1980, p. 6; Scheff, 2000; Scheff, 2003).

Recalling his discussion of the imaginative foundation of the self, we see that Cooley treats egoism, egotism, pride, vanity, and leadership; Montaigne (whom Emerson calls the "prince of egotists") is characterized with the disclaimer: "Montaigne, who says 'I' on every other line, and whose avowed purpose is to display himself at large and in all possible detail, does not, it seems to me, really make an impression of egotism upon the congenial reader, because he contrives to make his self so interesting in every aspect that the more we are reminded of it the better we are pleased" (Cooley, 1902, rev. ed. 1922, p. 222). Indeed, commentators on Montaigne agree with Cooley's assessment. One Montaigne scholar observes that in the first fifty lines of the essay "On Repentance," the first-person pronoun and its possessive adjective (*I* and *my*) occur forty times. Reversing Cooley's meaning of the terms egoism and egotism, Frank Bowman suggests that Montaigne practices "*égotisme*" but cannot be accused of "*égoïsme*," or self-satisfaction and self-admiration, for if some of the first-person sentences seem self-congratulatory, others are self-critical. Thus the "proud assertions here, as elsewhere, are the obverse of a critical analysis of mankind and the human condition, of an often derogatory portrait of one subject Montaigne can and does know, Montaigne himself." How significant that Bowman likens Montaigne to "a sort of Columbus discovering the new world of the self-in-flux and thus making a contribution to human consciousness" (Bowman, 1969, p. 46). The touchstone for us is the prefiguring of the study of the self by the behavioral sciences; but in Cooley's case Montaigne the essayist, more than an adumbrateor, is a collaborator in the elucidation of the social self.

By the same token, Cooley's discussion of vanity is more than peripheral to the understanding of the looking-glass self. Grounded in Montaigne's conception of the self as a communicative-conversational entity, and in the skeptical writings of the French moralists such as La Rochefoucauld, Jean de La Bruyère, and Henri Amiel, his insightful analysis is just as much a contribution to the essay tradition as it is to sociological literature. Louis Kronenberger, La Rochefoucauld's translator, speaks of the French moralists' cynical projection of others' motives: "What they do, systematically and untiringly, is gaze back and forth from their fellow-beings to themselves. From what they themselves are thinking, they postulate their neighbors' thoughts; from what they crave, they deduce their neighbors' desires; from what they themselves would conceal, they infer their neighbors' dissemblings" (La Rochefoucauld, 1959, p. 16). La Rochefoucauld, who follows Montaigne's lead, emphasizes vanity as the hallmark of the self. Vanity, viewed as a hypertrophied aspect of the self and its constitutive processes, is also invoked by Cooley to highlight the self as a social entity, but with an emphasis on the development of character. So he defines vanity to mean emptiness, indicating "either a weak or hollow appearance of worth put on in the endeavor to impress others, or the state of feeling that goes with it. It is the form social self-approval naturally takes in a somewhat unstable mind, not sure of its image" (1902, rev. ed. 1922, p. 234). On the other hand, "vanity, in moderation, may indicate an openness, a sensibility, a teachability, that is a good augury of growth" (p. 235).

Finally, Cooley suggests that "common sense approves a just mingling of deference and self-poise in the attitude of one man toward others" (p. 237).[11] While vanity may be perceived as an abnormality, Cooley, in the spirit of the essayists, discusses it as an aspect of daily life, and attempts to draw lessons from it about character and the self. As I have discussed in chapter 2, Cooley's contribution also stems from extensive self-observation—his inner work—as recorded in his personal journal (Jacobs, 1976, pp. 329–37). More than a personal habit, journal writing constitutes a literary tradition akin to the essay. Literate and literary journals have been considered literature in themselves, and the journal, especially when kept as Cooley did, is personal, fragmentary, and reflexive.

Cooley and Montaigne posit the consubstantiality of the writer and the book. Suggesting the book is the person also implies its opposite—the self is a book. Getting to know Montaigne's essays is, therefore, getting to know Montaigne. In the essays entitled "The Vanity of Words" (I, 51) and "Of Vanity" (III, 9), Montaigne "accepts the limitations of language . . . but uses them as a model for perceiving the limitations to human nature" (Bauschatz, 1980, pp. 281–82). The ultimate goal here is the cultivation of character through the deepening of one's understanding of the author. Simultaneously, one learns to study oneself like a book, and thus to sympathetically introspect. Hence, "through reading one objectifies one's concept of the self" (p. 284). On the other hand, the development of the self—personal evolution—can produce the dividend of better writing. Cooley tells us: "The only way to write better books is to make a better man of yourself" (*Journal* V. 18b [2/16/1908–1/1/1910] 4/29/1908, p. 9).

In *Life and the Student* (1927, pp. 65–66), contrasting Montaigne's style with the more private style of the journalkeepers Emerson and Thoreau, Cooley suggests that "his thinking seems conversational rather than private, not diary stuff at all, always intended for a public." Elsewhere Cooley similarly criticizes Emerson, yet here Emerson is included in the more private club of the journalkeepers.[12] This statement betrays a mild ambivalence toward Montaigne, as though retracting the compliment tendered in *Human Nature and the Social Order* in identical terms, and accusing him of pandering to the public. Some of this is, no doubt, sour grapes. How does one trump Montaigne! Perhaps ambivalence betrays a desire for distinction as a sociologist more associated with prosaic—if not more mundane—things, and perhaps it also evinces, as I also discuss below with respect to Walter Pater's influence, a nagging discomfort over the threat of precursor writers and texts to the writer's sense of autonomy and originality. At the same time, the struggle between living according to his stylistic lights and the equally compelling draw of scientifically attending to the bigger picture of the social world, is a creative tension that Montaigne prompts Cooley to ruminate on: "As compared with Montaigne . . . my thoughts at their best are perhaps more precise and fitted to a larger whole, but far poorer in discursive richness, in the flavor of experience, and in variety of human sentiment. A little thin for literature" (*Journal* V. 21 [11/1/1913–4/11/1919], 12/27/1914, p. 38). The placement of discursiveness here is interesting, for it testifies to Cooley's recognition of the multifarious character of the essay genre itself as promising the possibility of objectifying the social world.

Cooley's Emersonianism and His Donning of the Oratorical Self

Cooley's membership in the essay tradition is mildly idiosyncratic. From the standpoint of academic social science, however, it may in part reflect the insecurity and relative newness of sociology as a discipline, its boundaries still permeable. It also marks Cooley's own sense of distinctness from the discipline, and reflects his attempt in youth to develop an identity separate and distinct from that of his father. Recall that sociology, as it emerged from the nineteenth-century U.S. social science movement, broke away from economics and political science and found its legitimacy challenged by other disciplines contending it had no proper subject matter. Sociologists, perturbed at having "never really found a center," found themselves left with the detritus of the other social sciences and a tendency to venerate "great thinkers" (Furner, 1975, pp. 292–93, 311). This applies to Cooley, but with a twist: the thinkers he venerates are not social scientists, but literary ones. The scaffolding he constructs consists in part of his objectification of leaders of the essay tradition.

In addition, it bears remembering that Cooley borrows from Emerson the related concept of representative men, used in this case as a frame of reference for his understanding and emulation of his own literary models. In Emerson's version of transcendental philosophy, and for Cooley, the representative man fits with the American conception of the hero, which, unlike the European version, makes him an antidote to, as opposed to an instrument of, coercion (Schwartz, 1985, pp. 103–4). As Schwartz's astute analysis of Emerson's and Cooley's conception of the hero demonstrates, for the two writers the hero is drawn as "not a master but a servant whose true function is to represent and, by example, reinforce the values and aspirations of his time. Assuming great men to be *symbols* rather than *sources* of society's existing tendencies, Cooley's was the first sociological effort to render hero worship intelligible to democracy. In this effort he drew heavily, if not exclusively, on the writings of Ralph Waldo Emerson" (p. 105). As discussed in chapter 2 with respect to his conception of the self, Cooley derived this thinking from his Emersonian discipleship, first with respect to his own personal evolution. It remained a theme of his development throughout his life, to the point where Emerson himself would be exchanged for other, in this case literary, exemplars. And the concept appears throughout his work, associated with the development and operation of democratic ideals. As Cooley's biographer, Edward C. Jandy, tells us, "before he was eighteen, his Journals already were suffused with the spirit of Emerson, the first real master of his thought" (1942, p. 41). Jandy says that Emerson, with whom Cooley had many personality traits in common—an outer coldness concealing the "really turbulent emotionality within them"—supplied him with the inspiration for his thinking on democracy, emulation, success, institutions, formalism, "and the tentative nature of social processes and progress" (pp. 42–43). Here Barry Schwartz's language describing Emerson's impact on Cooley reveals the ambiguity of sociological treatment of matters of influence:

> Cooley's idea of the social self, which directly informed his conception of the hero, was not the product of Emerson's influence; it was a precondition of his susceptibility to it. Yet, the fact of the influence itself is undeniable. Thinking, perhaps of the sheer frequency with which Emerson is cited in Cooley's works, Lewis Coser (1977: 318–319) recognized that "Most of [Cooley's] writings stand under the shadow of this New England philosopher." (1985, pp. 108–9)

So which is the case? Is Emerson the *chief* influence on Cooley, or not? I am afraid I will have to disappoint the reader and avoid a cut-and-dried answer. Emerson the man and Emerson's *writing*—its textual form and content—*both* definitively shaped Cooley's work on the self and other ideas; social psychologically via his internalization of Emerson as, to borrow Cooley's concept, a personal idea; and from the standpoint of the myriad ways in which style and the ideas embedded in these texts shaped Cooley's own texts.[13] In the following chapter, I explore this question in depth with respect to the way Cooley moves as a writer from the Emersonian oratorical stance to that of stylist under the aegis of Walter Pater. Let us take a look now at the architecture of Emerson's thought.

The principles of Emersonian transcendentalism[14] (Emerson, 1929, pp. 1–47) include (1) idealism: the senses give us representations of things, including nature, which themselves are emblematic of spiritual facts; (2) language is constituted of signs of natural—hence, spiritual—facts; (3) man is located in the center of things, and human transcendental mediators, representative men, are the conduits of the oversoul or spirit, with "man thinking," or the scholar, ranking highest in the pantheon (pp. 327–414).[15]

As a young man Cooley finds in Emerson's writings stimulus for the formation and development of his own ideals. The journal of the young Cooley contains allusions to the alchemy of character development. Life is depicted as a "smelting process" whose final result is "one golden bead of truth." Indeed, life "must be a succession of smelting processes" from which all impurities are separated out (*Journal*, undated [1886?], p. 52). Juxtaposed with the theme of character development is the motif of the representative man who is hieratic—transcendentally emblematic. As a designation, this comes close in meaning to Cooley's assigning himself and the essayists the status of sub specie aeternitatis. The representative man appears in Cooley's journal as "man verifying," the "superior man," "antique man," "efficient man," the "sensitive man," the "man of character," the "man of the world," "man investigating," and, of course, Emerson's "man thinking."

Emerson blurs the line between philosophy and religion. He viewed the great man as a moral exemplar and as a model for society's self-improvement (Schwartz, 1985, p. 106). In his essay "Uses of Great Men," representative men "have a pictorial or representative quality, and serve us in the intellect. . . . Men are also representative; first of things, and secondly, of ideas" (Emerson, 1929, p. 328). Emerson therefore sanctifies them: "Our religion is the love and cherishing of these patrons" (p. 327). Following suit, the young Cooley tells us that "Common men study the law externally; try to imitate successful actions. . . . Great men feel the law in themselves; do not imitate but *are*; and know that things must follow them" (*Journal* V. 6 [5/11/90–7/9/90] 6/10/90, p. 23). Heroes serve the function for society of conveying a religiouslike "sense of immortality," that is of a "larger and more enduring life surrounding, appreciating, uphold-ing the individual, and guaranteeing that his efforts and sacrifice will not be in vain" (1918, p. 139; see also Schwartz, 1985, p. 113).[16] In 1903, having transmuted this notion into sociological material for the first edition of *Human Nature and the Social Order* (1902), he says, "It is the nature of tradition to transform the great men of history into types or symbols of human tendency. Mankind needs types to define its thought, and forms them out of the most suitable material" (*Journal* V. 17 [7/8/1903–8/28/1904] 10/16/03, p. 28).

For the young Cooley representative men were ideals of what he would like to actualize in himself, what he would like to grow up and become, and later to emulate. As an adult he conceived of them as examples and exemplars of social process, that is, as role models. In the chapter "Various Phases of 'I'" in *Human Nature and the Social Order* (1902, rev. ed. 1922, p. 243), he suggests as much when he says, "Every outreaching person has masters in whose imagined presence he drops resistance and becomes clay in the hands of the potter, that they may make something better of him. He does this from a feeling that the master is more himself than he is." Such persons refer their lives to their masters "for comment and improvement" (p. 242). Great men thus are internalized as personal ideas.[17]

It is Emerson's emphasis on the thinking man—the scholar—as hieratic, and, furthermore, his incorporation of the poet, and especially the *orator* into this type, that provides the young Cooley with his ego ideal. In "The American Scholar" (1929, p. 32) Emerson proclaims:

> The poet, in utter solitude remembering his spontaneous thoughts and recording them, is found to have recorded that which men in crowded cities find true for them also. The orator distrusts at first the fitness of his frank confessions, his want of knowledge of the persons he addresses, until he finds that he is the complement of his hearers;—that they drink his words because he fulfills for them their own nature; the deeper he dives into his privatest, secretest presentiment to his wonder he finds this is the most acceptable, most public, and universally true. The people delight in it; the better part of every man feels. [*sic*] This is my music; this is myself.[18]

Speech signifies power and action to the young Cooley, and the theme of the orator-scholar is prominent in his journal (Jacobs, 1976, pp. 218–25): it reflects Emerson's lauding of oratory as power: the effective orator "has his audience at his devotion. . . . He is the true potentate" (Emerson, 1929, p. 640). No doubt, too, Emerson impressed Cooley when in his essay "Eloquence" he tightly connected oratory to a conception of the audience as an organic entity cohering by the force of sympathy (terms nearly identical to those Cooley would use in describing the organic relationship between self and social organization): "*An audience is not a simple addition of the individuals that compose it. Their sympathy gives them a certain social organism*, which fills each member, in his own degree, and most of all the orator, as a jar in a battery is charged with the whole electricity of the battery [my italics]" (p. 639).[19]

In 1895, at the age of thirty-one, reminiscing about his weak and unhealthy constitution from childhood through young adulthood, Cooley notes that, "the discrepancy between my ambitions and my actual state was great and often painful. I lived much in imagination, dreaming tales of various kinds of glory and adventure of which I could have given no notion in words"(*Journal* V. 10 [7/21/95–4/26/96] 7/21/95, p. 3). At the same time he recalls: "I was "passionately eager for applause and a great part of my mental life was spent in imagining situations of which I was the glorious hero" (p. 2).[20] This is coupled with his perception of himself in adolescence as isolated from his peer group and a coward for backing down from strange boys out of shyness. Such a recollection prompts him to reflect on his desire to be an orator:

> My confidence in the future seems almost to have been in inverse proportion to
> my actual attainments or reasonable expectation. For a long time I cherished the
> belief that I could do literally *anything* that I chose to attempt. Although I had not
> voice enough for ordinary conversation and no ear for music, I soberly held that
> I could become a great public singer if I chose to apply myself to it. However, al-
> though I believed this career quite practicable I preferred that of a great orator and
> for many years cherished fervently the design of being such. For this I was, to all
> appearances, scarcely more suited than to public singing; yet I believe that I have
> something of the temperament of an orator and that if my organization had been
> a little more massive I might have excelled in moving men thro' [*sic*] speech. The
> idea of doing so thrilled me incredibly—I feel something of this still. (pp. 7–8)

Indeed, he recalls that "I was, for a bright boy, remarkably deficient in command of language," noting that "I could frame sentences, either spoken or written, only with a great effort," and, in order to overcome this deficiency "I used to write all my letters at least twice" (p. 5).[21]

These reminiscences are punctuated by his observation that compensatory effort has seen him through his difficulties. As a result, "Notwithstanding the tremendous gulf between fact and desire it was always my habit to set seriously and industriously about the realization of my ambitions" (ibid., p. 8). Twenty-one years later, he notes that "deficiencies, like partial deafness [such as his own], lameness, bad eyesight, stammering, or even that kind of inhibitory shyness with which Rutger [his son] is afflicted, become serious obstacles to success only as they are allowed to confine or intimidate the spirit." He concludes, "The way to treat these things is to recognize them frankly as obstacles, but only minor ones which will nearly or quite disappear before a courageous attitude" (*Journal* V. 21 [11/1/13–4/11/19] 7/13/16, pp. 90–91).[22]

No doubt Cooley, with his admiration of oratory, dogged by a weak voice and personal shyness took heart from Emerson's transcendental formulation of the notion of compensation, wherein

> The good are befriended even by weakness and defect. As no man had ever a point of pride that was not injurious to him, so no man had ever a defect that was not somewhat made useful to him. . . . Every man in his lifetime needs to thank his faults. As no man thoroughly understands a truth until he has contended against it, so no man has a thorough acquaintance with the hindrances or talents of men until he has suffered from the one and seen the triumph of the other over his own want of the same. . . . Our strength grows out of our weaknesses. (Emerson, 1929, p. 161)

Put another way, in the psychoanalytic fashion of Erik Erikson, Cooley's anal-retentiveness is counterbalanced, nay compensated for, by his desire to be an orally expulsive, or more extroverted, orator. It is through the North American tradition of oratory that Cooley seeks and begins to find his adult self. Vernon Dibble argues that Cooley locates his (oratorical) identity midway "between the florid tradition and the venerable tradition, in the English language, of earthy, straightforward talk" (1982, p. 12). That latter tradition, as we have seen, finds its written counterpart among the essayists, among whom Emerson is one. Nonetheless, the post-1901 journals evince a subtle shift in priority from oratory to writing. Cooley begins to carp about Emerson's garrulousness and literary egotism as early as 1897. He says (*Journal* V. 11 [5/7/96–3/21/97] 2/14/97, p. 60): "It is likely that from a reading of Emerson I have contracted a tendency toward an excessive indulgence of individual peculiarity in style. . . . Emerson's style is all details, a rich mosaic without architecture." Having chosen an academic career, and continuing on the path of a writer, Cooley retains Emerson as a leading light, but shifts his focus from cultivation of the oratorical to that of the authorial self.[23] Thus, as he had earlier sensed it, writing satisfies "a need thus to objectify ourselves for the sake of development. . . . The instinct of thought seems to be to go out to something" (*Journal* unnumbered, 1887–88, p. 8).

For the cultivation of his authorial self Cooley needs new role models, among them Shakespeare, Goethe, Montaigne, Charles-Augustin Sainte-Beuve, à Kempis, La Rochefoucauld, La Bruyère, and Walter Pater. The first three are part of Emerson's complement of representative men, and Montaigne and the French moralists we have already discussed, but it is Walter Pater who serves as Cooley's most temporal and temperamentally close model and guide. Pater becomes Cooley's stylistic exemplar, but so unsociological is the content of his writing that, had we not begun to engage in the process of tracing the lineaments of the essay tradition in Cooley's thinking, he might be consigned to a minor place in Cooley's *sociological* formulation.

Despite his evident importance, the impact of Pater on Cooley's sociology, especially his attribution of aesthetic qualities to society, also has gone unnoticed. We shall see how significant this aesthetic tint is in Cooley's thought: society and the social process are both aesthetically tinged, that is, they exemplify an agent-centered sociology. Cooley's approach to the understanding of social organization, as well as his more familiar conception of the social self, includes creativity as an intrinsic ingredient. More than an ornament of his thought, however, Cooley's aestheticism is not a mere fillip. It stems from his concern with style and the impact of Walter Pater on the formation of his writer's personality.

CHAPTER FIVE

COOLEY AND THE ESSAY TRADITION, PART II

The Aesthetic Template Completed

> By contrast with another personality, say of Pater in his essays a
> certain aspect of my ideal self is stimulated, brought into vivid
> consciousness. I can hardly tell thro' [sic] what I get the personal
> impression, what echo of sensation, if any, is aroused in my mind.
> There seems to be hardly any sense-basis. I conceive him as
> thinking, as thoughtfully and truly expressing himself, basing the
> conceptions on my own experience. By experience I am enabled
> to conceive him and by conceiving him I recall my experience.
>
> CHARLES HORTON COOLEY, *Journal,* October 10, 1898

We have already seen how the essay form influenced not only Cooley's writing
style but the very quality of his theorizing and the nature of his ideas. As we
know, the ubiquitous but elusive matter of style is often raised in treatments of
Cooley, but the issue remains a slippery one. It is almost universally acknowledged that he was deeply affected by literature, and it is often implied that his
literariness (sometimes used along with the word "insight") is the main factor accounting for nonsystematic, hence faulty, theoretical development of his
ideas. As a half-truth stemming from the truism of his literariness, this charge
begs the question: what is it about literariness that forestalls thorough theorizing? Thus further questions are raised about the literary style of sociological
theorizing that prompts the attribution in the first place. Much of the criticism
is the ill-considered parroting of Mead's critique, echoing the trigger words
"mentalism" and "solipsism," which implicate the stylistic differences in the
framing of Cooley's and Mead's ideas. Moreover, the obvious fact of Cooley's
literariness has not prevented sociologists from assimilating, acknowledging,

and borrowing the *content* of his ideas—but has not prevented them from impugning his theoretical acuity. Have sociologists forgotten the *heuristic* value of theory? If a theory and/or its components stimulate empirical research and further theoretical development, it must be doing something right.

Style or substance, form or content. . . . Which precedes which? It is facile to say they "interact," for this glimmer of an answer merely offers a tantalizing clue to the nature of their interpretation in Cooley's writing. Within most academic, and certainly all social science, disciplines the question is deceptively transparent, its answer deceptively obvious: substance takes precedence. In practice, that is, in the evaluation of sociological writing, style and the substantive contents of sociological writing are not treated as interpenetrable. They are entirely separate matters, the substance of the work purportedly the main interest of the professional sociologist. Style intrudes only when it is perceived as an impediment to conveying content. Otherwise, style is not even conceived as epiphenomenal; it is merely ornamental. Only deviations from academic discursive writing are noticed and they are treated as anomalous departures from "good" sociology.

In the arts and in literature we get a different picture. Style is not only important, it is both a signature of the writer or artist, viewed as essential to the manner of conveying pictorial, musical, or literary content, to the point that at times the content itself may be dwarfed in importance. Further, in some writers style may itself comprise the content, not merely as a topic but in the sense of a beautifully sculptured frame commanding an attention all its own. Cooley fully appreciating this, and translating its significance in an analysis of a book's appeal to an audience, tells us:

> Suppose that a work has true literary merit, like say, Pater's essays. The mass of readers will be wholly blind to this, and will care only for the definite content of the book. *A considerable number, however, will feel the merit though they could not separate and define it.* Only the last are fit to be critics; the second class help to make the reputation of a good book, though often timid in approval if it is new: the first will not read it until its reputation is established [my italics]. (*Journal* V. 16 [9/19/02–6/17/03] 10/14/02, pp. 21–22)

"Literary merit" and "style" are summarizing abstractions pointing in the same direction. A sociologist or natural scientist might decry the terms as ambiguous and inexact, but one who is familiar with literature, although not with the author or work in question, would want to know more, and would perhaps search the work out. In addition, notice how Cooley suggests that feeling, as opposed to cognition, is the vehicle for literary knowledge and understanding. Knowing how substantive style is in literature, how do we probe its place in a discipline that professes to view style as an extraneous issue?

Taking a look at Bryan Green's *Literary Methods and Sociological Theory* (1988), which analyzes and evaluates this subject using literary methods, we find ourselves immersed in an unfamiliar analytic realm. He informs us that style is only salient in a negative way, as a peripheral concern in the evaluation of socio-logical work. As he puts it: "First, writing style is an occasional, secondary, and peripheral topic: one sometimes mentioned in passing prefatory remarks, foot-notes, supplementary comments, and other marginalia. Even when noted more fully or made an issue, it is typically in a negative voice only: reactions against breaches of stylistic rules whose authority to govern sociological theorizing is left methodologically unexplicated" (p. 15). Green explains, as I have in compar-ing Mead and Cooley, that such ephemeral allusions in sociology stem partly from the importation of "evaluative criteria belonging to other areas of language use—in particular, natural science, literary art, and standard public language," and that these project us into "concepts of good writing [which] are imported across the boundaries of sociology from other writing realms." However, this becomes problematic because "there is no indigenous, discipline-specific con-cept of good writing to oppose them"; that is there are no clear guidelines telling us what the connections are between sociological writing style and theoretical acuity or empirical validity. We are then left with the predicament of method-ological marginality: "When we speak of stylistic choice it is in the voices of others" (ibid.). "Vacuity" would be another apt term! When we try to analyze style and the impact this occult subject has had on the evaluation of sociological writing, we find we may have to resort to outside, literary criteria to gain clarity about evaluating content. More importantly, we have to figure out what occult or unstated stylistic norms are operating among sociologists. Here we return to familiar sociological territory—the culture of disciplinary norms.

The professional norm concerning the "scientific ["truth"] value of socio-logical writing is to be found in content, not style. . . . Good style does not get in the way of empirical and discursive content" (p. 17). Thus, a corner must be turned in order to ascertain sociological opinions on good or poor, typical or atypical style, and, farther up the street, another one must be rounded to elucidate translation and comparison of literary norms among sociologists. Finally, a third corner must be navigated in order to import, and if warranted and/or permitted, to apply literary norms as guidelines for the evaluation of sociological style. Expanding on this rumination, Green urges that the "proposal to treat sociological theory as a particular form of literary work makes the stylistic *how* of writing—what the work is doing in the course of composing descriptive and expository content—crucial instead of marginal" to sociologists (p. 29): "The analytic challenge I wish to confront here is how to conceptualize a text in such a way that a question like What is it about? will be heard as a request for the dynamics of a compositional process, not for a summary of thematic content. . . . We are then led to think of the something that a given text, or genre, forms around, and to think of this as an active process" (p. 42). Because of Cooley's unusually incisive grasp of this issue, Green considers him an exemplar of the analytic method, which he calls the "transitive" concept of style, stressing the interpretation of stylistic identity, recognition, or a common generative principle of unity—style as person (pp. 35–41). Cooley calls this very principle the "personal element in style" or the "writer's personality," and differentiates it from the actual person outside his or her written product. It is, in effect, another social self. This motif is central to what I call Cooley's aestheticism. I shall treat it in detail in relation to the shift from Cooley's "oratorical" to his "literary" self as he passes from adopting the stylistic personality of Emerson to adopting that of Walter Pater.

Green notes that Cooley's description of Spencer as one who lacks "the stylistic requirements for truthful writing about social life: requirements that Spencer, in his life and writing style, is said to lack," serves as an exemplar of stylistic analysis of sociological theory (p. 38). He refers, in turn, to Cooley's organic view of society as a hallmark of stylistic analysis, where pattern rather than quantity serves as a basis of comparison. We can see how these patterns can make sense to sociologists if we view them as analogous to ideal types, models, or yardsticks for the measurement of social phenomena. The same emphasis applies to the textual analysis of both literature and sociological theory.

Utilizing Cooley's reference to the tentative method, which he recognized in the growth of a vine sending out tendrils on a trial-and-error basis, in order to anchor itself, and, which, in *Social Process* (Cooley, 1918, pp. 8–9) he likened to the growth of social organization, Green observes that Cooley himself looked at writing in the same way as he looked at social process and organization: "a text is an emergent organization of meanings within which nothing is fixed and where origin is absent" (Green, 1988, p. 45).

While I do not follow Green's deconstructive approach in analyzing Cooley's sociology or his literariness, I find his ruminations on style, and on Cooley's place in establishing its relevance as a means of analyzing sociological theory and theory construction consistent with my aim to explore Cooley's style and its interpenetrability with the content of his writing. Here I shall probe Cooley's own speculations on the subject and his thinking about the evolution of his authorial personality as he passes from Emerson to Pater.

Style and Authorial Self: The Connection with Walter Pater's Aestheticism

The eclipse of oratory by writing and his assumption of a self-identity as a scholar are signaled in Cooley's journal during the year of his marriage (1890) where he states that "A command over printed sources of information is one of the scholar's chief instruments. How to keep and classify such material?" Thence he outlines his use of bibliography cards for the purpose of organizing, classifying, and digesting information (V. 6 [5/11/90–7/9/90] 5/30/90, pp. 14–16). From then onward, style and writing supersede oratory. As he puts it in his discussion of personal ideas in *Human Nature and the Social Order* (1902, rev. ed. 1922, p. 109), "'The style is the man,' is the equivalent, in the artist's way of doing things, of those visible and audible traits of the form and voice by which we judge people who are bodily present."

Cooley had been thinking about the matter for some time. Style clearly has wide significance as a literary analogue to personality. Indeed, we also find here another connection to a broad social literary current that "envisions writers as instruments of 'the impulse of style' engaged in a work that transcends the time scale of an individual life, a generation, even a civilization" (Thomas, 1992, p. 8).

In a journal entry in 1895, marking the transition from his oratorical to authorial self, Cooley compares Emerson with Walter Pater (1839–94), a Victorian literary critic. Of Emerson he says, "every sentence is either an anecdote, a picture or an epigram. No writing could have less waste; it is all diamonds and no setting." While he finds in Pater "less vivacity," he argues that "you feel at once a contained and religious earnestness, an intense simplicity that makes Emerson seem almost frivolous." He adds that "it is a noble style but not one that many can take in" (*Journal* V. 10 [7/21/1895–4/26/1896] 11/19/1895, p. 50). At the end of 1897, in the midst of talking about the stiffness and lack of personal vitality of some of Emerson's writing, he says, "Style is the rhetorical equivalent or translation of those little peculiarities of personal movement, attitude and expression by which we judge of a man's character" (V. 12 [5/2/97–7/31/98] 12/14/1897, p. 58). Soon after, he mentions Pater, an essayist and noted stylist, as representative of "an attitude, a way of feeling, subtly communicated by a style religiously faithful to the writer's mind" (p. 59). Indeed, Pater's aestheticism contributes to Cooley's view on the self; but also relevant is his discussion of the personal elements of style.

Cooley mentions Pater frequently in his journal (see, for example, V. 12 [5/2/97–7/31/98], 12/14/1897, pp. 58–59; V. 13 [8/8/1898–4/26/1899], pp. 5 (9/4/1898), 14–15 (10/10/1898), 38–39 (12/14/1898), and 62–63 (4/22/1898); V. 14 [1/2/00– 12/20/01] 11/30/00, pp. 34–35; V. 15 [12/24/01–9/12/02] pp. 6–7 (1/2/02) and 17 (2/6/02); V. 16 [9/19/02–7/17/03] pp. 10 (10/2/02), 21–23 (10/14/02) and 38 (12/7/02); V. 18b [2/16/08–1/1/10] 12/18/08, p. 33; V. 22 [4/20/19–5/25/25] 7/30/22, p. 82), but it is not the frequency of these allusions that interests us so much as their appearance at the time of Cooley's maturation—his ripening. Most of the references are to Pater's mastership of style, and even, following Emerson's transcendental motif, his hieratic quality: "It might be read in church, while some rite was in performance" (V. 16 [9/19/02–6/17/03] 10/2/02, p. 10). It is "as if a sort of supersensuous fragrance surrounded Walter Pater's book as it lies on my table. It is the living essence of the yearning after art in literature" (V. 16 [9/19/1902–6/17/1903] 10/14/02, p. 22). Examination of Pater's writing (see, for example, Hale), 1901, pp. ix–xxii, 123–53, 204–18, and passim; Pater, 1873; Pater, 1987 [1889]; Pater, 1891) reveals a philosophy, psychology, and practice of writing highly congenial to Cooley's thinking and action. It is in Pater, whom Kenneth Burke calls an "adept at 'pure' literature" (1953, pp. 9–15), that we find Cooley's most important (next to Emerson) *literary* alter ego. I hazard the judgment that Pater is in fact the most important, because of their closeness in sensibility and their substantive intersections—with their clear bearing upon Cooley's writing style and his aesthetic conceptualization of society. I read this too in the feelings Pater evokes in Cooley.

What sort of impact does Pater's aestheticism have on Cooley's sociology? The musings on Pater's philosophy of art and literary style in Cooley's journal reveal a concordance of sentiment and sensibility that surfaces in his published work in (1) illustrative and interpretive examples highlighting discussions of self (such as the comment on style and personal ideas) and social organization; (2) a root metaphor characterizing society and individual and collective mental life as works of art; and (3) an analysis of social process in a differentiated and socially diverse society proceeding through the operation of "social intelligence." It is important first to understand Pater's aesthetics, based as it is on a phenomenology of aesthetic impressions having an affinity with Cooley's perspective on imagination and personal ideas.

Walter Pater was associated with the pre-Raphaelite and Aesthetic movements in nineteenth-century English art and letters, especially painting and poetry (Iser, 1987; McGrath, 1986, p. 1; Seiler, 1980, pp. 4–6). The Aesthetic movement and pre-Raphaelites included Dante Gabriel Rossetti, John Everett Millais, Holman Hunt, and Edward Burne-Jones.[1] The school sought the "primitiveness" of painters before Raphael (1483–1520) but often merely discarded the conventions of the schools while imitating the painters who came before them. They are considered (Canaday, 1959, pp. 280–96) romantics of the Victorian period who self-consciously rebelled against commerce, industrialization, and urbanization through "adulation of the middle ages, noble aesthetic aspirations, religious yearning, morbid sentimentality, historical delusions, faulty archeology, and debilitating literary preoccupations" (p. 280). They are characterized by a near-contemporary as "intense" to the point of caricature (Hale, 1901, p. xxv), although Pater himself was quite reserved, indeed reticent, in manner.[2]

As much as it may have been a personal mannerism of some, intensity or the passionate love of beauty is more a value of the movement than a personal affectation. As Kenneth Burke suggests, in Pater's case, "being an oddity but untroubled, being exceptional without strain, he could simplify his work through sheer lack of sympathy for anything but the restricted world in which he lived." His existence cloistered at Oxford, "while removing him from the specific issues of his times, permitted him to hear discussed the various key ideas underlying these issues" (Burke, 1953, p. 10). In manner and temperament, he was strikingly similar to Cooley: to lecture was a trial to him, and "in a room, if he was not among very intimate friends, Pater was rarely quite at ease" (Symons, in Pater, 1873, p. xx). In company "he was often silent, withdrawn, and when he consented to speak he spoke hesitantly, with long pauses between the words, as if he found conversation at regular speed and vivacity an effort" (Donoghue, 1995, p. 54). This shyness filtered through "in intellectual matters

and [he] shrank from engaging on equal terms with the personages of scholarship and rhetoric. He remained the don who got the poor second" (pp. 163–64).
Finally, "he was quite content that his mind should 'keep as a solitary prisoner
its own dream of a world'; it was that world that it was his whole business as a
writer to remember to perpetuate" (Symons, n.d., p. xxiv). Indeed, Cooley also
was accused, although, as we have shown, somewhat unjustly, of solipsism.

Pater's philosophy was communicated in two ways: (1) semifictional novels and essays employing the foil of a character in a particular historical and
philosophical context through which these currents, often in transition, are re-
constructed and perhaps somewhat reconstituted (as in *Marius the Epicurean*
(1891), *Gaston de Latour* (1896), and *Imaginary Portraits* (1910), and (2) the literary essay.

In his well-known essay "Style," Pater views art as not so much an expression of fact as of the artist's *sense* of it. Prose for Pater (as for Cooley) is an art
form: "how wholesome! How delightful! As to identify in prose what we call
poetry, the imaginative power, not treating it out of place and a kind of vagrant
intruder, but by way of an estimate of its rights, that is, of it achieved powers,
there" (Pater, 1987 [1889], p. 6). Pater does not concern himself with objects
or works of art, but with the types of *feeling,* representing an unusual sense of
life or skewed consciousness embodied in them (Donoghue, 1995, p. 139). Significantly, echoing Montaigne, Pater chooses the essay as "'the literary form
necessary for a mind for which truth itself is but a possibility, realisable not as
a general conclusion, but rather as the elusive effect of a particular personal
experience; to a mind which, . . . must needs content itself with suspension
of judgment . . . to the very last asking: *Que scais-je?*'" (quoted in Iser, 1987,
p. 18). Moreover, consistent with the fragmentary character of the essay, it is
an open form "which deconstructs itself in order to represent open-endedness,
unrelatedness and endlessness as facts of experiential reality" (ibid.). In Pater's
words, the essay is "'that characteristic literary type of our own time, a time so
rich and various in special apprehensions of truth, so tentative and dubious in
its sense of their *ensemble,* and issues'" (quoted in Iser, ibid.). This is close to
Montaigne's sense of the essay. And it is no accident that in *Gaston de Latour*
(1997 [1910], p. 85), Pater pays homage to Montaigne, whose "essays owed their
actual publication at last to none of the usual literary motives—desire for fame,
to instruct, to amuse, to sell—but to the sociable desire for a still wider range of
conversation with others." For Montaigne, opines Pater, "the essential dialogue

was that of the mind with itself." Alert to his motives, Pater notes, too, that Montaigne's essays "were a kind of abstract" of "that endless *inward* converse" stimulated by the conversation and social life surrounding him (ibid.).

According to Pater the essay form, opening itself to the inward vision and self-discovery, is a vehicle giving form to subjective reality. Thus, to "the mind sensitive to 'form,' the flood of random sounds, colours, incidents, is ever penetrating from the world without . . . and it is just there, just as those doubtful points that the function of style, as tact or taste, intervenes" in order to refine, enlarge, and correct "at a hundred points" the welter of stimuli (Pater, 1987 [1889], p. 31). As with Simmel's evocation of urban reserve (which in the modern and postmodern contexts refers to "hipness" or a "cool" personal style), Pater evokes style, which disciplines the writer through the removal of surplusage and "a skilful economy of means, ascesis . . . that frugal closeness of style which makes the most out of a word, in the exaction from every sentence of a precise relief, in the just spacing out of a word to thought, in the logically filled space connected always with the delightful sense of difficulty overcome" (p. 17).

Imagination is the key ingredient distinguishing art from artifice, and it is imagination that transforms the world by shaping the writer's sense of fact through the formation of impression. "For just in proportion as the writer's aim, consciously or unconsciously, comes to be the transcribing, not of the world, not of mere fact, but of his sense of it, he becomes an artist, his work *fine* art; and good art . . . in proportion to the truth of his presentiment of that sense." In other words, "whereever this sense asserts itself . . . there, 'fine' as opposed to merely serviceable art, exists" (pp. 9–10). To communicate one's sense of the world is the mission of the artist. And just what does the artist's "sense" of the world refer to? For Pater, it means the artist's or critic's impression of the world. Thus:

> "To see the object as it really is," has been justly said to be the aim of all true criticism whatever: and in aesthetic criticism the first step towards seeing one's object as it really is, is to know one's own impression as it really is, to discriminate it, to realize it distinctly. The objects with which aesthetic criticism deals— music, poetry, artistic and accomplished forms of human life—are indeed receptacles of so many powers or forces: they possess, like the products of nature, so many virtues or qualities. What is this song or picture, this engaging personality presented in life or in a book, to *me*? What effect does it really produce on

me? . . . And he who experiences these impressions, and drives directly at the discrimination and analysis of them, has no need to trouble himself with the abstract question what beauty is in itself, or what its exact relation to truth or experience—metaphysical questions, as unprofitable as metaphysical questions elsewhere. (Pater, 1873, pp. xxv–xxvi)

Pater does not believe that one can know an object in an independent sense. As soon as one's mind has produced an impression, the source or object of it fades into a minor issue. As a scholar has recently remarked, "Pater doesn't feel enough piety toward the object to maintain its rights. . . . Pater, having displaced 'one's object' in favor of 'one's own impression,' treats the impression as if it were an object held in place by the attention of the verbs 'to know,' 'to discriminate,' and 'to realize.'" Thus the feeling or sensation aroused by looking at an object becomes a "virtual object," which Pater calls an impression, which now has "superseded the object that provoked it to begin with, and it has fulfilled the mind that has set it astir" (Donoghue, 1995, p. 124).

So too, as the vehicle by which impressions are conveyed and communicated, "literary art . . . is the representation of such fact as connected with soul, of a specific personality, in its preferences, its volition and power" (Pater, 1987 [1889], p. 10). By soul, the literary artist "reaches us . . . through vagrant sympathy and a kind of immediate contact" (p. 25). Speaking of the personal element in literature, Pater tells us, "there are some to whom nothing has any real interest, or real meaning, except as operative in a given person; and it is they who best appreciate the quality of soul in literary art" (p. 27). And as Cooley would have it, literature "is personal because personality appeals to persons, and also because in our personality, as distinct from our specialty, we know life more simply, originally and intensely" (*Journal* v. 20 [10/30/11–11/1/13] 1/14/12, p. 10).

Cooley's notion of the writer's personality or the embeddedness of the personal idea in writing, as much as it is rooted in Montaigne's "rolling around in the self," also derives from Pater's sense of the personal element in style. For Cooley, an "artistic personality is a special sense of self . . . both more and less than his usual self, and is, in fact, the original work of art of which all his other works are children" (1927, p. 68). Furthermore,

any work of art, literary or other, has it origin in a personality, but takes on an organic development of its own to which the rest of the personality is irrelevant. Indeed, this includes scientific work and all special development of the mind:

but it is most interesting (notable) in general literature because there the distinction between the man and his specialty is least obvious (apparent). Any of these specialties involves a special self, a system of attributes which may or may not be conscious and deliberate, but to which habit gives stability. This is style in the sense of 'Le style c'est l'homme même.' And beyond this, still more distinct from the general personality, though springing from it, are the fictive personalities which a writer or other artist may create, Romeo, Monna [*sic*] Lisa, Apollo or what not. (*Journal* V. 23 [6/6/25–10/4/28] 8/26/26, p. 33)

Here he echoes Pater, who tells us style "is truly the man himself." It follows that "style, the manner, would be the man . . . in absolutely sincere apprehension of what is most real to him" (1987 [1889], p. 36). Thus, "since style gives form to subjective reality, it is ultimately to be identified with art" (Iser, 1987, p. 47). Moreover, for Pater what is most real is intensified experience. Art for its own sake represents a heightening, an intensification of reality. Since a "counted number of pulses only is given to us of a variegated, dramatic life," it is necessary to "be present always at the focus where the greatest number of vital forces unite in their purest energy" (*The Renaissance,* "Conclusion," 1873, p. 197). Thus follows Pater's famous adage: "To burn always with this hard, gemlike flame, to maintain this ecstasy, is success in life" (ibid.).

Deigning the "facile orthodox[ies] of Comte, or of Hegel," Pater (ibid.) reminds us that scholarship also serves art: "The literary artist is of necessity a scholar, and in what he proposes to do will have in mind, first of all, the scholar and the scholarly conscience."[3] Furthermore, the medium of the literary scholar is intertextual since "the material in which he works is no more a creation of his own than the sculptor's marble." Rather, it is the product "of a myriad various minds and contending tongues" (1987 [1889], p. 12). And the matter works both ways, in terms of his precursors' influences on Pater, as well as Pater's influence on other writers, for which Donoghue suggests, intertextuality "is a better word than 'influence' because it establishes a field of action and leaves readers free to consider many lines of force, affiliations, trajectories" (1995 p. 8).[4] As Cooley puts it, next to an entry quoting Pater's essay on Coleridge regarding the attainment of clarity of expression (*Journal* V. 16 [9/19/02–7/17/03] 2/18/03, pp. 68–69), "Literary prose uses not only words handed down from the past, but phrases, cadences, artifices of arrangement and contrast, a whole spirit and practice of fine art. It is not well to take on these things too consciously, but to be saturated with them and to give them forth as they arise spontaneously out of one's being. Thus, if one has a character of his own, he will not imitate but assimilate." Here influence meets intertexuality, for Cooley suggests that immersion in rich and prolific textual waters will activate the writer's chemistry. The degree to which he interweaves intertexuality and volition is interesting: the writer is urged not to consciously imbibe texts handed down from the past, but to immerse himself or herself in them, allowing them to meld with the writer's own texts. So Cooley edifies us on the connection between reading and writing and the decentering of the text.

On the other hand, the art of writing clearly presupposes the centrality of the self and the cultivation of an authorial personality functioning as a magnetic center, absorbing and transforming textual materials, and creating new ones out of one's being. In this respect, Pater's philosophy of style and writing is a central point of reference for Cooley's development as a writer. Pater is a fulcrum, and a target as well, for Cooley's ambivalent sentiments about his own and the Victorian's writing. Cooley states that he is drawn to Pater because "it is the man I care for, infinitely more than any separable merit in his work" (*Journal* V. 16 [9/19/1902–6/17/1903] 10/14/02, pp. 22–23).

The quote from Cooley's journal at the beginning of this chapter ostensibly establishes a connection between him and Pater, but its nature is ambiguous. What, for example, do "stimulation," "personal impression," "echo of sensation," "conception," "expression," and "experience" convey? Cooley's sense of Pater's impact on him is unclear, yet his language is redolent of Pater. "I can hardly tell thro'[ugh] what I get the personal impression" of Pater, says Cooley. One might perceive the connection as an osmotic or contagious one. Clearly the derivation is textual, but the apparent inaccessibility of the mechanism by which the writing affects him does not deter Cooley from speaking of Pater as a "personal idea." He describes Pater as communicating "a chastened and withdrawn yet intense self-feeling" (*Journal* V. 15 [12/24/1901–9/12/1902] 2/6/01, p. 17). Indeed, opacity prompts Cooley to concretize Pater as a personal idea. He frames his contact with Pater by means of sympathetic introspection: "I conceive him as thinking, as thoughtfully and truly expressing himself, basing the conceptions on my own experience." Cooley forms his image of Pater following the process conceived by Montaigne, the reader plumbing the author's and therefore his or her own subjectivity. But we are still left with Cooley's own puzzlement over the exact nature of Pater's influence. As we shall see, this reflects his *ambivalence* toward Pater. A clue appears about two months later when Cooley jots in his diary, "How quiet Pater is: so simple and direct that there seems nothing to note particularly, yet one feels that there is intense feeling and sure thought underneath. It is the quiet of an eager, sensitive personality which has mastered itself and subordinated all to art. Compared with this my writing is nervous, incontinent, immature" (*Journal* V. 13 [8/8/1898–4/26/1890] 12/14/98, pp. 38–39). Thus Pater is now a looking-glass for Cooley, who suffers by comparison as an incontinent child! Pater's style shames him. How then to learn from this master, absorb him while retaining one's dignity and composure? The intertextual affinities in Cooley and Pater, and their common apotheosis of style, do not sufficiently explain Pater's *influence* on Cooley. What is telling is the manner in which Cooley appropriates Pater's sensibility.

In his journal two years later, Cooley is no more sure of the source of his attraction to Pater, but he answers his own question, this time with ambiguity verging on ambivalence: it is Pater's consummate style, his means of expression that attracts him:

> There is something strangely and lastingly attractive to me in Pater's style. I know it is labored: indeed it is the effect of painstaking or of perfect maturity of thought that I like. I do not altogether see what it is; repose is one element, but that is not all. . . .
>
> At least one thing may be learned from Walter Pater—how much a simple sentence may be made to mean. It is possible so to say a thing as to make the very manner of saying it convey your way of thought, even your character. (V. 14 [1/2/00–12/20/01] 11/30/00, pp. 34–35)

Further down the page, following a paragraph announcing his completion of the first draft of *Human Nature and the Social Order,* he refers to Montaigne's statement concerning those who "make excuses that they cannot express themselves and pretend to have their fancies full of a great many fine things. . . . They are nothing but shadows of some imperfect images." Perhaps this coda underscores his passing insecurity about his own writing and reveals the source of ambivalence toward Pater, which becomes more explicit. Thus, three years later, in lightly veiled language, he describes his feeling toward Pater's intellect, again in mildly ambivalent terms: "Pater's work well illustrates how the endeavor after a high ideal, however imperfectly successful, elevates a man and makes him interesting. It would almost seem that we may be more conscious of the ideal in a writer who mostly fails to attain it, than in one whose apparent ease makes us forget the process. Doubtless the latter is the greater artist, but the former may be nearer our sympathy" (*Journal* V. 16 [9/19/02–7/17/03] 2/4/03, pp. 64–65).

Cooley gauges his own subject matter as paltry compared with Pater's quest for the attainment of beauty and high art. The mature Cooley is warmed by Pater's style and at the same time (1908) assesses his own by comparison; he is still laboring in the shade of the oratorical Emerson, producing something too much like speech: "There is something luxurious about Pater's style; a very subtle sensuousness, a glow that makes one feel something as he does before a good work in color. . . . My style is too much like talking to have anything of this kind" (*Journal* V. 18b [2/16/08–1/1/10] 12/18/08, p. 33). As a reflection of his ambition to divest himself of the garment of oratory, Cooley's respect for Pater appears straightforwardly to be a matter of writing style. A few pages later Cooley explains, with full-blown ambivalence, that "Pater, for a mind perhaps second-rate, has notable attractiveness. It is largely his very great seriousness and painstaking; partly also his subtle seriousness and avoidance of all that is in the least harsh or coarse; partly that he treats well of deep themes. . . . His qualities are, in a way, more negative; he very subtly shuns the disagreeable: intellectually fresh and invigorating he is not" (p. 39). And scarcely more than thirty pages later he remarks that Pater holds continuing interest for him: "I read again passages I have already read twenty times." The secret is partly in Pater's subject, "Art in Life—and partly a kind of smothered passion there in his paragraphs." Cooley finds him "academic, decorous, refined, a little decadent; but he is on fire underneath" (p. 71). The next day (11/22/09) Cooley sees "an intensity of brooding insight and long-pondered passion in Pater," next to which "my writing is nervous, facile, conversational." And again he interprets the matter as one of style; Pater's intensity lies "in a kind of rhythm or slow and subtle music that he loves to set his words to" (pp. 71–72).

What is the motivation to read and reread a second-rate mind? Perhaps it is the similarity of temperament and intellect—of sense and sensibility, that both fascinates and repels Cooley. Academic decorousness and suppressed passion are qualities they share, and ones that kept the Oxford don at arm's length from the stuffy Victorian literati. Pater's aestheticism initially made him a reluctant rebel—it was bold and original, but he later suffered for it, being passed over for academic advancement, and suffering hostility from the university establishment (Monsman, 1980, pp. 2–3).

The "smothered passion" keeping Pater on fire underneath is something Cooley identifies with, and which undoubtedly reminds him of his own outward shyness, weak voice, shunning of the disagreeable, and dreams he must more and more surrender as he ages. Broadly speaking, Cooley embraces Pater's aesthetic philosophy about communicating sensibility in writing, and, thus, the aesthetic construction of reality, yet he disrespects Pater's mind; he is both attracted and repelled by the image reflected in the mirror held up to him by Pater. This ambivalence manifests Bloom's "anxiety of influence." Bloom posits that literary texts are a misreading of those that precede them. In addition to this "misprision" there is the denial of influence that these prior texts exercise on the author's works. In Cooley's case, his ambivalence, his ambiguity regarding Pater's influence on him, stems partly from their similarity, partly from Cooley's wresting Pater's aestheticism out of his literary and artistic context and superimposing it on society itself. According to Cooley, Pater, having nothing of great moment to say, nevertheless says it splendidly! Nearly fetishizing Pater's style, Cooley adopts his aestheticism without crediting him fully for it.

Cooley's Creative Misprision: Society as a Work of Art

In the same year that he commented on Pater's emphasis on art in life, Cooley posited a foundational component of his organic view in *Social Organization:* "Both consciously and unconsciously the larger mind is continually building itself up into wholes—fashions, traditions, institutions, tendencies, and the like. . . . *Visible society is, indeed, literally, a work of art, slow and mostly subconscious in its production—as great art often is—full of grotesque and wayward traits, but yet of inexhaustible beauty and fascination* [italics mine]" (1909, p. 21). If society is a work of art, who is or are the artist(s)? Mightn't the reference to an artwork presume a creative agent or agency? This sounds teleological, as though there were a social mind (Spencer's sensorium), or perhaps some other outside agent, planning, directing, and coordinating, subconsciously or otherwise. On the other hand, today it is possible to conceive of art as not agent-centered, just as in Cooley's, and before him in Emerson's, time it was possible to conceive—as Durkheim does—of religion without God. Viewing society as an artwork still entails study of the constitutive social processes of growth, development, and change. Postmodernist thinking decenters the artist and conceives of art as work and not a variety of extraordinary privileged perception and understanding (Woolff, 1981). Thus all those participating in the practice of an art including the artist, his or her teachers, patrons, pupils, critics, members of other associated occupations, even spectators (audiences) and those who make it possible for the artist to practice his or her art, must be considered, not to mention prevailing traditions and cultural influences. Viewed from this standpoint the dividing lines separating society, art, and the artist grow hazy. This brings us closer to the meaning of Cooley's simile because decentering art, creativity, and the processes and social networks associated with them, in effect embeds them in society in fields and in institutions not necessarily circumscribed by the artist in his or her studio. Cooley stipulates that society itself is a work of art. A close social science usage is the notion of transculturation, coined by the Cuban anthropologist Fernando Ortiz (1947, pp. 97–103), to capture the creative synthesis exemplified by Cuban culture. This term represents the multilayered, transformative processes initiated and pursued by the common, albeit socially diverse, carriers of a culture as well as the more lauded agents of cultural development. It was developed by Ortiz to counter the term "acculturation," which emphasizes culture change as a one-way development stemming from contact between so-called primitive and civilized societies, resulting in the loss of primitiveness and putative gain of civilization. Ortiz's term, as used by himself and contemporary writers, has been most closely associated with the development of the popular culture in Cuba. In this respect, the notion closely approximates Cooley's view of society as a work of art.

More recently Paul Willis (2000, p. ix) has developed a conception nearly identical to Cooley's by asking: "what happens if we understand the raw materials of everyday lived cultures as if they were living art forms?" Viewing art as creative of meaning, Willis places it "at the heart of everyday human practices and interactions" that produce cultural forms (p. 3); thus life and society are themselves art. Here Willis wants "to reclaim art as a living, textual thing and as inherently social and democratic," thus in opposition to the prevailing individualistic view, collectively embedding creativity in cultural forms (pp. 3, 4).

While Cooley is inspired by Pater's ecstatic view of art, he democratizes it, extending its boundaries to the masses, insisting that art "increases the more we share it, taking us out of the selfish atmosphere of every-day competition" (1918,

p. 410). Art enlarges human sympathy and animates collective ideals. In this light he views popular art as a necessity and abjures those who "deprecate . . . the poor taste of the masses, as if art were a matter of mere refinement, and not of urgent need" (1918, p. 411).

As early as 1902 Cooley analogizes society to art in *Human Nature and the Social Order,* in Chapter IV, "Sympathy or Understanding," where he says the aesthetic quality of the individual and collective aspects of mental life run in parallel: "our mental life, individual and collective, is truly a never finished work of art, in the sense that we are ever striving . . . to make of it a harmonious and congenial whole. Each man does this in his own peculiar way, and men on the aggregate do it for human nature at large" (p. 157). Society itself as a work of art is simply the collective side of the onward movement toward making life a harmonious unity. As for art itself, Cooley calls it "joyous self-expression" (1918, p. 410). Narrowly speaking, this view also derives from Pater's aestheticism which represents art with a capital A. For Pater, art *is* for art's sake: "Of such wisdom, the poetic passion, the desire for beauty, the love of art for its own sake, has most. For art comes to you proposing frankly to give nothing but the highest quality to your moments as they pass, and simply for these moments' sake" (Pater, 1873, pp. 198–99).

For Pater, "the inner world whose walls are inscribed by experience finds freedom through expression" (Iser, 1987, p. 27). In this context expression is originality; art, an enhancement of subjectivity detached from ordinary modes of existence, "creates a heaven resembling an earthly paradise" (p. 32). For Cooley, on the other hand, art could—indeed, should—be a *social* expression as much as an individual one. Thus, using the example of the medieval cathedral builders, he says: "The people who built the cathedrals were no more patient, by nature, than you and I; but they had an ideal that would not let them off with small things; age by age, progressively building church after church, each very like the preceding but better, they had learned to conceive of great architectural wholes and of the processes by which they are achieved" (*Journal* V. 16 [9/19/02–6/17/03] 1/18/03, p. 53). As for the artist, Cooley says: "He may turn his artistic sense upon the organic movement of society, see life as a play, and strive to fulfill the action; not hating the villain but requiring that he give way at the fitting time" (1927, p. 142). Thus in both his analogical and substantive uses of art, Cooley removes it from the charmed circle of a romantic/ecstatic, indivualized conception of the aesthetic experience as Pater conceives it, to the societal orbit of a democratic one. He develops this further in discussing diversity.

The Aesthetic of Societal Growth and Difference in Cooley's Sociology

Coupled with the metaphor of society as a work of art, Cooley's democratization of art diffuses the aesthetic throughout social organization, extending its operation through the social process. He builds on the social aspect of the aesthetic impulse in discussing the manner in which individualism is channeled into specialization in a differentiating society. This also derives from Pater's aestheticism, but at first blush appears so far removed from it that it is difficult to recognize.

A hint at Pater's influence here is provided by the inclusion of the *grotesque* in Cooley's description of society as a work of art "full of grotesque and wayward traits," which also recalls Pater's aestheticism. In his "Postscript" to a volume of essays (1987 [1889], pp. 247–48), Pater characterizes the romantic love of beauty as one that embraces even the grotesque: "Its desire is for a beauty born of unlikely elements, by a profound alchemy, by a difficult initiation, by the charm which wrings it even out of terrible things; and a trace of distortion, of the grotesque, may perhaps linger, as an additional element of expression, about its ultimate grace. Its eager, excited spirit will have strength, the grotesque, first of all—the trees shrieking as you tear off the leaves."[5]

If society is a work of art, then so must its least favored groups and types, its atypical, its unrecognized and unrewarded, its eccentric and its downtrodden groups, be part of that beauty. One student of Cooley's work describes his depiction of the social process as "characterized by social differentiation, cultural diversification, individual specialization, and personality individualization" (Hinkle, 1966, p. xli). In Cooley's elaboration of the process of social change the grotesque is permuted as diversity, and this discussion also is laced with aestheticism. Thus he says that "our democracy might be a work of art, a joyous whole, rich in form and color, free but chastened, tumultuously harmonious, *unfolding strange beauty* year by year. Each of us would be spontaneously functional, like the detail in great architecture [my italics]" (1927, p. 143). Some of the groundwork for Cooley's discussion of diversity is laid in *Social Organization* (1909, pp. 93–95, 126–30) in discussions of social differentiation, individuality, and communication, wherein he says that individuality and communication foster specialization, which, in turn, is enhanced, balanced, and mediated through public opinion. This resembles Pater's embracing of the relative spirit, which, initially surfacing in Montagine, is encapsulated in the appreciation of difference that Pater regards as "charming" (Donoghue, 1995, p. 275).

For Cooley, social change is emancipated from Spencerian and other organismic views of societal evolution. Society evolves as a manifestation of "the higher organic life," based on "systematic differentiation" increasingly finding its expression through democracy, and guided by the social intelligence thriving in "a corresponding diversity of environments" (Cooley, 1918, pp. 365, 369). Here we see the prosaic sociological idea of societal differentiation joined by the issue of social difference. Intelligence, identified as "the power to act successfully in new situations" is part of the social heritage, is "inseparably bound up with communication and discussion, and has always functioned for the common life which embraces the most cogent interests of the individual" (pp. 351, 355). Thus Cooley could easily find a place in an evolving democratic society for all sorts of heresies and for radical movements that prompt discussion of basic principles: [6] "It is essential to the intelligent conduct of society that radical groups, however small and unpopular, should develop and express their views. Their proposals do good by forcing the discussion of principles and so leading to an illumination otherwise impossible" (p. 368). Moreover, the university is an arena "where ideas that shock prevalent habits of thought can hardly be advocated without resisting social and academic pressure, and, perhaps, endangering one's position, or advancement that might otherwise be expected." These ideas include socialism and "other social and economic heresies, such as birth control, pacifism, or what-not, that in time may become entirely respectable" (p. 367).

As the grotesque in art challenges yet amplifies the conception of beauty, so does radicalism offer a perspective-widening "challenge to thought" (p. 368). Diversity, for Cooley, is also group differences. Thus in strikingly contemporary terms he defends immigration and immigrants "because their various temperaments and capacities enrich our life"; this is "true biologically, as regards diversity of natural stocks, and applies also to the ideals and habits of thought that immigrants bring with them" (p. 370). Likewise, with respect to the issue of language, "a common language, at least, is necessary to assimilation, but this will come naturally if our social attitude is hospitable and our schools efficient" (p. 371). One might extrapolate from this the views Cooley might entertain today regarding bilingual education; no doubt his liberalism would prompt him to advocate it, especially considering the large body of research supporting its programmatic installation in schools.

Cooley's liberal extrapolation of an appreciation of the social contributions of radicals and immigrants from an aesthetic of difference, given its origin in Pater's inclusion of the grotesque in art for art's sake, might be interpreted as patronizing. This impression is magnified by consideration of his aforementioned views on race. On the other hand, as Jandy states, Cooley had a "healthy tolerance" for the forces challenging the status quo (1942, p. 201). He, too, quotes the following passages on this subject from *Life and the Student*: "There are three irrefutable reasons why views that seem dangerous, unpatriotic or otherwise abominable should be freely expressed. 1. Discussion is the only way to modify or control them. 2. It is the only way to mobilize conservative views in order to combat them intelligently. 3. They may be right" (Cooley, 1927, pp. 21–22).

In view of this, we are reminded of the importance of contextualizing Cooley's views historically. Doing so tilts the balance back to perceiving Cooley as both reflecting his times, and, in critical ways, departing from prevailing social and political sentiments. The "Red Scares" and corresponding Palmer raids of 1919–20 testify to the growing intolerance of the times. Returning to the matter of immigration, for example, the 1920s saw the passage of the Quota Act of 1921, and the Johnson-Reed Immigration Act of 1924 that shut immigration down to a trickle. In addition, the period comprising Cooley's academic career, roughly 1891 through 1929, is overlapped by what has been called the "lynching era" of 1889 to 1945 (McMillen, 1989, p. 229). Considering these prevailing national sentiments and practices regarding difference, one is impelled to agree with Jandy's judgment. Indeed, beyond restating the sociological truism of differentiation as a corollary of modernization, Cooley integrated difference as a social issue into his conception of social organization. We cannot take lightly the aestheticism that facilitated his doing so.

Cooley's view on tradition and its role in modern society articulates well with his aesthetic conception of society. He conceives of tradition that it "comes down from the past, as opposed to convention, which "arrives sideways, as it were from our contemporaries" (1909, p. 335). They are not two separate, even opposite things, though, for a "traditional usage is also a convention within the group where it prevails." Similarly, conventions may also be traditions, new fashions adaptations of old ones (p. 337). In modern society tradition is "so intricate and spread out over the face of things that its character as tradition is hardly to be discovered; influences seems to come in sideways and fashion rules over custom." With the proliferation of "facile communication," Cooley, in line with his aesthetic view, says that tradition provides the palette from which social intelligence selects elements of social change. Hence, "all the known past becomes accessible anywhere, and instead of the cult of immediate ancestors we have a long-armed, selective appropriation of whatever ideas suit our tastes" (p. 339). Consonant with this approach, Cooley sees tradition, which other sociologists might view as backward and deterministic, "as a set of resources" to be drawn upon "eclectically and pragmatically" (Clark, 1994, pp. 279–80).

Viewing "our mental life, individual and collective, [as] truly a never finished work of art," Cooley informs us that selection in social development is a process guided by the two streams of heredity and the social heritage. These prompt us to welcome or reject "suggestions of the moment," according to whether every new influence is judged "as the painter judges every fresh stroke of his brush, by its relation to the whole . . . and to call it good or ill according to whether it does or does not make for a congruous development" (1902, rev. ed. 1922, p. 157). As an element of the selective process, aesthetics again is societally formative. Here Cooley strikingly echoes Walter Pater's praise for the prophetic quality writers attain by "immediate sympathetic contact . . . called soul . . . in style," which is "a faculty of choosing and rejecting what is congruous or otherwise, with a drift towards unity" (Pater, 1987 [1889], p. 26). According to Cooley, we do this "without deliberate reasoning," our heredity and social past serving as the filtration screen determining which influences arouse our enthusiasm or antipathy.

Likening the process of societal growth and selection of form to picking a book off a shelf in one's library, Cooley explicates the unconscious and meandering quality of social selection—the tentative method resembling the sympodial growth of a vine—using the analogy of the subconscious influence of an author on oneself:[7] "Thus if one likes a book, so that he feels himself inclined to take it down from time to time and linger in the companionship of the author, he may be sure he is getting something that he needs, though it may be long before he discovers what it is" (1902 rev. ed. 1922, p. 157). He concludes that "it is quite evident that there must be, in every phase of mental life, an aesthetic impulse to preside over selection" (ibid.). This process, however, is guided by social intelligence, a kind of imaginative mental staging or prevision wherein intelligence "as applied to social life, is essentially dramatic in character. That is, it deals with men in all their human complexity, and is required to forecast how they will act in relation to one another and how the situation as a whole will work out. The most intelligent man is he who can most adequately dramatize that part of the social process with which he has to deal" (1918, pp. 358–59).

The organic nature of the social process may require "another sort of rationality and sequence, not mechanical, consistent with a kind of freedom, which makes possible an organized development of social knowledge" consistent with it (p. 401). Cooley suggests that the "supreme aim of social science is to perceive the drama of life more adequately than can be done by ordinary observation," but that this "seems to include a creative element which must be grasped by the participating activity of the mind rather than by computations." Later on, in "The Roots of Social Knowledge" (1926 in 1930), he elaborates on this theme in a masterful treatise on qualitative methodology. In the end, the right method "is the one that may be found to give the best results" (1918, pp. 403, 401). This fits in well with what Joas adduces as intrinsic to American pragmatism, "a *theory of situated creativity*. . . . for it is a theory of the creativity of human action [Joas's italics]" (1996, 133).[8] Cooley's aestheticism enables him to move a step beyond this precept since his organic view, as much as his interactional one, incorporates spontaneous development as intrinsic to social organization and process. Thus he triangulates from the standpoints of social action and social organization, visualizing both as infused with the same principle. Hence, "the constructive part of science is, in truth, a form of art" (1918, p. 404). By extension, the drama and other literary forms "may be regarded as intelligence striving to interpret the social process as art" (pp. 359–60). All of this requires "sympathy and participation in the currents of life," and the sociologist therefore "can no more stand aloof than can the novelist or the poet, and all his work is, in a certain sense, autobiography" (1918, pp. 401–2).

Cooley's Aesthetic Misprision and His Sociological Genius

Although Cooley's conceptions of society as art and art in society in great measure derive from Pater's aestheticism, when placed in the context of his democratically tinged architecture of social organization, they turn Pater's ideas around. Pater sees art as an instrumentality heightening the individual's experience. He is a connoisseur of taste, and somewhat elitist to my taste. For Pater, art is "a detachment from and contradiction to man's ordinary modes of

existence" (Iser, 1987, p. 32). The Bloomian anxiety of Pater's influence on Cooley lies in the latter's appropriation of the former's notion of art for art's sake,
which is turned back onto society, whose ideals it animates. In this respect Cooley adapts Pater's conception of the aesthetic to the exceptionlist ethos in much
the same way as the Emersonian hero or representative man is: it is democratized, and instead of enhancing individualized experience, provides unifying
ideals for society.[9] Cooley's idealization of democracy, his incorporation of the
aesthetic of diversity into social organization, turns around the thrust of Pater's,
for it makes art plebian.

Cooley's interpolation of aestheticism into sociology is thus a "misprision,"
a creative distortion of Pater's conception. It is also a trump card establishing Cooley as a sociologist with a unique vantage point deriving from sources
outside the discipline. Aestheticism supplies the creative impetus—and the
metaphors—through which Cooley can reaffirm his faith in democracy as the
best crucible for the operation of social intelligence and the consummation
of social selection. As a metaphor describing mental (individual) and social
life, society-as-art catalyzes Cooley's thought about social organization and the
social process moving society in new directions. In retaining the humanistic
element of creativity, aesthetics is pivotal in setting Cooley's organicism apart
from cruder organismic approaches such as Spencer's. Bypassing the blindness
of purely *botanical* sympodial development, for example, he inserts novelty into
the system. It is the filigreed *image* of meandering sympodial growth—that is,
the tentative method—that attracts Cooley. The methodological implications
of the tentative, creative social process are taken up in chapter 6, reminding
us once again of the parallels between the nature of social phenomena and the
tools we use to study them.

Writ large, fine art and popular art provide society with animating ideals;
writ small, creativity permeates society in the scenaric/imaginative staging of
conduct—the operation of social intelligence—employed by various actors in
the social process. Diversity in illuminating these processes by the social issues
they entail, enriches social organization. Metaphors concerning the selection of
pigments from the painter's palette or volumes off the library shelf retain plausibility because their reference points always are social; they closely articulate
with the aesthetically laden social process. Aestheticism thus supplies the form
and contents of a unique organic view, incorporating Cooley's vision of society
and the individual as aspects of a unity.

Clearly, in Cooley's case, as with the other creative writers, the distortion of a precursor's thought does not discredit current work or author. As Bloom tells us, the work (in this case, Cooley's schemata of social organization and process) itself is "an anxiety achieved in and by the story, novel, play, poem, or essay." Thus the "strong" work "is the achieved anxiety" (1997, p. xxiii). While Cooley's work was, and perhaps continues to be, thought of as anomalous, the reasons for this also explain the fertility and usefulness of his insights for us. The essay tradition frees him from the perspectives and jargon of sociological fashion, and the humanistic frame of reference in his prose evokes "sympathy in his readers at the same time that his thoughts prod our intellects" (Gutman, 1958, p. 255).

The Relevance of Cooley's Literariness

The literary strain in Cooley's writing is a bridge to his thought and intellectual concerns. Commentators' ignorance of literary presuppositions and criteria concerning matters of literary style has led to the errors in evaluations wherein he is viewed both as an acute thinker and, paradoxically, as diffuse, or bereft of theoretical acuity. Such is the case with Mead's evaluation of Cooley's notion of the self. Speaking to a similar point is a comment made in 1958 by a sociologist (Gutman, p. 253) who remarks on "his limited capacities as a theoretician" and cites his preference for concrete experiences, arguing that as opposed to being a "virtuoso of abstraction" such as Talcott Parsons, Cooley "fill[s] in the conceptual 'boxes' with images of specific events or persons" (p. 254). Cooley's use of analogies, allegories, and other literary devices is here mistaken for a kind of a-theoretical literalism or abstracted empiricism. Despite his misperception, this commentator understands that "almost no sociologist uses the man of letters as his reference group in the way that Cooley compared himself to Goethe, Emerson and Thoreau" (ibid.).

It is clear that the essay tradition decenters the intellectual vantage point. This decentered aspect of his writing contributes to the perception of Cooley as both literal and literary, and as "diffuse," with limited theoretical capacity, whereas the issue is one of stylistic distance and not theoretical capacity at all. Certainly it is true that Cooley is not a discursive or "systematic" theorist (nor would he have been flattered to have been lumped together with Parsons, whom he would have viewed much as he did Spencer), but it should be clear that, in line with the norms of the essay tradition, the appearance of fragmentariness does not denote triviality or lack of thoroughness. Cooley's aestheticism, more than ornamentally pleasing or even intuitively suggestive of possibility, is incorporated into his understanding of the intrinsic qualities of social process and culture. The view of society as art is only just now being suggested as offering a perspective looking beyond the arts into the more mundane realms of social organization; it will be interesting to see where this is taken.

Cooley's discussion of the operation of intelligence within the social process, as an extension of his aestheticism, resonates well with the appreciation, beyond mere toleration, of difference. Such a revitalizing point of view is essential to understanding the differences of social reality "experienced most acutely by those in the excluded positions in Western society: women, homosexuals, the poor, the working class, nonwhites, the third world" (Lemert, 1992, pp. 38–39). In the contemporary broadening of the boundaries of ethnographic textuality, the discourse of the essayists is instructive, for it is centrifugal rather than centripetal, inclusive rather than exclusive, objective as well as subjective. It involves the opening of the self and the ethnographic writing genre to a wider spectrum of thought.

As I suggest in the following chapter, Cooley's shy and retiring demeanor suggests that his quietness makes him not removed, rather thoughtfully engaged, as a listener. His emphasis on reading as well as writing, which he assimilated from the essay tradition, and which is brought home to us through his congenial style, represents an openness necessary in qualitative sociological research. Deriving from his literary aestheticism, it presumes openness to context and the multitextuality of life itself. Such a premise applies to teaching as well as to theorizing and research, and this is what Cooley means when he observes that he is not so interested in creating or contributing to a graduate school research colossus as in allowing students to find their own sociological voices.

Cooley the litterateur tells us that "It is the nature of art to build languages, of which the verbal is but one. In sound, color, form and motion we beget evolving incarnations in which the human spirit can live and grow" (1927, p. 137). So too does he conceive of sociology and the sociological forum as the beneficiary of new "onward" perspectives or incarnations, including his own work. Sociology, as part of the life it seeks to understand, shares in life's dynamic unfinished beauty. Having been inspired, continuing to be inspired, and inspiring such movement within the evolving discipline he helps shape in his nonparochial manner is a cardinal virtue of Cooley's work.

CHAPTER SIX

LIFE AND DEATH AT THE AESTHETIC CENTER

Cooley's Methodology

To know men perhaps the surest way is to have simple and necessary relations with them, as of man and wife, father and child, buyer and seller, employer and workman, teacher and scholar.

CHARLES HORTON COOLEY, *Journal,* November 23, 1902

There is, no doubt, a way of knowing people with whom we do not sympathize which is essentially external or animal in character. An example of this is the practical but wholly behavioristic knowledge that men of much sexual experience sometimes have of women, or women of men—something that involves no true participation in thought and feeling. . . . Or, to put it rather coarsely, a man sometimes understands a woman as he does a horse; not by sharing her psychic processes, but by watching what she does.

CHARLES HORTON COOLEY, "The Roots of Social Knowledge"

When I imagine myself dead and forgotten I feel no such despair as might be expected in one whose sense of self is so intense. I think of the general life going on just the same, and it does not seem to matter much. . . . I wonder if my studies have not given me a consciousness of the general movement of things, and a faith in its beneficence, beyond that of most minds.

CHARLES HORTON COOLEY, *Journal,* December 7, 1902

Knowing that the essay tradition in large part formed Cooley's intellectual practice, and that aestheticism shaped his writing style and substance, it should come as no surprise that this tradition also palpably shaped his thinking on research method. Commenting on the hybrid nature of sociology Cooley says that "The sociologist needs to be at once a disinterested accumulator of facts and a vivid sympathizer with active life—things not easy to reconcile. He must have the spirit of the naturalist with much of the sentiment of the novelist and the poet" (*Journal* V. 17 [7/8/03–8/28/04] 3/29/04, p. 72). More than narrowly framing his methodology, this statement typifies Cooley's work as a whole. More than any other figures even more closely associated with the symbolic interactionist tradition, the tradition identified with the "Chicago School," whether of the so-called first or second generation, Cooley unifies the theory and method that jointly came to define it. Recent evaluations of the Chicago department and its legendary figures bear this out. In the first generation, neither Mead nor W. I. Thomas, although brilliant expositors of the theory of the self, or practitioners of its methodology, did formulate *both* theory and qualitative methodology. Cooley did do so. The same generalization largely holds for its second generation—including, for example, Herbert Blumer and Everett C. Hughes— and even for the third, which distinguished itself as carriers and expositors of the tradition (Fine, 1995; Colomy and Brown, 1995; Reinharz, 1995; Fine and Ducharme, 1995). It may be objected that Blumer did formulate both theory and method, and it is clear that he largely organized, refined, and rationalized Mead's approach, adapting it to a distinct methodological perspective (Blumer, 1969; Holstein and Gubrium, 2000, p. 32). From that perspective my generalization stands corrected.

Cooley's reading of the essayists played a deciding role in his development of a perspective holding qualitative inquiry (participant observation and broadly based ethnographic methods) as essential to sociological research methods. This methodological perspective also incorporates his approach to the self and social process based on sympathy, taking the form of a methodological tool Cooley called "sympathetic introspection." It immediately follows his opening critique of the Cartesian *cogito* and precedes his adage, "Self and society go together, as phases of a common whole" in the opening pages of *Social Organization.* Thus, qualifying Descartes's notion of introspection, Cooley informs us that this principal method of the social psychologist consists of "putting himself into intimate contact with various sorts of persons and allowing them to awake in himself a life similar to their own." In this fashion "he is more or less able to understand . . . children, idiots, criminals, rich and poor, conservative and radical—any phase of human nature not wholly alien to his own" (1909, p. 7). Throughout his life Cooley maintained this position, but seventeen years after its introduction in his published work it becomes the linchpin, based on his knowledge of the essay tradition, of an essay setting forth the foundations of qualitative methodology.

This remarkable essay, "The Roots of Social Knowledge," unlike most treatments of qualitative methodology, treats the question of method *epistemologically*, deriving it from the intersubjective character of social interaction, social process, and social organization. Moreover, his analysis also extends to the social nature of science and social science, that is, to the research process employing quantitative methods and their presuppositions. Cooley's analysis prefigures later critiques of quantitative methods such as Blumer's, which were instrumental in establishing a foundation for symbolic interactionism (Blumer, 1937 in 1969; 1939 in 1969; 1956 in 1969).

Cooley and Pascal Speak across the Ages

"The Roots of Social Knowledge" (1926 in 1930, pp. 289–309) begins with an epistemological distinction between the natural sciences and the social sciences, abjuring the positivist sensibility (social facts as measurable things) so tightly embraced by Durkheim.[1] At the outset Cooley sets up a dichotomy, deriving from one made by Blaise Pascal, whom he refers to in a 1920 journal entry. This opposes natural and social knowledge, and the sciences studying them, as divergent sensibilities, "spatial" versus "social," each deriving from the character of the phenomena they represent:

> We may, then, distinguish two sorts of knowledge: one, the development of sense contacts into knowledge of things, including its refinement into mensurative science. This I call spatial or material knowledge. The second is developed from contact with the minds of other men, through communication, which sets going a process of thought and sentiment similar to theirs and enables us to understand them by sharing their states of mind. This I call personal or social knowledge. It might also be described as sympathetic, or, in its more active forms, as dramatic, since it is apt to consist of a visualization of behavior accompanied by imagination of corresponding mental processes. (1930, p. 290)

This dichotomy reflects Pascal's opening distinction, in the aphoristic *Pensées*, between the "intuitive" and "geometric" or mathematical minds (Jacobs, 1979). As he puts it, the mathematical mind rests on palpable ("exact and plain") principles removed from ordinary life, whereas the intuitive mind rests on principles which, "found in common use, . . . are before the eyes of everybody" (Pascal, 1958, p. 1). How well this complements Cooley's aestheticism; the reader can easily see which sensibility is preferred and to where he or she is being led: feeling and seeing are subsumed under sympathy and imagination, the key components of Cooley's method of "dramatic" visualization of social processes.

When it comes to the gulf between those who reason mathematically and those who think intuitively, Pascal says that intuitive minds "cannot turn their attention to the principles of mathematics," and mathematicians cannot think intuitively because "they do not see what is before them" (ibid.). For intuitive minds, "accustomed to judge at a single glance," principles are "felt rather than seen." Moreover, the principles "are so fine and numerous that a very delicate and very clear sense is needed to perceive them." To understand and derive them mathematically "would be an endless matter" (p. 2).

It is certain that Cooley's distinction rests upon Pascal's, for in his 1920 journal entry he states, "Pascal's discussion of the *esprit géomêtre* and the *esprit de finesse* is in Art. VII," whereupon, with a very brief introduction, he sets about copying passages in French from the *Pensées:* "Of the *choses de finesse* he says, '*Il faut tout d'un coup voir la chose d'un seul regard, et non pas par progrès de raisonnement, au moins jusque un certain degré. Etaines il est rare que les géomètres soient fins, et que les fins soient géomètre*'" [We must see the matter at once, at one glance, and not by a process of reasoning, at least to a certain degree. And thus it is rare that mathematicians are intuitive, and that men of intuition are mathematicians.] (*Journal* V. 22 [4/20/1919–5/25/1925], 7/30/20, p. 30; Pascal, 1958, p. 2). This passage lies at the heart of Pascal's ruminations on the mathematical-intuitive distinction, and, of course, of Cooley's on the difference between spatial and social science.[2]

Thus Cooley nearly directly transforms Pascal's distinction into a credo of sociological methodology, incorporating the dictum that the plethora of intuitive principles are felt rather than seen, that the social-research process—observation—is implemented through sympathetic introspection, which is a refinement of the sympathy serving as the basis for social interaction—that is, social processes among selves. Cooley notes as well the observational faculty's distance from natural (mensurative) science's hallmarks of precision and prediction:

The social processes of actual life can be embraced only by a mind working at large, participating through intellect and sympathy with many currents of human force, and bringing them to an imaginative synthesis. This can hardly be done with much precision, nor done at all except by infusing technical methods with a total and creative spirit.

The human mind participates in social processes in a way that it does not in any other processes. It is itself a sample, a phase, of those processes, and is capable, under favorable circumstances, of so far identifying itself with the general movement of a group as to achieve a remarkably just anticipation of what the group will do. Prediction of this sort is largely intuitive rather than intellectual. (1926 in 1930, p. 308)

But how does the human mind participate? Again, the comparison between social and spatial science is invoked: while spatial knowledge is mensurative, social science is "dramatic," that is, it rests on the observer's capacity to replicate the configurations of thought and conduct of the observed. It is a repetition of the discussion of social intelligence in *Social Process* (1918, pp. 395–97, 400–401, 403–4). Thus, "in social life . . . [t]he dramatic element, which in biology is revealed only to a titanic imagination, becomes the most familiar and intimate thing in experience. . . . We can know it by sympathetic participation. Many find this fact embarrassing, and are inclined to escape it by trying to use only 'objective' methods, or to question whether it does not shut out sociology and introspective psychology from the number of true sciences" (pp. 396–97).

Social knowledge is based on "the inter-communicating behavior of men and experience of the processes of mind that go with it" (1926 in 1930, p. 294). Thus "human knowledge is both behavioristic and sympathetic: the perception and imagination of the external trait is accompanied by sympathy with the feeling, sentiment, or idea that goes with it" (1929 in 1930, p. 295). Social science knowledge therefore rests on "sympathetic introspection, or the understanding of another's consciousness by the aid of your own" and thereby gives "full play to the mental-social complex" (p. 300).[3]

Shuttling back and forth between principle and example, Cooley illustrates the distinction between positivist science and social science by telling us that spatial knowledge "may be resolved into distinctions among our sensations, and hence among the material objects that condition those sensations," whereas social knowledge is based on "perceptions of the intercommunicating behavior of men, and experiences of the processes of mind that go with it." The crux is that "[I]t is these latter sympathetic elements which make the difference between our knowledge of a man and our knowledge of a horse or a dog. The latter is almost wholly external or behavioristic" (1926 in 1930, p. 294). Thus, "although our knowledge of people is . . . behavioristic, it has no penetration, no distinctively human insight, unless it is sympathetic also." Here Cooley illustrates the observation that there is "a way of knowing people with whom we do not sympathize which is essentially external or animal in character" with an earthy example of "the practical but wholly behavioristic knowledge that men of much sexual experience sometimes have of women, or women of men—something that involves no true participation of thought and feeling. . . . Or to put it rather coarsely, a man sometimes understands a woman as he does a horse; not by sharing her psychic process, but by watching what she does" (pp. 294–95). So much for behaviorism!

Pascal provides the perfect lever allowing Cooley to turn the tables on mathematical or quantitative claims to exclusive certainty. The mathematical-intuitive mind distinction offers him a springboard to deny foundationalism—the monopolization of truth by the scientific or any vantage point—and to analyze the socially consensual basis of natural science. He states that spatial knowledge's affinity for measurement is no guarantee of absolute truth since "this sort of knowledge consists essentially in the measurement of one material thing in terms of another, man, with his senses and his reason, serving only as a mediator between them" (p. 291). Measurement is contingent on group consensus, as is the body of hypothesis and theory arising out of it. Thus, "what we judge to be true . . . is largely a social matter . . . yet it is far from infallible," with assent "induced by conforming influences not wholly different from those operating in religion or politics" (pp. 291–92). As he says in his journal a few pages after pronouncing "I would like to make a connecting link between science and poetry,"

> Verification is simply the consensus of competent minds. What minds are competent depends largely on the nature of the matter. If it is one of the senses all sane men may agree. If it is a remoter induction only expert judgments are competent. And as we get into social and moral questions the organization of the competent mind must match that of the phenomena to be judged. There is no line of division between things universally admitted to be verifiable, and those,

like conscience or aesthetic judgments, commonly held unverifiable. (*Journal* V. 16 [9/19/02–6/17/03] 10/14/02, pp. 18, 23–24)

Thus "there are no yardsticks in social knowledge, no elementary perceptions of distinctively social facts that are so alike in all men, and can be so precisely communicated, that they supply an unquestionable means of description and measurement" (1926 in 1930, p. 297). And "while spatial knowledge is precise and communicable, and hence cumulative, the dramatic and intuitive perceptions that underlie social knowledge are so individual that we cannot expect that men will be able to build them up into an increasing structure of ascertained truth." Hence, "I do not look for any rapid growth of science that is profound, as regards its penetration into human life, and at the same time exact and indisputable" (p. 296). As for quantitative reasoning in social science, in *Social Process* Cooley states that "while I ascribe the utmost importance to precision in preparing the data for social science, I do not think its true aim is to bring society within the sphere of arithmetic. Exact prediction and mechanical control for the social world I believe to be a false ideal inconsiderately borrowed from the provinces of physical science" (1918, p. 398). As he characterizes it, "Much statistical work, especially that based upon questionnaires or interviews, is vitiated by a lack of dramatic insight into the states of mind of the people who supply the information" (1926 in 1930, pp. 303–4). This is a radical statement, considering the scientific pretensions of many in the social sciences of his and our own times. Cooley's skepticism, abjuring "ascertained truth" and the cumulativeness of social science, might be perceived as apostasy, or at least eccentric. In short, viewing sympathetic introspection as constitutive of the self, social interaction, and social scientific understanding (*verstehen*), anchors Cooley's demystification and revelation of the presuppositions of the sciences as perspectivally spatial or social. It is a totalizing perspective, unifying society and its study.

Scientific objectivity he sees as a chimera replaceable by the recognition "that all knowledge is subjective . . . in the sense . . . that . . . it is . . . a construct of mind" rendering even the "so-called physical sciences . . . after all, part of the social heritage and creatures of the mental-social complex" (1926 in 1930, p. 297). Here Cooley's relativization of scientific methodology anticipates T. S. Kuhn's discussion of "normal" science and the essentially *social* processes and practices underlying a science's consensual template he calls a "paradigm," or a shared basic image of the science's subject matter (Ritzer, 2000, p. 461). Lack of familiarity with the essayistic basis of Cooley's thinking might make him appear "quirky" and, moreover, serve to alienate him from the central aims and ambitions of the fashionable sociological community in his and even our own day. At the same time, it makes his point of view congenial by bringing the locus of social reality closer to home to social scientists, as "the field" or site of humanistic study of society. This makes the guidelines of sociological research different, and somewhat more indistinct—that is, nonlinear—so that the highly rationalized hypothetical deductive method is replaced by a more tentative one in the sequencing of hypothesis testing, now replaced by the "hunch" or working hypothesis that may be revised, reformulated, or discarded in the course of research. Moreover, the research itself, while more systematically pursued in a given time, may be interrupted by other investigatory projects and events in one's life and then resumed, having perhaps been enriched by these interruptions in a myriad of accounted for and unaccounted ways. Such is the tentativeness presupposed by social knowledge.

The Tentative Method: Neither a Priori nor a Posteriori

Cooley's stated approach to sociological research is by the tentative method, the same process by which society, guided by intelligence, develops and changes. Simply put, "intelligence . . . has to feel its way" (Cooley 1918, p. 353).[4] Again, this takes the form of imagined scenarios: "our mental staging of what is about to happen is almost never completely true, but it approaches the truth, in proportion as we are intelligent." Darwin, whom Cooley admires as an exemplar of scientific intelligence, "felt his way among observations and hypotheses," and so also do "composers, sculptors, painters, and poets: their rapid accomplishment is the fruit of a long disciplines in trial and error" (pp. 353–54). Similarly, in a little essay, "Sumner and Methodology," Cooley informs us "that methodology is a little like religion," being "something we need every day, something we are irresistibly impelled to talk and think about, but regarding which we never seem to reach a definite conclusion." The crux of the matter is that "a working methodology is a residue from actual research, a tradition of laboratories and work in the field" (1928 in 1930, p. 326).

Here Cooley speaks from his own experience and practice. Following the spirit of the essay tradition, the tentative method is a kind of tactics initially without strategy. The strategy, or larger conspectus of research methodology, is actually uncovered, discovered, or emerges and is inextricably tied to the author's personal evolution, and so appears to be meandering, zigzagging back and forth as a kind of conversation between the sectors of one's life. In Cooley's case, this is illustrated through the evolution of his ideas on the self, whose architectonics I have laid bare in relation to the essay genre and its tradition, which Cooley adopts in his journalkeeping and his writing style—and earlier, in his published treatise *Human Nature and the Social Order.* There, as we have seen, resting on its foundation of a plastic human-social nature, Cooley methodically lays out the architecture of this "organic view," maintaining that the individual and society are two aspects of the same thing, a mental social complex constituted of and framed by the imagination, which, building on impressions and operating via sympathy, creates personal ideas and the reflexive triumvirate of the self. This treatment is extensive and includes ample illustrative—we would now call it "ethnographic"—material on Cooley's first two children that appears in notes and in his journal. In short, the concept of the looking-glass self, with its supporting theoretical infrastructure, appeared in a complete articulated form in 1902, in the first edition of *Human Nature and the Social Order.*

Six years later, however, an essay appeared, almost ex nihilo, in the form of a research report, "A Study of the Early Use of Self-Words by a Child," in the *Psychological Review.* Its rationale states that the researcher is interested in the initial use by children of names for the self in the context of everyday life and that "I was especially attracted by the interest of the matter for sociology—as throwing light on the question how far and in what sense the self-idea is a social conception—but I suppose it has a bearing on other aspects of psychology, and perhaps on metaphysics." This is followed by the statement: "Having already made some scanty observations in the development of two of my children I determined, in the case of a third, to give especial attention to this point and make as full a record as practicable of the use of self-words and whatever seemed to bear upon it, up to the time when they were thoroughly mastered" (1908 in 1930, p. 229). Finally, the report investigates the general problem "How is 'I' learned and what does it mean?'," which is peculiar owing to the "apparent impossibility of learning its proper use by direct imitation" (p. 230). Nine category listings[5] follow, each containing a summary statement or generalization and an appended listing of month-day (child's age) observations (such as 14–26, referring to the child at fourteen months, twenty-six days of age). Finally, the summary category listings are followed by detailed observations, derived from notes and observations for each month-day designation. These comprise the balance of the article; there is no extended discussion of the findings, nor any conclusion. The piece is starkly data-laden—even mundane in form and tone—containing little theory and analysis.

What is the significance of this article, the most empirically based of all Cooley's writing? He does not engage in ongoing research on the self, at least not what we usually call "research." Rather, his thought grows organically, much as he sees society growing, its different facets evolving together and separately at different rates. In the years preceding publication of the article his most intensive project was the writing of *Social Organization* (1909). It would appear that the article is redundant in his writing. In the period between the first edition of *Human Nature and the Social Order* (1902) and *Social Organization* there is no mention made of this piece in Cooley's journals, but there are frequent entries describing the behavior of Mary Elizabeth, his third child, whom he often appears quite taken with. Thus on January 27, 1907, he observes that "M. E. sits before me in the arm chair holding her Cock Robin book in her lap, wriggling about and making up stories about the pictures, often acting them; i.e., ringing the bell with her arm. She is very pretty with blue dress, blonde hair curling about her shoulders and sweet face. She is the most human and sympathetic of the family" (*Journal* V. 18a [9/9/1904–2/11/1908], pp. 106–7. Is it possible that Cooley's enthusiasm for his child prompts him to revisit his work on the self? This might be so, but he does not continue to publish on the topic, at least not in the *form* of an enduring research project. On the other hand, the stark contrast between the data-driven article and his other stylistically distinct writing might be symptomatic of the difficulty in reconciling the opposing tendencies he sees comprising sociology: "The sociologist needs to be at once a disinterested accumulator of facts and a vivid sympathizer with active life—things not easy to reconcile. He must have the spirit of the naturalist with much of the sentiment of the moralist and the poet" (*Journal* V. 17 [7/8/1903–8/28/1904] 4/28/04, p. 72). Sure enough, a note referring to "A Study of the Early Use of Self Words" appears in the first chapter ("Social and Individual Aspects of Mind") of *Social Organization* (1909, p. 8) where the Cartesian ego is refuted.

Cooley's aim as a sociologist is not to have the last word on anything. He does not view social science as an enterprise entailing the cumulative accretion of knowledge with predictability and mastery as its goals, as in spatial or natural science. Problematic configurations, whose dimensions change over time, loom larger or smaller, disappear and reappear in altered—or sometimes anachronistically identical—costume, are the stuff of his intellect. During the period in question he describes his method:

> Certainly I have not been a thorough student of fact, at least in any ordinary sense. My book-knowledge is only tasting, and I have done no personal investigation worth mentioning, *except in certain matters of child study.* Why is this? I do not lack patience, when I see that it is necessary, and enjoy study.
>
> My mind has been focussed *on problems of which the* <u>*data*</u> *were common and required no research: the thing needed was insight and synthesis.* In gaining this I have displayed patience and courage. When one intends his mind in this way he is apt to be impatient of collection unless he can see that it contributes some definite value to his result. Now the facts I have *not* gathered are of a sort that could not much have influenced my central line of thought. I need such facts for illustration, hardly as foundation. . . .
>
> Yet no doubt my method, measured by the highest standards, is hasty, and my results would be solider if I sought more for knowledge and did not strain so hard for principles [my italics]. (*Journal* V. 18b [2/16/1908–1/1/1910] 10/4/08, pp. 25–26)

Note again the *tentative* tone of this abjuration of concentrated data gathering, one that also recognizes the qualified need for such material. The article on the self *is* thus incongruous in form and style among his other work, including short essays. Cooley is not one to publish empirical research reports, and although this is not characteristic, it has dipped into his substance, that is, into his continuing interest in the self, whether the transcendental or social "I." As Robert Cooley Angell states in the conclusion to his introduction to the centennial Festschrift published in Cooley's honor, he "was neither a rigorously deductive nor inductive thinker." Nor did he "frame specific hypotheses and test them." In fact, "the best empirical work he ever did—on the self-words of a child—was exploratory in character and reached ex post facto, though important, conclusions" (1968, p. 11). Angell tells us that Cooley's gift is his talent for "brooding over common experiences and distilling from them more than what had yet been recovered from them," and of course he follows this comment up with a well-worn reference to Cooley's literary reference group, the essayists (pp. 11–12).

We can better understand what integrates and unifies our understanding of Cooley's intellectual practice by gaining familiarity with the most significant part of his intellectual back region, his journal. My work on Cooley's journal has given me a longer view and more breadth of perspective in understanding the themes of his life and work (Jacobs, 1976). Thus charting themes such as his identity passage from the oratorical to the authorial self, style in writing, representative men and inner work, provides a larger perspective from which we can more accurately and clearly perceive Cooley's intellectual process. On the face of it the article on the self comes out of the blue, but the self and its vicissitudes are of unending fascination to him because his observations of his own self and of those around him are of continuing interest. His credo is: "Following my thought, I incline to see every person as a part of myself, as a phase of that 'we' which all express" (*Journal* V. 19 [2/16/1908–1/1/1910], p. 23). We need to imagine his life as a whole in order to comprehend his intellect—"imagine" because there is no one true depiction of his, or any, life.

Cooley's diary-keeping hews to a venerable literary tradition, abounding with commentary on his reading, art and music, and all sorts of observations of his inner life, his family, friends, colleagues, fellow sociologists, professional life and travels to meetings and conventions, townspeople (mostly in Ann Arbor and surrounding communities), and travels to cities near and far. It is, as I have referred to it, the back region of his theory building (Jacobs, 1976). In his journal are the textual traces of Cooley's self and its vicissitudes. His commentary, above, on his own method does not do justice to the consistency and richness of his journal, which, among other things, provides him with what we now call "fieldnotes" on what he calls commonplace facts. True, he does not assiduously focus on one setting, group, organization, activity, institution, or set of processes. He remarks and comments on everything he comes across, leaving the maturation of his subject matter to its successive emendation in his journal, its ripening to his published writing. Thus it is with his perception of Jews, the settlement house, and the broader significance of life and death. Among his observations, a trip to New York's Jewish community on the Lower East Side in 1904, and visits to Chicago's Hull House and with Jane Addams are revealing of Cooley's intellectual practice.

These segments move between Cooley's view of the social world and of his personal and inner life and between what he observes and his own and others' thinking. Although they are not, strictly speaking, ethnographic fieldnotes, since they are not portions of extended or prolonged focused research, they come close to these in their immediacy and in the format—journal entries— in which they are done. At the same time, as we look at the larger contexts of Cooley's journals and his theory, these entries are framed in dialogue *with* these contexts. Their aim is not merely to derive, or build theory from the ground up, or, working the other way round, to interpret observed situations as exemplars of theoretical generalizations. Broadly speaking, they illustrate his tentative method as a variant of what Michael Burawoy calls the "extended case method," or the improvement of theories by "turning anomalies into exemplars," wherein we begin with "our own conjectures" and eventually "turn to some existing literature [in this case, Cooley's own theory as well as others'] with the goal of improving it" (1991a, pp. 10, 11; 1991b). Burawoy's formulation is a somewhat more rationalized one linked to the positivist hypothetico-deductive framework, but its dialogic, or, if you will, its dialectical aspect is useful here. So also is Clifford Geertz's assertion that "the essential task of theory is not to codify abstract regularities but to make thick description possible, not to generalize across cases but to generalize within them" (1973, p. 26).

Cooley's notion of sociology as systematic autobiography is his shorthand for his transposition of the essayists' conversational yardstick, via his journal among other things, into sociological methodology. The conversational discourse framing the essay tradition brings the street onto the printed page. It is but a short step from there to making participant observation a methodological credo: "The surest way to know men is to have simple and necessary relations with them—as of buyer and seller, employer and workman, teacher and scholar" (1918, p. 70). How like the mundane from of Montaigne's world, which, like Thoreau's later, was more and more deeply mined for what Cooley calls "principles" anchored in this world, as opposed to the concocting of transcendent systems. "It is for this reason," says Geertz "that the essay . . . has seemed the natural genre in which to present cultural interpretations . . . and why, if one looks for systematic treatises in the field, one is so soon disappointed, the more so if one finds any" (1973, p. 25).

Cooley as Urban Ethnographer: The Lower East Side

The essential fragmentariness of the journal has been a literary genre of its own, and broadly speaking it can be conceived as integral part of the essay tradition.[6]

In one of the most interesting extended vignettes (taking up six pages) in his journal, Cooley describes a trip to New York City in September 1904. Here his observations on the people he met and some of the events he attended are vivid and sensitively drawn. On the other hand, the spaces—what is not said—are equally intriguing. For example, we are not told why he is traveling and under what auspices, although at one point he mentions three names with their institutional affiliations; one of these, Parmelee, is immediately recognizable as a sociologist, so it is probable that Cooley was in New York for a professional meeting.[7] This material never makes its way into Cooley's published work, but it *is*, as part of his journalwriting, significant.[8]

The entry opens as follows: "Sat. Sept. 9, 1904. New York. Visited two synagogues with Mr. Billikopf (Jacob). The old men rather earnest though barely reverent, conversation, apparently of a general character, going on all the time. The young perfunctory" (*Journal* V. 18a [9/9/1904–2/11/1908] 9/9/04, p. 1). This is followed by a more detailed "visit with a woman regarding a question of charity," referring to thoughts and doubts she had about taking her mother in to live with her family in a three-room apartment. These are described as follows:

> Her mother had applied for some kind of aid to get support from her husband and children. This was one of the daughters. She explained her mother's case as due chiefly to change in environment. "In Europe the man is the only boss," etc. "You know how it 'tis in America." The wife wanted her own way. Her daughter would be willing to take her in but she (the mother) objected to the well-grounded criticism of her manners—spitting on the floor, etc., from her son in law. "Not his (the father's) fault, not her fault, not our fault."
>
> The daughter had three children and another coming. They live in three small rooms, but decent, for which they pay $18.00 a month. She was willing to take in her mother and her mother's child (own brother). B[illikopf] thought it not unlikely they were taking in a boarder." (pp. 1–2)

Cooley does not ask any questions—at least he doesn't report that he does—and offers little commentary. One might ask what he is referring to as the son-in-law's "well grounded criticism" of his mother-in-law's manners. Did she spit in front of him or behave vulgarly? There are no descriptions of the characters' appearance and dress. Beyond his agreement with the son-in-law's assessment, we do not hear about any feelings he has or judgments he made; nor is there any description of the neighborhood and environs. And preceding this, what is meant by the old men's earnestness and irreverence? One is tempted to infer that Cooley is sketching in Jewish traits. Is the perfunctoriness of the young shorthand for youthful postures taken with adults, or with visitors, or does it appear to be a typical ethnic pattern?

The following day, Sunday, he attends Jewish vaudeville in the evening: "a song called 'Columbus mit sein golden[m?] Land' (Yiddish) was one of the features." He goes to the Subway tavern, to an Italian *festa* on Elizabeth Street, and to the Haymarket on Sixth Avenue and 31st Street, "a large saloon and dance hall where prostitutes go to dance, drink and seek assignments. A few were handsome, one or two not very coarse looking." He apparently is escorted by a Jewish graduate student, and notes: "Most of the Jewish young men and girls graduate first at the City College. 80% (?) of the students are Jews" (p. 2). On Monday he goes to the Yiddish theater and sees a pessimistic play about intermarriage between a Jewish woman and gentile man that ends with a child not recognizing his origins and snowballing his maternal Jewish grandfather in the street and with the separation of the couple. He also describes visits to an Italian settlement house and discussions with labor figures. The travel entry ends a week later, on a Sunday, with a conversation with a precocious eight-year-old boy, Isidor, who is described as follows:

> Isidor says: My mother says I am 8, but I think I am 9 because I am so far ahead in school. He says he is a socialist and a free-thinker, and does not believe in God. He does not know whether he wants Debs to be elected because he does not know what kind of a man he is. He wants to read a book about him. The most determined individuality is expressed in all Isidor's conversation. He does not like his teacher, because, he says, she "picks out the wrong boy to hit." He is bent on judging everything for himself and withholds his decision in doubtful cases. He likes Longfellow and Stevenson, and especially the poet who wrote "Stitch, stitch, stitch" because he "recognizes what that woman would feel." He means to be a poet and makes little poems which he likes to say to himself. (p. 6)

There are two striking attributes of Cooley's notes: the awareness of multiple perspectives meeting within the situation, and the striving for understanding of the perspective of the actors—empathy or sympathy. Completeness of detail for its own sake is not a signal feature of his observations, but the attempt to convey the perspective or point of view of those he observes is. Thus, in the example of the daughter pondering taking her mother in to live with her and her family,

we do not need a florid description of their emotions to imagine the agony each
character faces. The situation is described from the standpoint of the mother,
daughter, and son-in-law in spare terms capturing the conflicts in points of
view and loyalties between the nuclear family and the in-laws ("Not his . . .
fault, not her fault, not our fault") as well as conflicts between the cultures of
Europe and the United States.

The description of Isidor captures the richness of the subject and his world.
The narrative is augmented by Cooley's brief, matter-of-fact observations ("The
most determined individuality is expressed in all Isidor's conversation. . . . He
is bent on judging everything for himself and withholds his decision in doubtful
cases"). One comes away with a delicately crafted image of Isidor's precocity,
but also of his childish qualities, especially in the concluding segment of the
description where Cooley transcribes the following poem written by Isidor,
followed by Cooley's coda:

> As I [sic] walking in the street
> I met my little friend
> I says to him "Hello."
> He says to me back "Hello;"
> But he never knew who I am."

He asked my name. Perhaps he means to send me his first book of poems as I
requested him to do. (pp. 6–7)

The poem, awkwardly simple and childish, is redolent of a child's sense of the
streets (the likely setting of Isidor's encounter with his friend) of the Lower
East Side. Given Isidor's straightforward opinions, preferences, and observations ("she 'picks on the wrong boy to hit'"), does one need more detail than
is offered here? Cooley's descriptions induce lively, insightful images. How can
an image be insightful? By parsimoniously conveying a rich sense of the subjective and intersubjective realities of the actors (presenting characters simply
and vividly), the richness of the subject matter itself preempts any need to resort to purple prose. In short, Cooley's descriptions, their vividness and apt
juxtapositions with commentary—that is, their positioning within the diary
text—convey meaning.

On the other hand, how Cooley selects his subject matter is not conveyed
here, nor of course, is a description of all he sees. The images of Jews one re-
ceives is that they are struggling with their share of familial conflicts, a common

theme among observers of immigrants, and that they are interested in education. Some of this verges on stereotypical "model minority" images cultivated even among Jews themselves, but Cooley gives few clues in his writing of his feelings about them. In his essay "Genius, Fame and the Comparison of Races" (1897 in 1930), however, he cites research on British Jews, comparing the well-to-do West End with poorer working-class East End Jews, which indicates that the former are anthropometrically on a par with Englishmen of the same class, whereas the latter "employed for the most part in sweat-shops upon the manufacture of cheap clothing [as were their brethren in the United States], averaged more than three inches less in stature, and were inferior also in the size of skull and in every particular covered by the measurements."[9] This, of course, implies that somatic differences are driven by social factors. On the whole this summary appears to be a "value free" assessment, but when we look at his comments on Jews and anti-Semitism in *Life and the Student* (1927, pp. 30–31), the work with the greatest affinity with his journalwriting, we find an ironic concluding paragraph that no doubt benefits from his New York experience, which must have served as a priming for his later experiences with Jews: "What is peculiarly disgusting in the Jews is their proneness to the so-called Christian virtues—humility, long-suffering, family loyalty [!], succor to the weak and the like—so repugnant to those sound principles of individual competition and the survival of the fittest by which we Christians are guided."

Reminiscences of an Ethnographer's Guide

A letter written in 1942 by Jacob Billikopf, Cooley's guide on the Lower East Side, to Edward C. Jandy, his biographer, is a significant coda to discussion of Cooley's merits as an ethnographer. This (Billikopf, 1942) states that having learned of the publication of Jandy's intellectual biography, Billikopf ordered the book. As an undergraduate at the University of Chicago he had read Cooley's *Human Nature and the Social Order,* and had met faculty "who were privileged to know this truly great man." Upon graduation he became associated with the Industrial Removal Office in New York, "whose purpose was to direct immigrants, crowding the East Side, to the vast American hinterland." At the time he lived at the University Settlement on the Lower East Side.

Billikopf recalls the visit: "Presumably Cooley wanted to know how the Other Half, particularly recently arrived immigrants, were making adjustments to their new milieu—social, economic and political." He remembers that "mine was the privilege to act as Cooley's guide, and to interpret to him the life of Jewish immigrants" and adds that "many a time we would walk up and down stairs of the tenement houses, visiting any number of families, making inquiries which would be of particular interest to Cooley." Cooley did not merely encounter immigrants in agency offices, courtrooms, or other official venues.

He remembers "as though it were yesterday, his saying to me not once but several times that it was truly wonderful how the immigrant families, with three, four and five children, living in two or three rooms, managed somehow or other to find accommodations for one or more landsleute [countrymen]." And continues,

> Cooley was deeply impressed with the type of service which the immigrants were extending to others less fortunate than themselves, and this is what he said—although I cannot reproduce his exact words: "In Ann Arbor we have large and spacious houses, small families; but when a relative comes to visit us we begin to wonder how long he will stay. An extra person or two forces a readjustment in our habits and modes of living; but here, in the fearfully crowded East Side, there is always room for relatives and landsleute.

In addition, Billikopf relates how Cooley, about to return home, expressed a desire to purchase a samovar, "the only thing he wished to bring back home with him." Knowing that he was a member of the Samovar Club at the University in Ann Arbor, "I can understand his eagerness to possess that . . . precious article"; Billikopf accompanied him to an antique shop on Allen Street (whose sign read "ANTIQUE ARTICLES MADE HERE") which had a number of samovars for sale. He reminisces that the shop owner, prevented from overcharging Cooley for a samovar, remarked to Billikopf in Yiddish that "I was not the kind of customer he craved to have in his store because I knew too much. . . . This of course with a smile on his face." When Billikopf informed Cooley about this conversation, he "was immediately pleased not to have been obliged to pay an exorbitant price, but he was also amused."

It is noteworthy that Cooley, so reputed to be shy and in an environment both geographically and socially distant from the one he inhabited, plunged into the milieu and walked up and down stairs to visit a good number of immigrant families in tenements. Moreover, his commentary on the folkways of immigrant adjustment—their willingness to accommodate *landsleute*—more than evincing simple appreciativeness, records what was for him a significant contrast with the folkways of his own people. Finally, Billikopf's letter bears witness to Cooley's curiosity, his analytic capacity in the field, and his empathic understanding—his *verstehen*.

Give and Take between the Theorist and the Settlement House: Jane Addams

Surely Cooley's love of good writers and writing, and his journalkeeping, which made writing a continuous practice for him, served him well as a sociological observer. His writing is never prolix or jargon-ridden; tutelage by the essayists has prevented him from falling into this academic trap. His love of Shakespeare and of poetry, and his reading of world literature and novels as well, all lead toward simplicity and elegance of expression; these carry through into his journal, the staple of his observation of all spheres of his life.

An emphasis on sympathy, some of it derived from Cooley, in addition to the many and varying qualities of urban immigrant realities, would be adopted by Jane Addams in her practice as an activist and social scientist. Cooley's description of Jane Addams is instructive, for it conveys the very qualities Addams admires and adopts from him in her own work in the gritty world of Chicago's immigrant neighborhoods.

In August 1906, in a one-paragraph journal entry, Cooley describes Hull House as "a very genuine place. There is no pose about it. It makes no formal pretensions and is all it seems and more. It is not doctrinaire, not overstrenuous, not denunciatory, simply honest and human" (V. 18a [9/9/04–2/11/08] 8/11/06, p. 83).[10] A few lines down, after a paragraph describing his daughter riding a tricycle, he lists his Chicago trip expenses; five pages and three weeks later, on September 2, he writes a two-page cameo of Jane Addams. What is striking about the two entries is the implicit identity of the institution (Hull House) and Addams, for they are described in similar terms. The key phrase in both is, "There is no pose about her [*or* it]." He describes Addams as follows:

> The evening I went to Hull House—about 9:30 P.M.—Miss Addams was sitting at the phone answering calls of some sort. She dresses very plainly, not looking untidy but with nothing that indicates expense or special attention. Apparently

any laborer's wife might dress as well. Her manner is kind but very undemon-strative; she talks straightforwardly, smiles little but is never cross or censorious. There is no pose about her—not even the pose of not posing, for she makes no objection to having her picture taken. She appears and is a simple, kindly, de-termined woman of much executive ability who finds a congenial career in living among the poor and sharing their problems. She is very busy—just now a member of the Board of Education, an office of great responsibility—and appears at times just a little strained and anxious. Although she took no pains to show it, I felt that she understood me as well as need be and wished to help me. I did not hear her mention religion and there was no "grace" or anything of that sort at Hull House.

If asked why I think her great I should perhaps say it was her downright human sympathy, conviction and power. She is a large, strong character dominated by love and expressing itself in a perhaps epoch-making way. In her humanity renews itself and puts forth a vital shoot.

Her "non-resistance" is simply moral resistance rather than brutal. I heard her tell of organizing a demonstration among the passengers on a ship in behalf of ill-treated steerage passengers, and threatening publicity if the conditions were not remedied.

In her immediate presence it does not occur to me to think that she is ex-traordinary, still less would one dream of saying anything of the kind to her. She would think such an observation trivial and would not take the trouble to ask herself whether it were true or not. (9/2/06, pp. 88–89)

It is clear that Cooley prefers personal portraiture to situational and organi-zational description. Hull House is given a sparse one-paragraph description, which might as well have been of a person, for it foreshadows in manner the extended description of Addams. For Cooley, the personal idea is a method-ological and stylistic tool as well; as his cameo of Addams does, it represents a concrete image grounding his observational style. One might object that this is not really sociological, until we understand clearly that he sees persons as types; they represent and are represented by their social and institutional contexts. As I have argued, this derives from Cooley's adaptation of Emerson's notion of representative men. Addams is such a representative person, particularly in the moral terms in which Cooley describes her. She defies the stereotypical images of women of the time: she has evident executive ability; she is an activist and organizer who leads a public life; she is a founder of an institution serving both as a meliorative force and as a staging area for urban reform—the settlement house—which becomes a key institution in America's growing industrial and corporate cities; and she is an intellectual, actually a trained sociologist who has interacted closely with the men of the most influential and productive sociology department of the time, at the University of Chicago (Deegan, 1988).

While Cooley and Addams certainly do not have identical perspectives, there are points of convergence in their approaches to understanding the social world. Lengermann and Niebrugge-Brantley, in their treatment of Addams's sociological perspective, state that this activist-sociologist "develops an organic rather than a linear theory, proceeding by means of narrative or illustration rather than argument, and presenting through narrative the major themes of her sociology" (1998, p. 74). This is not entirely the case for Cooley, who is not an activist and who does write abstract sociological treatises, but his literary style, and his observational material, some of which I have excerpted from his journal, do have this quality. Moreover, Cooley describes his own sociology as the organic view. In addition, Niebrugge-Brantley and Lengermann note that a key principle for Addams is to obtain knowledge of social life through direct social experience, that is, through sympathetic understanding (p. 75). Deegan makes the same point in her study on Addams and her connection with the sociologists of the Chicago school. She adds that by 1911 Addams asserts that sympathetic knowledge is the most effective way of approaching human problems and that she advocates "the use of 'sympathetic introspection,' a methodological technique later formalized by Charles H. Cooley in 'The Roots of Social Knowledge,'" and implies that Cooley's "formalization" of the notion stems from her influence (Deegan, 1988, pp. 233, 245 f.). This stretches the point, since by 1902 Cooley already had written extensively on the subject of sympathy as a key social building block and an ingredient of understanding, in *Human Nature and the Social Order*. By 1909 he had already formulated the notion of sympathetic introspection, which appears in *Social Organization* (p. 7). On the other hand, he had read Addams's work, admired it, and learned from it.[11] Suffice it to say, they influenced each other.

Another principle of Addams, which resonates well with Cooley's field reportage, is her emphasis on analyzing the "situation at-hand as a narrative of multiple vantage points." This is evident too in Cooley's vignette of the Lower

East Side, and reflects his emphasis on diversity and democratic values. Likewise, Addams states that "diversified human experience and resultant sympathy . . . are the foundation and guarantee of Democracy" (in Lengermann and Niebrugge-Brantley, 1998, p. 95). For Addams such diversity underlies a principle of action as well, as when she describes the conflict between the perspectives of Hull House resident staff and neighbors regarding the burial of a foundling child (quoted in Niebrugge-Brantley and Lengermann, 1998, p. 77), in her discussion of the relation of the charity visitor and the client in *Democracy and Social Ethics* (pp. 77–78), in her recounting of the mythical "Devil Baby" at Hull House and the variations of the rumor among the Italian and Jewish neighbors, and in her discussion of the settlement's role in bringing together Russian-Jewish male tailors and Italian and Irish seamstresses for the purpose of organizing them (pp. 90–94).

Cooley's portrait of Addams as sympathetic and with no pose about her presupposes her as a person whose role is historic, and, as he might say, one who lives in the larger life. In this case his transcendentalist leanings are muted, but still drive his portrait of her.

Facing Death from the Vantage Point of the Larger Life

Throughout his adult life Cooley maintained an abiding interest in his spiritual development. Intellectuals may or may not seek to integrate their spirituality into their professional life, but I would hazard a guess that a considerable proportion do, depending on how one defines "spiritual." In nineteenth- and early-twentieth-century sociology in the United States there is certainly a predilection to do so. Many of the first generation of American sociologists (the generation preceding Cooley—Ward, Giddings, Small, Sumner, Vincent, Hayes, and others) came from backgrounds where either their parents or they themselves were ministers, and their reformism can be seen as "a direct outgrowth of religious antecedents in their personal lives" (Hinkle and Hinkle, 1954, p. 3).[12] This is not the case for Cooley, who is not obviously a reformist, but to a certain extent the Hinkles' generalization does hold true for him because he sees in his unpublished and published work a connection between the social and the spiritual or religious spheres. Throughout his journal there are abundant thoughts about the connections and tensions between the mundane pursuits of career, reputation, fame, and business success and the "larger," or spiritual, life and aims. As a young sociologist, at age thirty-one, avoiding the mention of class, Cooley spells out some of the connections between the societal and spiritual realms, implying that reaching the spiritual summit is an affordable luxury:

> To forget self and live the larger life is to be free, free, that is, from the racking passions of the lower self, free to go onward into that self that is joyful, boundless and without remorse. To gain this freedom the principal means is the control and mortification of sensual needs and personal ambitions. But this may be carried to an extreme that is anti-social—e.g. monasticism; so the freedom of the soul may be a luxury not to be indulged. But as society progresses there arises a social freedom—a greater economic plenty and a decline of war and other forms of hostility—which permits a more general and beneficent development of moral freedom of the soul. There is a freedom of institutions which is not the freedom of the soul but is a necessary foundation. (*Journal* V. 12 [5/2/1897–7/31/1898] 2/27/1898, p. 80)

We are already familiar with the way in which Cooley's spiritual practice figures in his formulation of the looking-glass self, and it is applied more widely in his daily observations. Many of the judgments he makes about the characters of those he encounters (such as Jane Addams, whose reformist life and work makes her more acutely conscious of class) emanate from this schema: yes, there is a structural tension between social life, daily affairs, occupations and obligations, and the spiritual realm; but it is possible to transcend these, and when one does, it may show in the kind of repose and lack of pose so evident in Jane Addams. In this way Cooley brings the spiritual dimension into the social, into everyday life, and vice versa—making the mundane an arena for spiritual development.

Society challenges us in various ways, but these limitations at the same time set the conditions and tasks for our spiritual work. One thing is certain, however: one who lives the larger life is sub specie aeternitatis, that is, a dweller in another dimension transcending the everyday world. For Cooley, work on himself (his inner work) induces a kind of role distance or detachment from the social—the occupational, communal, familial, and economic provinces he lives and travels in. It is an ingredient in his stance as a participant observer of his life and the life around him. Nowhere is this more poignantly the case than in his observations of the events and behavior connected with death of his daughter, and, lastly of his own approaching death. Here detachment does not obliterate feeling, but enables Cooley to better observe his own and others' feelings and behavior. The power of his gaze and his effectiveness in harnessing it in writing invite us into the reality he lives and observes.

Journaling Death and Bereavement

Cooley's description of the death of Margaret (born August 4, 1897), his second child, evokes pathos in the way in which a dispassionate narrator in a novel might coolly convey it. The passage is bracketed by entries about proofreading the manuscript of his last book, *Life and the Student,* which he is about to send off to the publisher. The entry concerning Margaret's death begins "5/29[/26] Margaret died yesterday morning about half past eleven" (*Journal* V. 23 [6/6/1925–10/4/1928], p. 20). Most of the following page consists of a description of her stay in the hospital for childbirth, the Cesarean section done to save the baby, and the medical complications leading to her death by eclampsia. This is followed by a description of his daughter:

> M. was sweet, charming, above all, as she seemed to me *gallant.* She was not deeply sympathetic and tender—yet she loved children and quaint weak things, like kittens—you would hardly think of her as maternal. She was simple in intention, frank, loyal, witty—and gallant. She gave the impression of being rather slight to meet life, but that she would always meet it with a smile and a jaunty gesture. She was pretty, graceful and very "taking": she had many friends among women and most men admired her. She had rather a brilliant mind, and much common-sense and practical wisdom, did most things quickly and well, as if by intuition. A beginning deafness which she feared would increase, gave a slightly pathetic touch. (5/31/26, p. 22)

This is followed immediately by a reflection—actually, an observational generalization—on being gratified by the responses of others to the bereaved and a reflection on his own behavior when encountering a bereaved person: "A bereaved man is gratified by any indication that his friends, or even his acquaintances, recognize and appreciate his grief. There is some tact and art in conveying this without being awkward or intrusive. I have never been able to do it with any grace, mainly, I fear, because I do not readily feel sympathy." Note how he sympathetically introspects the feelings and behavior of those offering condolence by reminiscing about his experience of having done so, and thence, now that he is on the other side of the fence, appreciating "the tact and art in conveying this." He does not need to wallow in his pain for us to plumb it. There is no description of any encounters he has as a bereaved person with others, only a distillation of his experiences, but these are reflective. Earlier, he tersely describes his wife, Elsie, in response to Margaret's death, as "the most stricken, but is very brave," and his son-in-law, Jim, as "wonderful, considerate of every one, not at all broken" (p. 22). His description of his daughter's dying and her personality does convey pathos, shall we say, *induces* this feeling in the reader, and his observations of his wife and son-in-law, now that he has triangulated the feelings of the bereaved, need no further description to convey the family's shared sense of loss.

This observation is followed by a statement concerning Margaret's cremation and burial, then by a visit to the hospital where Cooley, his son-in-law, and daughter Mary Elizabeth see the baby for the first time: "It seemed a promising child, placid, poised and intelligent. There were a number of other babies of about the same age, some of them, I thought, with rather villainous physiognomies" (p. 23). He does not say if his pride compensates him for his grief.

Another entry, on June 6, announces that Jim and his new granddaughter will come to live with him, and concludes with a philosophical reflection on the meaning of life and death: "An individual life is a process, a strangely intensified and integrated form of that which, in diffusion, is present all about us. There is perhaps nothing essentially mysterious about its beginning and close, any more than there is in the kindling burning and extinction of a fire" (ibid.). Strange, how such objectivity conveys even greater pathos concerning the agony of our poor lives and the brevity of it all. Cooley's shift from the events surrounding Margaret's death to contemplation of the life process conveys an aesthetic appreciation of this event, as, indeed, do his writings in general. As John Dewey tells us, "because the actual world, that in which we live, is a combination of movement and culmination, of breaks and re-unions, the experience of a living creature is capable of esthetic quality" (in McDermott [ed.], 1973, 2:538). This is captured in Cooley's rendition of his daughter's death, its rippling out to the family, and its universal significance.

This passage is not stylistically different from the rest of the journal. Its fragmented character, its shuttling back and forth between descriptions of events, family members' responses to them, and reflections upon their meaning, induce in us as readers reflections on the events presented and on similar ones in our lives. This is the essence of the essay genre's reflexive character. While it would seem that writing fieldnotes is the "natural" accompaniment to doing participant observation research, until recently little thought has been given to fieldnotes themselves as professional texts. They become a part of thought as much as they reflect and embody it; they objectify the author's thought and thus are embodied by and incorporated into future thinking, whether this is confined to the informal mental process of the author or appears in writing.

In some sense this is attested to by the juxtaposition in the journal of all sorts of activities and reports of events such as the writing and preparation of Cooley's last book, which contains the most aphoristic and fragmented of all of his writing. As he puts it, "My MS Life and the Student is essentially an autobiography; a record, that is of spontaneous thoughts where unity and value, if any, is relative to my personality: that is the organizing principle" (*Journal* V. 23 [6/6/1925–10/2/1928] 8/26/26, pp. 32–33).[13]

The last words in Cooley's journal, written a month before he died, following his return home from an operation for cancer, are in the same spirit as that of his observations on Margaret's death, and, indeed, as most of his other writing. They read as follows:

> I look from my window out into the lovely April landscape, the busy men at work on the new building, the blood-roots in the garden below, and think: This is *our* world, the world of the social heritage and the cumulative achievements of men, of great traditions, of history, literature and arts, of great men, great hopes and great endeavors; the world which has been growing from immemorial time, and will continue to grow for unmeasured time to come.
>
> I think also: this is *my* world; the world in which from earliest childhood I have rejoiced to live and strive and have a part. Where I have learned and experimented and aspired, begotten children, formed and executed projects, failed and succeeded, made in the whole a helpful and honorable incarnation of myself. In this world I shall go on living; for the immediate future in my known works, and in the memories of men, for all time as an influence absorbed into the whole.
>
> The change which is about to take place is this: that my organism, and my consciousness which is a part of it, will dissolve, losing that separate and precarious height of being attained and exhausted during the years of my life, "immerging [*sic*] again into that holy silence and eternity out of which, as a man, I arose." This is a notable change, but in so far as I have lived and do live as a man, in our world,

in the great world, by no means a calamitous one; for what I care most about shall not die but live hopefully on. (*Journal* V. 24 [10/4/1928–4/7/1929] 4/7/29, pp. 17–18)

What is unique about Cooley's reflections on his own imminent death, and earlier, on his health and the possibility of dying, is that he is not preoccupied with them. The beginning of the journal volume (number 24), in the preceding October, notes he is in good health, as does a line in January 20. The first inkling of something wrong appears on February 15, where he states: "Indisposed for about 3 weeks: pulse *47*. I have had a sort of break-down of the digestion, manifested by loss of appetite and inability to digest more than a very little of very mild food" (p. 15). On February 26 he mentions having had an X-ray of his stomach, with no pathological finding. In March 15 he is in the hospital: "I am reduced to about 112 lbs., am rather yellow with jaundice and quite weak, but do not feel properly sick." He mentions that the university staff have taken over his work (*Journal* V. 24 (10/4/1928–4/7/1929), p. 16).

Throughout, with the exception of the paragraphs quoted above, there is no preoccupation with his posterity, and there is no evident melancholia. There is also a clear absence of any apparent belief in an afterlife, at least in the customary sense of a "next world," which might appear surprising considering his spiritual practice. He is a man with no regrets, satisfied with his life and accomplishments. The expostulator of the tentative method, Cooley simply sees himself, if not a discoverer of, then as "showing the way to new knowledge" (p. 3). Yet when this is juxtaposed with his foreknowledge of his death, we are moved by its emotional understatedness and simultaneous sense of the *scale* of his life, counterpoising thoughts about impending death with an appreciation of nature and the gardeners at work in it. We are given a bird's-eye view of the world he is about to leave, as though it were a Brueghel painting. As we move into this world, where he has "learned and experimented and aspired, begotten children, formed and executed projects, failed and succeeded," he evaluates his impress on it as lasting for a while. He feels confident that what he has cared for and has assisted in effecting will live on after his reabsorption into "that holy silence and eternity" from whence he came.

The absence of hand-wringing does not detract from the emotional tone of the *situations* Cooley describes. Although the events of his daughter's and his own impending death are presented in the same tone as experiences on the Lower East Side and at Hull House, one does not come away feeling that he has been coldhearted and detached. Rather, the descriptions are rich; if not teeming with detail, they are thick with meaning. A literary context has been presumed and established. Cooley is clearly an adept writer, and his delicately crafted descriptions, evocative but not effusive, aesthetic while evincing ascesis, that is, shorn of "surplusage" (as his stylistic exemplar Walter Pater called it) but providing a wealth of meaning, suffice to evoke emotion in the reader. Whether in his published work or his journal, Cooley always evokes and engages the reader's personality alongside that of the author. He does not tell the reader what to feel, knowing that his skilled writing will enable him or her to experience emotion, if not in the way he does, then at least so as to encourage the summoning of the reader's own emotional ensemble. Since feeling is the sine qua non of stylistic effectiveness, this becomes the armature from which meaning is suspended—yet again, feeling does not drown the reader. Put another way, Cooley's writing engages the reader by stimulating his or her imagination. The point is expressed beautifully by the narrator in a recent novel, *The Book of Illusions*, by Paul Auster, who in discussing his preference for black-and-white silent films over the modern cinema, tells us, "The addition of sound and color had created the illusion of a third dimension, but at the same time it had robbed the images of their purity." Sound and color "had weakened the language they were supposed to enhance," because "too much was given, I felt, not enough was left to the viewer's imagination, and the paradox was that the closer movies came to simulating reality, the worse they failed at representing the world—which is in us as much as it is around us" (Auster, 2002, p. 14). Imagination, that bugaboo of tight-sphinctered scientism, is squeezed out of the picture by positivism, aroused by literature, and awakened by thick ethnographic description. Or, as Geertz says, "To construct actor-oriented descriptions . . . is clearly an imaginative act" (1973, p. 15).

The Politics of Methods: Blurring the Boundaries of Science, Art, and Literature

Once the underpinnings of positivism are stripped away, what are we left with in the social sciences, and where does this place Cooley and his aesthetically based sociology? A recent essay, which reconceptualizes social science as a discursive practice and social structures as structures of language invented through speech acts, conceives of science as a "conversation that takes place over time" (Brown,

1992, p. 227). These are the exact terms of Cooley's own discourse. Similarly, an anthropologist's essay on postmodern ethnography terms this enterprise "in a word, poetry" (Tyler, 1986). Consider the following passage from Cooley's journal, musing on a practitioner's description of art history as a continuing poem: "Is not science an art in this large sense, and the generalizations of science a kind of interpretive poem? The sciences are intellectual arts interpreting the world for the delight and edification of men somewhat as painting and sculpture do" (*Journal* V. 22 [4/20/19–5/25/25], p. 142). This aesthetic interpretation of science was written twenty-three years after the publication of Cooley's first book, *Human Nature and the Social Order* (1902, rev. ed., 1922, p. 21), where he states that "visible society is, indeed, literally, a work of art." In chapter 5, social intelligence (discussed in *Social Process*) is conceived as dramatic and scenaric. From this standpoint social science is an extension of social intelligence employing sympathetic introspection, which works by a "dramatic method." Here "the supreme aim of social science is to perceive the drama of life more adequately than can be done by ordinary observation. . . . Or I may say that the constructive part of science is, in truth, a form of art" (1918, pp. 404–5).

To be sure, a few natural scientists might agree with these statements as a metaphoric description, but most sociologists would hesitate calling science art and its "creations" poetry, and they certainly would wince at calling society itself a work of art. Despite the claim of many denizens of the academy that they do not see research and writing as work but as fun, the view of science as a pleasurable, even passionate, pastime aesthetically engaging both its practitioners and those witnessing its performance, is far from the more familiar notion of science as contributing to cumulative discovery and the accretion of truth, or of social science as contributing to the solution of the social problems impeding human progress. Scientific work may, indeed, be described by its practitioners as a passionate undertaking, but such passion is usually explained by its importance to well-being, or its contribution to truth. Indeed, Cooley's thinking is akin to postmodern views, according to which "one reads and writes not in pursuit of truth or knowledge" but "for the pleasure of the experience" (Rosenau, 1992, p. 26). In other words, pleasure is what remains as the motivation for intellectual work once foundational pleading is removed. As Cooley proclaims, "Write only in joy. . . . *To be what you wish to write* is the first thing, then to write it—just that and nothing else, in simplicity and patience [Cooley's italics]" (*Journal* V. 16 [9/19/02–6/17/03] 3/29/03, p. 82).

Elucidating Cooley's subscription to the essay tradition clarifies how his aestheticism can be linked to current approaches stressing social science's rhetorical kinship with literature. Thus, when James Clifford informs us that "I treat ethnography itself as a performance emplotted by powerful stories," and goes on to discuss past and current ethnographic writing as allegorical (for example, as salvage of once pristine societies) "at the level of both its content and its form" (Clifford and Marcus, 1986, p. 99), we can surmise that he is motivated by something akin to Cooley's predilection to see science as an interpretive poem. So too John Van Maanen's urge to explore "how social reality . . . conveyed through writing involves, among other things, authorial voice," is akin to Cooley's casting of style as a regnant principle not only of writing, but of the practice of sociology itself (1988, p. ix). In any case, we are now witnessing a shift in perspective away from scientism among social science subdisciplines, such as ethnography, which are friendlier toward artistic and literary approaches. Thus, Van Maanen notes that the thread uniting all fine ethnographers is good writing, that is, style: "Good writing is characteristic of these figures, and it is of a kind that goes well beyond the competent ethnographic writing read by the more specialized audiences. Artful ethnography is evocative in addition to being factual and truthful. Since the descriptions and interpretations given by many of these authors are so vivid and convincing, attention to literary style and writing quality in general is heightened among ethnographers" (p. 34).

Such credence lent to style opens scientific discourse to newly emerging norms used to evaluate scientific work. In view of this, one is indeed tempted to interpret—given the pervasiveness of intertextuality—Cooley's designation of the essayists and their great conversation as sub specie aeternitatis, as a form of literary (social) interaction. Sociological notions such as the "invisible college" indeed move us toward a grasp of literary and scholarly discourse (Crane, 1972). For the time being, stuck as we are in our academic seven-league boots, let us content ourselves with the understanding that literature and art are not anomalous but contain their own strategies for grasping social truth. When their boundaries are crossed, appreciation and enrichment are our reward. Indeed, some ethnographers see the potential of the essay genre for their work. As one anthropologist suggests: "The modern essay permits, or rather sanctions, the ultimate hedge—it legitimates fragmentation, rough edges, and the self-conscious aim of achieving an effect that disturbs the reader. The essay in this postmodernist sense is thus a particularly appropriate self-conscious posture for the most radically experimental ethnographies. They want to change the conventional focus in ethnography and thus the perception of readers" (Marcus, 1986, p. 191). The reason lies partly in the postmodernist debunking of foundationalism—"the modernist belief that there are essential single truths to history" (Lemert, 1992, p. 38; see also Brown, 1992, p. 239). This is not to say Cooley was a postmodern thinker. But regardless of how we may pigeonhole him, some of his perspective can be considered congenial to postmodernism, for it is a relativizing one.

The fragmentary or reflective essay, as we have seen in Montaigne's case, in Barthes's embrace of it, and in Cooley's stylistic inspiration by it, dispenses with pretensions to objective truth because it has "renounced the economy of a philosophic system that commands the idea of Mastery" and "appears as one of those rare literary texts in which literariness asserts itself from beginning to end: as a *tactics without strategy*" (Bensmaïa, 1987, p. 54). Cooley's sociological practice embodies the essay sensibility. His research methodology shares in the essentially reflexive practice of his writing, which is manifested, as we know, in his nonlinear treatment of data as it appears in his published work. Cooley's scientific praxis—what he calls the tentative method—thus may appear as a tactics without *apparent* strategy, but now we can appreciate his agenda as embodying something quite other than the naive attribution of diffuseness leads us to believe. Conceiving of the reflexive self emerging out of conversation with itself and others counts as insightful, but, as we have seen with respect to his inner work in chapter 2, observing onself with impartiality transcends simple seeing: *this* seeing is a means of developing oneself—that is, it conduces toward *being*. Thus Cooley urges us to see more clearly, to feel more deeply, and to evolve! Viewed in this light his sociological methods, methodology, and theory merge and we see them as more than academic erudition—they are emblematic of his wisdom.

CHAPTER SEVEN

THE ECONOMY AND THE WHOLE

The Theory of Pecuniary Valuation

> I may say that the economic theorist appears like a man who
> should observe only the second hand of a watch: he counts the
> seconds with care, but is hardly in a position to tell what time
> it is.
>
> CHARLES HORTON COOLEY,
> "Political Economy and Social Process"

With a space of fourteen years separating each of two periods, Cooley's work on
the economy, undertaken at the beginning and in the latter half of his scholarly
writing career,[1] is notable for its quintessentially social character and for being
rooted in a theory of value. Cooley began his career as an economist, taking his
doctorate at Michigan under Henry Carter Adams, an advocate of regulation.
His earliest writing on the economy, beginning with his doctoral dissertation
on transportation, takes a sociological standpoint, and his earliest publication,
his work on economics—on transportation—is integrated by the organic view,
stated as follows: "transportation is a highly organic activity, requiring to be
conducted according to a comprehensive plan and by unified instruments and
methods. . . . It is an agency by which every part of society is brought into
relation with every other, and interdependence, specialization, in a word, organization, made possible." The development of transportation, reflecting and
enhancing specialization and societal differentiation, is intimately associated

with communication. In fact, transportation may be considered "the means of material communication between one place and another" (1894 in 1930, p. 104). Thus Cooley's formulation of the social is initially articulated in work done on the economy. There was no need to separately hammer out an ex post facto sociological rationale for the economy; in this respect, there is a remarkable consistency between his earliest and his later work, whether it concerns economics, the self, or social organization.

Unlike contemporary sociologists attempting to integrate the economy and society, Cooley from the beginning had effortlessly done so. On the other hand, in the process of formulating his ideas on the economy he left unquestioned certain assumptions, such as the shift in emphasis from production to distribution or exchange (Sklansky, 2000, p. 99). As we shall see, this places him as following the liberal exceptionalist ideology, supporting corporate capitalism, and therefore makes his views kindred to those of economists he criticized. Although he advocated regulation, as Adams had, he was critical of much of the economic thinking his mentor expressed. As in the case of his disagreement with his contemporaries with respect to his formulation of the social, Cooley's conceptualizing of economic institutions, based on his theory of value deriving from his organizational perspective and his notion of the primary group, stands out from the motley assortment of economic doctrines of his time.

Cooley's understanding of the economy is a noneclectic attempt to "re-embed" it in society. Moreover, it does not attempt to do so using anything analogous to a rational choice approach, which is simply a reified version of neoclassical economics to begin with. In 1918, noting that his doctorate was in economics, and that he had "only recently . . . endeavored to recover my economic foothold," Cooley asks, "What should we expect of a doctrine of economic process?" (1919 in 1930, p. 251). His answer is that such a doctrine should enable us to understand its human significance. Instead, actual treatment of the economy is "almost wholly a short-range study of mechanism . . . not at all remarkable for breadth or any light it throws on the wider economic and social significance of the mechanism which it treats" (pp. 251, 252). Thus, "the economic theorist appears like a man who should observe only the second hand of a watch: he counts the seconds, but is hardly in a position to tell what time it is" (p. 252).

Cooley's Conception of Competition as the Procrustean Bed of Society

A plausible case can be made for the continuity between Cooley's ideas about the economy (beginning with transportation as an exchange of goods and its analogy to communication as an exchange of ideas), and his ideas about social psychology, including that of the self (Sklansky, 2000, pp. 100–101). Sklansky cites Cooley's essay "Personal Competition," where he states that success, or what it is that is worth doing, is "a function . . . of what other people think," that is, the standard of living is a social psychological phenomenon "fixed by what others think" (1899, p. 222). But recalling Cooley's recollection of his emancipation from Spencerianism and the simple fact that his published formulation of the looking-glass self appears just three years later, in 1902, this comes as no surprise. Cooley's notion of the social, though somewhat further developed by 1909, was clearly in mind by 1894.

A more recondite, although original, source of Cooley's ideas about competition and the economy is Emerson's transcendental adage that "every man's condition is a solution in hieroglyphic." Jandy tells us that both Emerson and Goethe taught Cooley "to seek universals behind particulars" (1942, p. 43). Here Cooley could have remembered Emerson's corollary: "property . . . is the surface action of internal machinery, like the index on the face of a clock." In "Nominalist and Realist" Emerson says that "money, which represents the prose of life . . . is, in its effects and laws, as beautiful as roses. Property keeps the accounts of the world, and is always moral" (1929, p. 307). These ideas certainly may have prompted Cooley to state in advance of any of his published writing that "all men are constituted into a detective agency to discover what you are good for," and that "society is a vast machine the purpose of which is to organize goodness and power" (*Journal* Unnumbered [1889–91] [n.d.], p. 27).[2] Later, justifying the distinction between mental and menial or manual labor, he would comment, "Those who think govern those who toil. And, for a like reason they must control commerce and finance—because production in its complexity, is also thought" (*Journal* V. 16 [1902–3] 9/16/03, p. 99). In addition, Cooley's statement conveys his Emersonian veneration of representative men—the hero is viewed as "a valuable instrument for the elevation of morality . . . over commercial culture" (Schwartz, 1985, p. 108). Below I show how he incorporated this idea into his excoriation of the domination of the economic institutions by pecuniary values.

These are the underpinnings—the infrastructure—of the invisible hand adjusting the division of labor underlying Cooley's view of competition, class, and economy. Competition itself, as I have discussed in chapter 3, is not so intrinsically brutal as it is imperfect: it demands improvement by opening opportunity chiefly through industrial regulation and education. Since its only alternative is the "status principle" that orders caste, competition itself is rescued with the suggestion that its abuses are not intrinsic but rather caused by local groups and conditions, vices associated with other abilities of successful men, and the temporary success of speculator types. In other words, "competition simply enforces the conditions, *as a whole,* upon all competitors . . . [and] levels down or up, just as may happen" (1899 in 1930, p. 199). The solution to its excesses, as Cooley tells us in his essay on transportation (1894 in 1930, p. 104), lies in regulation: "As economic organization becomes more complicated and the various parts more interdependent, it constantly happens that the securing of general freedom demands particular regulation."

During a time when crises of corporate anarchy, as a manifestation of the capitalist contradiction between monopoly and competition, demanded a solution in policy and practice, social scientists such as Cooley hammered out the lineaments of corporate liberalism, providing ideological support and guidelines as U.S. business, big labor, government, and the public, responding to social upheavals of the 1880s, sought a modus operandi for the coming decades. Cooley's economic sociology influenced a rising group of liberal economists. As one writer surveying economic theories of the time observes, "While Cooley was less heretical in detail than some of his broad propositions might indicate, their very breadth and his emphasis on social change within the framework of the existing system helped to feed the stream of liberal economic thought" (Dorfman, 1949, p. 407).

The Theory of Pecuniary Valuation: The Social Basis of Value

The explicit formulation of Cooley's approach to the economy as a social institution appears in three papers published in 1913, reprinted as three chapters in *Social Process* (1918, pp. 293–348) and including an additional fourth chapter of *Social Process* (pp. 283–92) and a paper published during the same year as *Social Process* (1918 in 1930, pp. 251–89).

Cooley's analysis opens with a discussion of the social basis of value: "a system of values is a system of practical ideas or motives to behavior" (p. 283).
From there Cooley pursues the discussion in language reminiscent of George
Herbert Mead's description of the act: "It would seem that the essential things
in the conception of value are three: an organism, a situation, and an object."
The organism "is the heart of the whole matter" because it "is necessary to give
meaning to the idea," which translates into the organism being one of a sundry
lot comprising a person, a group, an institution, a doctrine—"any organized
form of life will do" (1918, p. 284). The situation "is the immediate occasion
for action, in view of which the organism integrates the various values working
within it . . . and meets the situation by an act of selection." The object is "in-
determinate unless we bring in the organism and the situation to define them,"
thereby imparting value designations to them. So "we speak of grain-values,
stock-values, the values of books, of pictures, of doctrines, of men" (pp. 284–85).

Despite the promise of an action perspective, a speedy exit is made from the
organism-situation-object schema to the social grounding of value and a distinction between human nature values and institutional values. Values are part
of the ethos, the mores, "or whatever you choose to call the collective state of
mind" (p. 289). They are part of organic mental life, and valuation "is only another name for tentative organic process." Thus an "organic mental life has for
one of its phases an organic system of values" (pp. 285, 288). Values can be distinguished according to whether they derive from human nature ("human values")
and primary ideals (love, ambition, fear, loyalty, honor), or from the realm of
institutions—which, containing special values, including technical ones, shape
and transform them. All human values are "mediated by social conditions" (pp.
286, 287). The process that generates values is mental but not conscious: "it
works by suggestion, influence, and the competition and survival of ideas" in a
tentative manner (p. 290).

Every sort of institutional development has special values. "Human nature
enters into them but is so transformed . . . by the system that we regard the
latter as their source" (p. 286). Moreover, human and institutional values often conflict, and "an institution . . . seldom or never corresponds so closely to a
phase of human nature that the institutional values and the immediately human
values on the whole coincide." Consequently, "no institutions . . . express adequately the inner need for beauty, truth, righteousness, and religion as human
nature requires them at a given time" (p. 289). When human nature values "are

led to take on organization and an institutional character, which carries them far away from human nature," a reassertion of the latter occurs through "the initiative of individuals and small groups" (p. 288).

Institutions have precise methods for the appraisal of values (tests of membership, sacraments, creeds, medals, exhibitions, titles, academic chairs, and so on). The pecuniary estimates people make are determined by discussion and suggestion and vary with the group and time. They are products of the same social forces that create other phases of sentiment and tradition (pp. 293–94). Social complexity is enmeshed in the value process. Consequently, "the study of value-making institutions becomes, then, the principal means of arriving at practical truth" (p. 296). Viewed this way the market—"a vast and complicated social system . . . wielding incalculable prestige"—is as much an institution as the state or church and should "by no means be understood from a merely individual point of view" (pp. 296–97).

At this juncture it is needs to be stressed that Cooley, by the standard of Joas's (2000) analysis of the social derivation of value, is making another significant mark by simply addressing the subject of value as measured by both the sociology and the economics of his and our own times. As his biographer Edward C. Jandy stresses, "sociologists in America have never paid much attention to the problem of values" (1969 [1942], p. 221). It is the institutionalists in economics (of whom Cooley is considered one), most conspicuously represented by Veblen, who take up the question, and it is they who shift the ground in economics from the fixation on price to an emphasis on group behavior and on the place habit, custom, law, and institutions occupy in determining and influencing economic behavior, and are thus able to detach themselves from the allure of economistic, that is, tautological, thinking about the economy.

According to Cooley, a flaw of contemporary political economy, with its fixation on demand (which is at its base a class phenomenon) as its root datum, is that it is not cognizant of the notion of institutions (1918 in 1930, pp. 252–53). In other words, political economy, insufficiently treating the valuation process, "starts with demand as a *datum,* assuming that each individual has made up his mind what he wants and how much he wants it" (1918, p. 297). Consequently, political economy has planted the market institution in human nature, thereby divorcing it from society (1918, pp. 7, 65, 72–73 and passim).[3] Cooley, like several contemporary proponents of economic sociology, wishes to re-embed the economy in society. As Joas observes, Cooley is "opposed to a 'naturalization' of the market and to a conception of it as a self-regulating, problem-solving mechanism. It is precisely the consequences of the interconnection of actions having economic ends that require a collective interpretation and assessment" (1993, p. 23).

Cooley's approach to value employs his understanding of institutions as crystallized phases of the "public mind" or as "phases of a common and at least partly homogeneous body of thought . . ." (1909, p. 314). On the other hand, while he views the market as an institution, it bears repeating that "an institution . . . seldom or never corresponds so closely to a phase of human nature that the institutional values and the immediately human values on the whole coincide" (1918, pp. 288–89). Thus, institutions are "human nature formulated, cut-and-dried. That which is fresh and forward cannot be formulated. So to the progressive mind institutions are ever commonplace, tyrannical and disgusting" (*Journal* V. 16 [9/19/02–6/17/03] 6/17/03, p. 116). Here he insures himself against fetishizing the economy and the market by alerting us to the kind of mechanical thinking institutions induce in us.

Cooley implies a tension among human nature, values, and institutions. Institutions are eschewed when their mediation of human nature becomes overformalized or transformed into a dead mechanism (1909, pp. 342–45). Institutional formalism is evil when "it interferes with growth and adaptation, when it suppresses individuality and stupefies or misdirects the energies of human nature" (p. 342). The apparent uniformity of the market is due to the molding of individual estimate by that institution, at first inchoately and then more narrowly channeled in the process of pricing. Thence the individual and the market interact reciprocally. As an institution the market has duration and continuity, and is no more a summation than fashion is a summation of individual ideas about dress. As individuals conform to other institutions, they do so, in a general way, to pecuniary ones. People manifest a certain individuality in their choices and thus can depart from the norm and initiate new tendencies. As we shall see, the proponents of the "new" economic sociology discuss innovation as a major stumbling block for conventional economics.

In journal material anticipating his essays on pecuniary valuation we see reflections on the marketplace that display Cooley's ambivalence toward the competitive system. The material is instructive because it reveals how his own conceptions of value run into a cul-de-sac:

Market Value, or Power in the Market is expressive of the whole social order, in all that grandeur and confusion with which nature everywhere presents herself to the finite mind. Most values, perhaps, are vital or organic, springing from the very nature of life, and such as are justified as we come to understand that life, like the commercial power of men of organizing genius. Other values or powers we must regard as parasitical, like that of the clever speculator, or the law-abiding swindler. Others again are secondary, incidental, like those of diamonds or first editions. Yet among the incidental values, derived from the taste or caprice of a few, are the values—so far as they have any in the market—of men of genius in art, letters and pure science. In general the values of the market are those of the actual world, in all its grossness: spiritual values in the higher sense, the values of the future or of the finest minds of today, are little felt in it; they are not organized. (*Journal* V. 16 [1902–3] 5/3/03, pp. 95–96)

Cooley's ambivalence about the market reflects the fragility of idealism as it runs up against obdurate reality; its venality prevents it from measuring up to the higher values he prefers. Evoking the transcendental formula, he states that the market is emblematic, expressive of nature mediated by the social order. Higher artistic and spiritual values are included among other, secondary, in-cidental, often "whimsical," yet "worldly" market values. Borrowing the tran-scendental formula of heroism embedded in representative men, he runs into a contradiction, for in democratizing the hero he must simultaneously vener-ate and excoriate the commonplace. The representative man both symbolizes and leads the age; he and the values he upholds reflect and yet must liberate society—as democracy must reflect yet emancipate a people from its baseness, lift it to meet its vaunted ideals. Cooley's antinomianism and its object, and his antipathy to the market, is strained. What then of money? Predictably, it falls into the realm of the deadly sins: "Money is rather a derivative than an original motive, except as we may come to love it for its own sake; it is a mechanism in-dispensable to the organization of life. . . . But this sort of motivation is wholly inadequate to the higher incitement of human nature. *It takes hold of us, for the most part, in a somewhat superficial way, and if allowed to guide rather than fol-low the deeper currents of character, it degrades us into avarice and materialism* [my italics]" (1918, p. 129). Here Cooley's ambivalence surfaces again. The pecuniary motive is derivative but can become primary. It is a mundane necessity and fails to "incite" the higher aspects of human nature. Character is the bulwark against it; idealism must go toe-to-toe with materialism.

The distinctive function of money, according to Cooley, is "to generalize or assimilate values through a common measure," thereby giving them reach and flexibility (1918, p. 309); it transcends any sort of value. Money thus resembles language, since it furnishes a medium of communicative growth, just as language and social organization are extended in scope by cheap printing, mails, telephones, and telegraphy. Pecuniary valuation operates through uniform currency and devices of credit and transfer. It is an expression of the total life of society (p. 310); this makes it supple, and it appears to be automatic.

Money permits the weighing of one value against another. For example, honor may call for saving to pay a debt, and friendship, righteousness, and beauty are gauged in terms of it. If there is "anything attractive about a man he soon learns to collect pay for it" (p. 313). Hence the values we think of as absolute are only "relatively absolute": "Life itself is not the absolute value, since we constantly see it sacrificed to other ends: chastity is sold daily by people not radically different in nature from the rest of us, and as for honor it would be hard to imagine a kind which might not, in conceivable situations, be renounced for some other and perhaps higher aim" (ibid.). Hence we have the notion of money as a leveler, the economic lingua franca. In this respect, Cooley's conception is similar to one taken by Talcott Parsons later. However, the Parsonian case uses money as a root metaphor for the economy as a whole: it can be used as the model for the understanding of the operations of the economy *and* of symbolic communication—"actually a language." Money thus is the model for the understanding of the "generalized media" of other institutional subsystems—the polity, kinship, and others. Society is grounded in money, and money is the detached first member of an imaginary series (Parsons, 1969, pp. 311–16). In other words, Parsons's structural functionalist schema confronts the same cul-de-sac, for money is both a derivative of, and a root metaphor describing, society. So symbolically robust, and therefore a plausible symbol of both the economy and society, it here becomes a snake swallowing its tail, for, while appearing to re-embed the economy in society, actually re-embeds the economy in the economy! Here Cooley avoids the trap of fetishizing money à la Parsons. Instead, he seeks to rescue society from pecuniary crassness by aesthetics—the craft ideal.

In Cooley's schema there is a gap as to money's origin and the relationship between value, price, and profit. Values are expressions of organizations and also are motives: we weigh one kind of value against another and our conduct is guided by the decision. So "apart from any definite medium of exchange there is a system of mental barter . . . by which values are compared definitely enough to make choice possible" (p. 332). Pecuniary valuation supplements this psychic barter by making it communicable and uniform. In effect Cooley is positing a *social* marginal utility schema in place of the more individualized, doctrinaire psychological schema of his colleagues in economics.

Pecuniary standardization ignores or depreciates some kinds of value otherwise held in high esteem, and exaggerates others that may appear to have merit—it warps life (p. 333). This is because two types of institutional conditions mediate the expression of psychical value via pecuniary ones: (1) those operating within exchange after pecuniary demand is formed; and (2) those operating antecedent to actual demand. The first is illustrated by the case of the artist who cannot sell his or her product according to its merit because of his or her ignorance of the market. The artist may lack contact with buyers, and, as in case (2) above, a buying segment may be absent to begin with because of a "low state of taste."

As to considerations underlying pecuniary demand, a technical class is involved, which stands "in the same relation to the pecuniary institution as the clergy, politicians, lawyers, doctors do to other institutions" (pp. 334–35). Their intimate knowledge of the system enables them to guide its operations in partial independence of the rest of society. This they do partly in the spirit of public service and partly for personal aggrandizement, so that the commercially ascendant class possesses—in addition to tangible (including buying) power—prestige and initiative, which enables it to set fashions and control the market. This repudiates the economists' cherished notions on economic freedom "and makes it necessary to look for pecuniary recognition of values to the goodwill of the class that has the most pecuniary power" (p. 336). Unfortunately, however, Cooley, notwithstanding his strained attitude toward privilege, shares this tendency with the upper class, for what is the ultimate difference between upper-class good will and spiritual good will? Both ultimately rest on a kind of individualistic charitable sentiment.

In addition to this commercial establishment, there is the fact that the market translates into pecuniary terms values that have already become institutionalized: the institutions the market serves—for example, the artist and circles of connoisseurs, wealthy amateurs, other taste-making and manufacturing networks, and publics which establish values translated into pecuniary terms (pp. 337–38). Values that are innovative, nonconformist, and righteous may pay least "not because moral value is essentially non-pecuniary . . . but because pecuniary valuation is essentially an institution, and values which are anti-institutional naturally stand outside of it" (p. 338). To be well-paid, initiative and originality must have power to enhance established market values. Thus the problem is to provide a standard of originality that will not become conventional. "The higher values remain . . . untranslated" (p. 321). In the final analysis this is resolved by the concentration of actual buying power of the "richer class, which is largely the same as the commercial class" (p. 335).

In short, the market is administered by a class. Class control is exerted through control of purchasing power (demand) and through actual administration of the business system, giving that class opportunities to increase its power. Note here that demand is shifted, not extirpated! The ideals of the controlling class consist of acquisitive commercialism (including the pecuniary display noted by Veblen) and caste. The class in power "is for many purposes a real historical organism acting collectively for its own aggrandizement" (pp. 305–6). Cooley comes very close to developing a notion of the power elite:

> We are all, especially in pecuniary matters, ready to join forces with those whose interest is parallel to our own: bankers unite to promote the banking interest, manufacturers form associations, and so on. The whole business world is a network of associations, formal and informal, which aim to further the pecuniary interest of the members. And while these groups, or members of the same group, are often in competition with one another, this does not prevent a general parallelism of effort as regards matters which concern the interest of the business class as a whole. The larger the group the less effective and it can hardly be denied that the capitalist-manager class . . . acts powerfully as a body in maintaining and increasing its advantages over other classes. (p. 306)

In this fashion the ruling class controls the actual administration of the market in the same manner as a powerful party controls offices with the influence of patronage. Persons having access to opportunities have enhanced market value: "They are enabled by their advantageous position to draw from the common store salaries, fees, and profits not at all explicable by natural ability alone. The effect is multiplied by the fact that limitation of the number of competitors gives an additional scarcity value to the services of the competent. . . . And the same principle is quite generally required to explain the relatively large incomes of the class in power, including those of the more lucrative professions" (p. 307).

Finally, although such a situation does not bespeak a closed upper class or caste, while "partly free from the hereditary character of the European upper classes, it is yet a true historical successor to the latter, and dominates the weaker classes in much the same way as stronger classes have always done" (p. 308). The powerful classes are still free to use their power for their individual and class advantage.

This description is hard-hitting and still apropos. So too, apparently, is Cooley's criticism of the political economists of his time. But as he excoriates their fixation on demand we actually find him suggesting a shift of the demand function rather than making a fundamental critique of it. Thus, he accuses them of failing to view demand as an expression of economic power, that is, as a class phenomenon responsible for "all the vices and degeneracy of the actual social system" (1918 in 1930, pp. 253, 254). Which is to say that the economists "assume productivity as judged on the market as the righteous or approximately righteous basis of distribution, and in so doing of course accept demand . . . as the standard of economic justice" (p. 254). This affords "no basis for a judgment of the social value of the present distribution of wealth" (p. 255). Moreover, the economists abstract competition, "the very heart of the economic process," from other aspects of society, thereby isolating and idealizing it. As for combination (monopoly, oligopoly), they have treated it only as a disturbing condition. Contemporary political economy presupposes competition as a static condition. A static condition "must destroy free competition and give rise to a rigid and non-competitive kind of organization" (p. 256). Contrariwise, free competition is actually "a phenomenon of social change."

In the tendency of competitors to "get together" (ibid.), monopolistic enterprise is created.[4] Thus the economists are inconsistent, says Cooley. He is correct on both counts, for himself and for the economists. In effect he is positing economic revisionism. The marginal utility paradigm—about which I will have a bit more to say—posits a static equilibrium through competition. Cooley tells us that free competition can only be ensured, under present monopolizing conditions, by government regulation (pp. 256–57).

Cooley is saying that competition always was and will be free only under dynamic conditions; the idealized past will be preserved by social change via government regulation. Neither he nor the economists are able to face squarely the contradictions of monopoly and competition—Cooley because he assumes the possible coexistence of the best of both worlds, the latter because they persist in promulgating the myth of perfect competition, and, at best, treat monopoly as exceptional or pathological. In actuality, Cooley's formulation exactly represents the compromise economics was working out as it was becoming a liberal social science. Cooley is in its vanguard. He believes he is incorporating a by-product of sociality—ethics—into economics. He opts for a social science that is an ethical science as well, one affording a basis for the "social value of the present distribution of wealth" (p. 255).

Cooley's criticism of political economy is tautological because it is leveled from the standpoint of political economy itself. While he accuses the economists of taking demand for granted, he does little but emend the limitations of their thinking. His discussion of class control and determination of demand does little to clarify the real source of domination of the ruling class—its control over the means of production of goods and services, except as he sees it, through consumership, taste making, and pricing. In other words, beyond the regulation of competition, Cooley adduces no other mitigating influence on class control. Hence, "pecuniary value provides a motive to serve the pecuniary organism, a motive that penetrates everywhere, acts automatically, and adjusts itself delicately to the conditions of demand and supply. . . . Thus there is everywhere an inducement to supply these goods and services which the buying power in society thinks it wants, and this inducement largely guides production" (p. 310).

Production thus simply remains a function of supply and demand; labor does not immediately enter into the picture. While Cooley understands that profit begets profit ("Commercialism tends to fix attention rather on the acquisition than the use of wealth"), he concludes that there is another sphere of production inaccessible to the market. This, outside of pecuniary valuation, becomes romantically tinged for him. He tells us that the pecuniary motive

> can serve as an effective guide only in the case of deliberate production, for the sake of gain, and with ownership of the product. The production must be deliberate in order that *any* rational motive may control it, and the pecuniary motive will not control it unless it is for the sake of gain and protected by ownership. These limitations exclude such vast provinces of life that we well may wonder at the extent of trust in the market process.
>
> They shut out the whole matter of the production and development of men, of human and social life; that is, they indicate that however important the pecuniary process may be in the field it can never be trusted to control it, not even the

economic side of it. This is a sphere in which the market must be dominated by other kinds of organization. (p. 317)

In other words, Cooley does not discuss the productive sphere itself—the workplace—as a *contestable* site, nor does he discuss class control over it as actually or potentially contested by workers. While he recognizes that the production of commodities is incidental to the nurturance and development of people and that the market's forces stunt human potential, the productive sphere is left inviolate, except perhaps through the setting apart of an *idealized* sphere of production outside the pecuniary sphere. In sequestering production, Cooley subtly shifts the focus of political economy away from labor and industrial capital to exchange and social interaction (Sklansky, 2000, p. 99). This returns us to the issue of values. Thus "personal and social development must, in general, be sought through rational organization having a far wider scope than the market, though co-operating with that in every helpful way, and including, perhaps, radical reforms in the pecuniary system itself" (Cooley, 1918, p. 318). In other words, as regards "the finer human values . . . [t]hese higher goods do not really come within the economic sphere. They touch it only incidentally, their genesis and interaction belonging mainly to a different kind of process, one in which ownership and material exchange play a secondary part" (pp. 318–19). These "higher values remain for the most part untranslated, even though translatable, and the material and technical aspects of the process have acquired an undue ascendancy." Commercial ascendancy represents the split between the ideal and the material, stifling the self-expression of "the artist, the poet, the skilled craftsman in wood and iron, the born teacher or lawyer" (p. 321). Hence *"the pecuniary motive may be said to be an extrinsic one, as compared with the more intrinsic character of those others which I have called the motives of self-expression* [Cooley's italics]" (p. 322). How could one who sees competition, albeit regulated competition, as a transcendentally directed process of social selection, think otherwise?

Rescuing Production: Creativity versus the Market

Within this framework of pecuniary valuation Cooley envisions production as sublimated into an ideal; the ideal of self-expression becomes the quintessence of production: "When I say that self-expression is a regulator of productive activity I mean that, like the pecuniary motive, though in a different way, it is the expression of an organic whole, and not necessarily a less authoritative expression" (p. 322). From here on self-expression as the apogee of production becomes somewhat mystified:

> Self-expression springs from the deeper and more obscure currents of life, from subconscious, unmechanized forces which are potent without our understanding why. It represents humanity more immediately and its values are, or may be more vital and significant than those of the market; we may look to them for art, for science, for religion, for moral improvement. . . . The onward things of life come from men whose imperious self-expression disregards the pecuniary market. (p. 323)

Thus production is conceived as a refuge from the market. The sphere of production becomes the idealized preserve of artists, writers, scientists and those with the leisure to cultivate the inner life, and is not the province of the ordinary factory laborer. Exchange is synonymous with communication, the integument of society as Cooley sees it. As one scholar analyzing the compatibility of his sociology with the emergent ideology of corporate capitalism says, "By envisioning a 'democracy of sentiment' instead of an oligarchy of property, a society governed by 'self expression' rather than 'self-interest,' he issued a sharp cultural critique of the 'pecuniary values' of American capitalism" (Sklansky, 2000, p. 92). This perspective fit in with the ethos of Progressive-era reform, which nonetheless "was wedded in complex ways to the logic of corporate capitalism" (p. 93).

Romantic and idealistic at its base, "Progressive reform" is implicitly a hierarchical sentiment, that is, a form of what we now call "moderate Republicanism." For Cooley this is exemplified by the service ideal among "producers" who are presently "guided by no ideals of group function and service. . . . This attitude is anti-progressive" (1918, p. 342). "Producers" here connotes the anachronistic preindustrial skilled craftsman and the artist: "A shoe manufacturer is no more justified in making the worst shoes he can than an artist in painting the worst pictures" (p. 342), as though, in fact, standards of factory production could feasibly be identical with those of artisanship. Quickly lapsing into nostalgia, Cooley notes that production has not always lacked ideals, "nor does it everywhere lack them at present" (p. 343). They come "when the producing group gets a corporate consciousness and a sense of the social worth of its function."

Today such ideals may be seen in some of the trades and professions, and this hearkens back to the "medieval guilds [which] developed high traditions and standards of workmanship, and held their members to them" (ibid.).

Cooley's solutions to the rapacity of capitalism are both "progressive" (that is, in tune with the spirit of reform during the Progressive era, roughly 1900–15) and anachronistic (for example, his apotheosis of guild craftsmanship, or the rejuvenation of the service ideal among the rich). The corporation of his time was well on its way toward achieving the cooperation of labor leaders, politicians, and academicians in forming a new, "responsible" business ethic (Weinstein, 1968). Cooley wishes for a new solidarity, a new spirit of cooperation among producing groups. His ideal is the syndicate and the guild, wherein the ideals of production

> come when the producing group gets a corporate consciousness and a sense of the social worth of its function. The medieval guilds developed high traditions and standards of workmanship, and held their members to them. They thought of themselves in terms of service, and not merely as purveyors to a demand. In our time the same is to some extent true of trades and professions in which a sense of workmanship has been developed by tradition and training. . . . The same principal ought to hold good throughout society, each functional group forming ideals of its own function and holding its members to them. Consuming and producing groups should cooperate in this matter, each making requirements which the other might overlook. . . . The general rule is that a stable group has a tendency to create for itself ideals of service in accord with the ruling ideals of society at large. (1918, p. 343)

In this apotheosis of the guild he comes remarkably close to Durkheim extolling the coming occupationally (based on corporations or syndicates) versus territorially organized state (Durkheim, 1933, pp. 5–10, 190). For Cooley, the puritan ideals of function and service should be embodied "in a system of appealing images by the aid of art." Likewise, in keeping with his aestheticism, we "need to *see* society—see it beautiful and inspiring—as a whole and in its special meaning for us, building up the conception of democracy until it stands before us with the grandeur and details of great architecture. Then we will have a source of higher values from which the pecuniary channels, as well as others, will be fed" (1918, p. 344). This "liberal-syndicalist" motif (Schwedinger and Schwendinger, 1974, pp. 124–29) might represent the corporatist tinge developed in capitalist ideology as it sought a nostalgic return to community without the ruling class having to relinquish its hold over the means of production.

Cooley and the Economics of His Time: The Marginal Utility Paradigm

How does Cooley's economic sociology compare with the theories of his contemporaries in economics? This calls for a more extensive discussion. Cooley took his doctorate in economics (with a minor in sociology) under the tutelage of Henry Carter Adams, a moderate reformer who had a brief romance with socialism during the labor conflicts of the mid-1880s, but who, because of threats to his position at Michigan, soon recanted, and respectably and safely became "a pioneer in search of ways for scholars in a technological, interest-oriented society to influence traditional values and policies without arousing resistance" (Furner, 1975, p. 142).

Cooley's early work on transportation and competition attest to his sharing of his teacher's and his father's views on the relations between government and business.[5] As Adams put it: "Both governmental activity and private enterprise are essential to the development of a highly organized society, and the purpose of constructive thought should be to maintain them in harmonious relation" (quoted in Dorfman, 1949, p. 168). The state does not curtail competition but determines the manner in which it operates (regulates it). By outlawing undesirable practices, it "raises the plane of competition." The state might interfere in business "to secure to the public the benefits flowing from the inevitable organization of those 'natural monopolies' which were the outgrowth of modern industrial development" (ibid.). Both Adams and Cooley favored government control as opposed to government ownership, and both preferred the expansion of municipal and state powers, as opposed to federal powers, on the grounds that "responsibility should be as close as possible to those upon whom it is exercised" (p. 171).

From the time that economics in the United States left its amateur phase (in the 1870s), its key doctrinal issue was the conflict between laissez-faire and the positive state (reform). This was fought along with that of deduction versus induction, or as Karl Polanyi would call it, "formalism" versus "substantivism" or the opposition between formal classical economic theory and the substantive historical and social issues viewed as the context for economic policies and problems (Polanyi, Arensberg, and Pearson, 1971 [1957]; Smelser and Swedberg,

1994, p. 15). The reformists were led by Richard T. Ely, who championed the "new" inductive, historical, and ethical approach. The substantivists included the institutionalists, who are discussed below.

The issues U.S. economists confronted were in part a reflection of the experience of a sizable contingent of the first generation of professional social economists and sociologists, Cooley among them, who had studied in Germany, many of them having been tutored under the exponents of the German historical school, the *Verein für Sozialpolitik* ("Union for Social Policy") or *Kathedersozialisten* ("Socialists of the Chair")—Roscher, Kneis, Wagner, Conrad, Hildebrand, and Schmoller. These German political economists, some of them advisors to Chancellor Bismarck, replaced the laissez-faire premises of English classical economics with a conception of the positive state, which was envisioned as guiding the evolution of the economy and spreading the benefits of industrialism to all classes (Furner, 1975, p. 48; Herbst, 1965; Dorfman, 1949, pp. 87–96; Hutchison, 1953, pp. 130–37, 180–86; Schwendinger and Schwendinger, 1974, pp. xvii, 86–95).[6] While their historical focus led them to study economic institutions, classes, and economic progress, they rejected utopian plans for wholesale social reorganization—socialist or liberal—and "regarded as premature historical generalizations, and the attempt to promulgate laws of historical development" (Hutchison, 1953, p. 182).

The *Verein*, organically involved with the state, were sometimes affiliated with, occasionally fought, and sometimes overlapped the "Austrian School." This school (Bohm-Bawerk, von Wieser, Menger) developed and shared the "marginal utility" perspective of Jevons (and later, Marshall) in England, Walras in France, and J. B. Clark in the United States (William Breit and Roger L. Ransom, 1971, pp. 1–30; Mary O. Furner, 1975, pp. 185–89; Joseph Dorfman, 1949, pp. 83–87, 190–205; T. W. Hutchison, 1953, pp. 32–49, 138–79, 197–215, 251–62). Essentially, the marginal utility approach was a consumer-based economics beginning with demand (the element Cooley is so critical of) or the "final degree of utility" rather than the cost of production, as in the case of the classical school. The value of commodities is thus established by the individual buyer's cost-benefit psychology.[7] It comes remarkably close to the rational choice schemes in economics and sociology.

According to this concept of consumer sovereignty, *cost ultimately is determined by consumer evaluations or the rationally calculating human who balances marginal expenditures and marginal utilities.* Commodity production serves consumption. Since an increase in production (serving demand) of a given commodity involves a withdrawal of resources from the production of another commodity, an increase in cost (or decreased consumer benefit utility) results for the other commodity. Appropriate or "ideal" production for the economy is achieved when neither an expansion nor a contraction of output can increase welfare (Breit and Ransom, 1971, pp. 10–11). Economic, moral, and social equilibrium is thereby attained. Equilibrium for the total system is attained when there is perfect competition and when supply and demand are equal.

The doctrine of perfect competition is the requisite corollary of marginal utility theory via consumer sovereignty, because only under perfect competition is it guaranteed that the entrepreneur submits to the will of the consumer. The rationality of the consumer will always induce him or her to measure the use value of the commodity by its price, and producers will adjust their prices to demand. "With consumers and producers so motivated, the conditions of competition create an equilibrium where marginal costs always equal marginal benefits" (Breit and Ransom, 1971, p. 12). The regnancy of consumption is for the marginalists an end in itself:

> To summarize, the marginalists redefined consumption not as a means to achieve the ends of the state but as an end—an individual end—in itself. Consumption, no matter how idiosyncratic, was viewed as the creator of demand and the motive for producers to create goods. The marginalists thus dramatically shifted the conceptual status of consumption from a potentially disruptive aspect of the macroeconomy to an axiomatic aspect of individual microeconomic behavior and the motive force for the entire economy. (Frenzen, Hirsch, and Zerillo 1994, p. 405)

These neoclassicists, as the marginalists are now called (recall the centrality of perfect competition to this doctrine), thus relocate the economic root—production—behind the illusion of household economy (Furner, 1975, p. 188). In this case, as Cooley observes, disturbances of demand—insufficient demand—are automatically interpreted as the fault of human nature; all of the evils of the economic system are due to the consumer (Cooley, 1918 in 1930, pp. 252–53). By sleight of hand, productivity, as judged and determined on the market, is assumed the righteous basis of distribution, and becomes the standard of economic justice. In Cooley's terms, market values thus come to supervene all other values. In this way, social class and class inequality are obscured. If "the market were perfectly free, both capital and labor would constantly follow the highest possible return," each would get its fair share, and economic social equilibrium would be attained (Furner, 1975, p. 187). The result is a patchwork affair (Cooley, 1918 in 1930, pp. 252–53).

Economics, for which the widespread acceptance of the marginalist perspective served as numbing force against social conflict, became micro-oriented and shifted its focus away from distasteful matters of class exploitation and class struggle—that is, socialism. The advent of neoclassical economics marks the true emergence of economics from political economy; neoclassicism became the hegemonic paradigm of first and last resort (Ross, 1991, pp. 118–28, 172–218).

Institutional Economics

Institutional economics is actually a congeries of approaches attempting to tunnel back to society, albeit for the most part less sociologically than Cooley. Institutional economics did not, however, rival the ascendancy of the marginal utility schema, which achieved great respectability and preeminence (Ross, 1991, p. 172). Thorstein Veblen is the most noteworthy economist associated with the early institutional approach. The term, promising a societal touchstone for economics, refracted the social whole. Besides Veblen, Cooley and B. M. Anderson in particular are the institutionalists who borrow more than an abstract premise or two from sociology. It would be arbitrary to separate institutional economists from the reformists, among whom they should be included. Thus John Commons's institutional economics is essentially a euphemism for ameliorative legislative reform and social engineering (Dorfman, 1949, pp. 276–99; Gruchy, 1972, p. 72; Weinstein, 1968, pp. 172–213); as one commentator says, "his attempt to build a complete and systematic theory was also ultimately unsuccessful, and his legacy consists of a number of episodic insights and sometimes incompletely developed theoretical notions" (Hodgson, 1994, p. 59).

Veblen, earning his reputation for radicalism by his personal lifestyle and the individuality of his thinking, but not for political activity or crusading, was a marginal man who attained the status of grand academic maverick. Along with Simon Patten, he was one of "the first American economists . . . to sense the

growing importance in modern capitalist society of consumption and its conventional character" (Ross, 1991, p. 206). His *Theory of the Leisure Class* traced
the "conspicuous consumption" of the owners of modern industry back to the
propensity to emulation and its evolution down to the present from hunters
and warriors, agriculturalists, and barbaric and feudal overlords, among whom
the wealthy leisure class displayed their power "by developing to a high art their
conspicuous disdain of work and usefulness." Their successors were the modern
owners and managers of industry "whose concern with pecuniary gain led them
to engage in and admire the same predatory behaviors as their ancestors, and
adopt the same genteel standards of reputability." For them conspicuous consumption replaced the conspicuous leisure of their feudal forebears (p. 209).[8]

Veblen is the most interesting economist of Cooley's generation because he
produced a thoroughgoing critique of the marginal utility perspective and its
methodological individualism, as well as advancing a holistic view of economic
institutions as essentially social ones. Instead of the bundle of intellect and
sensations constituting the individual as propounded by the marginalists, he
sees institutions as repositories of habit and custom providing the context for
economic behavior. This derives from and fits the view of habit and its role
in human behavior advanced by pragmatists such as Peirce (Hodgson, 1994,
pp. 60–64).

Veblen sees the marginal utility theorists as classicists in modern garb taking for granted the institutional roots of industrial and pecuniary employments
(1909 in 1947, pp. 231–51). Their static approach has "nothing to say to the
growth of business usages and expedients or to the concomitant changes in
the principles of conduct which govern the pecuniary relations of men, which
condition and are conditioned by these altered relations of business life or which
bring them to pass" (p. 233). As Cooley would notice a few years later, "pecuniary accountancy . . . extends . . . to many facts which properly have no pecuniary bearing and no pecuniary magnitude, as for example, works of art,
science, scholarship and religion" (pp. 245–46, 247). On the other hand, when
it came down to economic issues, the irrevocable split Veblen perceived between "pecuniary and industrial employments" induced him to cynically view
the encroachment of pecuniary values on all spheres of life as ineluctable.

Veblen views technology as the institution responsible for material progress.
The industrial arts, their transmission and evolution, are the clockwork of society. Businessmen appropriate this process through control of funds. From their

mad competition to outdo each other crises, depressions, and industrial disorganization result (1932 [1904]). As for the unskilled worker, it was not always
the case that the craftsman was denuded of his or her pecuniary function: specialization has now *exempted* him or her from it (n.d. in 1945, pp. 293–95). In
an essay bearing the same title, Veblen distinguishes between "Industrial and
Pecuniary Employments," and production gets lost in the shuffle. On the one
hand, "the pecuniary employments do not properly fall under . . . Production."
On the other, the laborer is only mechanically engaged in the production of
goods and is "primarily occupied with the phenomena of material serviceabil-
ity [use value], rather than those of exchange value" (n.d. in 1969 [1919], pp.
295, 294)—thus as opposed to the Marxian view, in which the labor of the
worker is, indeed, a commodity *embodying* exchange value. Thus, in Veblen's
view "[t]he business man enters the economic life process from the pecuniary
side" and is concerned with people's convictions and beliefs regarding market
values, whereas the industrial employments "begin and end outside the higgling
of the market" (p. 294).

Veblen conceives the movement that promises restoration of societal wholeness by practice—socialism—as the "most insidious and most alarming malady,
as well as the most perplexing and unprecedented that threatens the modern
and political structure. . . ." Echoing the sentiments of *The Theory of the Leisure
Class* (1912), he states that the socialist-leaning labor unionists' "disaffection has
been set down to discontent with their lot by comparison with others, and to a
mistaken view of their own interests" (p. 319). Later, in *The Theory of Business
Enterprise* (1932 [1904], pp. 158–70), he would entertain a slightly more san-
guine view of socialist thinking, regarding it as an inevitable corollary of trade
unionism.

Putting aside Veblen's views on production and craftsmanship, it is clear
that he epitomized the institutionalist rejection of economic formalism or
neoclassicism, with its individualistic fallacy. Hodgson's characterization of
Veblen's work clarifies its importance: "It is important to note . . . that Veblen's
critique was directed not only at neoclassical economics . . . but at all theories
in which the individual is taken as given. This would include much work in
the new institutionalist camp" (1994, p. 62). More broadly, Veblen increasingly
came to take the stance of the dispassionate scientist, not simply to ape the
natural sciences, but, as Ross says, to afford himself the opportunity to adopt
"the subversive stance of the radical Enlightenment and the Marxist tradition,

that science was inherently the tool of delegitimation," which, in his own case allowed as well the comfortable, ambiguous interpretation of his writing as either "tough-minded realism" or satirical debunking (Ross, 1991, p. 215).

The economist B. M. Anderson (1911, pp. 72–89) attempted to develop a theory of social value in part deriving from Cooley's organic approach in *Social Organization* and *Human Nature and the Social Order*. Anderson may be considered an institutional economist deriving his approach to value directly from sociology. He took courses from Giddings at Columbia, but criticized the latter's emphasis on an identity of content for a definition of the social mind and preferred Cooley's conception of a highly differentiated unity, including "the dissenters" (p. 82). Rebuking the economic imperialism of his colleagues he jettisoned the eighteenth-century notion of the economic man making "goods reflect the habits of men" (Dorfman, 1949, p. 418).[9] Yet Anderson's virtue was also his vice, for he confined his analysis to a highly academic critique of professional economics without actually engaging in a concrete analysis of the social foundation of economic institutions or extending it to economic and social policies. J. B. Clark, comparing Cooley's and B. M. Anderson's approaches to values and economic institutions, obliquely recognizes this by narrowly, and, in Cooley's case fallaciously, stating that both "writers demonstrate forcibly that economic values are dependent on the legal institutions of personal and property rights, and other legal regulations:

> Anderson is extremely preoccupied with the establishment of a concept of economic value as an absolute entity which shall be distinctively economic. . . . This quest leads him through paths of dialectic in which the present writer does not wholly follow him. Cooley's more realistic treatment avoids these difficulties, exhibiting the institutional character of the process underlying financial values in ways which hinge not at all on any particular definition of the tangible economic phenomenon on which these forces take effect. (quoted in Jandy, 1942, p. 228)

Considering that both Anderson and Cooley were critical of Clark's marginal utility approach, this compliment is somewhat puzzling, unless we surmise that Clark's narrow acknowledgment, confining the meaning of institution to legal ones, rests his mind about the veracity of Cooley's thinking and enables him to dissociate his critique from one leveled at the marginal utility approach as a whole.

Most of the economists of the turn of the twentieth century, with the exception of Veblen—including proponents of institutionalism in its early forms and the reformists—did little to identify capitalism itself as *the* social problem.[10] For Veblen and Cooley social institutions are inserted into the economic process as the source of pecuniary values, which, in turn, guide the relations of production frequently; but while both view "pecuniary efficiency" with a jaundiced eye, for Cooley productive relations evaporate into the halcyon spirit of the past as an idealized form of feudal artisanship, whereas for Veblen there is no rescue from the relentless contamination of "pecuniary standards of efficiency [that] invade (contaminate) the sense of workmanship" (Veblen, 1914, pp. 348–49). For virtually all economists, if the modern unskilled worker seemed such a sorry sight, how could *he or she* (not the machine process) be the foundation of the economy? The spawn of the cities, rough, improvident, occasionally militantly violent, and, in Veblen's thought reduced to the iconoclastic socialist doctrine of labor unionism—this was no economic bedrock for the nation. It was only an improvidential source of social problems. Institutionalism's unification of economy and society thereby produces its opposite, fragmentation, by dividing that whole into pecuniary and industrial sectors (Veblen), or by merely extending utilitarianism cloaked in the metaphor of social institutions (J. B. Clark, Commons).

In sum, Cooley and the most sociological of the institutionalists viewed the methodological individualism of the economics of their time as diversionary, seeing the driving force of the economy in the individual consumer or demand, thus perverting the basis of economic value or of values in general. Of course, as Karl Polanyi (1944) tells us, this posture can be taken as symptomatic of the rise of the autonomous market economy itself. The key issue then, as critics of economic formalism see it, concerns the matter of "embeddedness," or conceiving the economy and economic processes as essentially social, as opposed to seeing them as a special class of behavior so isolated or autonomous that they are not capable of being assessed as other social processes and phenomena might be. Here Cooley's approach is the most essentially sociological.

Looking back at the economic doctrines of Cooley's time, that is, the Progressive period, it is apparent that most economists adopted or worked out compromises with the marginalist paradigm, for it was compatible with mild reform and provided "simple, abstract logic for disparate economic phenomena" (Ross, 1991, p. 216). It also was compatible with, and in fact championed, quantitative

reasoning, and so provided scientific legitimation of the liberal capitalist order. This validated a social context within which the market had come to occupy a key position in the absence of a centralizing state that had conditioned
the growth and development of professional economics, as in Germany and
France. In the United States the rapid professionalization of economics was a
response to the development of research-oriented universities and an emerging
elite of full-time academicians. Thus, "American university professors had to
conquer their own legitimacy and social standing in a culture that had never
been strongly deferential to intellectual authority, and they relied upon professionalization to accomplish that goal" (Fourcade-Gourinchas, 2001, p. 426).
Marginalism smacked of scientific objectivity, salable skills, and a more plausible strategy to influence public policy.

On the other hand, the institutionalists and others touched by (German)
historicism, faced with the possibility of historical engagement that this perspective implied, were neither willing nor able to challenge the new capitalist order of enlarged corporate and industrial scale. Veblen's work, providing a
model for the institutional economists following him, "showed how economists
could accept history and legitimate change, even radical change, while assuming a stance of scientific objectivity; how they could undermine convention,
yet speak in the name of universal truth" while envisioning a "world of perpetual liberal change" (Ross, 1991, pp. 215, 216). But Veblen's jaundiced view
of the economy and society provided a very narrow ledge for his successors to
walk on and most, as Clark had done, either fell into untenable contradictori-
ness or made less discomfiting accommodations with scientism or neoclassical
syntheses.

In short, economics was congenial to and helped hammer out corporate
liberal social policy. For reformists such as Richard T. Ely, J. R. Commons,[11]
Henry Carter Adams, and other moderates and left centrists who had ventured
into social criticism and then taken their lumps, if not in the name of academic
freedom then as leading actors in academic-freedom cases, the historical school
and institutionalism served a purpose similar to marginalism, although they
were forced to refashion historicism in order to make it inoffensive enough to
maintain academic and political legitimacy. With the exception of Edward Be-
mis, virtually all the reformers who had been fired from their academic positions
surrendered their prolabor, anticapitalist, quasi-socialist, even bimetalist views

for the sake of professional and academic respectability (Furner, 1975). Professional acceptance as civic and government economic advisors and consultants afforded them greater ease in swallowing their pride. As a result, most of the dissidents fled to the more acceptable realm of applied marginal utility economics where the presumption of fair share was the moral corollary of perfect competition. Since economic morality was centered on demand and distribution, the solution of social problems would never entail more than vociferous dickering, at most, about who was getting their due. Finally, marginalism fit well with reform among moderate liberals such as E. R. A. Seligman,[12] because it "eventually provided the programming capability and much of the inspiration for welfare economics and supplied the means to welfare capitalism" (Furner, 1975, p. 189). Simon Patten was unique in recognizing the coming age of consumption brought on by the new industrial economy. He recognized that social forces were open to direction and could be used to lessen the burden on the worker. He felt, however, that capitalist progress "depended on the survival of the intelligent and the elimination of the ignorant in the 'struggle for subsistence.'" (Ross, 1991, p. 197). Eventually his view hardened and he advocated "'eradication of the vicious and inefficient [quoted in Ross]'" (p. 199).

The virtue of Ross's view of the history of these ideas lies in its bringing together under the banner of exceptionalism an often confusing array of perspectives and viewpoints. As a historical motif this works very well as a summarizing abstraction. The marginalists provided a scientific defense of the liberal capitalist order, and the liberal reformers attracted to historicism and institutionalism saw history as a counterforce to the capitalist market and conceived of it "as limiting conditions upon fundamentally beneficent economic principle." Thus, in America, the threat to exceptional historical identity posed by the "late nineteenth-century traumas of state formation and rapid industrialization" made historical change plausible and fostered in the next generation of economists and sociologists the impetus to develop what Ross calls new models of American liberal change (pp. 217–18, 303–89). Despite the apparent sophistication of current methods of analysis, recent attempts at reappropriating the economy as sociological territory have run up against the obstacles and obfuscations of methodological individualism, the uncomfortable implications of the analysis of value, the ambiguities of scale, and the problem of action—all bespeaking the heritage of their theoretical forebears.

Old Wine, New Bottles: The Contemporary Scene

Cooley, in step with some of the institutionalists, called his economist contemporaries to task for their obscurantism, that is, for enshrouding the social essence of economic behavior in the cloak of "methodological individualism" or the rational calculating individual (Smelser and Swedberg, 1994, p. 8). The issues he raised are still debated within economics and among sociologists discussing the "new economic sociology" concerning the nature of economic processes and institutions and their relationships to and within society (see Smelser and Swedberg, 1994; Zafirovski, 1999, 1997; Granovetter, 1993, 1985; Swedberg, 1990). The calculating individual, for example, motivated by utility and exercising rational choice, which mainstream economists still take without question to be the locus of economic action, remains a key point at issue among both contemporary sociologists and economists attempting to redraw the lineaments of the economy according to sociological principles.

Cooley's approach to the economy is congenial to current tendencies among sociologists seeking to truly ground the economy in society. In seeking to make economics an ethical as well as a social science, in tackling the problem of value, he attempted to do what Durkheim strove to do: to make social science moral science as well. For a number of reasons Cooley traveled further sociologically than his contemporaries and than current economic sociologists. Since it is by no means certain that the methodological individualism of the rational choice model of orthodox economics has been laid to rest, or that new structural models or neoinstitutionalists have resolved the question of value, attempts to ground the economy in society—to develop an economic sociology—are frequently caricatures of what they are pretending to be or are seeking to replace.

Added to the above is the fact that although sociological discussions of the economy have for a long time been associated with sociological theory, the grounding of economic activity in its social context means different things to different scholars (Smelser and Swedberg, 1994). Taking embeddedness as a watchword, Mark Granovetter, for example, did some pathbreaking studies concerning the sociological side of economic activity and action; but whereas earlier he narrowly equated the notion of social embeddedness with networks and thus veered toward a more rational-instrumental analysis (1985; 1989; 1994), he has more recently put networks into perspective by attempting to develop a conspectus of social economic structural phenomena on a more general scalar level, and at the same time appears to be on the verge of either abandoning or enriching network analysis itself (2002). Thus, decrying the dangers of the tunnel vision that network analysis can induce, he calls for a more complex synthesis and to connect social networks to the body of more central concerns of sociological theory such as solidarity, power, and norms; their "very definition relies on social relations, and they are produced in networks, as is well understood in the 'classics' of Durkheim, Weber, Simmel and Marx" (2002, p. 54).

Grannovetter would do well to take his cue from the interpretive understanding Weber offers but which the pragmatic tradition actually fleshes out, because at this juncture his analysis faces the risk of being detoured into another rationalistic cul-de-sac. He needs to explore the "relational," going beyond describing "network configurations," as he wishes to, but not explaining them, as he expects to, by resorting to mechanistic metaphors used in describing the structures ("highly decoupled," "weakly coupled" and "highly coupled") that are the contexts for economic action.[13] This ambiguity is the source of an uncertain future for network analysis. In this way, although attempting to find the linkage between structure and agency, he runs into a dead end as soon as he confronts concrete issues of trust and cooperation, incentives, power and compliance, and norms and identities, all which "condition" economic actors. As he says, "While I naturally believe that many of the important contributions of economic sociology stem from its interest in network analysis [cf. Granovetter, 1985], a focus on the *mechanics* of networks alone is not sufficiently distinctive theoretically from instrumentalist theories to lead us toward the more complex synthesis that we seek in understanding the economy [my italics]" (2002, p. 54). Hence Granovetter is still talking around the subject, explaining it away by resort to a higher scalar structural architecture, or confining it to an ever more snarled, mechanistic network topography. Although he sneers at values, he might also benefit from Cooley's linked value-action-institutional perspective.[14]

Explicitly pursuing the theme of embeddedness, Jens Beckert's discussion (1999) takes the interpretive tack, placing economic action within a Meadian or symbolic interactionist context. Beckert attempts to develop an alternative to the rational choice model. He argues that the meaning and perceptions of rationality are intersubjectively established in the action process, thereby making embeddedness comprise the social construction of meaning in interpretative acts. Thus he attempts to develop an understanding of economic actions explaining what actors actually decide to do in complex economic situation. Here economic action is viewed as noncalculative because it is based on unreflected routines; but when routines fail, reflexive forms of intentionality emerge and actors begin experimenting and innovating, leading to conceptions of possible future states. Such reflection makes rationality (now as a social construction) possible without implying its objective existence, as formal economic reasoning does (pp. 12–14). Reflection also enables one to account for the inherent complexity and novelty of economic life, which eludes the rational choice model. To this end, Beckert adapts John Dewey's notion of "ends-in-view" in which economic scenarios, action plans, ideas, and theories are formulated and continually revised (p. 27). This comes strikingly close to Cooley's conception of intelligence as dramatic, which appears in *Social Process*, in a chapter following his discussion of the process of pecuniary valuation (1918, pp. 358–59):

> It seems that intelligence, as applied to social life, is essentially dramatic in character. That is, it deals with men in all their human complexity, and is required to forecast how they will act in relation to one another and how the situation as a whole will work out. . . . [W]hat is the stock market but a continuous drama, successful participation in which depends upon the power to apprehend some phase of it as a moving whole and foresee its destiny?

In other words, Beckert has arrived at the point where Cooley left off. His analysis, however, remains on the level of social psychology.

Interestingly, Beckert's Meadian approach and Veblen's earlier institutional one both hearken back to the pragmatists, the first via the problem-solving approach of Dewey and the symbolically mediated interaction processes of Mead, and the second via the application of the pragmatists' notion to economic social institutions. Unfortunately Veblen's lead has not been followed by today's scholars calling themselves the neoinstitutionalists, most of whom share the common proposition "that the individual can, in a sense, be taken for granted," since "the individual, along with his or her assumed behavioral characteristics, is taken as the elemental building block in the theory of the social or economic stystem" (Hodgson, 1994, pp. 69–70). Many of the new institutionalists express disdain for the contributions of their namesake predecessors. It appears that they have thrown out the baby with the bathwater, and along with contemporary rational choice sociologists returned to the fold of the neoclassicists, thus having continued the ambiguous tradition of the earlier institutionalists in seeking scientific respectability via a compromise with individualism.

Rational choice *sociologists* such as Coleman have turned around and reified *Homo economicus* by superimposing that model, that is, a model of rational choice and methodological individualism, onto the social world (Coleman, 1994: Smelser and Swedberg, 1994, p. 17). Such attempts seem to have great plausibility, for they appeal to the Enlightenment conceit of having reason on their side. On the other hand, as Hodgson says, discussion of Veblen has been revived along with other conceptual developments, such as "path-dependency, cumulative causation, and lock-in, all of which have a strong institutionalist ring." Yet, at the same time it appears that "[i]nstitutionalism is not yet sufficiently developed to replace orthodoxy" (Hodgson, 1994, p. 71). All in all, the matter of institutionalism has not been settled, possibly because at base it, like its predecessors, must confront the normative basis of all institutions, thus forcing sociologists to once again face the problem of value. As a result, many of the same problems, dilemmas, and debates regarding the putative social foundations of the economy (and of economics) persist. What does all of this suggest in terms of Cooley's position and relevance to economic sociology today?

Since Cooley is not even mentioned in the works of contemporary economic sociologists, it is clear that they are unaware of, or do not consider useful, his pathbreaking approach to the economy. At the very least, the precedents he set need to be addressed, particularly his approach to pecuniary values and institutions. Second, his implicit critique of market values and appeal to resurrect the guild ethic, which can be considered anachronistic, nevertheless—like Durkheim's parallel apotheosis of the communal corporate ethic (1933, pp. 22–30)—bears hearing in this day of the so-called global eclipse of community and even of nation-states, for it brings back into focus a truly sociological way of discussing economic processes, institutions, policies, and events. His discussion of economic institutions can bear fruit, for while many agree that other social institutions are integrally related to economic ones such as the market, there currently is great ambiguity in deciding "which social structures are necessary, the conditions that are necessary for markets to exist, and which of these issues are important to study" (Fligstein, 2002, p. 70). Cooley's approach sheds light on this question.

Finally, Cooley's analysis of value, despite its contradictions, if rendered more appreciative of the constructive side of social conflict, and closely aligned with his discussion of creative social intelligence, could provide welcome leads in the discussion of how novelty and change originate and figure in the economy.

This could also foster the building of models of economic action as alternates to the rational choice model, which he criticizes. Cooley's economic sociology thus provides a reference point or forum for the convergence of key issues integrating economics and sociology. His confident venture into the realm of values as it encompasses economic action and institutions stands outside the periphery of a controversy dividing sociologists who "view human action as the pursuit of self-advantage or clear interests, or at the very least stable and largely context-independent preferences, and those who emphasize the irreducible character of the normative dimension of human action" (Joas, 2000, p. 13). For Cooley, the higher "primary" values or deals both derive from and serve as points of reference for democracy: they reflect the prevailing values of society and its constituent communities, institutions, and associations. While all may not agree with his prioritization of higher and lower values, the method he uses to analyze their place in the economy, and his critique of the fashionable economics of his time, which essentially prefigure the dilemmas of our own time, stands as an exemplar of how analysis may proceed.

APPENDIX

A Note on Cooley's Journal and Its Use Herein

> My journals might conceivably be published just as I wrote them,
> deriving unity and interest from their natural relation to my life;
> but to use the material otherwise requires a new effort and syn-
> thesis. It is only fragments, rudiments of thought. I must select
> and develop what is fresh and germinal.
>
> CHARLES HORTON COOLEY, *Journal*, April 25, 1919

Cooley's journal begins in 1882, when he was eighteen years old. He kept it for about forty-six years, until just a few weeks before his death on May 8, 1929, the last entry being on April 7. Examination of the journal, in addition to his published writing, discloses the deeper and more subtle infrastructure of his theory building. His journal served, among other things, as an intellectual laboratory and staging area for his ideas. In it he recorded his observations on himself and his chagrins, joys, satisfactions, failures, and accomplishments; on his family, the people he met and knew, his ruminations and speculations about society; on tentative plans for future sociological writing projects; on art, philosophy, religion, what he read, and his experiences and travels. It served also as a commonplace book in which he copied passages of others, sometimes several pages long.

As a genre unto itself, the diary adds yet another dimension to Cooley's literary background. Elsewhere, I have analyzed it as a "back region" of Cooley's thought (Jacobs, 1976). It represents what authors have called the journal genre: a sheltered and relatively unguarded, if not entirely private, medium. It also conforms to what some say is a frequently multifaceted genre, shifting in intellectual posture, voice, candor, purpose, and content (Lowenstein, 1987). Thus, it is a medium lending itself to speculation and experimentation, and to the rehearsal and phrasing of ideas. Likewise, Cooley's journal entries serve many purposes identified as quintessential to this medium, running the gamut from "pragmatic"—more public and interpersonal in terms of their desired impact and long- and short-term outcomes—to "mathetic" utterances of the speaker-as-observer; a commentary or sometimes a simple naming, more private, solitary and poetic in tone and purpose (Summerfield, 1987, p. 35). In the latter sense, the journal represents "the stringing together of exploratory discourse for the self" (Elbow and Clarke, 1987, pp. 30–31).

One intellectual historian perceptively characterizes the Cooley journals as the "most direct route to an understanding of Charles Horton Cooley's thought." Cooley's journals, in contrast to more mundane diaries,

> are a detailed and painstaking analysis of Cooley's intellectual and personal convictions. Year after year, Cooley raked over the same themes, recasting them, refining them, sometimes overturning them altogether. Quite often he dwelled on his childhood and how it informed his adult life. At other times, he speculated about his children's inner mental lives. Always he laid out detailed projects for intellectual self-improvement, chastising or praising himself as he saw fit. In these pages he sowed the seeds of his sociological theories, but they shared ground with the minutiae of daily life; no idea was too insignificant for treatment in the journals. What is more, Cooley appears to have reread these entries, going back and amending portions to clarify his meaning for himself. Though his published writings are self-revelatory, the journals are, even by nineteenth century standards of journal-keeping, a remarkably introspective record of a man in conversation with himself. (Winterer, 1994, p. 20)

Perusal of Cooley's journal leaves one with the sense that he strove to know himself and often succeeded in this quest. On the other hand, the reader will see that there seldom is a feeling of rawness in the journal, for it truly is a genre of literature resembling the essay—spontaneous or extemporaneous in feeling, and of course auto-referential, fragmentary, and conversational in tone. In perpetual conversation with himself, Cooley could be candid but seldom totally unguarded. Thus, the journal, despite this fragmentariness, conveys a sense of being polished, and of course always highly literate. It is an integral link between the development of Cooley's intellect and his personal evolution and the written corpus, his intellectual production.[6] I have relied upon it as a key source corroborating Cooley's published writing. In line with my identifying it as a back region of his theory building, I here often introduce his ideas in their nascent journal form and then in their slightly more polished published format. In this way I have striven to convey Cooley's intellectual method and to flesh out the generalizations I make regarding his literary background and his approach to sociological theorizing. The table below lists the Cooley journals, giving dates and volume numbers where applicable. It was not until 1890 that Cooley numbered them by volume. Volumes 7, 8, and 9 Cooley destroyed because he thought them "too priggish" (Jandy, 1942, p. 294).

THE CHARLES HORTON COOLEY JOURNALS, CHARLES HORTON COOLEY PAPERS, BENTLEY HISTORICAL LIBRARY, UNIVERSITY OF MICHIGAN

UNNUMBERED	NUMBERED	
UNDATED		BOX 5
	V. 6	[5/11/1890–7/9/1890]
BOX 2	V. 10	[7/21/1895–4/26/1896]
1/1882–3/1/1882	V. 11	[5/7/1896–3/21/1897]
1882 (*trip to Colorado*)	V. 12	[5/2/1897–7/31/1898]
1887–1888	V. 13	[8/8/1898–4/26/1899]
1889–1891	V. 14	[1/2/1900–12/20/1901]
	V. 15	[12/24/1901–9/12/1902]
BOX 7	V. 16	[9/19/1902–7/17/1903]
1883 (*trip to Smoky Mountains*)	V. 17	[7/8/1903–8/28/1904]
	V. 18a	[9/9/1904–2/11/1908]
	V. 18b	[2/16/1908–1/1/1910]
	V. 19	[2/6/1910–10/15/1911]
		BOX 6
	V. 20	[10/30/1911–11/1/1913]
	V. 21	[11/1/1913–4/11/1919]
	V. 22	[4/20/1919–5/25/1925]
	V. 23	[6/6/1925–10/4/1928]
	V. 24	[10/4/1928–4/7/1929]

NOTES

1. From Leo Chall, who stalwartly maintained the principle of open international sociological discourse, I grasped the subtle as well as grosser political and economic aspects of sociological information as a commodity. It was Leo who early opened my eyes to the fact that "America" and "American" were not synonymous with the United States and its citizens, and that it is as important for sociologists in the United States and Europe to read, for example, Mexican and Indian journals as it is for "them to read us."

2. Much of my work in the present book relies heavily on Cooley's journal. See the Appendix ("A Note on Cooley's Journal and Its Use Herein"), which details its format and use.

INTRODUCTION

1. A treatment of the social class theories of the key "fathers" (Ward, Sumner, Giddings, Cooley, and Ross) of American sociology by Charles Page, barely more than a decade past Cooley's death (Page, 1969 [1940], p. 21), does starkly summarize them all as generalists and, ironically, sets Cooley apart as follows: "A wide erudition typified all of them: to the greatest extent in the cases of Ward and Giddings, perhaps least so with Cooley; though Cooley compensated with a thorough knowledge of literature."

2. This portrait largely derives from Edward C. Jandy's biography of Cooley (1942, pp. 9–78).

3. Charles Cooley's comments on his father and his father's siblings in a journal entry reveal how the family's humble beginnings are manifested in Thomas McIntyre Cooley's attitudes toward education and social standing:

> My father's oldest brother was a cabinet maker in Buffalo. . . . His second and third brothers were farmers. They were all taught reading and writing after a fashion, but he believes that all except himself learned these arts very imperfectly. He mentioned a letter from his sister (Mrs. Newton?) in which sugar was spelt with an "h." So far as he knew none of the 15 children except himself ever showed marked capacity of any sort. He does not know how many are now living: one has recently died in Oregon. He himself acquired a very large part of all he has of general education by reading in bed. He regrets the stress of his life as having led to inevitable collapse and left him without any fund of general reminiscence to draw on. His mind was always concentrated on his work and he has little memory for matters unconnected with it. So far as he knows his only relative of any note was his second cousin Timothy Mather Cooley, a clergyman much beloved in Granville [?] Mass. and a descendant on his mother's side of Cotton Mather. It seems clear that if there had been any noted name in the connection it would have been preserved in the family. This seems to me the more remarkable as my father's ability is of a kind—intense energy and strong, well-balanced mind—that make a man notable in any career. If any of his relatives had resembled him it would seem that they must have been heard from. (*Journal* V. 10 [7/21/1895–4/26/1896] 7/21/1895, pp. 1–2)

Also revealing is the air of mild incredulity in this entry. Ironically, it seems as if Cooley, who asserted the importance of the social heritage in determining genius and fame (1897 in 1930), is puzzled by the paucity of notable family members in his father's generation, as though it were a trick of fate that made his father such an exception. In actuality, taking a broader historical view, it was the family heritage as part of a broader social milieu that contributed to T. M. Cooley's eminence. The Protestant immigrants to New York were "reviled by socially elevated observers from the settled, Puritan realm east of the Hudson River, who thought that moral and religious degradation pervaded western New York" (Carrington, 1997, p. 504). These settlers "were among the first to identify themselves as citizens of a nation as well as a state. People who crossed the mountains, unlike those who remained in Massachusetts, mingled with Irish and Germans and others to form a different collective consciousness" (p. 507). The steamboat traffic on Lake Erie, soon extended by the Erie Canal, tied New York to "the infant western frontier," propelling "the stream of migrants to northern Ohio and southern Michigan. These migrants were joined by nineteen-year-old Cooley, who arrived in the village of Adrian in 1843, to commence his career" (p. 511). Hence it was the creative churning of the migrant cultures that in a wider sense created new social and cultural worlds and a new national consciousness, among them famous and infamous characters, out of the moving frontier.

4. This chapter builds on my earlier discussion (Jacobs, 1979) of Cooley's economic sociology.

5. In *Social Process* the dramatic-scenario operation of social intelligence is described as the capacity to understand the "group in living interaction," and offers an example apropos of the economy: "In the cases of statesmanship . . . and the stock market, which represent "but a continuous drama, successful participation depends upon the power to apprehend some phase of it as a moving whole and foresee its tendency" (1918, p. 359).

CHAPTER I

1. Benoit-Smullyan used this term to describe Durkheim's synthesis of positivist methodology with his maintenance of "the reality *sui generis* of the causal priority of the social group *qua* group" (1948, p. 499).

2. As to this matter of the imagination, Smith tells us: "it is the impressions of our own senses only, not those of his, which our imaginations copy." Thus "we enter as it were into his body, and become in some measure the same person with him, and thence form some idea of his sensations, and even feel something which, though weaker in degree, is not altogether unlike them" (1976 [1759], p. 9). It is critical to emphasize that this is the sense of Cooley's use of the imagination, for, as I discuss below (in chapter 2), it is not solipsistic with respect to an identity of feeling and cognition—which is the corollary of Mead's attribution of solipsism to Cooley's formulation of the social psychology of the self.

3. I will have more to say about Cooley's theory of the self in chapter 2.

4. One might speculate that the ideas in *The Theory of Moral Sentiments* perhaps could have served, given their potential as a psychological bulwark of social control, as a model for a social psychology of market relations supplying an explanation of market stability beyond that of the invisible hand. Instead Smith contended, in accordance with his "contemplative utilitarianism," that a sort of trickle-down effect operating through the "Stoic doctrine of harmoniously developing nature . . . lies behind the . . . 'invisible hand' which leads the selfish rich in pursuing their own ends to cause a 'distribution of the necessaries of life' tending to promote human happiness" (Ross, 1995, p. 167). Ross contends that Smith's idea of sympathy served as an explanation of benevolence, a key component of Smith's adoption of the Stoic ideal of "self command" (p. 163).

5. The fact that Cooley took his doctorate in economics leaves little doubt that he read *TMS*, though I can find no mention of Smith in his books, papers, or journal. Could this be a symptom of what Harold Bloom calls the "anxiety of influence," causing the creative writer defensively to omit mention of a central precursor of his work? Some evidence of a mild form of this, as we shall see, appears with Cooley in the case of Walter Pater. In the case of Smith's influence, the fact that Giddings, whose work entailing the use of Smith's *TMS* was familiar to Cooley, and who from New York submitted the sociology questions for Cooley's doctoral exam in economics at Michigan, somewhat justifies our suspicions. Giddings's work, as I discuss below, despite its purported basis in Smith's, actually only uses the notion of sympathy as a vehicle of the identity and contagion of feeling.

6. Spencer's key postulate is: "Evolution is an integration of matter and concomitant dissipation of motion; during which the matter passes from an indefinite, incoherent homogeneity to a definite, coherent heterogeneity; and during which the retained motion undergoes a parallel transformation" (quoted in Martindale, 1981, p. 83).

7. Westby comments that this, among others, is a central contradiction in Spencer's conception of social change. Thus, while Spencer is convinced of the inevitability of the good society, he fails to provide a convincing sociological account (as Durkheim did) of its moral basis. Similarly, knowledge and science are regarded as evolutionary outcomes facilitating human adaptability, but Spencer does not—indeed, cannot—follow through on the implication that the growing significance of intelligence is manifested in

"increasingly effective intervention and greater control over evolution" by the organized altruism of the state. Likewise, Spencer's confining of the proper uses of knowledge to private ends contradicts his theoretical imperative regarding the increased differentiation and need for state coordination that the development of knowledge in society implies (Westby, 1991, pp. 166–67). By contrast, Durkheim does do this, and criticizes Spencer for not recognizing the connection between increased societal differentiation and the correlative widened role of the state (Durkheim, 1933, pp. 219–22).

8. Here Spencer's theory, including his exposition of dichotomous military and industrial societies, is thwarted, as Westby says, by events in Europe as early as the late nineteenth century, with the rapid pace of industrialism continuing "in concert with an expanding colonialism and intensifying jingoistic militarism" (Westby, 1991, pp. 165–66).

9. Consonant with Ward's criticism of Spencerian laissez-faire is his analysis of plutocracy, the abuse of democracy through the protection of economic privilege by the state. Plutocracy is created and perpetuated by the distrust of government and the belief in laissez-faire, which is occasioned by extreme individualism (Ward in Commager [ed.], 1967, pp. 168–77, 178–92). Ward's antipathy to plutocracy is shared by his curmudgeonly rival, the conservative William Graham Sumner, who believed that the leveling of the laissez-faire playing field is retarded by plutocracy.

10. This reflects the facts that Cooley took his doctorate in economics under Charles Francis Adams, a well-known economist who advocated regulation, and that his father, Thomas McIntyre Cooley, an eminent legal scholar at the University of Michigan law school, was also a proponent of regulation and the first chair of the federal Interstate Commerce Commission, under President Cleveland.

11. Martindale (1981, pp. 93–94) provides a short summary of Schäffle's system, influenced by Spencer, Lilienfeld, and Darwin, which like Spencer's thought conceives of society using organic analogies, but which is not confined to them. Thus these organic analogies are transcended by the inclusion of "social tissues" and a conception of group life sui generis in which it is seen as "the unit of conflict, mutual aid and survival" (p. 93).

12. House (1936, p. 224 ff.) describes the organizational history leading up to the creation of the American Sociological Society following the fragmentation of the American Social Science Association: "To be quite accurate, the National Conference of Charities and Corrections was founded as a division or department of the American Social Science Association in 1874 and became independent of it in 1879. The American Historical Society was launched under the auspices of the American Social Science Association in 1884. While the American Economic Association was founded more or less independently of the American Social Science Association, but by no means independent of it, in 1885. *The American Sociological Society originated in 1905 at a meeting of the American Economic Association (which had a similar origin meanwhile)* [my italics]. Thus, the National Conference of Charities and Corrections (later the National Conference of Social Work) arose from the American Social Science Association somewhat more directly than the American Sociological Society."

13. This is an expression Cooley himself used to define the mission of sociology with respect to social problems (1909, p. 299).

14. Clearly the expansion of the universities and the professionalization of the social sciences offered opportunities for academic entrepreneurship such as exhibited by Small,

who is described as follows by a historian of the professionalization of the social sciences in the United States:

> As a professional social scientist Small was a complicated mixture of the old-style moral philosopher and the modern rationalist with administrative inclinations. . . . Urbane, erudite, and dignified, Small was an academic entrepreneur who wrote one of the first textbooks in sociology, started the new discipline's first journal, and became fourth president of the American Sociological Society he helped to found. His ethical inclinations were always balanced internally by ambition and externally by a habit of handling situations in the most diplomatic way. (Furner, 1975, p 176)

15. Here Small is unable to transcend the individual. Thus, "'the social process is incessant reaction of persons prompted by interests that in part conflict with the interests of their fellows, and in part comport with the interests of others. . . . Human experience composes an associational process. The elements of that process are interests lodged in individuals'" (quoted in Barnes, 1948, pp. 783–84).

16. Page (1969 [1940], p. 25) observes that Veblen, who is admired and respected by many of the first generation of sociologists, does not return the favor to Small and "found little of value in Small's works, regarding him, while at Chicago, as an administrative official rather than an 'intellectual equal.'"

17. An interesting footnote to this matter is Small's letter to Cooley of December 2, 1902, acknowledging receipt of a copy of *Human Nature and the Social Order,* in which he congratulates Cooley for the book being "easily in the first rank of contributions to sociology." He notes, however, that he has only had "time to run a preliminary survey through it but shall keep it at my elbow till it has become a part of my everyday thinking," which unfortunately it did not (Small to Cooley, 1902).

18. Tarde in his essay on "Quantification and Social Indicators" (reprinted in Clark (ed.) 1969, 222–41) advocated the use of statistics to gauge "the quantitative oppositions of societies . . . whether simultaneous or successive, symmetrical or rhythmic" (p. 222). Tarde was the director of the French census.

19. Furner states that "Ross was an inveterate racist . . . inordinately committed to the superiority of Aryan stock" (1975, p. 309). At the beginning of his career he ran into difficulty at Stanford, in 1900, because of comments he made regarding the inevitability of public ownership of the railroads and because of an inflammatory speech before a group of San Francisco labor leaders extolling racial purity and condemnation of the supporters of "coolie" immigration, which ran counter to the Stanford family interests (p. 235). Ross viewed cities as "artificial growths" that placed Aryan populations at a disadvantage because they fared less well "than the Latins, Slavs, and Asiatics—normally Catholic or non-Christian—who adapted better to crowded, regimented life. The only hope for survival was a set of new set of restraints, imposed by society, to control the irresponsible individual. In that context, *Social Control* was more than an empirical study. It was a program for survival" (Furner, 1975, p. 309). Thus, the superficiality of the Tardian mentality—"segmental pluralism"—cloaked in the fear of being overrun by the minions, the massing, multilayered tide of populations of color threatening to deluge the so-called Aryan core of American society and culture.

20. Faris erroneously states that this "essential definition of the subject matter of sociology was effectively imported from France [that is, from Durkheim] by the quiet and modest scholar at the University of Michigan" (p. 9). Cooley clearly did not derive

his theory from Durkheim. I have found only one mention of Durkheim in Cooley's published material and none in his personal journals; the former is a brief reference to discussion of altruistic suicide in *Social Process* (1918, p. 400).

CHAPTER 2

1. Cooley says of the Cartesian ego: "Seeking an unquestionable basis for philosophy, he thought that he found it in the proposition 'I think, therefore I am'." Cooley finds this reasoning unsatisfactory because it implies "that 'I'-consciousness is a part of all consciousness, when in fact, it only belongs to a rather advanced stage of development [i.e., maturation]" (1909, p. 6). Thus Cartesian introspection is illusory for it is conceived as a private matter, which Cooley quickly rebuts in his discussion of introspection as "an act of public communication" (Schubert, 1998, p. 11). Schubert notes that Cooley's critique is shared with the pragmatists', especially Peirce's, critique of Cartesian doubt (pp. 11–15).

2. Cooley also discusses the processes of *social* selection in *Social Process* (1918). I take up this discussion in my analysis of Cooley's perspective on diversity as an offshoot of his aestheticism in chapter 5.

3. This statement serves in advance as a demurral to Parsons's critique of Cooley, which states that "Cooley needs to be supplemented by Durkheim" insofar as Durkheim recognizes that society "is just as immediately primordial, just as 'given,' as is the individual," that is that "the situation of action is neither individual nor social, but the matrix from which the individual and the social eventually come to be differentiated" (Parsons, 1968, p. 68). Social process, in effect, as Cooley conceives it, forms this matrix of action. As fundamental is Cooley's formulation of the primary group, the elemental foundation of social organization.

4. Here I bypass his discussion of suggestion and choice, which is not germane as merely serving Cooley's purpose of clearing the path of Tardean pluralistic behaviorism, to wit, his preference for the term "suggestion" over "imitation," which "writers, like Professor Baldwin and M. Tarde . . . adopt . . . and give . . . a wide and unusual application" (1902, rev. ed. 1922, p. 52).

5. Here again Cooley uses a simile resembling the field of corn image referring to the individual versus society. The cognitive mapping of one's personal ideas is described as "electric light bulbs, each of which represents a possible thought or impulse whose presence in our consciousness may be indicated by the lighting up of the bulb. Now each of the persons we know is represented by such a scheme, not by a particular area of the wall set apart for him, but by a system of hidden connections among the bulbs which causes certain combinations of them to be lit up when his characteristic symbol is suggested. If something presses the button corresponding to my friend A, a peculiarly shaped figure appears upon the wall; when that is released another figure appears, including perhaps many of the same lights, yet unique as a whole not in its parts; and so on with as many people as you please" (pp. 131–32).

6. Simmel (1955, p. 141), sounding like Cooley, notes: "As the individual leaves his established position within *one* primary group, he comes to stand at a point at which many groups intersect." Below (chapter 4) I compare Cooley with Simmel from the

standpoint of their similar style with respect to the literary and aesthetic character of Cooley's thought.

7. The earliest writing of Mead containing his full-blown notion of the self appears in an article of 1913, "The Social Self" (Reck [ed.], 1964, pp. 142–49). In an earlier survey of social psychology written in 1909 (pp. 94–101) he approvingly cites Cooley's work (*Human Nature and the Social Order* and *Social Organization*) as an exception to his generalization that "the sociologists have no adequate social psychology with which to interpret their own science" (p. 96).

8. I mention Gurdjieff, not because Cooley knew him or knew of him, but because of the identical conceptions they had of vanity and staking one's self-esteem on the perceived judgments of others, which comprises the focus for work on oneself. C. S. Nott, a student of Gurdjieff, recalls the following reply by Gurdjieff to a question concerning what he means by "considering": "'I will give you a simple example. Although I am accustomed to sitting with my legs crossed under me, I consider the opinion of the people here and sit as they do, with my legs down. This is external considering. . . . As regards inner considering. Someone looks at me, as I think, disapprovingly. This starts corresponding associations in my feelings; if I am too weak to refrain from reacting, I am annoyed with him. I consider internally, and show that I am annoyed. This is how we usually live; we manifest outside what we feel inside. . . . But why should I be annoyed or hurt if someone looks at me disapprovingly?—or if he doesn't look at me, doesn't notice me? It may be that he himself is the slave of someone else's opinion; perhaps he is an automaton, a parrot repeating someone else's words'" (Nott, 1961, pp. 37–38).

9. Consider how Cooley distilled the following aphorisms about vanity and pride from La Rochefoucauld, although without the latter's cynicism: #294: "We always like the people who admire us; we do not always like the people we admire"; #254: "Humility is often just feigned submissiveness employed to dominate others"; #152: "If we did not flatter ourselves, the flattery of others could do us no harm"; #144: "We dislike to bestow praise, and we never do it without a selfish motive. Praise is a clever, delicate and masked form of flattery which differently satisfies the recipient and the donor; the one accepts it as a reward of merit, the other bestows it to prove how fair-minded he is, and how discerning"; #228: "Pride does not wish to owe and vanity does not wish to pay"; #254: "It is a stratagem of pride, which lowers itself that it may raise itself; and though pride wears a thousand masks, it is never better disguised or better able to deceive than when it wears the mask of humility itself" (1959).

10. Joas, in his volume on Mead, notes that he is unable to find any evidence of contact between Mead and Cooley at Michigan despite frequent allusions to it in the secondary literature (1985, p. 219 f.). Nonetheless, at this juncture, it bears repeating that Cooley exerts a formative influence on Mead. Andrew Reck (1964, p. xxv) says that "from Cooley, his colleague at the University of Michigan from 1891 to 1893, Mead learned that in consciousness there is 'a social process going on, within which the self and others arise.'" While Mead may not have borrowed this idea at that time, it is likely that he read the first edition of *Human Nature and the Social Order* in 1902 or thereafter.

11. Ross (1991, p. 168) does not let the matter rest on the face value of Cooley's stated ambiguousness regarding Dewey's influence at the turn of the century, averring Dewey's

broader influence, even when not discussing Cooley, on other liberal intellectuals at Michigan. Among these is George Herbert Mead, whom Joas states Dewey befriended (1985, p. 20).

12. Cooley's notes of Dewey's lectures in political philosophy in 1893 are unnumbered. The page numbers indicated are my own.

13. Of the latter three, since they are extraneous to this discussion, I have little to say save that sovereignty is defined as "the completed social activity so far as that is made effective by embodying itself in definite institutions—this embodiment having two sides, that of structure and that of function." Law is viewed as the "definite, conscious expression of sovereignty" (p. 46). Political law as the expression of sovereignty is "the statement of some social fact from the standpoint of the whole community" (p. 59). Government is the organ—"a more or less determinate body of men"—expressing the common will (p. 64).

14. Mills tells us that "Peirce's precision . . . is overrun by James, who cannot anywhere in his writing about pragmatism be termed overly precise." He is thus "gossiping with these audiences about what the philosophers are up to: he is letting them in on things" (Mills, 1964, p. 223). By the same token, as I say below, William Barrett in his treatise on existentialism observes that James is considered by contemporary pragmatists "as the black sheep of the movement" owing to the "unashamedly personal tone of his philosophizing, [and] his willingness to give psychology the final voice over logic where the two seem in conflict" (1958, pp. 18–19).

15. Durkheim (1983; see also Joas, 1993, pp. 55–78), who takes a more jaundiced view of pragmatism, interprets it as an attack on rationalism and empiricism. Durkheim associates pragmatism with romanticism, and this is entirely consistent with his classical and positivist approach to sociology as the study of social facts as things. As I discuss below, it also stands in stark contrast to Cooley's aesthetically and pragmatically based conception of social science method as "tentative," as opposed to the moral implications of Durkheim's positing of *rules* of sociological method. As John B. Allcock, the editor of the English edition of Durkheim's *Pragmatism and Sociology* states, "His attack is based upon the premise that the weakness of pragmatism is a *moral* weakness. What he finds in pragmatism is no less than *intellectual anomie,* in that there is insufficient regulation of that which passes for truth in society" (1983, pp. xxxvi–xxxvii).

16. Mills tells us that for James pragmatism's mediatory element is so pervasive in his thinking . . . that it may be made a typical component of his 'pragmatic' style of thought" (1964, pp. 225–26). Thus science and religion, science and philosophy, the one and the many are examples of it. Most importantly, that the mediation does not occur for him "upon a sheerly syntactical level, that it is not a 'logical' reconciliation, is a mark of his penetration" (p. 228). In other words, it is the key to James's genius, for by the mediation of diversities James succeeds in "relativizing each mode of experience and style of thinking to its purpose" (ibid.). As I discuss below, Cooley does the same with aesthetics and sociology—as his main exemplar for literary style, Walter Pater, does for art and sense experience, art and religion, and so on (Loesberg, 1991, pp. 24–25).

17. Thus, in the introduction to the section on the self in their now classic reader, Stone and Farberman (1970, p. 370) describe Cooley as a "profound observer if not the

trenchant theorist" who made incisive observations without incorporating them into his explanations, as, for example, his insistence that the "I" always must consider others but instead roots the "I" in a sense of appropriation that "Cooley thought of as instinctive," or that his creative inclusion of self-feeling as an integral component of the self is accompanied by a "less than adequate" explanation, thus laying bare his solipsism. Ironically, more mention is made of, and greater space is devoted to, Cooley's contributions than any other author, including Mead.

18. Parson's critique of Cooley, appearing in a Festschrift (Reiss ed., 1968) of largely tangential and strained tributes, suggests: "The most important starting point for criticism of Cooley concerns, as Mead rightly said, his predilection for interpreting social phenomena as 'mind'." He states that Cooley's recognition of the individual as given needs to be "supplemented" by Durkheim's recognition of *social systems* as objects, since Durkheim recognizes that society "is just as immediately primordial, just as 'given,' as is the individual," that is, that "the situation of action is neither individual nor social, but matrix from which the individual and the social eventually come to be differentiated" (Parsons, 1968, pp. 67, 68). It would seem that Parsons has forgotten Cooley's organic view of social organization and the self, of society and the individual. Social process, in effect, as Cooley conceives it, forms this matrix of action. As fundamental is Cooley's formulation of the primary group serving as an elemental foundation of social organization. So why the selective perception of Cooley's approach?

19. Reck (1954, p. xxv) interprets the first part of the quote as formative of Mead's thinking.

20. Of this Cooley says: "Meantime the feeling itself does not remain unaltered, but undergoes differentiation and refinement. . . . And concrete self-feeling, as it exists in mature persons, is a whole made up of . . . various sentiments, along with a good deal of primitive emotion not broken up" (1902, rev. ed., 1922, p. 171).

21. As I demonstrate here, as a leading "first generation" Chicago figure, Mead himself, if not a thorough positivist, nonetheless took on positivist trappings to legitimate his perspective. Fine (1995), Platt (1995), and Galliher (1995) inform us that both the first and second Chicago "schools" were not unitary entities, either theoretically symbolic interactionist, or solely qualitatively methodological. Rather, the University of Chicago contained a variety of interests and perspectives. Its reputation as a symbolic interactionist stronghold belies a perspectively factionalized department (Fine, 1995, p. 4). Similarly, the associated impression of a department with predominantly qualitative methodological leanings is a "postwar invention" providing "a banner around which sympathizers can rally" (Platt, 1995, pp. 93, 97).

22. Mead's more academic mien, although not necessarily a more scientific one, inclines him away from the use of sympathy as a theoretical mainstay. Only after Mead discusses mind and self does he discuss sympathy, and then almost as an afterthought (1962 (1934), pp. 298–303).

23. Cooley's contribution to the latter is the *most* noteworthy of "first-generation" U. S. sociologists, as I discuss in chapter 6.

24. Turner says this approvingly, however, for he feels there is a virtue in symbolic interactionists refraining from building strained linkages between theirs and structural

perspectives while refraining from pursuing what he takes to be their viable microsocial mission.

25. Alfred McClung Lee's *Multivalent Man* (1966, p. 118), in part hearkening back to William James's multivalent social self, defines group in a more subtle and nuanced way, that is, in a manner incorporating difference:

> A group is an aggregate of two or more people who have occasion to associate or at least to identify themselves with one another once or repeatedly. Group members may associate in a face-to-face sense or may merely have an explicit identification only with the aggregate and thus, perhaps quite tenuously, with one another. The members may have a sense of holding one or more shared or compatible interests even though they may define those interests differently. . . . Regardless of how transient or continuing the group might be, it is a social reification, a social thing which is different from the individuals making it up.

26. Blumer formulated the symbolic interactionist perspective as an attempt to offset structural functionalism, which dominated the discipline in the 1950s and early 1960s. As opposed to the view quoted above, Blumer states that other sociological conceptions "generally lodge social action in the action of society or in some unit of society." He goes on to offer examples wherein "some conceptions, in treating societies and human groups as 'social systems,' regard group action as an expression of a system, either in a state of balance or seeking to achieve balance," or represent group action as "an expression of the ' functions' of a society or of a group" (1968, p. 84).

CHAPTER 3

1. This theme is explored in chapter 5, where I discuss Cooley's aestheticism as an outgrowth of his reading of the essay tradition and Walter Pater. I also discuss it in chapter 6, in relation to his methodology and its affinity with current ethnographers' turn toward a literary sensibility.

2. Regarding the Bosanquet reference, House states: "So closely does this treatment of the life of the family parallel Cooley's discussion of 'primary groups,' that it is surprising to discover from the index of Cooley's *Social Organization* that Mrs. Bosenquet's work was apparently unfamiliar to him when he wrote the latter volume. Of course, the fact that both books appear in the same year excludes the possibility of plagiarism on either side." On the same page House states in a footnote that "there is in the Small and Vincent *Introduction to the Study of Society* (New York, 1894) a chapter entitled 'The Primary Social Group: the Family,' but this chapter is not mentioned by Cooley in *Social Organization*" (1929, p. 141).

3. "The first function which a newspaper supplies is that which formerly was performed by the village gossip" (Park, 1916 in 1952, p. 45). Cooley states that the bulk of the matter comprising the newspaper "is best described by the phrase organized gossip. The sort of intercourse that people formerly carried on at cross-road stores or over the back fence, has now attained the dignity of print and an imposing system." This is owing to three traits: it is "copious," being designed to occupy the mind without exertion; it consists mostly of personalities, appealing to superficial emotion; and it is untrustworthy (1909, pp. 83–84).

4. I take this matter up again in my discussion of Cooley's economic sociology in chapter 7.

CHAPTER 4

1. As "'mosaic[s]' or 'tissue[s] of quotation without quotation marks, without a pre-existent author exercising agency," texts thus constituted in certain respects resemble types of what sociologists once called "collective behavior," especially fashion and public opinion, which operate and manifest themselves transpersonally, if not impersonally (Friedman, 1991, p. 149). Certainly the semioticians would consider fashion and public opinion textualities. Derrida's use of metaphors of sexual insemination and dissemination and poisoning and healing (the "pharmakon") in describing the processes entailed in interextuality, and, coming from the direction of influence, qua Bloom's punning reference to "influenza" (1973, 1997, p. 95), resembles descriptions of the social processes entailed in the behavior of the crowd and mob, or fashion and public opinion, which archaic sociology often ascribed to a collective psyche (the "group mind" or "crowd mind") on the one hand, or to processes akin to those underlying intertextuality, such as Tarde's imitation, suggestion, and contagion. In either case, intertextual and collective behavior processes can be read *contextually,* that is, as socially, culturally, and historically situated.

2. Friedman observes that the discourses of intertextuality and influence emanate from European and North American contexts, the former reflecting "the fall-out of two massive wars fought on European soil" and the ultimate intellectual rejection of the transcendental ego, the latter reflecting the "cultural ideology of the Self" which is deeply rooted in United States history and culture, and which I spoke about in connection with Cooley's work on the self. In this case groups "who have been denied the agency and status of the individual for reasons of race, class, gender, religion, ethnicity, sexual preference . . . have traditionally felt excluded from 'the American Dream.'" Consequently, the study of literary influence has retained a stronghold among scholars in the United States where "appropriation of the discourse of the Self, however redefined, has been and still is a central characteristic of cultural and political movements of the marginalized in the United States" (1991, pp. 156–57). This discourse is thus culturally related to the content of Cooley's work as well as useful in analyzing the influences upon it.

3. Réda Bensmaïa's analysis of Barthes's writing suggests that Barthes revives the original fragmented spirit of Montaigne's essay form—the "reflective text" (1987). Richman tells us that Barthes's essay style "goes to the extreme of destroying its own discursive category." As a practice of writing Barthes's work both embodies Montaigne's spirit and serves as an innovative contribution within the essay tradition because "the text is generated from fragments outside established classifications which refuse a fixed center or totalizing scheme" (Richman, 1987, p. xi). Bensmaïa suggests that what gives the Barthian essay its unity in spite of everything is that "it works," that is, "from start to finish in an Essay, fragments remain fragments," and its unity is denoted in the spirit of Montaigne as "'My book and I are one'" (1987, p. 35). Coincidentally, "the unifying concept" Green draws from Cooley's sociology, "through which Cooley draws together natural, social, and linguistic forms of life is that of 'working'" (1988, p. 43). The essay's unit stems from its very polysemy—the myriad of meanings and associations—that is its essence. Bensmaïa informs us that, as Montaigne instructs, some word in the essay—often a title word—will resonate mnemonically in the author's digressions to create a totality out of the heterogeneous parts. This is what Barthes calls the *mana* word, which for him is the word "body." Thus this four-hundred-year-old genre antedating

the "modern" novel serves contemporary literary needs admirably well (Bensmaïa, 1987, p. 11–18).

4. In the essay "Of Liars," among other places, Montaigne proclaims his faulty memory, and tells us, using the guise of confession, that "there is nobody less suited than I am to start talking about memory. I can hardly find a trace of it in myself; I doubt there is any other memory in the world as grotesquely faulty as mine is! All my other endowments are mean and ordinary: but I think that, where memory is concerned, I am most singular and rare, worth of both name and reputation." A few lines down however, after mentioning that those who hear this confession often reprove him for denigrating himself, he notes that "they see no difference between memory and intelligence," and that this makes his case seem worse than it is. Furthermore, his interlocutors do him wrong, for "experience shows us that it is almost the contrary: an outstanding memory is often associated with weak judgment" (1991 [1588], p. 32). Montaigne turns this weakness into a virtue and uses it as a foil to commence his discussion of lying, "an accursed vice" (p. 33). Thus abjuration of memory provides a basis for the free play of ideas in the essay.

5. Montaigne criticizes pedantic mimicry, confesses his intertextual borrowing under the protective coloration of personal style, asserts his freedom, and appears to hide nothing. In acknowledging the influence and use of prior texts on his own work, he playfully baits his reader with this game of allusion. As he tells us in the essay "On Books" (1991, p. 458), "Where my borrowings are concerned, . . . I get others to say what I cannot put so well myself, sometimes because of the weakness of my language and sometimes because of the weakness of my intellect." Then he boasts shamelessly that "I do not count my borrowings: I weigh them; if I had wanted them valued for their number I would have burdened them with twice as many." Now he challenges the reader's pride and plunges into the maw of the anxiety of influence, using other, prior texts as shields and decoys:

> They [my borrowings] are all, except for very, very few, taken from names so famous and ancient that they seem to name themselves without help from me. . . . I sometimes omit to give the author's name so as to reign in the temerity of those hasty criticisms which leap to attack writings of every kind, especially recent writings by men still alive and in our vulgar tongue which allow anyone to talk about them and which seem to convict both their conception and design of being just as vulgar. I want them to flick Plutarch's nose in mistake for mine and to scald themselves by insulting Seneca in me. I have to hide my weakness beneath those great reputations.

6. After Montaigne, "the essay split into two modalities: one remained informal, personal, intimate, relaxed, conversational, and often humorous; the other, dogmatic, impersonal, systematic, and expository" (Richman, 1987, p. x). In the former, the fragmentary essay or "reflective text," in contrast to the discursive expository essay, the writer serves as the primary intellectual object for eclectic digressions. Thus the autobiographical sensibility has become a hallmark of literary technique, and, in Cooley's case, sociological methodology. To some degree, as discussed below, this applies to recent thinking in ethnographic methods.

7. This journal passage appears in Part Seven, "Larger Life," in *Life and the Student* (1927, p. 239). The allusion to the social heritage recalls Cooley's discussion in *Human Nature and the Social Order* of the "two lines of transmission" of human life; the one a

road, the other a stream. The road is communication or social transmission; the stream is heredity. The latter "flows through the germ plasm"; the former "comes by way of language, intercourse, and education. The road is more recent than the stream; it is an improvement that did not exist at all in the earliest flow of animal life, but appears later as a vague trail alongside the stream, becomes more and more distinct and travelled, and finally develops into an elaborate highway, supporting many kinds of vehicles and a traffic fully equal to the stream itself" (1902, rev. ed. 1922, pp. 4–5). Clearly, the essay tradition, signifying communication and social interaction, inspires much of Cooley's view of human nature, which, in turn, serves as the foundation for his conception of the self. As he says, the "social origin of . . . [the individual's] life comes by the pathway of intercourse with other persons" (p. 5).

8. Cooley probably derives the image of the "higher tribunal" from Adam Smith, who traces the sources of conscience from "the great judge of the world" or "great tribunal" by devising the impartial spectator, and says "whatever may be the source of this inferiour tribunal [other men] . . . which is continually before their eyes . . . men may appeal . . . and call upon a superior . . . tribunal, the tribunal established in their own breasts" (Smith, 1976 [1759], p. 128). As I point out, Cooley adopts as well Emerson's notion of representative men to flesh out his conception of the essayistic reference group constituting his literary matrix.

9. In Montaigne's words, "I have no more made my book than my book has made me—a book consubstantial with its author, concerned with my own self, an integral part of my life; not concerned with some third-hand, extraneous purpose, like all other books" (1958, II, 18, 504 c).

10. This passage appears in Chapter VII, "Some Phases of Culture" in *Social Process* (1966 [1918], p. 70).

11. Much of Cooley's discussion of vanity hearkens back to his reading of the maxims of the French moralist La Rochefoucauld. Consider the relevance of the following examples to Cooley's conception of the looking-glass self: # 119: "We get so much in the habit of wearing a disguise before others that we finally appear disguised before ourselves"; # 256: "On all occasions we assume the look and appearance we want to be known for, so that the world in general is a congregation of masks" (1959, pp. 55, 81). Following Montaigne the French moralists begin with the assumption of the social mask and, as Erving Goffman calls it, the arts of performance and impression management as essential aspects of social life (1959, pp. 16–76, 208–37).

12. In this respect. Donald M. Frame points out in his introduction to his translation of the *Essays* (1958, pp. v–vi) that the criticism that they are not frank enough rings hollow, since the *Essays* are not confessions. Moreover, Montaigne "has no use for the introvert's anguish over the impenetrability of ultimates, the absurdity of man's place in the universe, or the discrepancy between our ideals and our attainments." The first two are accepted as the unfathomable data of human life; the third "he seeks to resolve by introspective study of human nature and human conduct." As Cooley elsewhere implies, Montaigne's aims are thus identical to his own: to deepen the reader's understanding of self and society by sympathetic introspection.

13. Note how Schwartz marshals his case by bringing in Coser, which really adds nothing but a quoted testimonial from his *Masters of Sociological Thought,* whose two

editions (1971, 1977) are distinguished by its presentation of the masters' ideas into sections representing "The Work," "The Man," "The Intellectual Context," "The Social Context," and a summary statement. Coser thus serves as a persuasive, propagandistic, element here. To be fair to Schwartz, it must be noted that his excellent treatment follows these quoted passages with Cooley's own autobiographical material on Emerson's felt influence (Schwartz, 1985, p. 109). Yet how revealing this is of the subliminal presumptions of discursive sociological style. Note too that I have inserted Cooley's own ideas to explain the mechanics of Emersonian influence and intertextuality, for Cooley is a creative agent in these processes, and conceiving him as potent an influence on his own work as any other, I wish to include his presentation of himself in the matrix of his writing and ideas.

14. These Emersonian principles are explicitly proclaimed in three well-known essays (in the 1929 edition), "Nature," (pp. 1–24) "The American Scholar," (pp. 25–36), and "An Address" (pp. 37–47) delivered to the senior class at the Harvard Divinity School. It is significant that Emerson also views property, for example, in the essay "Nature" (p. 12) as emblematic of spirit or the oversoul: "Property . . . is the surface action of internal machinery, like the index on the face of a clock." In "Nominalist and Realist" Emerson says, "Money, which represent the prose of life . . . is, in its effects and laws, as beautiful as roses. Property keeps the accounts of the world, and is always moral" (p. 307). Elsewhere (Jacobs, 1979), and herein, in chapter 7, I analyze the economic assumptions in Emerson and in Cooley's theory of pecuniary valuation.

15. In "The American Scholar" Emerson introduces the theme of representative men. Lamenting the fragmentation of original man into the "*divided* or social state [that is, by the division of labor] . . . the individual, to possess himself must sometimes return from his own labor to embrace all the other laborers." The scholar is best fitted to restore the lost unity: "In this distribution of functions the scholar is the delegated intellect," for "in the right state he is *Man Thinking* (1929, p. 25).

16. Schwartz states that Cooley's focus on the symbolic hero is widened "to incorporate, in his later writing on democracy, a more explicit appreciation of instrumental talents and achievement. Yet, Cooley displayed very little of Emerson's fascination with genius itself. He never dwells on the particulars of the hero's qualities" (1985, p. 114). This generalization is qualified by the fact that although these qualities are not emphasized in his published writing, in his personal life and in his journal—which Schwartz also drew heavily on—and as attested to herein, Cooley did focus on the *literary-personalities,* or particular traits of his exemplars, who, in a sense, again as types, served as models for his style and intellectual practice.

17. Schwartz correctly suggests that Cooley, who "dwells on motivation, not exploits" was not "impressed by the spectacle of impressive force" of the Emersonian hero, or representative men. Instead the "image was fashioned according to a stoic, not romantic ideal." In other words, "[b]readth of vision, unselfishness, desire for truth rather than fame, and . . . inner dedication to the quest for its own sake—these are hallmarks of the Cooleyan hero." He says these convictions stemmed from a deep puritanical strain derived from Cooley's New England family background, and the heroic image was "fashioned according to a stoic, not romantic, ideal (1985, p. 109). It is likely, however

that his background resonated well with Adam Smith's confessed Stoicism incarnated in his notions of sympathy and impartial spectator, key components of self-command, embodied in the mechanics of sympathy and the impartial spectator, which undoubtedly influenced Cooley's formulation of the social self. Self-command articulates well with the Emersonian virtues of self-reliance and self-possession, which Cooley took to heart.

18. As to the theme of music and the orator, Emerson also says, "of all the musical instruments on which men play, a popular assembly is that which has the largest compass and variety, and out of which the most wonderful effects can be drawn." This quote is taken from the first page of the essay "Eloquence," where he discourses at length on oratory (1929, pp. 639–51), which Cooley read (*Journal* 1882, p. 24). The 1882 journal volume, in fact, contains much of the young Cooley's impressions, reflections, hopes, and desires regarding oratory, public speaking, and the like. As F. O. Matthiessen comments on the orator motif in American letters, "the orator could speak most directly and most deeply to men, breaking down their reserves, tugging them through the barriers of themselves, bringing to articulation their own confused thoughts" (1941, p. 17).

19. As explained in chapter 1, Cooley's model of society uses the language of organicism, that is, his "organic view" integrates the unity of society and "the autonomy of the self" (Schubert, 1998, p. 18). It thus greatly differs from the organismic approach of Spencer.

20. In the same long journal entry, Cooley looks insightfully into the possible psychosomatic context of his character development:

> From early childhood—perhaps the age of 8 or 10—until I was over twenty, my health was miserable, so that my youth was in the main very dreary. I desire nothing less than to live it over again. . . . I suffered from chronic costiveness of the bowels for which nothing effective was done. I can recall going two weeks without a passage. This I believe to have been the foundation of that dark period of poor health from which I am even now scarcely emerged. I have sometimes thought that the fierce eagerness of my inner life, exhausting my strength, was the cause of this physical trouble, but I cannot tell. The matter was made worse by an almost incredible shyness. I could never have brought myself voluntarily to speak of such a trouble, even had I understood its nature, which of course I did not. I believe this trouble and the depressing but obscure diseases that followed it had a great deal to do in making my character what it is. (pp. 3–4)

21. Somewhat earlier, reflecting on his weak and unresponsive voice, which always was a problem for him, he hopes "that by persistent and intelligent practice, especially in the open air, I can do anything I please with my voice."

22. On the other side of the looking-glass, despite his success as an author and lecturer, Emerson laments: "Why has never the poorest country college offered me a professorship of rhetoric? I think I could have taught an orator, though I am none" (quoted in Matthiessen, 1941, p. 18).

23. In *Life and the Student* (1927, p. 66), Cooley consigns Emerson to the same status as he did Spencer when comparing him with Montaigne: "Emerson should be read in youth. His boundless hope and his call to self trust are congenial then. Later, when you have become disillusioned, sceptical and lazy, you may find his exhortations a little tiresome."

CHAPTER 5

1. Burne-Jones, a painter Cooley was fond of, is mentioned several times in his journal.

2. Susan Sontag (1966, p. 277–93) in her "Notes on 'Camp'," includes the Renaissance mannerists and "19th century aestheticism" of Burne-Jones, Pater, Ruskin, Tennyson, and then Art Nouveau as within the "camp" sensibility, which she tersely describes as "a good taste of bad taste." It is "Dandyism in the age of mass culture" (pp. 290, 280). A large critical literature is appearing on Pater. For a compilation of his contemporaries' reactions and responses to his writings, see Seiler (1980).

3. Donoghue notes that both Emerson and Pater use the term "scholar" in the service of self-realization. This certainly is true for Cooley. Moreover, in line with the notion of the scholar as mediating the oversoul (speaking sub specie aeternitatis), he observes in Pater's case that "a scholar belongs to a clerisy of language, learned, monastic" (1995, p. 224).

4. Hence Donoghue carefully notes, in speaking, just before his statement on intertextuality, of John Ashbery: "To be specific: I do not claim that Pater influenced Ashbery, but I do note that on one occasion Ashbery's reading of a passage in Pater's *Plato and Platonism* led to his writing a poem. For that occasion, Pater was a presence to Ashbery; the two writers came into one field of force" (1995, p. 8). The opening chapter of Donoghue's recent study proclaims that "Pater is a shade or trace in virtually every writer of any significance from Hopkins and Wilde to Ashbery." Furthermore, it was Pater, "more than Arnold, Tennyson, or Ruskin, who set modern literature upon its antithetical—he would say, its antinomian—course." Thus, "Pater is audible in virtually every attentive modern writer—in Hopkins, Wilde, James, Yeats, Pound, Ford, Woolfe, Joyce, Eliot, Aiken, Hart Crane, Fitzgerald, Forster, Borges, Stevens, Ammons, Tomlinson, and Ashbery" (pp. 6–7). Regarding the manner in which Pater's voice appears in these writers' works, Donoghue says that the influence is decidedly *intertextual*, that is, palpably there although not by direct, or always explicit, reference. Nevertheless, one skeptically comes away from such a cold disclaimer of conscious influence reminded of Bloom's Freudian remonstration.

5. Wolfgang Iser (1987, p. 63), speaking of Pater's notion of beauty, states that his conception represents a break with the Platonic structure. For Pater, beauty is pure appearance, and, as such, necessarily includes the different—the grotesque. Thus, the "grotesque is the absolute antithesis of harmony, not least because it can only be defined through the different forms of appearance, whereas harmony is an a priori concept."

6. This line of thinking also predisposes Cooley to tolerate, if not embrace, another heresy of his time, psychoanalysis, which he sees as a useful although unscientific means of investigating "the history and working of the self." Perhaps psychoanalysis is a bit too close for comfort, given the way Cooley depicts its subject matter: "The human mind is indeed a cave swarming with strange forms of life, most of them unconscious and unilluminated." His chief objection to psychoanalysis is its "tendency to work too directly from supposed instincts without allowing for the transforming action of social institutions and processes" (1902, rev. ed. 1922, p. 262 f).

7. "Sympodial" is a term borrowed from Lester Ward, after the pattern by which a grapevine grows and divides its shoots. While the reference here seems to be biological, it is not to the biological nature of society, and is more metaphorical and aesthetic.

8. In discussing Mead and Dewey, Joas posits that according to the pragmatic view creativity is intrinsic to social interaction because habitual action "constantly encounters obstacles, goals prove to be mutually exclusive; attainable goals have doubts cast upon them by other actors"; these crises necessitate redefinition and prompt us to conceive that "every situation contains a horizon of possibilities which in a crisis of action has to be rediscovered" (1996, p. 133).

9. This is not to say that art does not serve Cooley personally in this sense. In his journals it is clear that for him art is inspirational, even ecstatic. This does not, however, nullify the point that in his writing about art and society such elevation is democratized, that is, articulated in society for society.

CHAPTER 6

1. About "social facts" Cooley says, "Strictly speaking, there are no yardsticks in social knowledge, no elementary perceptions of distinctively social facts that are so alike in all men, and can be so precisely communicated, that they supply an unquestionable means of description and measurement" (1926 in 1930, p. 297).

2. I note that in this essay Cooley does not use the expressions social and spatial *science*. That is a liberty I take. He always refers to social and spatial *knowledge,* because the emphasis rests on the object of contemplation, which, consistent with Cooley's thinking, dictates the method of approach to it.

3. Below I discuss Cooley's visits to Hull House and Jane Addams's adoption of his notion of sympathetic introspection.

4. This term—tentativeness—resonates on a number of levels: (a) the process of societal evolution and change, that is, the social process and the sympodial growth of society; (b) the method(s) of sociological research discussed herein; and (c) the process of development of Cooley's inner life. The second and third intersect frequently in his diary, particularly in ruminations about his vocation in relation to his personal growth, character, and spirituality. Thus he outlines the fit between his temperament and his intellect in a fashion that typifies the sensibility of the essayists and is filtered into his conceptual apparatus as the tentative method:

> I am drawn into the world by sympathy, and perhaps to my advantage. Only a thick skin can live in this world and not be of it: if we associate we assimilate. I doubt if I have that great delicacy of perception and susceptibility that works best in apparent solitude. I need the world, though it is often too much with me. From it I have learned to know and to appreciate men, common men, and to have them and their workings as a basis to my philosophy. I am of them, no better, in some respects below the average, but more reflective. My perturbations instruct me: I should grow sensual in quiet: perhaps, on the whole, I am getting the most out of life I could get. (*Journal* V. 18b [2/16/1908–1/1/1910] 3/14/08, pp. 4–5)

Tentativeness appears here as his shuttling back and forth between the pull of the world and solitude, the sensual and spiritual, ordinariness and distinction, commonness and sensitivity or reflectiveness. These polarities, among others, are also common themes in his life. They appear as problems, but they are never decisively resolved, for they are part of Cooley's character; they are the stuff to which is applied the tentative method of the essayists.

5. These are: *Inarticulate Self-feeling; The Correct Understanding of "I" and "You" when Used by Others; Imitative Use of "I" Phrases, Apparently Without a Sense of the Subjective*

Reference, or Indeed any Discrimination of "I" from the Rest of the Phrase; Suggestions as to How the True or Subjective Meaning of "I" is Grasped; Examples of the Earliest Correct Use of "I" and Other Pronouns of the First Person; Does "I" Mean Primarily the Visible or Tangible Body?; In What sense is "I" a Social Conception?; Others are Named Before the Self; Other Names for the Self.

6. Tyler (1986, p. 131) tells us that ethnographic writing itself is coming to be represented by this hallmark—fragmentariness—of the essay tradition: "A post-modern ethnography is fragmentary because it cannot be otherwise. Life in the field is itself fragmentary, not at all organized around familiar ethnographic categories."

7. The entry reads: "9/12 Barnett, Johns Hopkins man, Estabrook, Cambridge, Parmelee, Yale." The latter is probably Maurice Parmelee, a well-known sociologist at the time. Another person, Walling, is mentioned further on in the entry, but without any institutional or other identification.

8. Recently journals and fieldnotes have come into their own as a subgenre of sociological writing, which is now commanding some attention. See, for example, Sanjeck's anthology (Sanjeck ed., 1990) devoted to the subject.

9. Jack London's *People of the Abyss* (1977 [1903]) is a little-known but vivid participant observation of London's East End, carried out when London, delayed on an Asian assignment, was held over in London, and decided to sell his clothes, wear the attire of the down-and-out East Enders and live among them in the summer of 1902 when "I went down into the under-world of London with an attitude of mind which I may best liken to that of the explorer. I was open to be convinced by the evidence of my eyes, rather than by the teachings of those who had not seen, or by the words of those who had seen and gone before" (p. 9). Consistent with Cooley's reference to the East Enders' smaller cranial sizes, London reports throughout on their poverty-marked, stunted bodies.

10. In lecture notes dated 1902, Cooley devotes three and a half typed pages to a description of Hull House (which he had visited several times), including its environs and programs (Cooley, 1902).

11. In *Social Organization* he makes seven references to Addams, in *Social Process*, two.

12. I use the terms "spirituality" and "religion" interchangeably here, and while there are many who might object to this, Cooley's own practice does not rigidly separate the two, although he surely recognizes and remarks on the difference between normative and institutional religious practices and personal spiritual development.

13. He adds that the materials in the MS "are capable of development into sociological studies having quite another kind of value, that springing from the general organism of thought," implying the continuity and intertextual development of thought.

CHAPTER 7

1. A short abstract, "The Social Significance of Street Railways," appeared in the *Publications of the American Economics Association* in 1891. His doctoral dissertation first appeared as a monograph in *Publications of the American Economic Association* 9, no. 3 (May 1894), and was accepted by the economics faculty of the University of Michigan in June of that year. It was followed by a paper, "Competition and Organization," in the *Michigan Political Science Association* in 1894, and then "Personal Competition" in 1899 in *Economic Studies.* After that, the next work on economics, "The Institutional Character

of Pecuniary Valuation" was published in 1913 in the *American Journal of Sociology* 18, no. 4 (Jan. 1913), followed by two other papers on that subject in the same year, and then a paper on political economy and social process in 1918. *Social Process* (1918) includes the three papers on pecuniary valuation. All of these, with the exception of "The Social Significance of Street Railways," are included in the posthumously published collection of Cooley's essays, *Sociological Theory and Social Research* (1930).

2. See chapter 4 for a discussion of the Emersonian transcendental principles.

3. The economic theorists Cooley criticizes, he suggests, represent demand as "what the people want, and if there is anything wrong with what the people want we are to ascribe it to the corruption of human nature" (1918 in 1930, pp. 252–53).

4. Cooley first used this expression (to "get together") almost twenty years earlier in his essay "Personal Competition" (1899 in 1930, pp. 176–77), in discussing the relationship between competition and the mitigating factor of association or industrial combination. "Getting together" produces a tendency away from the desirable state of "symmetry" or organizational growth balanced by regulation. He feels that there is no great danger posed by this modern organizing tendency and that, if properly regulated, organization and competition could peacefully coexist.

5. Thomas McIntyre Cooley, a respected dean of the University of Michigan law school, and first chair of the federal Interstate Commerce Commission, "was a leading exponent of the federal judiciary's sustained effort to apply the classical principles of private property and free enterprise to a society newly dominated by industrial and finance capital and wage labor. As one of the most influential jurists and legal scholars in postbellum America, the elder Cooley joined [Stephen J.] Field as a principal author of the doctrine of 'substantive due process,' by which the constitutional protections of life, liberty, and property formerly reserved for individuals were gradually conferred upon business corporations" (Sklansky, 2000, p. 91).

6. Despite their nickname, they eschewed Marxian socialist economics, advocating instead "the piecemeal study and preparation of practical immediate measures of reform in relation to hours and conditions of work, social insurance, factory legislation and the like" (Hutchison, 1953, p. 181).

7. Furner (1975, p. 187) aptly sums up the approach of the perspective as follows:

Value was determined by the amount that a consumer would pay for the final unit of a particular good or service that he would add to his supply before switching his consumption to some other item. In any series of increments there was constantly diminishing return. Thus the value (or wages) of labor was determined by the final increment added to the total output of an enterprise such as a farm or factory by the last laborer who could be profitably added to the force. That was what an employer would pay for the last laborer he would hire, and what the last laborer would take before he would offer his services somewhere else. The value (rent or interest) of capital was determined by the amount added to industry by the last unit of capital (land, tools, machines, building) that could profitably be invested in a given industry. That was the amount of interest or rent that an entrepreneur would pay on the last land or other instrument of production he acquired, and the lowest amount that the capitalist would accept before he switched his investment to some other enterprise.

8. The only reference I have been able to find by Cooley to Veblen is in his discussion of democracy in *Social Organization,* where he says ideas of caste, domination, military glory, "'conspicuous leisure' and the like—sprang from a secondary and artificial system, based on conditions which forbade a large realization of primary ideals." In a footnote

on the page he refers to conspicuous leisure as "one of the many illuminating phrases introduced by T. V. [*sic*] Veblen in his work on The Theory of the Leisure Class" (1909, p. 119).

9. Anticipating contemporary rebuttals of the professional arrogance of the economists, Anderson states that "economic theory has sought to make itself too much a thing apart, to isolate its phenomena from other phases of social life, and has busied itself exclusively with 'utility' and 'cost' and 'prices,' and the like. And where the economist has consented to consider the relations between his own field and adjacent fields, he has done so with a preconception of the priority of his own phenomena" (1911, p. 153).

10. Veblen did refer to the "Social Problem" as the conflict of institutional forces between the "discipline of the machine process" which "cuts away the spiritual, institutional foundations of business enterprise," and the financial and credit manipulations of business enterprise bringing about periodic crises (1932 [1904], pp. 177–78 and passim). Veblen is inconclusive about the outcome: "Which of the two anatagonistic factors may prove stronger in the long run is something of a blind guess." He does hazard that either machine technology or "distracted Christendom" might prevail over business enterprise and ethics.

11. Ross views Commons's focus as an exeptionalist interpretation of the American labor movement as the natural outcome of the competitiveness of the American labor market, which would be "a distinctively American result" (1991, p. 203).

12. Seligman is described by Dorothy Ross as having bridged the liberal historicists (those who hearkened back to the German school, or the *Verein*) and the marginalists. He championed the eventual autonomy of the workingman, recognizing the historical inevitability of class and race competition, and hoped "that progress would someday abrogate scarcity and inequality and thereby end the domination of history by economic struggle." His economic interpretation of history "opened a well-traveled road along which historicists and marginalists could join together," regarding the "capitalist economy as the chief dynamic force of modern history" (1991, p. 189). Thus he kept one step ahead of prevailing doctrines, "'along positions that accorded with those of the enlightened business community'" [Dorfman quoted in Ross, 1991, p. 192].

13. So, when Granovetter (2002, p. 40) says "one central task of economic sociology is to lay bare the circumstances under which people may safely set aside suspicions that rational action would require them to have," and that "such a task cannot be conceived from within a theory of behavior that admits only of rational action," how else to conceive of it but from an interpretive perspective?

14. Of course, engagement with values might get Granovetter into waters he wishes to avoid because the sticky issues of power and domination, exploitation and opportunity hoarding, which Tilly groups under the heading of "durable inequalities," inevitably thrust one into the realm of normative judgments, and Granovetter, who otherwise seems comfortable in grouping structural functionalists, Weberians, Marxists, Durkheimians, and Simmelians together, may no longer find refuge in such indiscriminate, value-free herding (Tilly, 1998).

REFERENCES

Abbott, Andrew. 1999. *Department and Discipline: Chicago Sociology at One Hundred.* Chicago: University of Chicago Press.

Allcock, John B. 1983. Editorial Introduction to the English Translation to Emile Durkheim, *Pragmatism and Sociology.* New York: Cambridge University Press.

Allen, Graham. 2000. *Intertextuality.* London: Routledge.

Anderson, B. M. 1911. *Social Value: a Study in Economic Theory Critical and Constructive.* Boston: Houghton Mifflin.

Angell, Robert Cooley. 1968. Introduction to *Cooley and Sociological Analysis,* ed. Albert J. Reiss. Ann Arbor: University of Michigan Press.

Auerbach, Eric. 1953. *Mimesis: The Representation of Reality in Western Literature,* trans. Willard Trask. Garden City, N.Y.: Doubleday.

Auster, Paul. 2002. *The Book of Illusions.* New York: Holt.

Baldwin, James Mark. 1894. *Mental Development in the Child and the Race: Methods and Processes.* New York: Macmillan.

Barnes, Harry Elmer, ed. 1923. "Some Contributions of American Psychological Sociology to Social and Political Theory: Charles Horton Cooley." *Sociological Review* 15: 194–205.

———. 1948. "Albion Woodbury Small: Promoter of American Sociology and Expositor of Social Interests." In *An Introduction to the History of Sociology*, ed. Harry Elmer Barnes. Chicago: University of Chicago Press.

———. 1948. *An Introduction to the History of Sociology.* Chicago: University of Chicago Press.

———. 1948. "Lester Frank Ward: The Reconstruction of Society by Social Science." In *An Introduction to the History of Sociology*, ed. Harry Elmer Barnes. Chicago: University of Chicago Press.

———. 1948. "Spencer and the Evolutionary Defense of Individualism." In *An Introduction to the History of Sociology*, ed. Harry Elmer Barnes. Chicago: University of Chicago Press.

———. 1948. "William Graham Sumner: Spencerianism in American Dress." In *An Introduction to American Sociology*, ed. Harry Elmer Barnes. Chicago: University of Chicago Press.

Barrett, William. 1958. *Irrational Man: A Study in Existential Philosophy.* Garden City, N.Y.: Doubleday.

Barthes, Roland. 1974. *S/Z.* Trans. Richard Miller. New York: Hill and Wang.

Bauschatz, Cathleen M. 1980. "Montaigne's Conception of Reading in the Context of Renaissance Poetics and Modern Criticism." In *The Reader in the Text: Essays on Audience and Interpretation*, ed. Susan R. Suleiman and Inge Crosman. Princeton: Princeton University Press.

Beckert, Jens. 1999. "Economic Action and Embeddedness: The Problem of the Structure of Action." Unpublished MS.

Benoit-Smullyan, Emile. 1948. "The Sociologism of Émile Durkheim and His School." In *An Introduction to the History of Sociology*, ed. Harry Elmer Barnes. Chicago: University of Chicago Press.

Bensmaïa, Réda. 1987. *The Barthes Effect: the Essay as Reflective Text.* Minneapolis: University of Minnesota Press.

Benson, Arthur C. 1906. *Walter Pater.* New York: Macmillan.

Bernard, Luther Lee, and Jesse Bernard. 1965. *The Origins of American Sociology.* New York: Crowell.

Berry, Christopher J. 2003. "Sociality and Socialisation." In *The Cambridge Companion to the Scottish Enlightenment*, ed. Alexander Broadie. Cambridge, U.K.: Cambridge University Press.

Billikopf, Jacob. 1942. Letter to Edward C. Jandy. Bentley Historical Library, University of Michigan, Cooley papers.

Bloom, Harold. 1973, 1997. *The Anxiety of Influence: A Theory of Poetry.* New York: Oxford University Press.

Blumer, Herbert. 1930 in 1969. "Science without Concepts." In *Symbolic Interactionism: Perspective and Method*, ed. Herbert Blumer. Englewood Cliffs, N.J.: Prentice-Hall.

———. 1937 in 1969. "The Methodological Position of Symbolic Interactionism." In *Symbolic Interactionism: Perspective and Method,* ed. Herbert Blumer. Englewood Cliffs, N.J.: Prentice-Hall.

———. 1939 in 1969. "An Appraisal of Thomas and Znaniecki's *The Polish Peasant in Europe and America.*" In *Symbolic Interactionism: Perspective and Method,* ed. Herbert Blumer. Englewood Cliffs, N.J.: Prentice-Hall.

———. 1956 in 1969. "Sociological Analysis and the Variable." In *Symbolic Interactionism: Perspective and Method,* ed. Herbert Blumer. Englewood Cliffs, N.J.: Prentice-Hall.

Bowen, Ralph H. 1947. *German Theories of the Corporate State.* New York: McGraw-Hill.

Bowman, Frank. 1969. "Montaigne." In *The Art of Criticism: Essays in French Literary Analysis,* ed. Peter H. Nurse. Edinburgh: Edinburgh University Press.

Bramson, Leon. 1961. *The Political Context of Sociology.* Princeton: Princeton University Press.

Breit, William and Roger L. Ransom. 1971. *The Academic Scribblers: American Economics in Collision.* New York: Holt, Rinehart and Winston.

Broadie, Alexander, ed. 2003. *The Cambridge Companion to the Scottish Enlightenment.* Cambridge, U.K.: Cambridge University Press.

Brown, Richard Harvey. 1992. "Social Science and Society as Discourse: Toward a Sociology for Civic Competence." In *Postmodernism and Social Theory: The Debate over General Theory,* ed. Steven Seidman and David G. Wagner. Cambridge, Mass.: Blackwell.

Bryant, Christopher G. A. 1985. *Positivism in Social Theory and Research.* London: Macmillan.

Bryson, Gladys. 1945. *Man and Society: The Scottish Inquiry of the Eighteenth Century.* Princeton: Princeton University Press.

Bulmer, Martin. 1984. *The Chicago School of Sociology: Institutionalization, Diversity, and the Rise of Sociological Research.* Chicago: University of Chicago Press.

Burawoy, Michael. 1991a. "Reconstructing Social Theories." In *Ethnography Unbound: Power and Resistance in the Modern Metropolis,* ed. Michael Burawoy et al. Berkeley: University of California Press.

———. 1991b. "The Extended Case Method." In *Ethnography Unbound: Power and Resistance in the Modern Metropolis,* ed. Michael Burawoy et al. Berkeley: University of California Press.

Burke, Kenneth. 1953. *Counter-Statement.* Chicago: University of Chicago Press.

Calhoun, Craig J. 1994. *Social Theory and the Politics of Identity.* Cambridge, Mass.: Blackwell.

Calhoun, Daniel H. 1965. *Professional Lives in America.* Cambridge, Mass.: Harvard University Press.

Canaday, John. 1959. *Mainstreams of Modern Art.* New York: Holt, Rinehart and Winston.

Carrington, Paul D. 1997. "Law as 'The Common Thoughts of Men': The Law-Teaching and Judging of Thomas McIntyre Cooley." *Stanford Law Review* 49 (Feb.): 495–546.

Cave, Terence. 1982. "The Mimesis of Reading in the Renaissance." In *Mimesis: From Mirror to Method, Augustine to Descartes.* Hanover, N.H.: University Press of New England.

Chugerman, Samuel. 1939. *Lester F. Ward, the American Aristotle: A Summary and Interpretation of His Sociology.* Durham, N.C.: Duke University Press.

Clark, Michael D. 1994. "Charles H. Cooley and the Modern Necessity of Tradition." *Modern Age* 36 (Spring): 277–85.

Clayton, Jay, and Eric Rothstein, eds. 1991. *Influence and Intertextuality in Literary History.* Madison: University of Wisconsin Press.

Clayton, Jay, and Eric Rothstein. 1991. "Figures in the Corpus: Theories of Influence and Intertextuality." In *Influence and Intertextuality in Literary History,* ed. Jay Clayton and Eric Rothstein. Madison: University of Wisconsin Press.

Clifford, James. 1986. Introduction to *Writing Culture: The Poetics and Politics of Ethnography,* ed. James Clifford and George E. Marcus. Berkeley: University of California Press.

———. 1986. "On Ethnographic Allegory." In *Writing Culture: the Poetics and Politics of Ethnography,* ed. James Clifford and George E. Marcus. Berkeley: University of California Press.

———. 1990. "Notes on (Field)notes." In *Fieldnotes: The Makings of Anthropology,* ed. Roger Sanjeck. Ithaca: Cornell University Press.

Clifford, James, and George E. Marcus. 1986. *Writing Culture: The Poetics and Politics of Ethnography.* Berkeley: University of California Press.

Cohen, Marshall J. 1967. "Self and Society: Charles Horton Cooley and the Idea of Social Self in American Thought." Ph.D. diss. Harvard University.

Coleman, James S. 1994. "A Rational Choice Perspective on Economic Sociology." In *The Handbook of Economic Sociology,* ed. Neil J. Smelser and Richard Swedberg. Princeton: Princeton University Press.

Colomy, Paul, and J. David Brown. 1995. "Elaboration, Revision, Polemic, and Progress in the Second Chicago School." In *A Second Chicago School?: The Development of a Postwar American Sociology,* ed. Gary Alan Fine. Chicago: University of Chicago Press.

Commager, Henry Steele, ed. 1967. *Lester Ward and the Welfare State.* Indianapolis: Bobbs-Merrill.

Conlon, John J. 1982. *Walter Pater and the French Tradition.* Lewisburg, Pa.: Bucknell University Press.

Cooley, Charles Horton. 1893. Notebook of political philosophy lectures of John Dewey. Box 7, Cooley papers. Bentley Historical Library, University of Michigan.

———. 1894 in 1930. "The Theory of Transportation." In *Sociological Theory and So-cial Research: Being Selected papers of Charles Horton Cooley,* ed. Robert Cooley Angell. New York: Holt.

———. 1897 in 1930. "Genius, Fame and the Comparison of Races." In *Sociological Theory and Social Research: Being Selected Papers of Charles Horton Cooley,* ed. Robert Cooley Angell. New York: Holt. Reprinted and abridged as "Genius, Fame, and Race" in Russell Jacoby and Naomi Glauberman, eds. 1997, *The Bell Curve Debate: History, Documents, Opinions.* New York: Random House.

———. 1897 in 1998. "The Process of Social Change." In *Charles Horton Cooley: On Self and Social Organization,* ed. Hans-Joachim Schubert. Chicago: University of Chicago Press.

———. 1899 in 1930. "Personal Competition." In *Sociological Theory and Social Research: Being Selected Papers of Charles Horton Cooley,* ed. Robert Cooley Angell. New York: Holt.

———. 1902. *Human Nature and the Social Order.* Rev. ed., 1922. New York: Scribner's. Reprinted 1956 in *The Two Major Works of Charles H. Cooley.* New York: Free Press.

———. 1902. Lecture notes. Box 2, Cooley papers, Bentley Historical Library, University of Michigan.

———. 1908 in 1930. "A Study of the Use of Self Words by a Child." In *Sociological Theory and Social Research: Being Selected Papers of Charles Horton Cooley,* ed. Robert Cooley Angell. New York: Holt.

———. 1909. *Social Organization: A Study of the Larger Mind.* New York: Scribner's. Reprinted 1956 in *The Two Major Works of Charles H. Cooley.* New York: Free Press.

———. 1918. *Social Process.* Reprinted 1966. Carbondale: Southern Illinois University Press.

———. 1918 in 1930. "Political Economy and Social Process." In *Sociological Theory and Social Research: Being Selected Papers of Charles Horton Cooley,* ed. Robert Cooley Angell. New York: Holt.

———. 1920 in 1930. "Reflections upon the Sociology of Herbert Spencer." In *Sociological Theory and Social Research: Being Selected Papers of Charles Horton Cooley,* ed. Robert Cooley Angell. New York: Holt.

———. 1924 in 1930. "Now and Then." In *Sociological Theory and Social Research: Being Selected Papers of Charles Horton Cooley,* ed. Robert Cooley Angell. New York: Holt.

———. 1926 in 1930. "The Roots of Social Knowledge." In *Sociological Theory and So-cial Research: Being Selected Papers of Charles Horton Cooley,* ed. Robert Cooley Angell. New York: Holt.

———. 1927. *Life and the Student: Roadside Notes on Human Nature, Society, and Letters.* New York: Knopf.

———. 1927 in 1930. "Case Study of Small Institutions as a Method of Research." In *Sociological Theory and Social Research: Being Selected Papers of Charles Horton Cooley,* ed. Robert Cooley Angell. New York: Holt.

———. 1928 in 1930. "Sumner and Methodology." In *Sociological Theory and Social Research: Being Selected Papers of Charles Horton Cooley,* ed. Robert Cooley Angell. New York: Holt.

———. 1929 in 1930. "The Life-Study Method as Applied to Rural Social Research." In *Sociological Theory and Social Research: Being Selected Papers of Charles Horton Cooley,* ed. Robert Cooley Angell. New York: Holt.

Coser, Lewis A. 1971. *Masters of Sociological Thought: Ideas in Historical and Social Context.* New York: Harcourt Brace Jovanivich.

———. 1977. *Masters of Sociological Thought: Ideas in Historical and Social Context.* 2nd ed. New York: Harcourt Brace Jovanivich.

Costelloe, Timothy M. 1997. "Contract or Coincidence: George Herbert Mead and Adam Smith on Self and Society." *History of the Human Sciences* 10: 81–109.

Crabb, George. 1917. *Crabb's English Synonyms.* Rev. ed. New York: Grossett and Dunlap.

Crane, Diana. 1969. "Social Structure in a Group of Scientists: A Test of the 'Invisible College' Hypothesis." *American Sociological Review* 31 (June): 335–52.

———. 1972. *Invisible Colleges: Diffusion of Knowledge in Scientific Communities.* Chicago: University of Chicago Press.

Crapanzano, Vincent. "Hermes' Dilemma: the Masking of Subversion in Ethnographic Description." In *Writing Culture: The Poetics and Politics of Ethnography,* ed. James Clifford and George E. Marcus. Berkeley: University of California Press.

Creeland, Paul. 1987. "The Degradation of the Sacred: Approaches of Cooley and Goffman." *Symbolic Interaction* V. 10 (#1): 29–56.

Culler, Jonathan. 1981. *The Pursuit of Signs: Semiotics, Literature, Deconstruction.* Ithaca: Cornell University Press.

Dalton, George. 1961. "Economic Theory and Primitive Society." *American Anthropologist* 63: 1–25.

Daniels, George. 1968. *American Science in the Age of Jackson.* New York: Columbia University Press.

Deegan, Mary Jo. 1988. *Jane Addams and the Men of the Chicago School, 1892–1918.* New Brunswick, N.J.: Transaction Books.

Denby, David. 2004. "Northern Lights: How Modern Life Emerged from Eighteenth Century Edinburgh." *New Yorker.* October 11: 90–98.

Dibble, Vernon K. 1982. "The Young Charles Horton Cooley and His Father: A Skeptical Note about Psychobiographies." *Journal of the History of Sociology* 4 (Spring): 1–26.

Dickens, David R., and Andrea Fontana, eds. 1994. *Postmodernism and Social Inquiry.* New York: Guilford.

Dickens, David R., and Andrea Fontana. 1994. "Postmodernism in the Social Sciences." In *Postmodernism and Social Inquiry,* ed. David R. Dickens and Andrea Fontana. New York: Guilford.

Dingwall, Robert. 2001. "Notes toward an Intellectual History of Symbolic Interaction." *Symbolic Interaction* 24 (2): 237–42.

Donoghue, Denis. 1995. *Walter Pater: Lover of Strange Souls.* New York: Knopf.

Dorfman, Joseph. 1949. *The Economic Mind in American Civilization, Volume Three: 1865–1918.* New York: Augustus Kelley.

Doubt, Keith. 1990. "Autonomy and Responsibility in Social Theory." In *Current Perspectives in Social Theory: A Research Annual,* Vol. 10, ed. John Wilson. Greenwich, Conn.: JAI Press.

Durkheim, Émile. 1933. *The Division of Labor in Society.* Trans. George Simpson. New York: Free Press of Glencoe.

———. 1938. *The Rules of Sociological Method.* Trans. Sarah A. Solovay and John H. Mueller. Ed. George E. G. Catlin. Glencoe, Ill.: Free Press.

———. 1983. *Pragmatism and Sociology.* Trans. J. C. Whitehouse. Ed. John B. Allcock. New York: Cambridge University Press.

———. 1995 [1912]. *The Elementary Forms of the Religious Life.* Trans. Karen E. Fields. New York: Free Press.

Elbow, Peter, and Jennifer Clarke. 1987. "Desert Island Discourse: The Benefits of Ignoring Audience." In *the Journal Book,* ed. Toby Fulweiler. Portsmouth, N.H.: Boynton/Cook.

Emerson, Ralph Waldo. 1929. *The Complete Writings of Ralph Waldo Emerson.* Vol. 1. New York: William H. Wise. Includes "An Address Delivered before the Senior Class in Divinity College, Cambridge"; "The American Scholar"; "Compensation"; "Eloquence"; "Montaigne: or, the Skeptic"; "Nature"; "Nominalist and Realist"; "The Over-Soul"; "Self Reliance"; "Uses of Great Men."

Emerson, Robert, Rachel I. Fretz, and Linda L. Shaw. 1995. *Writing Ethnographic Fieldnotes.* Chicago: University of Chicago Press.

Emerson, Roger. 2003. "The Contexts of the Scottish Enlightenment." In *The Cambridge Companion to the Scottish Enlightenment,* ed. Alexander Broadie. Cambridge, U.K.: Cambridge University Press.

Faris, Robert E. L. 1967. *Chicago Sociology, 1920–1932.* Chicago: University of Chicago Press.

Fine, Gary Alan, ed. 1995. *A Second Chicago School?: The Development of a Postwar American Sociology.* Chicago: University of Chicago Press.

Fine, Gary Alan, and Lori J. Ducharme. 1995. "The Ethnographic Present: Images of Institutional Control in Second-School Research." In *A Second Chicago School?: The Development of a Postwar American Sociology,* ed. Gary Alan Fine. Chicago: University of Chicago Press.

Fine, Sidney. 1956. *Laissez Faire and the General-Welfare State: A Study of Conflict in American Thought, 1865–1901.* Ann Arbor: University of Michigan Press.

Fligstein, Neil. 2002. "Agreements, Disagreements, and Opportunities in the 'New Sociology of Markets.'" In *The New Economic Sociology: Developments in an Emerging Field,* ed. Mauro F. Guillen, Randall Collins, Paula England, and Marshall Meyer. New York: Russell Sage Foundation.

Fontana, Andrea. 1994. "Ethnographic Trends in the Postmodern Era." In *Postmodernism and Social Inquiry,* ed. David R. Dickens and Andrea Fontana. New York: Guilford.

Ford, Henry Jones. 1909. "The Claims of Sociology Examined." *American Journal of Sociology* 15 (Sept.): 244–59.

Fourcade-Gourinchas, Marion. 2001. "Politics, Institutional Structures, and the Rise of Economics: A Comparative Study." *Theory and Society* 30: 397–447.

Franks, David D., and Viktor Gecas. 1992. "Autonomy and Conformity in Cooley's Self-Theory: The Looking-Glass Self and Beyond." *Symbolic Interaction* 15, no. 1: 49–68.

Frenzen, Jonathan, Paul M. Hirsch, and Philip C. Zerillo. 1994. "Consumption, Preferences, and Changing Lifestyles." In *The Handbook of Economic Sociology,* ed. Neil J. Smelser and Richard Swedberg. Princeton: Princeton University Press.

Friedman, Susan Stanford. 1991. "Weavings: Intertextuality and the (Re)Birth of the Author." In *Influence and Intertextuality in Literary History,* ed. Jay Clayton and Eric Rothstein. Madison: University of Wisconsin Press.

Furner, Mary O. 1975. *Advocacy and Objectivity: A Crisis in the Professionalization of American Social Science, 1865–1905.* Lexington: University Press of Kentucky.

Galliher, John F. 1995. "Chicago's Two World's of Deviance Research: Whose Side Are They On?" In *A Second Chicago School?: The Development of a Postwar American Sociology,* ed. Gary Alan Fine. Chicago: University of Chicago Press.

Gardiner, Carol Brooks, and William P. Gronfein. 2005. "Reflections on Varieties of Shame Induction, Shame Management, and Shame Avoidance in Some Works of Erving Goffman," *Symbolic Interaction* 28, no. 2: 175–82.

Gebauer, Gunter, and Christoph Wulf. 1995. *Mimesis: Culture, Art, Society.* Trans. Don Reneau. Berkeley: University of California Press.

Geertz, Clifford. 1973. *The Interpretation of Cultures: Selected Essays.* New York: Basic Books.

Gerstl, Joel, and Glenn Jacobs, eds. 1976. *Professions for the People: The Politics of Skill.* Cambridge, Mass.: Schenkman.

Gerver, Israel, ed. 1963. *Lester Frank Ward.* New York: Crowell.

Giddings, Franklin Henry. 1896. *The Principles of Sociology.* New York: Macmillan.

Gilb, Corinne Lathrop. 1966. *Hidden Hierarchies: The Professions and Government.* New York: Harper and Row.

Goffman, Erving. 1959. *The Presentation of Self in Everyday Life.* New York: Doubleday.

Granovetter, Mark. 1985. "Economic Action and Social Structure: The Problem of Embeddedness." *American Journal of Sociology* 91: 481–510.

———. 1993. "The Nature of Economic Relationships." In *Explorations in Economic Sociology,* ed. Richard Swedberg. New York: Russell Sage Foundation.

———. 2002. "A Theoretical Agenda for Economic Sociology." In *The New Economic Sociology: Developments in an Emerging Field,* ed. Mauro F. Guillén et al. New York: Russell Sage Foundation.

Green, Bryan S. 1988. *Literary Methods and Sociological Theory: Case Studies of Simmel and Weber.* Chicago: University of Chicago Press.

Green, Dan S. and Edwin D. Driver. 1978. Introduction to *W.E.B. Dubois: On Sociology and the Black Community,* ed. Dan S. Green and Edwin D. Driver. Chicago: University of Chicago Press.

Gruchy, Allan G. 1972. *Contemporary Economic Thought: The Contribution of Neo-Institutional Economics.* New York: Macmillan.

Guillén, Mauro F., et al. (Randall Collins, Paula England, and Marshall Meyer), eds. 2002. *The New Economic Sociology: Developments in an Emerging Field.* New York: Russell Sage Foundation.

Guillén, Mauro F., et al. 2002. "The Revival of Economic Sociology." In *The New Economic Sociology: Developments in an Emerging Field.* Ed. Mauro Guillén et al. New York: Russell Sage Foundation.

Gutman, Robert. 1958. "Cooley: A Perspective." *American Sociological Review* 23 (June): 251–56.

Hale, Edward Everett, Jr., ed. 1901. *Selections from Walter Pater.* New York: Holt.

Herbst, Jurgen. 1965. *The German Historical School in American Scholarship: A Study in the Transfer of Culture.* Port Washington, N.Y.: Kennikat.

Highet, Gilbert. 1949. *The Classical Tradition: Greek and Roman Influences on Western Literature.* London: Oxford University Press.

Hinkle, Roscoe C. 1966. Introduction to Charles Horton Cooley, *Social Process.* Carbondale, Ill.: Southern Illinois University Press.

———. 1975. "Basic Orientations of the Founding Fathers of American Sociology." *Journal of the History of the Behavioral Sciences* 11 (April): 107–22.

———. 1980. *Founding Theory of American Sociology 1881–1915.* Boston and London: Routledge.

Hinkle, Roscoe C., and Gisela J. Hinkle. 1954. *The Development of Modern Sociology.* New York: Random House.

Hodgson, Geoffrey M. 1994. "The Return of Institutional Economics." In *The Handbook of Economic Sociology,* ed. Neil J. Smelser and Richard Swedberg. Princeton: Princeton University Press.

Hofstadter, Richard. 1955. *Social Darwinism in American Thought.* Boston: Beacon.

Holstein, James A., and Jaber F. Gubrium. 2000. *The Self We Live By: Narrative Identity in a Postmodern World.* New York: Oxford University Press.

House, Floyd Nelson. 1936. *The Development of Sociology.* New York: McGraw-Hill.

House, Floyd Nelson. 1929. *The Range of Social Theory: A Study of the Development, Literature, Tendencies, and Fundamental Problems of the Social Sciences.* New York: Holt.

Hutchison, T. W. 1953. *A Review of Economic Doctrines 1870–1929.* London: Oxford University Press.

İlter, Tuğrul. 1995. "Disciplinary Sociology in the United Methods of Empiricism: Marking the Boundaries to Keep the 'Poachers' Out." In *Current Perspectives in Social Theory,* ed. Ben Agger. Greenwich, Conn.: JAI Press.

Infantino, Lorenzo. 1998. *Individualism in Modern Thought: From Adam Smith to Hayek.* London and New York: Routledge.

Iser, Wolfgang. 1987. *Walter Pater: The Aesthetic Moment.* Trans. David Henry Wilson. Cambridge, U.K.: Cambridge University Press.

Jackson, Jean E. 1990. "I Am a Fieldnote": Fieldnotes as a Symbol of Professional Identity. In *Fieldnotes: The Makings of Anthropology,* ed. Roger Sanjeck. Ithaca: Cornell University Press.

Jacobs, Glenn. 1976. *Cooley's Journals: A Study of Sociological Theory Building.* Ph.D. diss., Temple University.

———. 1979. "Charles Horton Cooley and the Methodological Origins of Humanism in American Sociology." *Humanity and Society* 3 (Feb.): 1–15.

———. 1979. "Economy and Totality: Cooley's Theory of Pecuniary Valuation." In *Studies in Symbolic Interaction: A Research Annual,* ed. Normal K. Denzin. Greenwich, Conn.: JAI Press.

———. 2004. "Charles Cooley: Traveler in the Inner and Social Worlds." *Discourse of Sociological Practice* 6, no. 2 (Fall): 143–64.

Jacoby, Russell, and Naomi Glauberman, eds. 1995. *The Bell Curve Debate: History, Documents, Opinions.* New York: Random House.

Jacoby, Russell, and Naomi Glauberman. 1995. Introduction to *The Bell Curve Debate: History, Documents, Opinions,* ed. Russell Jacoby and Naomi Glauberman. New York: Random House.

James, William. 1890. *Principles of Psychology,* 2 vols. New York: Holt.

———. 1963 [1892]. *Psychology.* New York: Fawcett.

Jandy, Edward C. 1942. *Charles Horton Cooley: His Life and His Social Theory.* New York: Dryden. Reprinted 1969, New York: Octagon.

Joas, Hans. 1985. *G. H. Mead: a Contempoirary Re-examination of His Thought.* Cambridge, Mass.: MIT Press.

———. 1993. *Pragmatism and Social Theory.* Chicago: University of Chicago Press.

———. 1996. *The Creativity of Action.* Chicago: University of Chicago Press.

———. 2000. *The Genesis of Values.* Chicago: University of Chicago Press.

Johnson, Cathryn. 1992. "The Emergence of the Emotional Self: A Development Theory." *Symbolic Interaction* 15 (2): 183–202.

Jones, Robert Alun, and Sidney Kronus. 1976. "Professional Sociologists and the History of Sociology: A Survey of Recent Opinion." *Journal of the History of the Behavioral Sciences* 12: 3–13.

Kolb, William L. 1948. "The Sociological Theories of Edward Alsworth Ross." In *An Introduction to the History of Sociology,* ed. H. E. Barnes. Chicago: University of Chicago Press.

Kress, Paul F. 1970. *Social Science and the Idea of Progress: The Ambiguous Legacy of Arthur F. Bentley.* Urbana: University of Illinois Press.

Kristeva, Julia. 1980. *Desire in Language: A Semiotic Approach to Literature and Art.* Trans. Thomas Gora, Alice Jardine, and Leon Roudiez. Ed. Leon Roudez. New York: Columbia University Press.

———. 1984. *Revolution in Poetic Language.* New York: Columbia University Press.

Kronenberger, Louis. 1959. Introduction to *The Maxims of La Rochefoucauld.* Trans. Louis Kronenberger. New York: Random House.

Kuhn, Manfred H. 1964. "Major Trends in Symbolic Interaction Theory in the Past Twenty-five Years." *Sociological Quarterly* 5 (Winter): 61–84.

Kuhn, T. S. 1962. *The Structure of Scientific Revolutions.* Chicago: University of Chicago Press.

La Rochefoucauld, François de. 1959. *The Maxims of La Rochefoucauld.* Trans. Louis Kronenberger. New York: Random House.

Lederman, Rena. 1990. "Pretexts for Ethnography: On Reading Fieldnotes." In *Fieldnotes: The Makings of Anthropology,* ed. Roger Sanjeck. Ithaca: Cornell University Press.

Lee, Alfred McClung. 1966. *Multivalent Man.* New York: George Braziller.

Lemert, Charles. 1992. "General Social Theory, Irony, Postmodernism." In *Postmodernism and Social Theory: The Debate over General Theory,* ed. Steven Seidman and David G. Wagner. Cambridge, Mass.: Blackwell.

Lengerman, Patricia Madoo, and Jill Neibrugge-Brantley, eds. 1998. *The Women Founders: Sociology and Social Theory, 1830–1930: A Text/Reader.* Boston: McGraw-Hill.

Levin, Samuel M. 1941. "Charles Horton Cooley and the Concept of Creativeness." *Journal of Social Philosophy* 6 (April): 216–29.

Levine, Donald N. 1971. Introduction to *Georg Simmel on Individuality and Social Forms,* ed. Donald Levine. Chicago: University of Chicago Press.

Loesberg, Jonathan. 1991. *Aestheticism and Deconstruction: Pater, Derrida, and de Man.* Princeton: Princeton University Press.

Lowenstein, Sharyn. 1987. "Brief History of Journal Keeping." In *The Journal Book,* ed. Toby Fulweiler. Portsmouth, N.H.: Boynton/Cook.

McDermott, John J., ed. 1973. *The Philosophy of John Dewey.* 2 vols. New York: G. P. Putnam's Sons.

McGrath, F. C. 1986. *The Sensible Spirit: Walter Pater and the Modernist Paradigm.* Tampa: University of South Florida Press.

McMillen, Neil R. 1929. *Dark Journey: Black Mississippians in the Age of Jim Crow.* Urbana: University of Illinois Press.

Marcus, George E. 1986. "Contemporary Problems of Ethnography in the Modern World System." In *Writing Culture: The Poetics and Politics of Ethnography,* ed. James Clifford and George E. Marcus. Berkeley: University of California Press.

Martindale, Don. 1960. *The Nature and Types of Sociological Theory.* Boston: Houghton Mifflin.

———. 1981. *The Nature and Types of Sociological Theory.* 2nd ed. Prospect Heights, Ill.: Waveland.

Matthiessen, F. O. 1941. *American Renaissance: Art and Expression in the Age of Emerson and Whitman.* London: Oxford University Press.

Mead, George Herbert. 1930. "Cooley's Contribution to American Social Thought." *American Journal of Sociology* 35 (March): 699–706. Reprinted in Anselm Strauss, ed., 1964. *George Herbert Mead on Social Psychology.* Chicago: University of Chicago Press.

———. 1936. *Movements of Thought in the Nineteenth Century,* ed. Merritt H. Moore. Chicago: University of Chicago Press.

———. 1962 [1934]. *Mind, Self, and Society: From the Standpoint of a Social Behaviorist,* ed. Charles W. Morris. Chicago: University of Chicago Press.

———. 1964 [1909]. "Social Psychology as Counterpart to Physiological Psychology." In *Selected Writings: George Herbert Mead,* ed. Andrew J. Reck. Indianapolis: Bobbs-Merrill.

———. 1964 [1913]. "The Social Self." In *Selected Writings: George Herbert Mead,* ed. Andrew J. Reck. Indianapolis: Bobbs-Merrill.

———. 1964 [1922]. "A Behavioristic Account of the Significant Symbol." In *Selected Writings: George Herbert Mead,* ed. Andrew J. Reck. Indianapolis: Bobbs-Merrill.

———. 1964 [1923]. "Scientific Method and the Moral Sciences." In *Selected Writings: George Herbert Mead,* ed. Andrew J. Reck. Indianapolis: Bobbs-Merrill.

———. 1964 [1924–25]. "The Genesis of the Self and Social Control." In *Selected Writings: George Herbert Mead,* ed. Andrew J. Reck. Indianapolis: Bobbs-Merrill.

———. 1964 [1932]. *George Herbert Mead: On Social Psychology,* ed. Anselm Strauss. Chicago: University of Chicago Press.

Meltzer, Bernard N., and John W. Petras. 1970. "The Chicago and Iowa Schools of Symbolic Interactionism." In *Symbolic Interactionism: a Reader in Social Psychology,* ed. Jerome G. Manis and Bernard N. Meltzer. Englewood Cliffs, N.J.: Prentice-Hall.

Meltzer, Bernard N., John W. Petras, and Larry T. Reynolds. 1975. *Symbolic Interactionism: Genesis, Varieties and Criticism.* Boston: Routledge.

Miller, David L. 1973. *G. H. Mead: Self, Language, and the World.* Austin: University of Texas Press.

Miller, Gale, and Robert Dingwell, eds. 1997. *Context and Method in Qualitative Research.* Thousand Oaks, Calif.: Sage.

Mills, C. Wright. 1939 in 1963. "Language, Logic, and Culture." In C. Wright Mills, *Power, Politics, and People,* ed. Irving Louis Horowitz. New York: Ballantine.

———. 1964. *Sociology and Pragmatism: The Higher Learning in America.* New York: Oxford University Press.

Monsman, Gerald. 1980. *Walter Pater's Art of Autobiography.* New Haven: Yale University Press.

Montaigne, Michel de. 1958. *The Complete Essays of Montaigne.* Trans. Donald M. Frame. Stanford: Stanford University Press.

———. 1991. *The Complete Essays,* trans. M. A. Screech. London: Penguin.

Northcott, Clarence H. 1948. "The Sociological Theories of Franklin Henry Giddings: Consciousness of Kind, Pluralistic Behavior, and Statistical Method." In *An Introduction to the History of Sociology,* ed. H. E. Barnes. Chicago: University of Chicago Press.

Oberschall, Anthony. 1972. "The Institutionalization of American Sociology." In *The Establishment of Empirical Sociology,* ed. Anthony Oberschall. New York: Harper and Row.

Odum, Howard W. 1951. *American Sociology: The Story of Sociology in the United States through 1950.* New York: Longmans Green.

Odum, Howard W., and H. E. Moore. 1938. *American Regionalism.* New York: Holt.

Omi, Michael, and Howard Winant. 1994. *Racial Formation in the United States: From the 1960s to the 1990s.* New York: Routledge.

Ortiz, Fernando. 1947. *Cuban Counterpoint: Tobacco and Sugar.* Durham: Duke University Press.

Ottenberg, Simon. 1990. "Thirty Years of Fieldnotes: Changing Relationships to the Text." In *Fieldnotes: The Makings of Anthropology,* ed. Roger Sanjeck. Ithaca: Cornell University Press.

Page, Charles H. 1969 (1940). *Class and American Sociology: From Ward to Ross.* New York: Schocken.

Park, Robert E. 1922. *The Immigrant Press and Its Control.* New York: Harper and Brothers.

———. 1952. *Human Communities: The City and Human Ecology.* Glencoe, Ill.: Free Press.

Parsons, Talcott. 1968. "Cooley and the Problem of Internalization." In *Cooley and Sociological Analysis,* ed. Albert J. Reiss. Ann Arbor: University of Michigan Press.

———. 1969. *Politics and Social Structure.* New York: Free Press.

Pascal, Blaise. 1958. *Pascal's Pensées.* New York: Dutton.

Pater, Walter. 1873. *The Renaissance.* Introduction by Arthur Symons. New York: Modern Library.

————. 1889, 1987. *Appreciations with an Essay on Style.* Evanston: Northwestern University Press.

————. 1997. *Imaginary Portraits with the Child in the House and Gaston de Latour.* New York: Allworth.

Platt, Jennifer. 1995. "Research Methods and the Second Chicago School." In *A Second Chicago School?: The Development of a Postwar American Sociology,* ed. Gary Alan Fine. Chicago: University of Chicago Press.

Polanyi, Karl. 1944. *The Great Transformation: The Political and Economic Origins of Our Time.* Boston: Beacon.

————. 1968. *Primitive, Archaic, and Modern Economics: Essays of Karl Polanyi,* ed. George Dalton. Boston: Beacon.

Polanyi, Karl, Conrad Arensberg, and Harry Pearsons, eds. 1971 [1957]. *Trade and Markets in the Early Empires: Economics in History and Theory.* Chicago: Regnery.

Prus, Robert. 1996. *Symbolic Interactionism and Ethnographic Research: Intersubjectivity and the Study of Lived Experience.* Albany: State University of New York Press.

Rabinow, Paul. "Representations Are Social Facts: Modernity and Post-Modernity in Anthropology." In *Writing Culture: The Poetics and Politics of Ethnography,* ed. James Clifford and George E. Marcus. Berkeley: University of California Press.

Raison, Timothy, ed. 1969. *The Founding Fathers of Social Science.* Baltimore: Penguin.

Raphael, D. D., and A. L. Macfie. 1976. Introduction to Adam Smith, *The Theory of Moral Sentiments,* ed. D. D. Raphael and A. L. Macfie. New York: Oxford University Press.

Reck, Andrew J. 1964. Editor's Introduction to *Selected Writings: George Herbert Mead,* ed. Andrew J. Reck. Indianapolis: Bobbs-Merrill.

Reinharz, Shulamit. 1995. "The Chicago School of Sociology and the Founding of the Brandeis University Graduate Program in Sociology: A Case in Cultural Diffusion." In *A Second Chicago School?. The Development of a Postwar American Sociology,* ed. Gary Alan Fine. Chicago: University of Chicago Press.

Reiss, Albert J., ed. 1968. *Cooley and Sociological Analysis.* Ann Arbor: University of Michigan Press.

Reitzes, Donald C. 1980. "Beyond the Looking-Glass Self: Cooley's Social Self and Its Treatment in Introductory Textbooks." *Contemporary Sociology* 9 (Sept.): 631–40.

Richman, Michèle. 1987. Foreword to *The Barthes Effect: The Essay as Reflective Text,* ed. Réda Bensmaïa. Minneapolis: University of Minnesota Press.

Ritzer, George. 2000. *Classical Sociological Theory.* 3rd ed. New York: McGraw-Hill.

Rosenau, Pauline Marie. 1992. *Post-Modernism and the Social Sciences: Insights, Inroads, and Intrusions.* Princeton: Princeton University Press.

Ross, Dorothy. 1991. *The Origins of American Social Science.* New York: Cambridge University Press.

Ross, Ian Simpson. 1995. *The Life of Adam Smith.* Oxford: Clarendon Press.

Sanders, Clinton. 1996. "Producing, Presenting, and Professing Ethnography." *Journal of Contemporary Ethnography* 25 (July): 285–90.

Sanjeck, Roger, ed. 1990. *Fieldnotes: The Making of Anthropology.* Ithaca: Cornell University Press.

———. 1990a. "A Vocabulary for Fieldnotes." In *Fieldnotes: The Makings of Anthropology,* ed. Roger Sanjeck. Ithaca: Cornell University Press.

———. 1990b. "The Secret Life of Fieldnotes." In *Fieldnotes: The Makings of Anthropology,* ed. Roger Sanjeck. Ithaca: Cornell University Press.

Scheff, Thomas J. 1994. "Emotions and Identity: A Theory of Ethnic Nationalism." In *Social Theory and the Politics of Identity,* ed. Craig Calhoun. Cambridge, Mass.: Blackwell.

———. 2003. "Looking Glass Selves: The Cooley/Goffman Conjecture." Paper presented at the Memorial Session for Erving Goffman at the annual meeting of the American Sociological Association.

———. 2005. "Looking-glass Self: Goffman as a Symbolic Interactionist." *Symbolic Interaction* 28, no. 2: 147–66.

Schubert, Hans-Joachim. 1998. *Charles Horton Cooley: On Self and Social Organization.* Chicago: University of Chicago Press.

Schwartz, Barry. 1985. "Cooley and the American Heroic Vision." *Symbolic Interaction* 8 (Spring): 103–20.

Schwendinger, Herman, and Julia Schwendinger. 1974. *The Sociologists of the Chair: A Radical Analysis of the Formative Years of North American Sociology, 1883–1922.* New York: Basic.

Seidman, Steven, and David G. Wagner, eds. 1992. *Postmodernism and Social Theory: The Debate over General Theory.* Cambridge, Mass.: Blackwell.

Seiler, R. M., ed. 1980. *Walter Pater: The Critical Heritage.* London: Routledge.

Shalin, Dmitri N. 1990. "The Impact of Transcendental Idealism on Early German and American Sociology." In *Current Perspectives in Social Theory: A Research Annual,* Vol. 10, ed. John Wilson. Greenwich, Conn.: JAI Press.

Shott, Susan. 1976. "Society, Self, and Mind in Moral Philosophy: The Scottish Moralists as Precursors of Symbolic Interactionism." *Journal of the History of the Behavioral Sciences* 12: 39–46.

Simmel, Georg. 1955. *Conflict and the Web of Group Affiliations.* Trans. Kurt H. Wolff and Reinhard Bendix. Glencoe, Ill.: Free Press.

———. 1971 [1903]. "The Metropolis and Mental Life." In *Georg Simmel: On Individuality and Social Forms,* ed. Donald N. Levine. Chicago: University of Chicago Press.

———. 1971 [1918]. "The Conflict of Modern Culture." In *Georg Simmel: On Individuality and Social Forms,* ed. Donald N. Levine. Chicago: University of Chicago Press.

————. 1971 [1918]. "The Transcendent Character of Life." In *Georg Simmel: On Individuality and Social Forms,* ed. Donald N. Levine. Chicago: University of Chicago Press.

Simonson, Peter. 1996. "Dreams of Democratic Togetherness: Communication Hope from Cooley to Katz." *Critical Studies in Mass Communication* 13: 324–42.

Simpson, George. 1969. *August Comte: Sire of Sociology.* New York: Crowell.

Sklansky, Jeff. 2000. "Corporate Property and Social Psychology: Thomas M. Cooley, Charles H. Cooley, and the Ideological Origins of the Social Self." *Radical History Review* 76: 90–114.

Small, Albion W. 1909. "The Vindication of Sociology." *American Journal of Sociology* 15 (July): 1–15.

————. 1916. "Fifty Years of Sociology in the United States." *American Journal of Sociology* 21 (May): 721–864.

————. 1910. "The Sociological Stage in the Evolution of the Social Sciences." *American Journal of Sociology* 15 (July): 681–97.

Smart, Barry. 1996. "Postmodern Social Theory." In *The Blackwell Companion to Social Theory,* ed. Bryan S. Turner. Malden, Mass.: Blackwell.

Smelser, Neil J., and Richard Swedberg, eds. 1994. "The Sociological Perspective on the Economy," In *The Handbook of Economic Sociology,* ed. Neil J. Smelser and Richard Swedberg. Princeton: Princeton University Press.

Smith, Adam. 1976 [1759]. *The Theory of Moral Sentiments,* eds. D. D. Raphael and A. L. Macfie. Indianapolis: Liberty Classics.

Sontag, Susan. 1966. *Against Interpretation and Other Essays.* New York: Dell.

Spencer, Herbert. 1873. *The Study of Sociology.* New York: Appleton.

————. 1898. *The Principles of Sociology.* 3 vols. New York: Appleton.

Stone, Gregory. 1962. "Appearance and the Self." In *Human Behavior and Social Processes,* ed. Arnold M. Rose. Boston: Houghton Mifflin.

Stone, Gregory P., and Harvey A. Farberman, eds. 1970. *Social Psychology through Symbolic Interaction.* New York: Wiley.

Stryker, Sheldon. 1980. *Symbolic Interactionism: A Social Structural Version.* Menlo Park, Calif.: Benjamin Cummings.

Symons, Arthur. 1873. Introduction to Walter Pater, *The Renaissance.* New York: Modern Library.

Summerfield, Geoffrey. 1987. "Not in Utopia: Reflections on Journal-Writing." In *The Journal Book,* ed. Toby Fulwiler. Portsmouth, N.H.: Boynton/Cook.

Tarde, Gabriel. 1969. *On Communication and Social Influence,* ed. Terry N. Clark. Chicago: University of Chicago Press.

Thomas, Francis-Noël. 1992. *The Writer Writing.* Princeton: Princeton University Press.

Thomas, William Isaac, and Florian Znaniecki. 1958. *The Polish Peasant in Europe and America.* 2 vols. New York: Dover.

Tilly, Charles. 1998. *Durable Inequality.* Berkeley: University of California Press.

Truzzi, Marcello. 1966. "Adam Smith and Contemporary Issues in Social Psychology." *Journal of the History of the Behavioral Sciences* 2 (3): 221–24.

Turner, Jonathan H. 1985. *Herbert Spencer: a Renewed Appreciation.* Beverly Hills, Calif.: Sage.

Tyler, Stephen A. 1986. "On Post-Modern Ethnography: From Document of the Occult to Occult Document." In *Writing Culture: The Poetics and Politics of Ethnography,* ed. James Clifford and James E. Marcus. Berkeley: University of California Press.

Van Maanen, John. 1988. *Tales of the Field.* Chicago: University of Chicago Press.

Veblen, Thorstein. 1909. "The Limitations of Marginal Utility." Reprinted 1969 in *Veblen on Marx, Race, Science, and Economics.* New York: Capricorn.

———. 1919. "Industrial and Pecuniary Employments." Reprinted 1969 in *Veblen on Marx, Race, Science, and Economics.* New York: Capricorn.

———. 1932 [1904]. *The Theory of Business Enterprise.* New York: Mentor.

Waller, Willard. 1942. Introduction to Edward C. Jandy, *Charles Horton Cooley: His Life and His Social Theory.* New York: Dryden. Reprinted 1969, New York: Octagon.

Weinstein, James. 1968. *The Corporate Ideal in the Liberal State, 1900–1918.* Boston: Beacon.

West, Candace. 1996. "Ethnography and Orthography: A (Modest) Methodological Proposal." *Journal of Contemporary Ethnography* 25 (Oct.): 327–52.

Westby, David L. 1991. *The Growth of Sociological Theory: Human Nature, Knowledge, and Social Change.* Englewood Cliffs, N.J.: Prentice-Hall.

Willis, Paul. 2000. *The Ethnographic Imagination.* Cambridge: Polity.

Wilson, David, and William Dixon. 2002. "The Social Self in Classical Economy: Adam Smith and the Reverend Chalmers Meet G. H. Mead." Paper presented at the European Society for the History of Economic Thought (ESHET) conference in Rethymo, Crete, March 2002, and at the Scottish Economic Society conference in Dundee, Scotland, April 2002.

———. 2004. "Economics and the Act." *Social Epistemology* 5, no. 18 (Jan.–Mar.): 71–84.

Winterer, Caroline. 1994. "A Happy Medium: The Sociology of Charles Horton Cooley." *Journal of the History of the Behavioral Sciences* 30 (Jan.): 19–27.

Woolff, Janet. 1981. *The Social Production of Art.* London: Macmillan.

Ybarra, Peter R. 2001. "Feeling the Field: Tracking Shifts in Ethnographic Research." *Studies in Symbolic Interaction* 24: 195–221.

Zafirovski, Milan. 2000. "Economic Distribution as a Social Process." *The Social Science Journal* 37, no. 3: 423–43.

———. 1999. "Economic Sociology in Retrospect and Prospect: In Search of Its Identity within Economics and Sociology." *American Journal of Economics and Sociology* 58 (Oct.): 583–627.

———. 1997. "Economic Sociology Reformulated: The Interface between Economics and Sociology." *American Journal of Economics and Sociology* 56 (July): 265–84.

BIBLIOGRAPHY OF
CHARLES HORTON COOLEY

[Adapted from Marshall J. Cohen. *Charles Horton Cooley and the Social Self in American Thought.* New York: Garland Publishing, 1982.]

Abstract of "The Social Significance of Street Railways," *Publications of the American Economic Association* 6 (1891): 71–73.

"Competition and Organization," *Publications of the Michigan Political Science Association* 1 (1894): 33–45.

"The Theory of Transportation," *Publications of the American Economic Association* 9 (1894).

"'Nature versus Nurture' in the Making of Social Careers," *Proceedings of the 23rd Conference of Charities and Corrections* (1896): 399–405.

"The Process of Social Change," *Political Science Quarterly* 12 (1897): 63–81.

"Genius, Fame, and the Comparison of Races," *Annals of the American Academy of Political and Social Science* 9 (1897): 1–42.

"Personal Competition: Its Place in the Social Order and the Effect upon Individuals; with Some Considerations on Success," *Economic Studies* 4 (1899).

"The Decrease of Rural Population in the Southern Peninsula of Michigan," *Publications of the Michigan Political Science Association* 4 (1902): 28–37.

Human Nature and the Social Order. New York: Charles Scribner's Sons, 1902.

Discussion of Franklin H. Giddings, "A Theory of Social Causation," *Publications of the American Economic Association,* 3rd ser., 5 (1904): 426–31.

"Social Consciousness," *Publications of the American Sociological Society* 1 (1907): 97–109.

"Social Consciousness," *American Journal of Sociology* 12 (1907): 675–87. Previously published as above.

"A Study of the Early Use of Self-Words by a Child," *Psychological Review* 15 (1908): 339–57.

Social Organization: A Study of the Larger Mind. New York: Charles Scribner's Sons, 1909.

"Builder of Democracy," *Survey* (1909): 210–13.

Discussion of Simon Patten, "The Background of Economic Theories," *Publications of the American Sociological Society* 7 (1912): 132.

"Valuation as a Social Process," *Psychological Bulletin* 9 (1912). Also published as part of *Social Process.*

"The Institutional Character of Pecuniary Valuation," *American Journal of Sociology* 18 (1913): 543–55. Also published as part of *Social Process.*

"The Sphere of Pecuniary Valuation," *American Journal of Sociology* 19 (1913): 188–203. Also published as part of *Social Process.*

"The Progress of Pecuniary Valuation," *Quarterly Journal of Economics* 30 (1913): 1–21. Also published as part of *Social Process.*

"Builder of Democracy." *Survey* 36 (1916): 116.

"Social Control in International Relations," *Publications of the American Sociological Society* 12 (1917): 207–16.

"A Primary Culture for Democracy," *Publications of the American Sociological Society* 13 (1918): 1–10.

"Political Economy and Social Process," *Journal of Political Economy* 25 (1918): 366–74.

Social Process. New York: Charles Scribner's Sons, 1918.

"Reflections upon the Sociology of Herbert Spencer." *American Journal of Sociology* 26 (1920): 129–45.

"Now and Then," *Journal of Applied Sociology* 8 (1924): 259–62.

"The Roots of Social Knowledge," *American Journal of Sociology* 32 (1926): 59–79.

"Heredity or Environment," *Journal of Applied Sociology* 10 (1926): 303–7.

"Sumner and Methodology," *Sociology and Social Research* 12 (1928): 303–6.

"Case Study of Small Institutions as a Method of Research," *Publications of the American Sociological Society* 22 (1928): 123–32.

"The Life-Study Method as Applied to Rural Social Research," *Publications of the American Sociological Society* 23 (1929): 248–54.

"The Development of Sociology at Michigan," In *Sociological Theory and Research: Being Selected Papers of Charles Horton Cooley,* ed. Robert Cooley Angell. New York: Holt, 1930.

INDEX

Glenn Jacobs is an associate professor of sociology at the University of Massachusetts Boston, where he has been teaching since 1976. He received his Ph.D. in sociology from Temple University in 1976. He teaches in the areas of sociological theory, qualitative methods, urban sociology, race and ethnic relations, and social problems. He has published on the community response to the privatization of the Chelsea public schools by Boston University, the retention of Latino students in higher education, and Afro-Cuban music. Currently he is working on an ethnographic study of the occupational lives of folkloric musicians in a neighborhood of Havana. In 2004 the American Sociological Association presented him with a Distinguished Achievement Award for co-founding, editing, and publishing the *Journal of the History of Sociology,* 1977–1982.